**Pragmatics & Interaction, Vol. 4**

# Interactional Competence in Japanese as an Additional Language

# Pragmatics & Interaction
*Editor*
*Gabriele Kasper*

PRAGMATICS & INTERACTION, a refereed series sponsored by the University of Hawai'i National Foreign Language Resource Center, publishes research on topics in pragmatics and discourse as social interaction from a wide variety of theoretical and methodological perspectives. P&I particularly welcomes studies on languages spoken in the Asia-Pacific region.

Pragmatics & Interaction, Vol. 4
**Interactional competence in Japanese as an additional language**
Tim Greer, Midori Ishida & Yumiko Tateyama (Eds.), (2017)
ISBN 978-1-64007-188-9

Pragmatics & Interaction, Vol. 3
**Pragmatics of Vietnamese as native and target language**
Carsten Roever & Hanh thi Nguyen (Eds.), (2013)
ISBN 978-0-9835816-2-8

Pragmatics & Interaction, Vol. 2
**L2 Learning as social practice: Conversation-analytic perspectives**
Gabriele Pallotti & Johannes Wagner (Eds.), (2011)
ISBN 978-0-9800459-7-0

Pragmatics & Interaction, Vol. 1
**Talk-in-interaction: Multilingual perspectives**
Hanh thi Nguyen & Gabriele Kasper (Eds.), (2009)
ISBN 978-0-09800459-1-8

*Ordering information at nflrc.hawaii.edu*

**Pragmatics & Interaction, Vol. 4**

# Interactional Competence in Japanese as an Additional Language

Edited by
Tim Greer, Midori Ishida
& Yumiko Tateyama

©①⑤⓪ 2017 Tim Greer, Midori Ishida & Yumiko Tateyama
This work is licensed under the Creative Commons Attribution-
NonCommercial-ShareAlike 4.0 International License.
To view a copy of this license, visit http://creativecommons.org/
licenses/by-nc-sa/4.0/.

Manufactured in the United States of America.

The contents of this publication were developed in part under a grant
from the U.S. Department of Education (CFDA 84.229, P229A140014).
However, the contents do not necessarily represent the policy of the
Department of Education, and one should not assume endorsement
by the Federal Government.

ISBN: 978-1-64007-188-9

Distributed by
**National Foreign Language Resource Center**
University of Hawai'i
1859 East-West Road #106
Honolulu, HI 96822-2322
**nflrc.hawaii.edu**

## About the
## National Foreign Language Resource Center

The National Foreign Language Resource Center, located in the College of Languages, Linguistics & Literature at the University of Hawai'i at Mānoa, has conducted research, developed materials, and trained language professionals since 1990 under a series of grants from the U.S. Department of Education (Language Resource Centers Program). A national advisory board sets the general direction of the resource center. With the goal of improving foreign language instruction in the United States, the center publishes research reports and teaching materials that focus primarily on the languages of Asia and the Pacific. The center also sponsors summer intensive teacher training institutes and other professional development opportunities. For additional information about center programs, contact us.

Julio C. Rodríguez, Director
National Foreign Language Resource Center
University of Hawai'i at Mānoa
1859 East-West Road #106
Honolulu, HI 96822-2322
nflrc@hawaii.edu
nflrc.hawaii.edu

## NFLRC Advisory Board 2014–2018

Carl Blyth
*University of Texas at Austin*

Jeenna Canche
*Hawai'i State Department of Education*

Una Cunningham
*University of Canterbury, New Zealand*

Janis Jensen
*Kean University, Union, New Jersey*

Paul Sandrock
*ACTFL, Alexandria, Virginia*

Julie Sykes
*University of Oregon*


NFLRC Independent Evaluator:
Steven Thorne
*Portland State University*

*To the memory of our friend and colleague
Dr. Yuzuru Takigawa*

# Contents

| | | |
|---|---|---|
| | About the Authors | xi |
| | Acknowledgments | xv |
| | Transcription Conventions | xvii |
| 1 | Interactional Competence in Japanese as an Additional Language: An Overview<br>*Tim Greer, Midori Ishida, & Yumiko Tateyama* | 1 |

## Interactional Competence Across Social Activities

| | | |
|---|---|---|
| 2 | "My Japanese isn't that Good": Self-Deprecation, Preference Organization, and Interactional Competence<br>*Alfred Rue Burch* | 19 |
| 3 | Learning Technical Terms in Workplace Interaction<br>*Stephen J. Moody* | 51 |
| 4 | She Who Laughs First: Audience Laughter and Interactional Competence at a Rakugo Performance for Foreign Students<br>*Cade Bushnell* | 81 |
| 5 | Co-construction of an L2 Speaker's Interactional Competence: Recipient Responses in an Interview Activity<br>*Mari Yamamoto & Tomoharu Yanagimachi* | 115 |
| 6 | Multimodal Interactional Competence in the Use of Technology in L2 Japanese Classrooms<br>*Keiko Ikeda & Don Bysouth* | 141 |

| 7 | Collaborative Orientation to the 'Search for What-to-Say' in Pair Work Interactions<br>*Atsushi Hasegawa* | 175 |
| --- | --- | --- |
| 8 | Assessing Interactional Competence: Storytelling in the Japanese Oral Proficiency Interview<br>*Waka Tominaga* | 211 |

**Developing Interactional Competence**

| 9 | Developing Recipient Competence during Study Abroad<br>*Midori Ishida* | 253 |
| --- | --- | --- |
| 10 | Becoming a Conversationalist at the Dinner Table: Topic Management Practices by a JFL Student Living in Foreign Language Housing<br>*Junko Mori & Yumiko Matsunaga* | 293 |
| 11 | "Daijoobu desu ka?": Use of Formulaic Expressions by One Novice L2 Japanese Teacher<br>*Yumiko Tateyama* | 333 |
| 12 | L1 Speaker Turn Design and Emergent Familiarity in Opening Sequences of Second Language Japanese Interaction<br>*Tim Greer* | 369 |
| | Index | 409 |

# About the Authors

**Alfred Rue Burch** is a postdoctoral fellow at Rice University. His research interests include (a) respecifying SLA topics such as motivation and communication strategies from an EMCA perspective, (b) language learning and use "in the wild," and (c) applying findings from this research to task based/supported language teaching. He has published in *Language Learning* and has co-edited a special issue on TBLT to appear in *TESOL Quarterly*, and has co-authored chapters with Gabriele Kasper appearing in *Talking Emotion in Multilingual Settings* (Prior & Kasper, 2016) and *Authenticity, Language, and Interaction in Second Language Contexts* (van Compernolle & McGregor, 2016).

**Cade Bushnell** is currently an associate professor of Japanese linguistics and Japanese language pedagogy at the University of Tsukuba, where he teaches the Japanese language to international students, and conversation analysis, membership categorization analysis, and Japanese language pedagogy to master's and doctoral students. He has published articles on identity in interaction, L2 language play, and learning in participation. He received his PhD in Japanese Linguistics from the University of Hawai'i at Mānoa. His current research interests include participation, membership and learning; laughter and language play; and identity work in interaction—all particularly in the case of second language users.

**Don Bysouth** is Associate Professor in the Graduate School of Human Sciences at Osaka University, Japan. He holds a PhD in Psychology from Murdoch University, Australia. His recent research is focused on cross-cultural social interaction in technologically mediated settings and higher education internationalization in Japan. His most recent book is *A Handbook for Enhancing English-Medium Program Quality and Practice* (2015) from Osaka University Press.

**Tim Greer** is a professor in the School of Languages and Communication and the Graduate School of Intercultural Studies at Kobe University. His research uses Conversation Analysis to examine various aspects of bilingual talk and second language use, including Japanese-English bilingual interaction, repair and receipt practices and identity-in-interaction. Recently he has been using longitudinal CA to document the development of interactional competence in study abroad contexts. His work has been published in *Multilingua*, the *Journal of Applied Linguistics, Classroom Discourse* and the *Journal of Pragmatics*.

**Atsushi Hasegawa,** PhD, is an Assistant Professor of Japan Studies at the University of Kentucky, where he serves as director of Japanese language. He teaches all levels of Japanese, as well as sociolinguistics and SLA. His primary research interests include JFL classroom talk with a particular focus on pair/small group work interaction. His next project will examine the formation of social networks and language use by participants of study abroad in Japan. In this project, he uses social network analysis (SNA) and conversation analysis (CA) as primary analytical frameworks.

**Keiko Ikeda** is Professor in the Division of International Affairs at Kansai University, Japan. She received a Ph.D. from University of Hawaiʻi at Mānoa. Her research has examined a wide range of social interaction practices, for example laughter ("Laughter and Turn-taking: Warranting next speakership in multiparty interactions" in *Studies of Laughter in Interaction,* 2013) and human-robot interactions ("Interactions between a quiz robot and multiple participants" in *Gaze in Human-Robot Communication,* 2015). Her recent research focuses on EMI (English Mediated Instruction) curriculum development, online cross-cultural learning and teaching, and transnational educational programs.

**Midori Ishida** is a lecturer of Japanese in the Department of World Languages and Literatures at San José State University. While the areas of her previous research include acquisition of aspect and oral language assessment, her main research interest lies in the use of CA for the investigation of development of interactional competence in study abroad contexts. Her studies have been published in *Language Learning, Pragmatics and Language Learning,* and previous volumes of the Pragmatics & Interaction Series.

**Yumiko Matsunaga** is senior instructor of Japanese at the University of Colorado Boulder. She received her Ph.D. from the University of Wisconsin-Madison, where she studied Japanese Linguistics and Second Language Acquisition. Her primary research interest is in how learners' participation in various types of communities and their changing identities influence their language learning experience. To this end, she conducted a multi-year study of a foreign language housing (FLH) program at a Midwestern university. The results have been presented at various conferences, including the Second Language Research Forum (SLRF) and the American Association of Teachers of Japanese (AATJ) annual conferences.

**Stephen J. Moody** (PhD, University of Hawai'i) is an assistant professor in the Department of Asian and Near Eastern Languages at Brigham Young University. He received a Ph.D. in East Asian Languages and Literatures from the University of Hawai'i and an MA in Economics from The Ohio State University. His research interests are in the area of intercultural communication in institutions with a focus on how linguistic and cultural knowledge is used as social capital in those settings.

**Junko Mori** is professor of Japanese language and linguistics at the University of Wisconsin-Madison, where she is also a core member of their interdepartmental Doctoral Program in Second Language Acquisition. By using conversation analysis as a central analytical framework, she has investigated the relationship between linguistic structures and organizations of social interaction, classroom discourse, intercultural communication, and workplace interaction. Her work has appeared in a number of edited volumes, as well as in journals such as *Applied Linguistics, Foreign Language Annals, IRAL, Journal of Pragmatics, The Modern Language Journal,* and *Research on Language and Social Interaction,* among others.

**Yumiko Tateyama** is an assistant professor in the Department of East Asian Languages and Literatures at the University of Hawai'i at Mānoa. Her research interests include Japanese language pedagogy, teaching and learning pragmatics, classroom discourse, and translation and interpreting. She has published papers in these areas. Her current research projects include the examination of interactional practices in the Japanese as a foreign language classroom and its application to teacher training.

**Waka Tominaga** is an instructor of Japanese in Languages, Linguistics and Literature Department at Kapi'olani Community College. She received her Ph.D. from the Department of East Asian Languages and Literatures at the University of Hawai'i at Mānoa in 2014. Her research interests include conversation analysis, oral proficiency interviews (OPIs), speaking proficiency development, Japanese language pedagogy and assessment. She was certified as an ACTFL OPI Tester in 2008 and has conducted and rated OPIs for various program evaluations.

**Mari Yamamoto** is an Associate Professor at the Center for Japanese Language Education at Kwansei Gakuin University, Japan. She received her PhD in International Media and Communications from Hokkaido University. Her main research interests are recipient responses in both speakers of Japanese as a first and second language, grammar and interaction, and conversation analysis. Recently, her interests have expanded to include teaching Japanese conversation in the second language classroom. She has authored journal articles on *serifu* utterances (recipients' reported speech as voices of story characters) and interactive developments of stories in journals including *Shakaigengokagaku* (*Japanese Journal of Language in Society*).

**Tomoharu Yanagimachi** (Ph.D., University of Minnesota) is Professor of Applied Linguistics at the English Department of Hokusei Gakuen University in Sapporo, Japan. His research interests include second language studies, discourse analysis, conversation analysis, and recently, plurilingualism and English as a *lingua franca* in workplaces in Japan. He has authored and co-authored book chapters and journal articles on the microanalysis of interactions involving speakers of Japanese as a second language in journals including *Shakaigengokagaku* (*Japanese Journal of Language in Society*). He currently serves on the editorial board of the academic journal.

## Acknowledgments

We are grateful to the following external reviewers for their insightful comments on the chapters in this volume.

Evelyne Berger, *Université de Neuchâtel*
Mayumi Bono, *National Institute of Informatics*
Adam Brandt, *Newcastle University*
Matthew Burdelski, *Osaka University*
Donald Carroll, *Shikoku Gakuin University*
Gavin Furukawa, *The University of Tokyo*
Toshiaki Furukawa, *Otsuma Women's University*
Marta Gonzalez-Lloret, *University of Hawai'i at Mānoa*
Eric Hauser, *University of Electro-Communications, Tokyo*
John Hellermann, *Portland State University*
Yuri Hosoda, *Kanagawa University*
Younhee Kim, *National Institute of Education, Singapore*
Nathan Krug, *Saitama University*
Chris Leyland, *Newcastle University*
Ikuyo Morimoto, *Kwansei Gakuin University*
Emi Murayama, *University of Hawai'i at Mānoa*
Ian Nakamura, *Okayama University*
Yusuke Okada, *Osaka University*
Scott Saft, *University of Hawai'i at Hilo*
Aki Siegal, *Rikkyo University*
Kana Suzuki, *Hiroshima International University*
Hiroko Takanashi, *Japan Women's University*
Erica Zimmerman, *United States Naval Academy*

# Transcription Conventions

*Based on Jefferson (2004).*

| Symbol | Meaning |
| --- | --- |
| [ | Point of overlap onset |
| ] | Point of overlap ending |
| \| | Onset of embodiment in relation to talk |
| / | Denotes an embodied action that occurs during a marked silence |
| = | No break or gap in speech (latched speech), or continuation of the same turn by the same speaker on another line in the transcript |
| (number) | Silence, measured in tenths of a second |
| (.) | Micro-pause (0.1s or less) |
| : | Prolongation of the immediately prior sound; the longer the colon row, the longer the sound stretch |
| ↑ | Shift into especially high pitch in the next sound |
| ↓ | Shift into especially low pitch in the next sound |
| ! | Animated tone |
| . | Falling intonation |
| , | Continuing intonation |
| ¿ | Slightly rising intonation |
| ? | Rising intonation |
| WORD | Especially loud sounds compared to the surrounding talk |
| °word° | Especially quiet sounds compared to the surrounding talk |
| %word% | Pressed voice |
| word | Emphasized speech |
| **word** | A focal linguistic item [in **boldface**] |
| (word) | Transcriber's best guess of the words or speaker |
| word- | Cut-off sound |
| xxxx or ( ) | Unintelligible speech or unidentifiable speaker to transcriber |
| <word> | Slowed down sounds compared to the surrounding talk |
| >word< | Speeded up sounds compared to the surrounding talk |
| $word$ | Surrounds "smile" voice |
| .hhh | Audible inbreath |
| hhh | Audible outbreath |

| | |
|---|---|
| (h) | Plosiveness, associated with laughter, crying, breathlessness, etc. |
| ((description)) | Transcriber's description |
| → | Focal item in analysis |

## Abbreviations used in word-by-word glosses of Japanese transcripts

### A. Content and function words

| | |
|---|---|
| AT | address term |
| CP | copula (e.g., *da, desu*) |
| CS | change of state token (*ah*) |
| H | hesitation marker (e.g., *e::, ano*) |
| IP | interactional particle (e.g., *ne, sa, no, yo, na*) |
| LK | linking particle (*no*) |
| N | nominalizer (*no, n*) |
| O | object marker (*o*) |
| PT | other particle |
| Q | question marker (*ka* and its variants) |
| QT | quotation marker (*to, tte*) |
| RT | receipt token |
| S | subject marker (*ga*) |
| TP | topic marker (*wa*) |

### B. Speech styles, tense and aspect, and other relevant conjugation forms

| | |
|---|---|
| CND | conditional |
| CONT | continuous |
| FTR | future |
| HON | honorific |
| NG | negative (*-nai*) |
| PAS | passive |
| PLN | plain |
| POL | polite |
| POT | potential |
| PROG | progressive |
| PST | past tense (*-ta*) |
| VOL | volitional |

## Reference

Jefferson, G. (2004). Glossary of transcript symbols with an introduction. In G. H. Lerner (Ed.), *Conversation analysis: Studies from the first generation* (pp. 13–31). Amsterdam: John Benjamins.

# 1 Interactional Competence in Japanese as an Additional Language: An Overview

Tim Greer
*Kobe University*

Midori Ishida
*San José State University*

Yumiko Tateyama
*University of Hawaiʻi at Mānoa*

## Introduction

Speaking a language involves more than just knowledge of grammar, vocabulary, and pronunciation: It also requires the abilities to interpret what your interlocutor is saying, to formulate a relevant response, and to deliver it in a timely manner. In addition, it entails skills such as dealing with trouble in talk when it arises and being able to identify an appropriate moment to start speaking. In short, it requires interactional competence (IC).

As this applies to speaking a language other than one's first, this volume of *Pragmatics & Interaction* examines specific interactional competences (ICs) that speakers of Japanese as an additional language display publically and how those competences develop over time. The volume consists of empirical studies of IC in situations where Japanese is an additional language, representatively a "second" language (L2), of one or more of the speakers.

IC has been drawing increasing attention in recent years, especially in relation to L2 talk and within the field of pragmatics. For the most part, studies that locate pragmatics in theories of communicative competence (e.g., Canale & Swain, 1980; Hymes, 1972) consider L2 speakers' proficiencies primarily as reflecting each person's ability alone. However, the IC perspective holds that L2 speakers' competences should be examined not in isolation, but instead as co-constructed by everyone involved in the interaction, since utterances are a joint accomplishment (Kasper & Ross, 2013). As Young (2011) puts it, "IC is not what a person *knows*, it is what a person *does* together with others" (p. 430), and this is the reason IC studies examine language-mediated actions, embodied actions, and a range of other multimodal practices as they are publically displayed in interaction. Adopting such a stance toward L2 competence, the contributions in the present volume each employ conversation analysis (CA) to investigate the sequentially co-accomplished interactional practices that L2 speakers of Japanese use both inside and outside the classroom, as well as in oral proficiency assessment settings. In doing so, the collection explores issues of learning in social interaction and highlights development in terms of changes in ICs over time. Considering that IC was not specifically addressed in the handful of previous volumes that have targeted L2 Japanese pragmatics to date (Kasper, 1992; Ohta, 2001; Taguchi, 2009; Yamashita, 1996), this volume of *Pragmatics & Interaction* is the first of its kind to take up IC as its overarching theme.

It is not our intention to give a complete introduction to the field of CA here; plenty are currently available in the literature (e.g., Heritage & Clayman, 2010; Sidnell & Stivers, 2013). Nor is it our aim to review all that has been said about CA in relation to second language acquisition (SLA); for comprehensive summaries see Pallotti and Wagner (2011), and Kasper and Wagner (2011, 2014). Instead, the purpose of this introduction is to provide an overview of how IC has been studied in CA studies of Japanese, both in L1 (first-language) and L2 contexts, and to outline how the chapters in the current volume contribute to this work.

## The primacy of interaction

Although increasingly mitigated in the literature, Japanese culture is still often juxtaposed against Anglo-American norms as a series of dichotomized perspectives, such as collectivism/individualism, hierarchy/egalitarianism, and indirect/direct communication (e.g., Brown, Hayashi, & Yamamoto, 2013). These sorts of cross-cultural comparisons can in many ways be better termed cross-cultural *contrasts* in that they focus more on the differences between two languages rather than on the similarities, which often times results in misleading claims to uniqueness. On the other hand, the CA approach highlights the inherent universality of talk, shifting the focus from language and culture toward the social order of interaction itself.

While the current volume focuses on Japanese interaction, one of its fundamental underpinnings is that interaction is first and foremost concerned with *sociality*, not a particular variety of talk that is mediated in a given language. Although it is undoubtedly valid to consider the unique properties of a language or the variations that might exist between two languages, interaction itself is built on fundamental generic organizations, such as minimization, nextness, and progressivity (Schegloff, 2006). As Schegloff (2006) puts it, "the dimensions on which variability is observed and rendered consequential are framed by the dimensions of generality that render the comparison relevant to begin with" (p. 85). The default starting point for examining interactional organizations, therefore, must be their universalities, even though inevitable variations in their form will exist. Whether Japanese or English, or L1 or L2, the interactional practices of turn-taking, sequence, and repair have more commonalities than variances.

To date, the vast majority of CA research has been based on L1 English data, but the findings hold relevance to Japanese as well. By way of illustration, consider the following excerpt, adapted from Kushida (2011, p. 2721), in which M and S are eating pizza while watching TV.

**Excerpt 1.** (From Kushida, 2011; format modified using the transcription conventions of the present volume)

```
01 M      |atashi mo    kogeteru no hoshii.
          I      also   burned    N  want
          I want the burned one, too.
          |((pointing at a piece of pizza))

02        |(0.8)
          |((S turns her head and looks down at the pizza))

03 S      |kore?
          this
          This one?
          |((touching a piece of pizza with her hand))

04 M      nn

05        (0.3)

06 S      |ageru de:.
          give  IP ¹
          This is for you.
          |((handing the piece to M)
```

Without going into too much detail about this transcript, we can see that M initiates a request sequence in line 1 by asking for one of the pieces of pizza. In formulating this request as "I want the burnt one too," M indexes earlier talk (not shown) in two ways: (a) *mo* 'too' suggests that S has already taken a slice and that M's request is to be heard as relative to that action; and (b) the indefinite pronoun *no* 'the one' stands in place of a more specific word selection such as *slice* or *piece*, and therefore indexes one of those words. Similarly, in line 3 when S initiates an insertion sequence to clarify M's request, her use of *kore* 'this' is designed to be understood only in conjunction with her embodied action (touching one of the slices), and therefore M's confirmation token in line 4 signals that she has understood what S means by *kore* in this context.

These observations on indexicality, intersubjectivity, and sequentiality demonstrate the connections between turns and how participants display their moment-by-moment understanding of what they are doing, and thus point to the orderly nature of sociality in Japanese, just as they do in English and other languages. Likewise, cross-linguistic comparative CA studies have shown that the generic practices of repair are more similar in Japanese and English than they are different (Fox, Hayashi, & Jasperson, 1996; Fox et al., 2009). A range of CA scholarship on L1 Japanese also points to the overwhelming generic nature of social organization, including aspects such as turn-taking (Hayashi, 2002, 2005), sequence (Hayashi, 2009, 2010; Kushida & Yamakawa, 2015; Tanaka, 2000), repair (Hayashi & Hayano, 2013), epistemics (Hayano, 2011; Kushida, 2015; Tanaka, 2013), and multimodal interaction (Nishizaka, 2014; Nishizaka & Sunaga, 2015).

Moreover, it is not difficult to imagine that either one of the interactants in Excerpt 1 might be an L2 speaker of Japanese. The competence needed for initiating repair is no different for first- and second-language speakers, and thanks to the universality of IC as a procedural and transferable competence, even L2 speakers of Japanese who have very little linguistic knowledge can take part in interaction (Burch, 2014; Mori & Matsunaga, this volume).

## Interactional Competence in L2 Japanese

There has been a steady rise in the number of studies examining the interactional practices in which L2 speakers engage and the development of L2 speakers' ICs in languages other than Japanese (e.g., Hall, Hellermann, & Pekarek Doehler, 2011; Hauser, 2013; Nguyen, 2012; Young & Miller, 2004). Micro-interactional changes in L2 interaction over time are beginning to be studied longitudinally and cross-sectionally through the use of CA, both in the classroom (Pekarek Doehler & Fasel Lauzon, 2015; Sert, 2015) and beyond (Pekarek Doehler & Berger, 2016; Pekarek Doehler & Pochon-Berger, 2015).

Although English has dominated the focus of many of these studies, a few have targeted other languages, including Japanese, and together this body of research has been heading the field in promising directions. For instance, in their analysis of a conversation between L1 and L2 speakers of Japanese, Mori and Hayashi (2006) reveal how participants engage in embodied completion—a multimodal IC in which an iconic gesture is substituted for some element of a turn-in-progress—a finding which contributes to our understanding of language learning as occurring within socially situated practices. Tominaga's (2013) analysis of Japanese OPI practices highlights the importance of taking into account the sequential achievement of narratives in assessing L2 speakers' proficiency. Ishida (2009, 2011) investigates the development of L2 Japanese learners' IC in a study abroad setting, demonstrating long-term changes in the learners' use of the interactional particle *ne* and, as story recipients, their use of assessments as well. Ishida's (2006) study of a 10-minute discussion held between L1 and L2 speakers of Japanese reveals how the L2 speaker expands the range of action she makes in a series of decision-making activities, suggesting 'microgenesis' of competence. Greer (2013) examines the way that Japanese/English language alternation practices become interactionally established between strangers. By analyzing talk between a Japanese hair stylist and his non-Japanese client across a series of successive haircuts, Greer demonstrates changes in their code-switching practices as they become aware of each other's proficiency levels and preferred language choices.

How novices develop ICs is a topic of particular interest for CA-SLA researchers (Kasper & Ross, 2013). L2 studies that employ CA have revealed novice speakers' competencies in the use of certain linguistic resources (e.g., *ne* in Ishida, 2009), sentential structures (e.g., Taguchi, 2014) and narrative structures (Tominaga, 2013), as well as social actions that enable specific methods of participation (e.g., Ishida, 2006, 2011). CA has also been used to reveal how L2 speakers manage knowledge, identities (Hazel, 2015; Lee, 2015), and emotion (Prior & Kasper, 2016). Moreover, by focusing on repair (e.g., Tateyama, 2012), word search sequences (Mori & Hasegawa, 2009), and embodied completion (Mori & Hayashi, 2006), CA studies of interactional architectures have revealed how participants, both L1 and L2 speakers, orient to learning as a social activity, and how this potentially leads to change, both microgenetically (Ishida, 2006) and over an extended period of time (e.g., Hauser, 2013).

## IC development among novice professionals

In addition to IC development as an L2 speaker phenomenon, recent studies have also begun to examine development of ICs among novice professionals in work-related settings. Nguyen (2011, 2012), for example, documents how pharmacy interns in the U.S. became more effective in their consultations with patients over time. As shown in Nguyen (2011), one intern (an L1 speaker of English) used technical terms in early consultations when explaining drugs, which did not generate alignment from his patient. Over the course of two months, the intern adapted his talk to meet the patient's needs and expectations by using less technical terms and providing more detailed explanations relevant to a layperson. Nguyen's study finds that presenting detailed expert knowledge about drugs is less effective, and that the way a novice pharmacist shifts toward a more simplified method of presentation can be considered evidence of development. IC in this case is not evaluated in terms of its complexity, as is often the gauge for L2 linguistic competence. Instead it is evidenced by how well the language is "recipient-designed" for the patient to ease understanding.

Designing one's turn in a manner that aligns with that of an interlocutor's contributes to generating further follow-up turns. This has been documented by Leyland, Greer, and Rettig-Miki (2016) in their investigation into the interactional practices of one novice tester (a highly proficient L2 speaker of English) during a series of group discussion tests among EFL students in Japan. The tester initially utilized a rhetorical discourse structure whereby she played the devil's advocate. It was found, however, that such strategies did not generate significant follow-up turns from the students who participated in the test. As the tester aligned her turn design with that of the EFL students, more follow-up turns from the students were observed.

In both the Nguyen and Leyland et al. studies, novice professionals remained in the same role (pharmacy intern; tester), the same task (counseling a patient about medication; generating responses from test-takers), and the same setting (pharmacy; classroom) throughout their successive engagement in the activity. What seems to play a key role in the development of professional competence when novices are involved in self-guided, independent engagement is the modification of previous performances and the incorporation of the modification into new performances of the same task in order to meet institutionally defined goals more effectively (Nguyen, 2012).

Studies on teacher training tend to focus on class observations and interviews rather than detailed analysis of actual classroom interactions. However, longitudinal CA studies such as Rine and Hall (2011) and Hosoda and Aline (2010) provide insight into the process of how teacher trainees develop their professional competencies in order to become effective teachers. Another point to be noted in these studies is that the pre-service teachers were L2 speakers of the language that they were being trained to teach. Few studies to date have investigated the development of L2 speakers' professional competence from a CA perspective, making this another fertile area for further research. In the current volume, Tateyama focuses on a novice Japanese as a foreign language (JFL) teacher, who is an L2 speaker of Japanese, in order to document the development of his IC in the classroom. Such studies help underscore the idea that IC involves the competence of both expert and novice speakers, and that changes in their interaction over time provide evidence of their development.

## The current volume

With all the above CA research in mind, the chapters in this volume investigate L2 Japanese speakers' ICs in a variety of settings, including JFL classrooms, language assessment contexts, and non-instructional situations. Three chapters are situated in L2 Japanese classrooms, each with a different focus: Atsushi Hasegawa looks at student-student interactions; Yumiko Tateyama focuses on the teacher who himself is an L2 speaker of Japanese; and Keiko Ikeda and Don Bysouth consider multimodal L2 interaction augmented with the use of IT tools. Two chapters examine interactions in educational contexts outside the classroom: Mari Yamamoto and Tomoharu Yanagimachi analyze an interview that was recorded as a classroom project and Junko Mori and Yumiko Matsunaga look at dinner table conversation in an international dormitory where the aim of the gathering is to practice spoken Japanese. Waka Tominaga's chapter on oral proficiency interviews is the only study that is set in a purely assessment context.

The remainder of the chapters examine L2 interactions "in the wild," beyond educational contexts: Cade Bushnell observes participants attending a *rakugo* performance; Midori Ishida takes up conversations between friends during study abroad; Alfred Rue Burch looks at a series of conversations between friends; Stephen Moody picks up on workplace interactions recorded during an internship; and Tim Greer explores service provider-client conversations in a Japanese hair salon. The volume has been organized into two sections: (a) interactional competence across social activities and (b) developing interactional competence.

### Interactional competencies across social activities

In this first section, a range of ICs that L2 speakers of Japanese exhibit across social activities is examined throughout seven chapters. Focusing on self-deprecation or negative self-assessments, Burch's chapter examines mundane conversations between an L2 speaker of Japanese and her friend, an L1 speaker of Japanese. Through a meticulous multimodal analysis, Burch illustrates how the self-deprecation bears on the L2 speaker's IC as it arises out of the contingencies of the interaction. Burch demonstrates the L2 speaker's ability to achieve, maintain, and manage intersubjectivity through sequential, categorical, and interactional (linguistic and embodied) resources. Particularly noteworthy is the issue of the management of preference as a component of the L2 speaker's

IC: As issues of preference and dispreference are not clear-cut, the interactants must manage self-deprecations subtly and skillfully. Burch's chapter sheds light on this infrequently researched aspect of L2 IC.

Moody's chapter looks at interaction between L2 speakers and their L1-Japanese colleagues during internships in Japanese companies, focusing particularly on their repair practices when they come across unfamiliar technical terms. Moody treats the learning of new technical items as a socially co-constructed achievement, demonstrating how participants use word search practices to incorporate negotiation of unfamiliar lexical items into talk while embedding them into broader work-related objectives. Such specialized jargon is frequently job-specific and is therefore not generally taught in the classroom. Moody's analysis outlines the competences the interns need to acquire this knowledge on the job and also shows that these competences are therefore an essential part of their IC.

Through its intricate analysis of *rakugo* (a traditional Japanese comedic monologue), Bushnell's chapter documents the way audience members at a scripted performance reveal aspects of their IC through the well-timed production of laughter tokens. Although laughter appears to be a mere reflex, previous CA studies (e.g., Jefferson, Sacks, & Schegloff, 1977) have shown that a hearer can accomplish various actions through laughter. Through his analysis, Bushnell demonstrates that the L2 Japanese speakers exhibit their IC in claiming their understanding of what is going on in terms of the structural point of a laughter-relevant moment as well as the content of the enacted story. Bushnell's chapter opens up a new realm of research that CA-SLA researchers can explore further in the future.

The chapter by Yamamoto and Yanagimachi conducts a single-case analysis of an interview that an L2 speaker of Japanese conducted with a Japanese scientist as a part of an out-of-class project. The authors consider the L2 speaker's use of recipient responses and show how she used them: to invite the interviewee to elaborate on his answer to her question, to indicate understanding, and to demonstrate that understanding in a verifiable manner. The focused investigation of the interviewee's turn design, including its related prosody and embodied actions, reveals how the interviewer's competence in responding to the interviewee is co-constructed. This chapter highlights the importance of a multimodal analysis of all participants' actions.

In their chapter, Ikeda and Bysouth investigate IC in relation to the use of information technology (IT) in multiparty contexts. They consider how L1 and L2 speakers of Japanese accomplish small group interaction during classes that incorporate IT devices, and how these tools allow the participants to communicate with each other to complete group learning tasks. By examining intercultural communication interactions augmented through the use of devices like computers, tablets, and smart boards, the authors account for multimodal aspects of L2 IC that are specific to such technology-mediated interactional environments and explore the IC required to integrate technology into face-to-face talk.

In his chapter, Hasegawa also examines how multimodal resources are used in classroom interaction. He analyzes the way L2 speakers search for what-to-say in highly controlled grammar-consolidating exercises in a JFL classroom at a U.S. university. Faced with the task of filling in the blanks in grammar exercises, students engage not only in an individual search for what-to-say but also jump in to help their peers to formulate a response. Hasegawa's fine-grained analyses of gaze direction, facial expressions, and laughter particles show how students orient to the need to come up with what-to-say, indicate appeals for assistance, and at times, abort their search entirely. By expanding CA scholarship on forward-oriented repair, this chapter demonstrates the ICs that L2 speakers exhibit during L2 classroom learning activities.

Tominaga's chapter addresses storytelling competence during the assessment of spoken interaction in the Japanese *ACTFL Oral Proficiency Interview* (OPI), specifically focusing on the adequacy of the level descriptions within its text-type rating criterion. Tominaga presents analyses of two intermediate candidates' performances on the narration task as representative samples from her data set. She finds that the text-type rating criterion did not necessarily match the candidates' actual performances, and argues that candidates' ICs, which are co-constructed with the interviewer, should be adequately reflected in level descriptions. These ICs include a candidate's ability to produce sequentially appropriate actions (including extended turns), to organize turns in an orderly manner, to use available resources to achieve coherent and cohesive telling, and to accomplish intersubjectivity with the interviewer. Tominaga's study demonstrates the value of reconsidering established rating criteria in high-stakes testing in terms of IC and through the lens of CA.

**Developing interactional competence**
In the second section, each of the four chapters employ longitudinal CA to document how IC develops over an extended period of time. Rather than merely recording additions to participant vocabulary or changes in their grammar, these chapters focus on the developing methods the participants use to co-accomplish intersubjectivity through interaction.

The section begins with Ishida's chapter, which analyzes conversations between an L2 speaker and his Japanese friends during a yearlong study abroad experience. Ishida outlines the contingencies of interaction that facilitate and debilitate the L2 speaker's use of agreeing forms of receipt, showing that the function of a receipt form is made identifiable due to its sequential position and through accompanying embodied actions. Although corrective feedback was not provided on the L2 user's inapposite receipts, his interlocutors' next-turn actions served as implicit feedback on his recipient action. Ishida's analysis explores the relationship between an L2 user's development and what is actually going on in social interaction during study abroad, shedding light on aspects of L2 talk that may help or hinder "development."

The chapter by Mori and Matsunaga, which likewise adopts a longitudinal CA perspective, examines mundane talk among L1 and L2 speakers in a foreign language housing context, documenting how one novice L2 speaker of Japanese changes the way he participates in dinner table conversations over the course of an academic year. Despite a relatively limited formal classroom study of Japanese, the L2 speaker demonstrated a high level of engagement, initiating and sustaining topical talk and generating opportunities for learning new vocabulary. This chapter considers what sort of IC is necessary in order to become an active participant in out-of-classroom, free-flowing, multi-party conversation.

In her chapter, Tateyama shifts the focus from the student to the teacher. She examines changes in the ways a novice L2 teacher of Japanese uses the formulaic expression *daijoobu desu ka* 'Are you all right?' throughout one semester of teaching a basic Japanese course. While the teacher used *daijoobu desu ka* throughout the semester to accomplish functions such as checking understanding and closing activities, as the semester progressed he increasingly incorporated other formulaic expressions, such as *ii desu ka* 'Are you okay?', that are more commonly deployed by L1 Japanese teachers, and became more adept at managing turns, demonstrating his growing sensitivity to both student responses and his own interactional repertoire. Through a sequential analysis of his use of formulaic expressions, the study focuses less on claiming that he has learned the expressions and more on how he adapts language that he already has to suit the task of managing the class. This chapter contributes to our understanding of how a novice L2 teacher develops ICs that are integral to directing classroom interaction.

Finally, Greer's chapter moves the spotlight away from the novice speaker to explore recipient design and turn construction among L1 and L2 speakers of Japanese in a series of service encounters. Focusing on greeting sequences at a hair salon in Japan, Greer investigates how the L1 Japanese-speaking hairdressers formulate their turns during these initial moments of contact with new clients and how they adapt and adjust their talk based on the clients' responses and their emerging familiarity. Greer's data allowed him to track changes in the interaction with the same speakers across time, as well as to compare the way the hairdressers interact in Japanese with clients of different levels of linguistic proficiency. This chapter provides novel insight into the development of IC from the perspective of the L1 speaker, specifically with respect to how the L1 speaker learns to design talk for L2 speakers with varying degrees of proficiency.

As this book is the first volume to gather together CA research on IC and its development in relation to L2 Japanese, it is anticipated that it will be of use to scholars and language educators alike, providing them with new ways to conceptualize the language learning they encounter in their classrooms and beyond. The shift from communicative competence to ICs is not just a matter of changing terminology: At its core lies an understanding that all parties at talk work together to achieve communication and that language *use* is central to language *acquisition*.

**Notes**

1   Kushida (2011) uses the abbreviation "FP" to denote a final particle.

## References

Brown, S., Hayashi, B., & Yamamoto, K. (2013). Japan/Anglo-American cross-cultural communication. In C. Bratt Paulston, S. F. Kiesling, & E. S. Rangel (Eds.), *The handbook of intercultural communication* (pp. 552–590). Malden, MA: Wiley-Blackwell.

Burch, A. R. (2014). Pursuing information: A conversation analytic perspective on communication strategies. *Language Learning, 64*(3), 651–684.

Canale, M., & Swain, M. (1980). Theoretical bases of communicative approaches to second language teaching and testing. *Applied Linguistics, 1*, 1–47.

Fox, B. A., Hayashi, M., & Jasperson, R. (1996). Resources and repair: A cross-linguistic study of syntax and repair. *Studies in Interactional Sociolinguistics, 13*, 185–237.

Fox, B., Wouk, F., Hayashi, M., Fincke, S., Tao, L., Sorjonen, M. L.,..., & Hernandez, W. F. (2009). A cross-linguistic investigation of the site of initiation in same-turn self-repair. In J. Sidnell (Ed.), *Conversation analysis: Comparative perspectives* (pp. 60–103). Cambridge: Cambridge University Press.

Greer, T. (2013). Establishing a pattern of dual receptive language alternation: Insights from a series of successive haircuts. *Australian Journal of Communication, 40*(2), 47–61.

Hall, J. K., Hellermann, J., & Pekarek Doehler, S. (Eds.). (2011). *L2 interactional competence and development*. Bristol, UK: Multilingual Matters.

Hauser, E. (2013). Stability and change in one adult's second language English negation. *Language Learning, 63*(3), 463–498.

Hayano, K. (2011). Claiming epistemic primacy: Yo-marked assessments in Japanese. In T. Stivers, L. Mondada, & J. Steensig (Eds.), *The morality of knowledge in conversation* (pp. 58–81). Cambridge: Cambridge University Press.

Hayashi, M. (2002). *Joint utterance construction in Japanese conversation*. Amsterdam: John Benjamins.

Hayashi, M. (2005). Referential problems and turn construction: An exploration of an intersection between grammar and interaction. *Text, 25*(4), 437–468.

Hayashi, M. (2009). Marking a 'noticing of departure' in talk: *Eh*-prefaced turns in Japanese conversation. *Journal of Pragmatics, 59*, 5–25.

Hayashi, M. (2010). An overview of the question-response system in Japanese conversation. *Journal of Pragmatics, 42*, 2685–2702.

Hayashi, M., & Hayano, K. (2013). Proffering insertable elements: A study of other-initiated repair in Japanese. In M. Hayashi, G. Raymond, & J. Sidnell (Eds.), *Conversational repair and human understanding* (pp. 293–321). Cambridge: Cambridge University Press.

Hazel, S. (2015). Identities at odds: Embedded and implicit language policing in the internationalized workplace. *Language and Intercultural Communication, 15*(1), 141–160.

Heritage, J., & Clayman, S. (2010). *Talk in action: Interactions, identities and institutions*. Chichester, UK: Wiley-Blackwell.

Hosoda, Y., & Aline, D. (2010). Learning to be a teacher: Development of EFL teacher trainee interactional practices. *JALT Journal, 32*(2), 119–147.

Hymes, D. (1972). On communicative competence. In J. B. Pride & J. Holmes (Eds.), *Sociolinguistics* (pp. 269–293). Harmondsworth, UK: Penguin Books.

Ishida, M. (2006). Interactional competence and the use of modal expressions in decision-making activities: CA for understanding microgenesis of competence. In K. Bardovi-Harlig, J. C. Félix-Brasdefer, & A. Omar (Eds.), *Pragmatics and language learning* (Vol. 11, pp. 55–79). Honolulu, HI: University of Hawai'i, National Foreign Language Resource Center.

Ishida, M. (2009). Development of interactional competence: Changes in the use of *ne* in L2 Japanese during study abroad. In H. T. Nguyen & G. Kasper (Eds.), *Talk-in-interaction: Multilingual perspectives* (pp. 351–385). Honolulu, HI: University of Hawai'i, National Foreign Language Resource Center.

Ishida, M. (2011). Engaging in another person's telling as a recipient in L2 Japanese: Development of interactional competence during one-year study abroad. In G. Pallotti & J. Wagner (Eds.), *L2 learning as social action: Conversation analytic perspectives* (pp. 45–85). Honolulu, HI: University of Hawai'i, National Foreign Language Resource Center.

Jefferson, G., Sacks, H., & Schegloff, E. A. (1987). Notes on laughter in the pursuit of intimacy. In G. Button & J. R. E. Lee (Eds.) *Talk and social organisation* (pp. 152–205). Clevedon, UK: Multilingual Matters.

Kasper, G., (1992). *Pragmatics of Japanese as native and target language*. Honolulu, HI: University of Hawai'i, Second Language Teaching and Curriculum Center.

Kasper, G., & Ross, S. J. (2013). Assessing second language pragmatics: An overview and introductions. In S. J. Ross & G. Kasper (Eds.), *Assessing second language pragmatics* (pp. 1–40). Basingstoke, UK: Palgrave Macmillan.

Kasper, G., & Wagner, J. (2011). A conversation analytic approach to second language acquisition. In D. Atkinson (Ed.), *Alternative approaches to second language acquisition* (pp. 117–142). New York, NY: Routledge.

Kasper, G., & Wagner, J. (2014). Conversation analysis in applied linguistics. *Annual Review of Applied Linguistics, 34*, 171–212.

Kushida, S. (2011). Confirming understanding and acknowledging assistance: Managing trouble responsibility in response to understanding check in Japanese talk-in-interaction. *Journal of Pragmatics, 43*(2), 2716–2739.

Kushida, S. (2015). Using names for referring without claiming shared knowledge: Name-quoting descriptors in Japanese. *Research on Language and Social Interaction, 48*(2), 230–251.

Kushida, S., & Yamakawa, Y. (2015). Fitting proposals to their sequential environment: A comparison of turn designs for proposing treatment in ongoing outpatient psychiatric consultations in Japan. *Sociology of Health & Illness, 37*(4), 522–544.

Lee, Y. A. (2015). Negotiating knowledge bases in pedagogical discourse: Relevance of identities to language classroom interactions. *Text & Talk, 35*(5), 621–642.

Leyland, C., Greer, T., & Rettig-Miki, E. (2016). Dropping the devil's advocate: One novice language tester's shifting interactional practices across a series of speaking tests. *Classroom Discourse, 7*(1), 85–107.

Mori, J., & Hasegawa, A. (2009). Doing being a foreign language learner in a classroom: Embodiment of cognitive states as social events. *IRAL, 47*, 65–94.

Mori, J., & Hayashi, M. (2006). The achievement of intersubjectivity through embodied completions: A study of interactions between first and second language speakers. *Applied Linguistics, 27*(2), 195–219.

Nguyen, H. T. (2011). Achieving recipient design longitudinally: Evidence from a pharmacy intern in patient consultations. In J. K. Hall, J. Hellermann, & S. Pekarek-Doehler (Eds.), *Interactional competence and development* (pp. 173–205). Bristol, UK: Multilingual Matters.

Nguyen, H. T. (2012). *Developing interactional competence. A conversation-analytic study of patient consultations in pharmacy.* Basingstoke, UK: Palgrave Macmillan.

Nishizaka, A. (2014). Sustained orientation to one activity in multiactivity during prenatal ultrasound examinations. In P. Haddington, T. Keisanen, L. Mondada, & M. Nevile (Eds.), *Multiactivity in social interaction: Beyond multitasking* (pp. 79–107). Amsterdam: John Benjamins.

Nishizaka, A., & Sunaga, M. (2015). Conversing while massaging: Multidimensional asymmetries of multiple activities in interaction. *Research on Language and Social Interaction, 48*(2), 200–229.

Ohta, A. (2001). *Second language acquisition processes in the classroom: Learning Japanese.* Mahwah, NJ: Lawrence Erlbaum.

Pallotti, G., & Wagner, J. (2011). *L2 learning as social practice: Conversation-analytic perspectives.* Honolulu, HI: University of Hawai'i, National Foreign Language Resource Center.

Pekarek Doehler, S., & Fasel Lauzon, V. (2015). Documenting change across time: Longitudinal and cross-sectional CA studies of classroom interaction. In N. Markee (Ed.), *Handbook of classroom interaction* (pp. 409–424). Hoboken, NJ: Wiley-Blackwell.

Pekarek Doehler, S., & Berger, E. (2016). L2 interactional competence as increased ability for context-sensitive conduct: A longitudinal study of story-openings. *Applied Linguistics.* doi.org/10.1093/applin/amw021

Pekarek Doehler, S., & Pochon-Berger, E. (2015). The development of L2 interactional competence: Evidence from turn-taking organization, sequence organization, repair organization and preference organization. In T. Cadierno & S. Eskildsen (Eds.), *Usage-based perspectives on second language learning* (pp. 233–267). Berlin: Mouton de Gruyter.

Prior, M., & Kasper, G. (Eds.). (2016). *Emotion in multilingual interaction.* Amsterdam: John Benjamins.

Rine, E. F., & Hall, J. K. (2011). Becoming the teacher: Changing participation frameworks in international teaching assistant discourse. In J. K. Hall, J. Hellermann, & S. Pekarek Doehler (Eds.), *L2 interactional competence and development* (pp. 1–15). Bristol, UK: Multilingual Matters.

Schegloff, E. (2006). Interaction: The infrastructure for social institutions, the natural ecological niche for language, and the arena in which culture is enacted. In N. J. Enfield & S. C. Levinson, (Eds.), *Roots of human sociality* (pp. 70–96). London: Berg.

Sert, O. (2015). *Social interaction and L2 classroom discourse.* Edinburgh: Edinburgh University Press.

Sidnell, J., & Stivers, T. (Eds.). (2013). *The handbook of conversation analysis.* Chichester, UK: Wiley-Blackwell.

Taguchi, N. (Eds.). (2009). *Pragmatic competence.* Berlin: Mouton de Gruyter.

Taguchi, N. (2014). Development of interactional competence in Japanese as a second language: Use of incomplete sentences as interactional resources. *The Modern Language Journal, 98*(2), 518–535.

Tanaka, H. (2000). The particle *ne* as a turn management device in Japanese conversation. *Journal of Pragmatics, 32*(8), 1135–1176.

Tanaka, H. (2013). The Japanese response token *Hee* for registering the achievement of epistemic coherence. *Journal of Pragmatics, 55*, 51–67.

Tateyama, Y. (2012). Repair in request sequence during student-teacher interactions in Japanese. In E. Alcon Soler & M. P. Safont (Eds.), *Discourse and language learning across L2 instructional settings* (pp. 79–104). Amsterdam: Rodopi.

Tominaga, W. (2013). The development of extended turns and storytelling in the Japanese oral proficiency interview. In G. Kasper & S. J. Ross (Eds.), *Assessing second language pragmatics* (pp. 220–257). Basingstoke, UK: Palgrave Macmillan.

Yamashita, S. (1996). *Six measures of JSL pragmatics* (Technical report #14). Honolulu, HI: University of Hawai'i, Second Language Teaching and Curriculum Center.

Young, R. F. (2011). Interactional competence in language learning, teaching, and testing. In E. Hinkel (Ed.), *Handbook of research in language learning and teaching* (pp. 426–443). New York, NY: Routledge.

Young, R. F., & Miller, E. R. (2004). Learning as changing participation: Discourse roles in ESL writing conferences. *The Modern Language Journal, 88*(5), 519–535.

# Interactional Competence

# Across Social Activities

# 2

# "My Japanese isn't that Good": Self-Deprecation, Preference Organization, and Interactional Competence

Alfred Rue Burch
*Rice University*

## Introduction

I would like to start this chapter, somewhat unconventionally, with an example that struck me as a "curious sequence" (Maynard, 2003). First, some brief ethnographic information. Peony is a Taiwanese woman living in Japan, is married to a Japanese man, and is studying the language. Yui is her colleague and friend, an L1 speaker of Japanese. They are chatting over tea and desserts about Peony's language study and ability when this question and answer sequence occurred:

**Extract 1a.** (20140412PY) Lazy Housewife (Simplified)

```
01    Y      nihongo  de  onegai  shimasu↑ tte  iwanai ↓no.
             Japanese in  favor   do-POL   QT   say-NG N
             You don't ask him to speak in Japanese?

02    P      .hh hh:: [°ee::  (demo)  (.)  chotto-
                       uhm    but          litte

03    Y               [((laugh))

04    P      namakemono  no  tsu- tsuma des°.
             lazy person LK       wife CP-POL
             I'm kind of a lazy wife.
```

Peony's formulation here raises a number of questions. Why does she formulate it in this way? Why not just say "I'm lazy." and leave it at that? Is she accomplishing something different by calling herself a "lazy wife"? Is there some tacit cultural obligation that a wife has to speak her husband's language? Is this simply a matter of Peony being modest in a way expected of her as a learner of Japanese or as someone who is married to a Japanese spouse and resides in the culture?

A deeper look at the wider sequence this example came from, as will be done in this chapter, reveals a subtle and skillful ability to achieve, maintain, and *manage* intersubjectivity through sequential, categorical, and interactional resources. This study explores this management through Conversation Analysis (CA)—here, meant to broadly reference the wider field that includes sequential analysis (Schegloff, 2007), preference organization (Pomerantz, 1984), membership categorization analysis (Sacks, 1992; Stokoe, 2012), formulation (Bilmes, 2011; Deppermann, 2011), and embodied interaction (Streeck, Goodwin, & LeBaron, 2011)—in order to illustrate how self-deprecation brings to bear the speaker's interactional competence (Hall & Pekarek Doehler, 2011; He & Young, 1998; Nguyen, 2012), particularly in how the self-deprecation arises out of the contingencies of the interaction and also engenders further contingencies that must be managed.

## Self-deprecation, preference, and L2 interactional competence

First, some comments on definition are in order. While modesty and self-deprecation have been discussed in CA research (Golato, 2005; Park, 2007; Pomerantz, 1984; Tarpey, 2012), the general tendency has been to treat the notion as a lay category without an explicit definition. Kim (2014), in her discourse analytic work on Japanese and Korean, defines self-deprecation as cases "in which speakers lower or humble themselves towards their addressee" (p. 82). Looking back at Extract 1a, it seems difficult to argue that Peony is humbling herself toward Yui as the addressee—indeed, if Peony is humbling herself, it seems to be more toward her non-present husband. Perhaps a workable gloss can be borrowed from Lazaraton's (1997) work on self-deprecation in Oral Proficiency Interviews (OPIs), where they are discussed as "negative self-assessments." While greater nuance is undoubtedly possible, this gloss suffices for our current purposes, as the data centers around Peony's negative assessments of her Japanese language ability and the efforts she makes towards improving.

It is perhaps tempting, especially when dealing with a language such as Japanese, to view self-deprecation (and terms that are often used rather synonymously such as self-effacement, humility, or modesty; cf. *inter alia*, Heine, Takata, & Lehman, 2000; Kim, 2014; Kitayama & Uchida, 2003) as simply acting upon cultural norm-related politeness that any competent member of society ought to follow (Kim, 2014). Indeed, politeness in Japanese is often viewed in this light. Lebra (2007) states that "Japanese culture is among those which endorse ritual politeness, humility, and reserve" (p. 18), while Ide (1989) discusses politeness in regard to the notion of *wakimae* 'discernment,' a cultural obligation to "conform to expected norms" (Geyer, 2008). Even work on politeness that aims to provide nuance and show language in use, such as Siegal (1995), discusses the ability to humble oneself as a matter of appropriateness and cultural competence. While none mention self-deprecation explicitly, it seems reasonable to treat the notion as a way of being humble and polite, as Brown and Levinson (1987) and Kim (2014) do, and therefore as something that anyone learning Japanese might be expected to be able to do in the course of culturally appropriate interaction (Saito & Beecken, 1997; Siegal, 1995). At the same time, as work by Cook (2005, 2006) and Geyer (2008) has shown, politeness is an interactional achievement, co-constructed between participants, and can be used as a resource in interaction.

The cultural norm perspective is problematic from a conversation analytic perspective in two ways. First, as Kasper (2006) notes, politeness theories such as Brown and Levinson (1987) rely on a rationalist perspective (Bilmes, 1986) which views action as goal-oriented and based upon intention and internal states. This approach runs the risk of drawing attention away from and ignoring the sequential unfolding of the talk: how the participants interact with each other and construct further talk in response to what has already been said. Mori (2009) points out a further problem. Not only does an approach that starts with the notion of cultural norms and appropriateness ignore the co-constructed nature of talk, it reifies the native speaker as a standard against which learners will be compared, casting the learners as deficient and ignoring the competencies that they bring to bear in the interaction (see also Firth & Wagner, 1997).

This is not to say that the speaker's identity as a non-native speaker or concerns with linguistic deficiency are never relevant. Park (2007) notes that self-deprecation is one method that L2 speakers can use to orient to their own (self-perceived and assessed) deficiencies, making their situated identities (Zimmermann, 1998) as L2 speakers relevant at that point in the interaction. Thus, self-deprecation, like all identity work, is an *in situ* accomplishment (Antaki & Widdicombe, 1998; Zimmermann, 1998), but can also be used in turn to accomplish other interactional work. On a very simple level, self-deprecation can be used by L2 speakers as a "bid for reassurance" (Tarpey, 2012, p. 119). However, as Lazaraton (1997) shows, negative self-assessments can be used for much more complex actions. She found in ESL placement OPIs that students could produce self-deprecations to account for and reinforce their desired placement into lower level courses. Such self-assessments thus have implications for identity work and may have stakes beyond the immediate interaction.

Which brings us to work in CA regarding self-deprecation and *preference organization* (Golato, 2005; Levinson, 1983; Pomerantz, 1984). While the term "preference" in lay terms is often associated with psychological or affective states, in CA it is used to describe regular patterns appearing in talk-in-interaction that display a gross tendency towards certain types of actions and responses (Atkinson & Heritage, 1984; Pekarek Doehler & Pochon Berger, 2011; Pomerantz & Heritage, 2013; Sacks, 1987). Of particular concern for us here is the general preference for agreement with assessments or assertions (Pomerantz, 1984), although this holds true for other areas such as the acceptance of proposals or invitations (Davidson, 1984) or answering affirmatively to positively formulated yes/no interrogatives (Hayano, 2013a; Heritage, 2010; Sacks, 1987), and relates to the interrelated dimensions of response timing and response formulation. By and large, preferred responses are delivered straight away (Pekarek Doehler & Pochon Berger, 2011; Pomerantz, 1984). Furthermore, preferred agreements to assessments are often upgraded. These tendencies are clearly illustrated by examples presented in Pomerantz (1984, p. 69), where the responses occur immediately and the evaluative adjectives are upgraded.

```
(34)  (NB:PT:19:r)
      L: God it's good.=
  →   E: =Isn't that exci:ting,

(35)  (JS:I:17)
      B: Isn'at good?=
  →   E: =It's duh::licious.
```

On the other hand, if responses are absent, delayed through pausing, hesitation markers, pro-forma agreements (i.e. "Well, yes, but..."), or are downgraded (i.e. "good" to "okay"), they are considered to have been designed as dispreferred (Hellermann, 2009; Pekarek Doehler & Pochon Berger, 2011; Pomerantz & Heritage, 2013). As Pomerantz (1984) states,

> [A]cross different situations, conversants orient to agreeing with one another as comfortable, supportive, reinforcing, perhaps as being sociable and as showing that they are like-minded. This phenomenon seems to hold whether persons are talking about the weather, a neighborhood dog, or a film that they just saw. Likewise, across a variety of situations conversants orient to their disagreeing with one another as uncomfortable, unpleasant, difficult, risking threat, insult, or offense. (p. 77)

Self-deprecation complicates the situation, however. Not surprisingly, an agreement with a negative self-assessment is generally dispreferred, and will be delivered as such (i.e., with hesitation markers and delays)—indeed, to deliver an agreement to a negative self-assessment without such dispreferred marking would likely be grounds for conflict or an interpretation of the agreement as doing another action (e. g., joking or "tough love"). Instead, when it comes to self-deprecation, it is disagreements that are generally delivered straight away and without hesitation.

Sequentially, self-deprecation appears in the preference literature in two positions, each with its own complexities. In the first position, as a negative self-assessment, the tendency for disagreement as the preferred next turn can lead to a situation where the speaker's self-deprecation can be viewed as fishing for compliments (Golato, 2005; Pomerantz, 1984). In the second position, self-deprecation often appears as a response to compliments (Golato, 2005; Saito & Beecken, 1997), but as Pomerantz (1978) points out, this can lead to issues of conflicting preferences. That is, while agreement is generally the preferred response to an assertion, there is also a preference to avoid self-praise. In responding to compliments, speakers must decide between agreeing with the compliment, but then by implication praise themselves, or avoid the self-praise by being self-deprecatory but then by implication disagree with the compliment.

Given the complexities of producing and responding to self-deprecation, it is not a stretch to argue that these actions can require some nuanced management, especially as they can implicate identity, social relationships, and even moral judgments (Jayyusi, 1991). That is to say, this management of the contingencies that engender and are engendered by negative self-assessments constitutes a display of interactional competence (IC). As Jacoby and Ochs (1995) point out, IC involves the "joint creation of a form, interpretation, stance, action, activity, identity, institution, skill, ideology, emotion, or other culturally meaning reality" (p. 171; see also Hall & Pekarek Doehler, 2011), and while the literature on self-deprecation cited above generally does not reference IC, it is clear that the environments in which negative self-assessments arise provide opportunities for such "joint creation." At the same time, negative self-assessments create preferentially complex situations that make further work on the part of both speakers relevant, which is made especially clear in Lazaraton (1997) and Golato (2005).

This chapter explores the relationship between self-deprecation and IC, with a particular focus on the following: (a) how Peony's negative self-assessments are occasioned by the ongoing talk, (b) how the negative self-assessments influence the trajectory of the talk, particularly how Peony and Yui manage the preferential complexities that arise from the self-deprecations, and (c) what resources (sequential, categorical, linguistic, and embodied) Peony and Yui employ in managing the self-deprecations and their consequences.

## Participants and methodology

The data presented here are from a longitudinal corpus of conversations recorded in mundane settings by Peony, the L2 speaker of Japanese introduced earlier, across the span of approximately a year and a half. Peony is an L1 speaker of Mandarin with a high degree of proficiency in English. Particularly relevant to the data presented here, she is married to a Japanese man whom she had met during graduate studies in the United States, and with whom (by her own accounts) she primarily speaks English. Prior to relocating to Japan, she had studied Japanese formally in the university setting during two different stretches, once as an undergraduate and then again as a graduate student (with a roughly 13 year hiatus in between), but had only taken up to second year courses each time. At the time of the first recording presented here, she had lived in Japan for approximately a year. Yui, an L1 speaker of Japanese who also has some ability in English, is an acquaintance that Peony met through a mutual friend. The extracts presented here are from two conversations between Peony and Yui that occurred roughly two months apart, the first of which was the first lengthy conversation in Japanese the pair had engaged in and therefore centered around getting acquainted and topical talk (Maynard & Zimmerman, 1984), while the second centered on story telling (Burch & Kasper, 2016).

The conversations were recorded with both digital audio recorders and video cameras. While the talk was transcribed according to a slightly modified version of the standard CA conventions (Jefferson, 2004), embodiment was transcribed using special conventions developed by the author (Burch, 2014; Burch & Kasper, 2016; Kasper & Burch, 2016), which are included in the appendix. Further, screen captures are included where textual description may be insufficient in clearly illustrating gestures, posture, or actions.

## Analysis

The first extract occurs early in the first conversation between Peony and Yui. Prior to this extract, Peony is describing another married couple also consisting of one L1 speaker and one L2 speaker of Japanese, and how she had heard that couple uses Japanese at home. Yui describes the situations as being *gyaku* 'the opposite' of Peony's case, and we pick up here in line 01 with Peony's response. In the screen captures, Peony is on the right, while Yui is on the left.

**Extract 1b.** (20140412PY) Lazy Housewife

```
01    P         but shujin    wa itsumo eego::   e.
                    husband   TP always  English *
                But my husband always English.

02              (0.6)

03    P         eego   [o?
                English O
                English?

04    Y                [nn     nn    nn.=
                        yeah  yeah  yeah
                Yeah yeah yeah.

05    P         =hana:su  n:  des.
                  speak    N  CP-POL
                He speaks English.

         y      +nod
06    Y         +°hanasu n da°  ((sniff))
                  speak   N CP
                Oh, he does.
```

```
         p                     +LH circle forward
         p                     +LH palm up
         p                     +GZ>Y
07    P         °dakara:°(.) +sonna ni   +joo:zu ni
                 therefore    that much   well
                So, I haven't (become) that good...

08              (0.7)
```

```
09    Y        ↑nn[::
               hmmm
               Hmmm.


      p                +squints
      p                +shakes head
10    P        [nari, +(0.4) [↑nari↑
               become-        become-
               become- ... become-

11    Y                        [naranai?
                                become-NG
               You haven't gotten (good)?


      p        +shakes head
12    P        +naranai.   [°naranai.°
               become-NG    become-NG
               Haven't gotten, haven't gotten.


      y                        +slow nod
13    Y                        [+n↑n::
                                hmmm
               Hmmm


      y                        +tilts head left
14    Y        nihongo de +onegai shi↑masu↑ tte
               Japanese in favor   do- POL    QT

      p        +GZ away, grimaces
15    Y        +iwanai ↓no.
                say-NG  N
               You don't ask him to speak in Japanese?
```

## Self-Deprecation, Preference Organization, and Interactional Competence 27

```
              p              +GZ>Y, slightly shakes head
16            P      .hh hh:: [+°ee::(demo) (.) chotto-
                              uhm            but   little

17            Y                       [((laugh))

18            P      namakemono no  [tsu- tsuma des°.
                     lazy person LK       wife  CP-POL
                     I'm kind of a lazy wife.

              y                           +sits back, claps
19            Y                          [+khh khh khh .hh

              p              +GZ at Y
20            P      nn::   +eego   ga  benri     des.
                     hmmm   English S   convenient CP-POL
                     Hmm, English is convenient.

21            Y      aa↑:[::::
                     ah
                     Ah.

22            P           [eego    ga benri     [des.
                           English S  convenient CP-POL
                     English is convenient.

23            Y                              [naruhodo ↑ne-
                                              I see    IP
                     I see.

              p      nod
24            P      =nn::
                     hmmm
                     Hmmm
```

In lines 01 through 03, Peony begins by contrasting her husband with the husband in the other couple, saying that he always speaks in English. Although she encounters some difficulty and self-repairs her particle usage, she completes the utterance in line 05. The *extreme case formulation itsumo* 'always' (line 01) sets this statement up as a possible complaint (Edwards, 2000; Pomerantz, 1986), treating the language situation at home as unchanging and problematic. The formulation also invokes the *standardized relational pair* (Sacks, 1992; Stokoe, 2012) of husband and wife, and makes visible *category predicated features* (i.e., norms that are implied by the participants but not explicitly worked up in the interaction; Reynolds & Fitzgerald, 2015, p. 102) that are involved in the relationship between spouses who are L1 speakers of different languages.

That is, the spouse who is the L1 speaker of the language that the other spouse is learning bears some degree of responsibility to be a resource for language learning, though Peony's claim that her husband always speaks in English suggests that this expectation is not met in her household.[1]

After Yui has displayed her understanding (line 06), Peony begins to formulate a self-assessment with *dakara sonna ni joozu ni* 'so I (haven't become) that good' while withdrawing her gaze and circling her left hand forward, but then pauses, all of which suggest a word search (Goodwin & Goodwin, 1986; Hayashi, 2003), or more specifically a grammar search (Kurhila, 2006; Markee & Kunitz, 2013). Peony says *nari*, projecting the polite negative form *narimasen* 'not become' (suggested by the grammatical form *sonna ni joozu ni* and the pre-polite rendering of the verb stem), but pauses, squints, and shakes her head before she attempts it again (line 10). In overlap, Yui provides a candidate completion (Lerner, 2004) with the plain form version *naranai*, which Peony repeats twice while shaking her head, accepting Yui's completion through both the repetitions and physically embodying the negative semantics.

With this co-completion, Peony's first self-deprecatory formulation is fully on the table. There are two broad points about this negative self-assessment that bear attention. The first is that the formulation not only assesses her own abilities, but also completes the complaint that was made relevant earlier through the use of the extreme case formulation *itsumo* 'always' and thus explicitly places the blame for her perceived lack of improvement upon her husband not speaking the language at home. The second point relates to what leads up to the formulation in the first place. Unlike the examples of negative self-assessment illustrated by Tarpey (2012) or Park (2007), there is no specific language related assessable being explicitly oriented to at this point. Instead, the formulation orients to her overall Japanese ability. In this way, the formulation is reminiscent of the negative self-assessments in Lazaraton's (1997) OPI study, which also occur early in the interaction and are not aimed at specific assessables. As discussed earlier, her participants used negative self-assessments as a warrant for taking a lower level English course. While there is no institutional purpose involved here, perhaps Peony is doing something similar; by placing her self-criticism on the record, she prospectively works against expectations about her ability and provides license for any further difficulties she may face in the language.

In lines 14 and 15, Yui responds by asking the question presented at the beginning of the chapter, *nihongo de onegai shimasu tte iwanai no* 'You don't ask him to speak in Japanese?', as she tilts her head to the left. Framed with the final particle *no*, which treats the proposition behind the question (that Peony does not ask her husband to speak in Japanese) as surprising or counter to expectations (Hayano, 2013b, p. 182), the question places some degree of responsibility upon Peony herself for whether her husband will speak Japanese with her. By doing so, Yui's negatively formulated question takes a very strong stance (Heritage, 2002) and functions to strongly suggest that Peony indeed *should* make such a request of her husband.

As Yui says *iwanai no*, however, Peony grimaces and then responds to the question with *(demo) (.) chotto namakemono no tsu- tsuma des* 'but, I'm kind of a lazy wife' as she shakes her head. This self-deprecatory formulation accomplishes at least three things. First, it essentially skips the type-conforming yes or no answer to Yui's question, but puts an account for it on record by providing a reason for why she does not ask her husband to speak in Japanese. At the same time, it aligns with the implication behind Yui's question by accepting responsibility through claiming that she is a *namakemono* 'lazy person.' Lastly, by instantiating the category of wife, which is not grammatically obligatory here, she re-invokes the category used earlier when she blamed her husband for her lack of progress in the language, thus using the standardized relational pair (Sacks, 1992, p. 326; Stokoe, 2012) as a resource to walk back her previous explicit attribution of responsibility. It is, in a sense, reparative (though not a repair in the canonical sequential sense) of her previous talk, as it mitigates against the upshot of her previous talk.

In response, Yui sits back, claps, and laughs (line 19), which treats Peony's negative self-assessment as non-serious (Schnurr & Chan, 2011), and thus withholds an on-the-record agreement or disagreement. Peony then provides a much more neutral alternative formulation before the sequential slot for a full response can really open, saying *eego ga benri des* 'English is convenient' in line 20. This sidesteps the earlier question of who is responsible and accounts for why they speak English at home, and at the same time provides a specification of the object of her laziness (i.e., the language and not other domestic activities). It also functions to delete the space in which Yui's agreement or disagreement with Peony's negative self-assessment would come due. Yui's elongated *aa* in line 21 indexes a change of state (Heritage, 1984), claiming understanding but still non-committal in terms of agreement or disagreement with Peony's neutral assessment. Peony then repeats that English is convenient, which receives a stronger receipt with Yui's *naruhodo ne* 'I see.' This response, if taken with the previous change of state token, not only claims understanding, but also treats Peony's neutral formulation as "just what [Yui] was waiting for" (Morita, 2005, p. 146), and therefore accepts the formulation as reasonable and appropriate.

Thus, in Extract 1b, we see two self-deprecatory formulations that arise for different reasons. The first, Peony's negative assessment of her Japanese ability, arises out of the comparison of Peony and her husband to another couple in terms of language use at home, and is part of a complaint that places blame on her husband's behavior for her lack of improvement. It is notable that this self-deprecation does not lead to the preferred disagreements discussed by Pomerantz (1984) and Golato (2005), which may be for a number of reasons. One possibility relates to the formulation's status as a blame attribution, which

Yui addresses with her negative question-framed suggestion. Another possibility is that since this conversation occurs early in the pair's relationship, Yui may not be in the position epistemically to judge Peony's language ability. The question formulation allows Yui to avoid agreements or disagreements that she does not have the epistemic access to give while still dealing with the self-deprecation in a relevant fashion by asking for further information and treating the situation as one that Peony can do something about. The second self-deprecation, the self-attribution as a 'lazy wife,' arises in response to Yui's suggestion, and with it, Peony manages the implications of her complaint and blame attribution skillfully; that is, she acknowledges that she has some responsibility for the situation, and thus steps back the blame she has assigned to her husband. However, as the formulation again runs the risk of being difficult for Yui to agree or disagree with (given epistemic access and preference concerns), Peony's provision of a neutral formulation framing the situation as a matter of convenience (line 20) provides Yui with an interactional slot where she does not need to go on record with an agreement or disagreement with Peony's self-deprecation, while also working to neutralize the blame attribution and allowing Peony to take a degree of the responsibility upon herself.

Extract 2, which occurs roughly two months later, illustrates another case where Peony provides negative self-assessments, although they arise out of a very different interactional trajectory and engender different consequences.[2] Prior to this talk, Peony and Yui are talking about what Peony has been doing recently, which involves Peony studying Japanese by listening to language related podcasts that explain grammar points and expressions. Extract 2a picks up where Peony begins to provide examples of expressions she has learned, and illustrates the activity that Peony's later self-deprecation arises from.

**Extract 2a.** (20140601PY) Hatsu

```
           p              +GZ up, LH>chin
01    P    [kyoo: +#wa::#
            today    TP
           Today...

02    Y    [((clears throat))

03    P    °kyoo  no lesson wa(h)a hh (.) °nani ga.°
            today LK lesson  TP                  what  S
```

```
          p       +GZ>Y, BH>together
04                +hatsu           (0.5) nani nani hatsu.
                   supposed to*          what what supposed to*
                  Today's lesson was, what was that, it's hatsu* (hazu)
                  it's supposed to be such and such.

05        Y       nn.
                  hm
                  Hm.

06                (1.6)

07        P       °eto° (.) ashita   wa: (0.5) ame: #ga# (.)
                   uhm       tomorrow TP        rain  S

          p       +leans forward, face down toward table
08                +furu hats(h)u(h)u d(h)e [hh hh hh
                   rain supposed to*
                  Uhm, It's supposed to rain tomorrow.

09        Y                              [.khh .hn .hn .hh

10        P       [((laughing))

11        Y       [((laughing)) [hh hh hh

          p                     /sits up, GZ>Y
12        P                     [+°to y(h)uu k(h)ot(h)o°
                                  QT say    matter
                  As an example.
```

```
          y       {LHIF sweeps up-down
                  {   /     /
13        Y       na[ruhodo
                  I see
                  I see.

14        P          [.hhn

15        Y       aa ee:to: ashita   wa::(.) nn:::(0.8)
                  oh uhm    tomorrow TP
```

```
             y                         +head tilt left
16                  raibu    ga aru    +hazu       [tok(h)a(h)a
                    concert  S  exist  supposed to  for example
                    Oh, uhm, so like, tomorrow umm there is supposed to be a
                    concert?

17       P                                         [aa aa aa naru    n
                                                    oh oh oh become *

18                  ga aru   hazu         hai=
                    S  exist supposed to  yes
                    Oh oh oh, become, there is supposed to be, yes.

19       Y          =.hh
```

In line 01, Peony launches into talking about the topic of the lesson she had listened to earlier in the day, but then does a solitary word search (Goodwin, 1987; Goodwin & Goodwin, 1986; Hayashi, 2003), as marked by the upwards gaze and quieter speech, asking herself what the lesson was. She does a visible display of remembering by bringing her gaze to Yui and her hands together in a quiet clap in line 4, as she says *hatsu*, a mispronunciation of *hazu* (which is an evidential marker for expectation, roughly translatable as "supposed to"). She then provides it within the grammar display format *nani nani* ('blank blank' or 'something something', a common format for discussing grammar points in Japanese language classrooms). Yui, however, only provides a continuer. After a 1.6 second gap of silence, indicative of a further word search, Peony attempts an example with *ashita wa: (0.5) ame: ga (.) furu hatsu* 'It is supposed to rain tomorrow,' but continues to mispronounce the target form. As she finishes the example, she leans forward with her face down toward the table and breaks into laughter (line 08), suggesting that she finds something problematic about her example. Yui then joins in with affiliative laughter (Glenn, 2003; Jefferson, 1974) which continues for a couple of seconds until Peony closes the example and laughter by sitting up, looking at Yui, and saying *to yuu koto* 'as an example.' Yui then displays her recognition by smiling and swiping her left hand index finger up and down in rhythm with *naruhodo* 'I see' (line 13). She then provides an other-repair of the pronunciation with her own example, *aa ee:to: ashita wa:: (.) nn::: (0.8) raibu ga aru hazu* 'oh, umm, tomorrow there is supposed to be a concert,' which she also marks with a head tilt and *toka* 'so like' or 'for instance,' treating it as a candidate understanding and leaving other possibilities open. In line 17, Peony receipts the repair with repeated change-of-state tokens (Heritage, 1984), and after what seems like a mis-repetition of *aru* as *naru*,[3] repeats the correct pronunciation and closes with *hai* 'yes.'

From this point, during the 36 lines of talk omitted here due to space constraints, Peony provides three more evidential markers: *ka mo shirenai* 'maybe', and *deshoo* and *daroo*, which are forms of the copula (polite and plain) which, in the examples Peony provides, index probability. While she produces *ka mo shirenai* and *deshoo* without difficulties, she again faces pronunciation problems with *daroo*, which leads to a similar exemplification sequence as with *hazu*. Extract 2b re-enters the talk after the exemplification sequence has concluded, as Peony launches into a negative self-assessment.

**Extract 2b.** (20140601PY) I'm not that good

```
56      P       °yeah but-° (.) .hh senshuu- (.)
                                    last week

57              senshuu:: no   shuuma#tsu::#
                last week LK   weekend
                Yeah but, last week, last weekend

58      Y       n[n
                hm
                Hm.

59      P       [ka(h)r(h)a(h)a[(h)a
                    from
                since (last weekend)

60      Y                      [nn.
                                hm
                Hm.

        p       BH>ears
61              (0.8)

        y       +BHIF PNT>ears
62      Y       [+>kikinagara<]
                    listen-while
                While listening

63      P       [ki-         ] kiku   #n:::# (.) [°nn°
                 lis-          listen N              hmm
                Listening, hmm...

64      Y                                          [°nn::°
                                                    hmm
                Hmm.
```

```
              p        +RH 'so so'              +smile
65            P        de +sonna ni   joozu ja +na(h)i(h)i
                       and that  much  good   CP  NG
                       ...and, I'm not that good.

66                     [.hh

              y                  +RH wave
67            Y        [°moo    +daijoobu da to [omou.°
                         already okay      CP QT   think
                       I think you already do okay.

68            P                                   [°joozu(ku)
                                                    good (*)

69                     narima°se(h)n(h)n
                       become-POL-NG
                       I don't get better.

70            Y        $joozuku na(h)r(h)im(h)a[s(h)en$
                         good *   become-POL-NG
                       Don't get better.

71            P                                   [((laughing))

72            Y        [((cough)) joozu da to omoimas    kedo.
                                    good  CP QT think-POL but
                       I think you're good though.

              p        +nod
73            P        [+nn.
                         hm
                       Hm.

              p        +BH waving
74            P        +nn uh::

              y        +shakes head slightly
75            Y        +nn.
                         hm
                       Hm.
```

```
              p          +BH together     +smile
    76        P          +tomodach(h)i    [+hhe he
                           friend
                         Friend.
```

```
              y                           +eyebrows raise
    77        Y                           [+°(      )?°

              p          face in hands
    78                   (0.5)

              p          GZ up
    79        P          °↑nn↑°
```

This segment begins with Peony initiating a new sequence with *yeah but (.) .hh senshuu- (.) senshuu no shuumatsu:: kara* 'since last week- last weekend' (lines 56 through 59), but she does not reach the predicate. At line 61, during a 0.8 second pause, Peony moves her hands to her ears, projecting a completion related to listening.[4] Yui then similarly moves both of her hands to her ears as she provides a candidate completion with *kikinagara* 'while listening,' picking up on Peony's trajectory. At the same time, Peony attempts to provide a predicate but experiences some difficulty as she says *kiku* 'listen' then in a creaky voice stretches out *n:::* (which, at least as it starts, seems to function as the nominalizer, but then comes to signal trouble).

Peony then provides a self-deprecating formulation about her lack of improvement in Japanese, formulated in a very similar fashion to the one two months earlier, saying *sonna ni joozu ja nai* 'I'm not that good' while producing a 'so so' gesture that reinforces her negative self-assessment (line 65). However, unlike the previous case, which was a general assessment not orienting to a specific assessable, this formulation seems to be both specific and general. Regarding specific assessables, it can be seen as an account for both her current difficulties and the errors that she made in providing the examples of *hazu* and *daroo* earlier (as the negative self-assessment is linked via *de* 'and' to her previous utterance about having started to listen to the podcasts the previous week). As a general negative self-assessment, given the number of examples she has just provided and her display of 'doing being a diligent student,' the formulation also mitigates against an interpretation of her actions as having been a form of self-praise (Pomerantz, 1978).

However, as self-deprecation tends to lead to preferred disagreements (Pomerantz, 1984) that praise the speaker, they can also be treated as fishing for compliments (Golato, 2005). Indeed, this is how Yui responds to Peony's formulation, by saying *moo daijoobu da to omou* 'I think you already do okay,' while waving her hands, as if waving off the negative self-assessment. In overlap (line 68), Peony reformulates that she has not improved (seemingly in a somewhat non-standard form as *joozuku*), while laughing, which Yui repeats through laughter as well, treating the negative self-assessment as non-serious. After the laughter, in line 72, Yui provides another, upgraded compliment which further disagrees with the self-deprecatory formulation—*joozu da to omoimas kedo* 'I think you're good though.'

As discussed earlier though, compliments risk raising an interactional dilemma. While agreement with an assertion is preferred, self-praise is generally avoided (Golato, 2005; Pomerantz, 1984). A common strategy is to deflect or return the compliment (Golato, 2005; Shimizu, 2009). Here, Peony refuses the compliment by first waving her hands in front of her (line 74), and then by saying *tomodachi* 'friend' while smiling and holding her hands together near her face (see screen capture, line 76). By this, she is seemingly saying that 'you are complimenting me because you are my friend,' orienting to category bound predicates and obligations (Stokoe, 2012; Watson, 1978) inherent in the standard relational pair *friends*. This refusal also mitigates against an interpretation of Peony's self-deprecatory formulation as fishing for a compliment. However, the implied assertion here also runs the risk of challenging the sincerity of Yui's compliment. Yui responds inaudibly but with rising intonation and raised eyebrows, which can function as a repair initiator (Hosoda, 2006) and as a display of surprise (Peräkylä & Ruusuvuori, 2006); as her response is inaudible, the action is also unclear, but speculatively could range from being a simple repair initiation all the way to treating Peony's account as problematic (i.e., questioning the sincerity of her compliment). Speculation aside, Peony responds to Yui's inaudible turn by putting her face in her hands, doing 'being embarrassed' (line 78).

It is here that Yui then orients to Peony's negative self-assessment in a similar way to the way she did in Extract 1, with a reference to Peony being able to practice her Japanese with her husband. As we see in Extract 2c, however, the trajectory unfolds in a very different fashion.

**Extract 2c.** (20140601PY) Impossible

```
80      Y       go[shujin to    nihongo  de hanaseba ii  °jan°.
                husband   with  Japanese in speak-if good IP
                You should speak Japanese with your husband.

81      P         [°nn°

82              (0.6)
```

```
           p        +grimace
83         P        +nnnn (0.4) demo (0.4) mu:ri       des.
                     hmmm       but         impossible CP-POL
                    Hmmm, but that's impossible.

           y        +LH>mouth
84         Y        +hhaa [ha ha

85         P              [muri       des. (0.3) itsumo eego       de
                           impossible CP-POL       always  English in
                          It's impossible. We're always in English.

           y        +nod
86         Y        +↑nn[::

87         P              [uh. (0.9) eego     de::   n (1.3)
                                     English in        *

           p        +RH palm up toward Y
88                  +wakaranai     e (0.4) uh: <terebi:> (.) mo
                     understand-NG *             television    also

89                  miru to[ki?
                    watch time
                    Uh, in English, I don't know, uh, when we also watch TV?

           y                  ↓nod
90         Y                 [+↑°nn°↑

91         P        wakaranai     (.) koto ga (.) n hanasu.
                     understand-NG      thing S*     * speak
                    We talk about stuff I don't understand.

92                  (1.4)

93         Y        ((cough)) mm (0.6) [kiku n da.
                                        ask  N CP
                    Mm, you ask.

94         P                            [shitsumon=
                                         question

95                  =kiku n da. (0.4) ũ::
                     ask   N CP         *
                    I ask questions.
```

```
96              (0.8)

97    Y         ((cough))=

98    P         =nn.
                 hm
                Hm.

99    Y         ((sniff)) (°°ne°°) khnn.

100   P         °jaa°
                 well
                Well,

101             (2.2)

102   Y         kotaete kureru   no? [goshu:jin ga.]
                answer  for you  N    husband    S
                Does he answer? Your husband.

      p                              +nod
103   P                         [+nn    nn    nn]
                                 yeah  yeah  yeah

104             [nn.
                 yeah
                Yeah yeah yeah yeah.

105   Y         [↑nn:/::?
                 yeah
                Yeah?

106             (1.2)

107   Y         [((clears throat))]

108   P         [nn]

      p         +grimace
109   P         +muri        des ne: (0.4) <nihongo [#de:#>
                 impossible  CP  IP         Japanese  in
                It's impossible, in Japanese.

                ((talk continues on to joking sequence
                  about going to gookon (group blind date)
                  to learn and practice Japanese))
```

In line 80, Yui provides another suggestion about Peony speaking Japanese with her husband. Similar to the case two months prior, this suggestion is touched off by Peony's self-deprecatory formulation and carries the implication that Peony has at least some responsibility for the state of affairs. Unlike the case two months prior, however, this is produced as a strong suggestion with no smile: *goshujin to nihongo de hanaseba ii jan* 'You should speak to your husband in Japanese' (line 80). Furthermore, as this is the first time in this conversation that Peony's husband has been mentioned, this suggestion seems to be based upon a prior understanding of Peony and her husband speaking English at home (quite likely the discussion that occurred in Extract 1), and thus comes from a position of greater epistemic access than her previous question/suggestion. The stern tone of the suggestion also seems to be in response to Peony's prior attribution of the reason for Yui's compliment as having to do with friendship (i.e., questioning the sincerity of her compliment).

While Peony's grimace (line 83) as an embodied response to the suggestion is not unlike Extract 1 in projecting a dispreferred response, her answer takes a different, and less self-deprecatory tact. Here, rather, she states that it would be *muri* 'impossible,' which Yui receipts with laughter. Peony repeats this formulation in line 85, and proceeds to provide an account, which states that she and her husband use English to clear up cases of misunderstanding that arise when they watch television (first as *wakaranai (.) koto ga (.) n hanasu* 'we speak about things I don't understand,' and then repaired to *shitsumon kiku n da* 'I ask questions'). The implication being that it is not that there is no Japanese in the home, it is that English is a resource for dealing with Japanese that she does not understand. This account reinforces Peony's negative assessment of her Japanese ability and the invocation of her identity as an L2 speaker, though it is interesting to note that here she elaborates upon her activity rather than describing herself as *namakemono* 'lazy'.

After coughing, sniffing, and a rather lengthy pause, Yui responds by asking whether Peony's husband answers these questions. Peony nods and provides repeated affirmative tokens (lines 103 and 104), and Yui receipts this with an elongated and gradually rising *nn:/::?*. After another pause, Peony then grimaces again and repeats *muri* 'impossible', and adds *nihongo de* 'in Japanese', formulating a summary of her response to Yui's suggestion. After this point, Yui provides another, much more humorous suggestion of going to a *gookon* (similar to a blind date, but with multiple participants) in order to meet people with whom to practice Japanese, thus providing an alternative (and not particularly serious) suggestion and closing down the talk about Peony speaking with her husband.[5]

In Extract 2, we again see two self-deprecating formulations. The first, the comment about not improving, works on one hand to account for Peony's difficulty when providing the examples of what she has learned (i.e. *hazu*) as well as her immediate difficulties with formulating her talk, while on the other hand also working to manage possible interpretations of her actions as bragging. However, as it touches off compliments in response, it leads to a dilemma where Peony needed to manage the possible inference of her having been fishing for compliments. This leads to the second self-deprecating formulation, her attribution of Yui only making the compliments because she is Peony's friend, which, in turn, touched off Yui's strong suggestion. The extract thus provides an example of how self-deprecating formulations, while acting as a resource for accounting for past and future difficulties and for managing how a recipient will interpret the speaker's talk and actions, can also lead to interactionally delicate situations that then must be managed further.

## Discussion and conclusion

The interactional circumstances that occasioned Peony's self-deprecations illustrate the wide variety of situations and contingencies that can lead to negative self-assessments. While we find that there were indeed specific assessables, such as the interactional difficulties Peony faced in Extracts 2a and 2b (*hatsu* for *hazu*, and difficulties formulating her explanation regarding how long she had listened to the podcasts) that occasioned her assessment of her Japanese ability as not good, they also function as a more general assessment of her overall ability, accounting both retrospectively for any mistakes she had already made and prospectively for any that may occur later. Thus, both her specific and general negative self-assessments work to make her situated identity as an L2 speaker relevant and consequential (Park, 2007) for accounting for the talk up to that point and the trajectory of the interaction thereafter.

Similarly, the actions accomplished through these self-deprecations were also varied. In Extract 1, Peony uses a negative self-assessment as a resource for a complaint and to attribute blame for her self-perceived lack of proficiency to her husband, and then another self-deprecation to counter that very same blame attribution. In Extract 2b, she uses a negative self-assessment to account for trouble, and further to counteract a possible implication that she has been bragging, then another to mitigate against being viewed as fishing for compliments (Golato, 2005). Thus, Peony's self-deprecations not only do identity work (Park, 2007; Tarpey, 2012), but also help to manage moral implications (Jayyusi, 1991; Lee, 1987; Sacks, 1972) to portray herself as someone who would not brag nor fish for compliments.

At the same time, as discussed previously, a negative self-assessment puts a number of issues related to preference at play. The aforementioned issue of fishing for compliments is just one that can lead to delicate situations. Indeed, when Peony rejects Yui's compliment by claiming she only said it because they are friends (Extract 2b), she also calls Yui's sincerity into question. Such situations can require interactional management to maintain a comfortable interaction and relationship. Peony exhibits just such management ability in Extract 1 by providing a neutral account of English as convenient after her self-attribution as being a lazy wife, thus deleting the sequential position in which Yui would be expected to respond, and in a sense letting Yui off the hook in regards to putting an agreement or disagreement with Peony's self-deprecation on record. To reiterate, the management of these potentially sensitive contingencies accomplishes both identity and moral work, which allows the interaction to move forward.

The management of the interactional contingencies that engender and are engendered by negative self-assessments requires the employment of a variety of resources, or a "bricolage" (Levinson, 2006) that draws from sequential, categorical, and other interactional capabilities. The aforementioned example of claiming that English is convenient (Extract 1) is an example of utilizing sequential resources to manage the interactional consequences of a negative self-assessment. Likewise, Peony uses categorical resources, such as the invocation of her situated identity as an L2 speaker of Japanese (Park, 2007), as well as the standardized relational pairs and concomitant category bound predicates of 'husband/wife' (Extract 1) and 'friend/friend' (Extract 2), in dealing with the interactional trajectories that arose after her negative self-assessments. Finally, Peony deploys embodied resources as well, including shaking her head as part of an assertion that her Japanese has not improved (Extract 1), grimacing as a means for projecting negative responses (Extracts 1 & 2), and her posture, facial expressions, and gestures as she physically waves off Yui's compliment about her Japanese ability (Extract 2). In assembling these resources together, Peony both accomplishes and reinforces her negative self-assessments and manages the complexities that arise from them.

Interactional competence has generally been concerned most specifically with phenomena related to sequence, actions, and activities (Hall, Hellermann, & Pekarek Doehler, 2011; He & Young, 1998; Nguyen, 2011, 2012; Theodórsdóttir, 2011), and we certainly see evidence of such issues in this data. A focus on Peony's self-deprecation, however, brings another related and equally important aspect to the fore: The ability to manage the contextually sensitive complexities of preference organization, including the interactional consequences of preferred and dispreferred actions and responses, is also a key component of IC (Al-Gahtani & Roever, 2014; Pekarek Doehler & Pochon Berger, 2011), not only in terms of agreements and disagreements, but also in terms of managing the potential difficulties that arise when preference is not particularly clear cut. Peony's management of these complexities was an illustration of this area of IC.

There are at least two significant implications that can be drawn from the data presented in this chapter. This first relates to the study of politeness in

Japanese interaction, and particularly in Japanese as an L2 interaction. What on the surface looks like a speaker (L1 or L2) acting in a culturally appropriate manner can be much more complex than simply following prescriptive rules of politeness or displaying *wakimae* 'discernment.' It is not that such rules are necessarily irrelevant—as norms of behavior that participants may orient to or use as accounts for behaviors, such notions may be found to be influential on identity work and preference. However, to treat such prescriptive rules as the end explanation for the behavior runs the risk of missing what is accomplished through acting in a culturally appropriate (or even inappropriate) manner. In the data presented here, self-deprecation is both an interactional accomplishment and an interactional resource.

Another implication relates to research on IC in general. There has been some work focusing on the intersection of IC and preference (Al-Gahtani & Roever, 2014; Pekarek Doehler & Pochon Berger, 2011), and previous work on self-deprecations in CA (Lazaraton, 1997; Park, 2007; Tarpey, 2012) could easily be subsumed under the rubric of IC even if no explicit reference to IC was made; however, greater exploration of the management of preference as a component of IC could be very fruitful, particularly in cases where issues of preference and dispreference are not cut-and-dried and can lead to delicate situations where social relationships, identity, and ascriptions of moral character could be at stake. This has particularly strong implications, in turn, for language pedagogy (Pekarek Doehler & Pochon Berger, 2011; van Compernolle, 2011), as L2 speakers inevitably encounter situations in which preferred and dispreferred responses result in an interactional rock and a hard place.

Further studies are needed, of course, in order to discern the range of situations that can occasion negative self-assessments, the undoubtedly large variety of actions that can be accomplished through self-deprecations, and the equally varied methods speakers use to deal with the interactional, identity, and moral consequences that ensue afterwards. Furthermore, there are likely other types of phenomena that lead to complex preference organizations that require interactional management; many such phenomena may also relate to rules of cultural appropriateness and etiquette, and can therefore be sites of further exploration of how interactional competence is displayed in potentially delicate situations.

## Notes

1 Two points bear making regarding this analysis. First, while Peony claims that her husband always speaks English at home, data from later months evidences him speaking both languages with her. Therefore, the extreme case formulation is best understood as a device employed for the current interactional purposes and not meant to be taken literally. Second, the expectation that spouses be available as language learning resources comes up not only in the two conversations discussed

in this chapter, but also at least two other times in the overall corpus. Anecdotally, it has been talked about or assumed on multiple occasions in my own conversations in Japanese as well. It seems likely that these category bound expectations arise when talking about other couples, but may not be relevant to (or are possibly even contested by) such couples. Of course, this could be fruitful ground for further research.

2   Although the conversation occurs two months later than that of Extract 1, and Peony's response to Yui's suggestion that she speak Japanese with her husband (Extract 2c) is more involved and detailed, I do not wish to suggest that there is evidence of longitudinal development. It is possible that the differences could be fully accounted for based upon the different interactional trajectories.

3   Another possibility, pointed out by one of the editors, is that this is an approximate repetition of Yui's *raibu*. While this analysis certainly fits in terms of action and sequence, the phonological evidence makes it difficult to do more than speculate.

4   At first glance, this action looks like an "embodied completion" (Olsher, 2004) in that Peony seemingly completes her utterance with a gesture. However, as line 63 shows, the gesture is related to a word search that leads to a verbal completion of the utterance.

5   The topic of the *gookon* seems to be an inside joke between Peony and Yui, as it arises in all of the conversations between them. The suggestion is always made humorously, playing off the fact that it would be unlikely and untoward for a married person to engage in such an activity, but that it would be a good way to practice the language. On one occasion, Yui even suggests that Peony take her husband along to the *gookon* as part of a game.

# References

Al-Gahtani, S., & Roever, C. (2014). Preference structure in L2 Arabic requests. *Intercultural Pragmatics, 11*(4), 619–643.
Antaki, C., & Widdicombe, S. (1998). Identity as an achievement and as a tool. In C. Antaki & S. Widdicombe (Eds.), *Identities in talk* (pp. 1–14). Cambridge: Cambridge University Press.
Atkinson, J. M., & Heritage, J. (Eds.). (1984). *Structures of social action: Studies in conversation analysis* (pp. 299–345). Cambridge: Cambridge University Press.
Bilmes, J. (1986). *Language and behavior.* New York, NY: Plenum.
Bilmes, J. (2011). Occasioned semantics: A systematic approach to meaning in talk. *Human Studies, 34*(2), 129–153.
Brown, P., & Levinson, S. (1987). *Politeness: Some universals in language use.* Cambridge: Cambridge University Press.
Burch, A. R. (2014). Pursuing information: A conversation analytic perspective on communication strategies. *Language Learning, 64*(3), 651–684.

Burch, A. R., & Kasper, G. (2016). Like Godzilla: Enactments and formulations in telling a disaster story in Japanese. In M. T. Prior & G. Kasper (Eds.), *Talking emotion in multilingual settings*. Amsterdam: John Benjamins.

Cook, H. M. (2005). *Reanalysis of discernment from a social constructivist perspective: Academic consultation sessions in Japanese universities*. Honolulu, HI: University of Hawai'i, National Foreign Language Resource Center.

Cook, H. M. (2006). Japanese politeness as an interactional achievement: Academic consultation sessions in Japanese universities. *Multilingua, 25*, 269–292.

Davidson, J. (1984). Subsequent versions of invitations, offers, requests, and proposals dealing with potential or actual rejection. In J. M. Atkinson & J. Heritage (Eds.), *Structures of social action: Studies in conversation analysis* (pp. 102–128). Cambridge: Cambridge University Press.

Deppermann, A. (2011). The study of formulations as a key to an interactional semantics. *Human Studies, 34*(2), 115–128.

Edwards, D. (2000). Extreme case formulations: Softeners, investment, and doing nonliteral. *Research on Language & Social Interaction, 33*(4), 347–373

Firth, A., & Wagner, J. (1997). On discourse, communication, and (some) fundamental concepts in SLA research. *Modern Language Journal, 81*(3), 285–300.

Geyer, N. (2008). *Discourse and politeness: Ambivalent face in Japanese*. London: Continuum.

Glenn, P. (2003). *Laughter in interaction*. Cambridge: Cambridge University Press.

Golato, A. (2005). *Compliments and compliment responses*. Amsterdam: John Benjamins.

Goodwin, C. (1987). Forgetfulness as an interactive resource. *Social Psychology Quarterly, 50*(2), 115–131.

Goodwin, C., & Goodwin, M. H. (1986). Gesture and coparticipation in the activity of searching for a word. *Semiotica, 62*, 51–75.Hall, J. K., & Pekarek Doehler, S. (2011). L2 interactional competence and development. In J. K. Hall, J. Hellermann, & S. Pekarek Doehler (Eds.), *L2 interactional competence and development* (pp. 1–15). Bristol, UK: Multilingual Matters.

Hall, J. K., Hellermann, J., & Pekarek Doehler, S. (Eds.). (2011). *L2 interactional competence and development*. Bristol, UK: Multilingual Matters.

Hayano, K. (2013a). Question design in conversation. In J. Sidnell & T. Stivers (Eds.) *The handbook of conversation analysis* (pp. 395–414). Oxford: Wiley-Blackwell.

Hayano, K. (2013b). *Territories of knowledge in Japanese conversation* (Unpublished doctoral dissertation). Radboud University, Nijmegen, Netherlands.

Hayashi, M. (2003). Language and the body as resources for collaborative action: A study of word searches in Japanese conversation. *Research on Language and Social Interaction, 36*(2), 109–141.

He, A. W., & Young, R. (1998). Language proficiency interviews: A discourse approach. In R. Young & A. W. He (Eds.), *Talking and testing: Discourse approaches to the assessment of oral proficiency* (pp. 1–24). Amsterdam: John Benjamins.

Heine, S., Takata, T., & Lehman, D. (2000). Beyond self-presentation: Evidence for self-criticism among Japanese. *Personality and Social Psychology Bulletin, 26*(1), 71–78.

Hellermann, J. (2009). Practices for dispreferred responses using 'no' by a learner of English. *IRAL, 47*(1), 95–126.

Heritage, J. (1984). A change-of-state token and aspects of its sequential placement. In J. M. Atkinson & J. Heritage (Eds.), *Structures of social action: Studies in conversation analysis* (pp. 299–345). Cambridge: Cambridge University Press.

Heritage, J. (2002). The limits of questioning: negative interrogatives and hostile question content. *Journal of Pragmatics, 34*(10–11), 1427–1446.

Heritage, J. (2010). Questioning in medicine. In A. F. Freed & S. Ehrlich (Eds.), *'Why do you ask?': The function of questions in institutional discourse* (pp. 42–68). Oxford: Oxford University Press.

Hosoda, Y. (2006). Repair and relevance of differential language expertise in second language conversations. *Applied Linguistics, 27*(1), 25–50.

Ide, S. (1989). Formal forms and discernment: Two neglected aspects of linguistic politeness. *Multilingua, 8*, 223–248.

Jacoby, S., & Ochs, E. (1995). Co-construction: An introduction. *Research on Language and Social Interaction, 28*(3), 171–183.

Jayyusi, L. (1991). Values and moral judgement: Communicative praxis. In G. Button (Ed.), *Ethnomethodology and the human sciences* (pp. 227–251). Cambridge: Cambridge University Press.

Jefferson, G. (1974). Error correction as an interactional resource. *Language in Society, 3*(2), 181–199.

Jefferson, G. (2004). Glossary of transcript symbols with an introduction. In G. Lerner (Ed.), *Conversation analysis: Studies from the first generation* (pp. 13–31). Amsterdam: John Benjamins.

Kasper, G. (2006). Speech acts in interaction: Towards discursive pragmatics. In K. Bardovi-Harlig, C. Félix-Brasdefer, & A. S. Omar (Eds.), *Pragmatics and language learning* (Vol. 11, pp. 281–314). Honolulu, HI: University of Hawai'i, National Foreign Language Resource Center.

Kasper, G., & Burch, A. R. (2016). Focus on form in the wild. In R. A. van Compernolle & J. McGregor (Eds.), *Authenticity, language, and interaction in second language contexts* (pp. 198–226). Bristol, UK: Multilingual Matters.

Kim, M-H. (2014). Why self-deprecating? Achieving 'oneness' in conversation. *Journal of Pragmatics, 69*, 82–98.

Kitayama, S., & Uchida, Y. (2003). Explicit self-criticism and implicit self-regard: Evaluating self and friend in two cultures. *Journal of Experimental Social Psychology, 39*(5), 476–482.

Kurhila, S. (2006). *Second language interaction*. Amsterdam: John Benjamins.

Lazaraton, A. (1997). Preference organization in oral proficiency interviews: The case of language ability assessments. *Research on Language and Social Interaction, 30*(1), 53–72.
Lebra, T. (2007). *Identity, gender, and status in Japan.* Kent, UK: Global Oriental.
Lee, J. R. E. (1987). Prologue: Talking organization. In G. Button & J. R. E. Lee (Eds.), *Talk and social organization* (pp. 19–53). Clevedon, UK: Multilingual Matters.
Lerner, G. (2004). Collaborative turn sequences. In G. Lerner (Ed.), *Conversation analysis: Studies from the first generation* (pp. 225–256). Amsterdam: John Benjamins.
Levinson, S. (1983). *Pragmatics.* New York, NY: Cambridge University Press.
Levinson, S. (2006). On the human "interaction engine." In N. J. Enfield & S. C. Levinson (Eds.), *Roots of human sociality* (pp. 39–69). Oxford: Berg.
Markee, N., & Kunitz, S. (2013). Doing planning and task performance in second language acquisition: An ethnomethodological respecification. *Language Learning, 63*(4), 629–664.
Maynard, D. (2003). *Bad news, good news: Conversational order in everyday talk and clinical settings.* Chicago, IL: University of Chicago Press.
Maynard, D., & Zimmerman, D. (1984). Topical talk, ritual, and the social organization of relationships. *Social Psychology Quarterly, 47*(4), 301–316.
Mori, J. (2009). Commentary: The social turn in second language acquisition and Japanese pragmatics research: Reflection on ideologies, methodologies, and instructional implications. In N. Taguchi (Ed.), *Pragmatic competence* (pp. 335–358). New York, NY: Mouton de Gruyter.
Morita, E. (2005). *Negotiation of contingent talk: The Japanese interactional particles* ne and sa. Amsterdam: John Benjamins.
Nguyen, H. T. (2011). Achieving recipient-design longitudinally: Evidence from a pharmacy intern in patient consultations. In J. K. Hall, J. Hellermann, & S. Pekarek Doehler (Eds.), *L2 interactional competence and development* (pp. 173–205). Bristol, UK: Multilingual Matters.
Nguyen, H. T. (2012). *Developing interactional competence: A conversation-analytic study of patient consultations in pharmacy.* Basingstoke, UK: Palgrave-Macmillan.
Olsher, D. (2004). Talk and gesture: The embodied completion of sequential actions in spoken interaction. In R. Gardner & J. Wagner (Eds.), *Second language conversations* (pp. 221–246). London: Continuum.
Peräkylä, A., & Ruusuvuori, J. (2006). Facial expression in an assessment. In H. Knoblauch, B. Schnettler, J. Raab, & H-G. Soeffner (Eds.), *Video analysis: Methodology and methods* (pp. 127–142). Frankfurt: Peter Lang.
Park, J-E. (2007). Co-construction of nonnative speaker identity in cross-cultural interaction. *Applied Linguistics, 28*(3), 339–360.
Pekarek Doehler, S., & Pochon Berger, E. (2011). Developing 'methods' for interaction: A cross-sectional study of disagreement sequences in French L2. In J. K. Hall, J. Hellermann, & S. Pekarek Doehler (Eds.), *L2 interactional competence and development* (pp. 206–243). Bristol, UK: Multilingual Matters.

Pomerantz, A. (1978). Compliment responses: Notes on the co-operation of multiple constraints. In J. Schenkein (Ed.), *Studies in the organization of conversational interaction* (pp. 79–112). New York, NY: Academic Press.
Pomerantz, A. (1984). Agreeing and disagreeing with assessments: Some features of preferred/dispreferred turn shapes. In J. M. Atkinson & J. Heritage (Eds.), *Structures of social action* (pp. 57–101). Cambridge: Cambridge University Press.
Pomerantz, A. (1986). Extreme case formulations: A way of legitimizing claims. *Human Studies, 9*(2-3), 219–229.
Pomerantz, A., & Heritage, J. (2013). Preference. In J. Sidnell & T. Stivers (Eds.), *The handbook of conversation analysis* (pp. 210–228). Oxford: Wiley-Blackwell.
Reynolds, E., & Fitzgerald, R. (2015). Challenging normativity: Re-appraising category bound, tied, and predicated features. In R. Fitzgerald & W. Housley (Eds.), *Advances in membership categorization analysis* (pp. 99–122). London: Sage.
Sacks, H. (1972). Notes on police assessment of moral character. In D. N. Sudnow (Ed.), *Studies in social interaction* (pp. 280–293). New York, NY: Free Press.
Sacks, H. (1987). On the preferences for agreement and contiguity in sequences in conversation. In G. Button & J. R. E. Lee (Eds.), *Talk and social organisation* (pp. 54–69). Clevedon, UK: Multilingual Matters.
Sacks, H. (1992). *Lectures on conversation* (Vols. 1–2). Oxford: Blackwell Publishers.
Saito, H., & Beecken, M. (1997). An approach to instruction of pragmatic aspects: Implications of pragmatic transfer by American learners of Japanese. *Modern Language Journal, 81*(3), 363–377.
Schegloff, E. A. (2007). *Sequence organization in interaction: A primer in conversation analysis* (Vol. 1). Cambridge: Cambridge University Press.
Schnurr, S., & Chan, A. (2011). When laughter is not enough: Responding to teasing and self-denigrating humour at work. *Journal of Pragmatics, 43*, 20–35.
Shimizu, T. (2009). Influence of learning context on L2 pragmatic realization: A comparison between JSL and JFL learners' compliment responses. In N. Taguchi (Ed.), *Pragmatic competence* (pp. 167–198). New York, NY: Mouton de Gruyter.
Siegal, M. (1995). Individual differences and study abroad: Women learning Japanese in Japan. In B. F. Freed (Ed.), *Second language acquisition in a study abroad context* (pp. 225–244), Amsterdam: John Benjamins.
Stokoe, E. (2012). Moving forward with membership categorization analysis: Methods for systematic analysis. *Discourse Studies, 14*(3), 277–303.
Streeck, J., Goodwin, C., & LeBaron, C. (Eds.). (2011). *Embodied interaction: Language and body in the material world*. New York, NY: Cambridge University Press.
Tarpey, T. E. (2012). "I'm bad at grammar": Self-deprecation in undergraduate peer tutoring. *Language & Information Society, 16*, 109–139.
Theodórsdóttir, G. (2011). Second language interaction for business and learning. In J. K. Hall, J. Hellermann, & S. Pekarek Doehler (Eds.), *L2 interactional competence and development* (pp. 93–116). Bristol, UK: Multilingual Matters.

Van Compernolle, R. A. (2011). Responding to questions and L2 learner interactional competence during language proficiency interviews: A microanalytic study with pedagogical implications. In J. K. Hall, J. Hellermann, & S. Pekarek Doehler (Eds.), *L2 interactional competence and development* (pp. 117–144). Bristol, UK: Multilingual Matters.

Watson, R. (1978). Categorization, authorization, and blame-negotiation in conversation. *Sociology, 12*(1), 105–113.

Zimmermann, D. (1998). Identity, context, and interaction. In C. Antaki & S. Widdicombe (Eds.), *Identities in talk* (pp. 88–106). Cambridge: Cambridge University Press.

# Appendix

Special conventions for transcribing talk:
- #word#     creaky voice
- ~          nasalized production
- /          gradual rise in pitch
- * (in gloss)   non-target-like forms and untranslated particles.

Special conventions for transcribing embodiment:
- +          marks onset of embodiment in relation to talk (cases without + mean no clear onset)
- {          marks where two tiers of embodiment description are to be read together
- /          marks beats (i.e. downbeats or taps)
- >          direction of action
- RH, LH, BH   right hand, left hand, both hands
- IF         index finger
- GZ         gaze
- PNT        point

# 3 Learning Technical Terms in Workplace Interaction

Stephen J. Moody
*Brigham Young University*

## Introduction

Communication in the workplace is characterized by a need for high levels of precision in order to successfully perform job-related tasks. For second language (L2) speakers in international workplaces, then, knowledge of technical terminologies is a particular concern. However, because of the industry-specific nature of specialized jargons, materials for teaching and learning technical language tend to target broad professional audiences. As such, they focus on generic business situations, neglect specialized fields, and consist largely of lists of specialized vocabulary to be memorized (e.g., Azuma & Sambongi, 2001; Suzuki, Hajikano, & Kataoka, 2006). The reality is, L2 speakers must manage industry-specific technical terms in the inevitable social moments when they encounter new or unfamiliar words while doing work.

Workplaces, however, are not inherently learning-focused environments. As Wagner and Firth (1997) have observed, "speakers [in institutions] are more oriented towards meaning creation and sense-making than towards linguistic form" (p. 341). In other words, workplace interactions involve a tight focus on institutional activities and thus first-language (L1) and L2 speakers alike are reluctant to interrupt ongoing job tasks in order to explicitly focus on learning (Brouwer, Rasmussen, & Wagner,

2004; Firth, 2009; Kurhila, 2004, 2006; Theodórsdóttir, 2011b). This raises an important question: While working to achieve the level of intersubjective understanding necessary for accomplishing immediate institutional goals, do L2 speakers also pay enough attention to linguistic details to find opportunities for learning the specialized language that they may not be exposed to elsewhere? The present study explores this question in the case of American student interns employed in Japanese companies.

## CA and learning in institutional interactions

Traditional second language acquisition (SLA) perspectives on vocabulary acquisition view learning as a product wherein one fills some lexical gap, moving from a cognitive state of "not knowing" a word to that of "knowing" the word. As it pertains to the acquisition of lexical items through participation in social activities, SLA has been particularly concerned with so-called "incidental learning." These studies measure gains, usually quantitatively, following learner engagement with an L2 during tasks and social activities not focused on language learning per se (Ellis, 1994; Huang, Willson, & Eslami, 2012; Huckin & Coady, 1999; Newton, 1995). A typical argument is that effective activities for vocabulary development involve (a) drawing attention to an unknown word, (b) providing access to an authoritative source of information that provides a solution, and (c) encouraging L2 speaker production of the new word (Ellis, 1994; Huckin & Coady, 1999; Newton, 2013). While this appears to speak to the process through which learning occurs, given the focus on quantitative gains these studies are ultimately concerned with testing the end result (i.e., how many new vocabulary words a learner can recognize or produce following the activity), rather than describing the process through which a cognitive change occurs. Such learning is deemed "incidental" due to the fact that the activity is not ostensibly arranged for the purpose of learning. However, if the process indeed involves attending to and producing an unknown word as part of bringing about a cognitive change, it is reasonable to wonder whether or not such learning is truly incidental.

In examining detailed accounts of turn-by-turn interaction as it unfolds at the moment when L2 speakers encounter new words, studies using Conversation Analysis (CA) suggest that L2 speakers orient to learning even when the underlying purpose of the interaction is focused on accomplishing other social goals (Brouwer, 2003; Gardner, 2008). In this sense, the learning is not incidental. Furthermore, CA offers the perspective that when learning is embedded in social activities, managing it is part of L2 speakers' interactional competence (Theodórsdóttir, 2011b). For instance, when encountering the need to use or understand unknown technical terms, an L2 speaker may solicit a definition from a more knowledgeable person. This, in turn, may lead to an opportunity to learn that word. Alternatively, the speaker may talk around the term, avoiding it in order to maintain a focus on the task at hand. In such circumstances, a learning opportunity may not emerge. By looking for evidence of cognitive changes in records of public displays in social interaction, CA is able to show that in many cases, rather than something that happens incidentally, learning is occasioned by and embedded within other activities.

A particular challenge for CA stems from the notion that if learning is seen as a change in cognitive states which reside in one's mind, it is inherently unavailable for outside observation. This is a topic of much recent work on CA-for-SLA. For instance, Mori and Hasegawa (2009) show that cognitive states are embodied in public actions as learners *collaboratively* deal with unknown words, displaying cognitive happenings such as noticing and uptake through verbalizations, gestures, hesitations, and so on. This finding invokes the notion of "socially shared cognition" (Schegloff, 1991), which is the idea that the private content of one's mind is made public in the turn-by-turn details of interaction as interlocutors work together to reach an intersubjective understanding (Kasper, 2006; Koschmann, 2012; Seedhouse, 2004). Indeed, the nature of social interaction is such that internal cognitive states are frequently displayed publicly when they are relevant to creating meaning in collaboration with others. The perspective taken in this study uses this notion that while learning involves a change in internal cognitive states, because it is embedded in social interaction it manifests through and is thus observable in publicly available actions.

As the type of learning that is empirically observable is that which is publicly displayed, the learning that has been studied by CA work on L1-L2 interactions is not really incidental, as participants may, at times, focus on linguistic forms and meanings when necessary to accomplish other social goals. A pervasive finding in CA work on L2 talk in institutions is that because institutionally situated interactions are first and foremost oriented toward institutional activities, speakers work primarily to establish just enough intersubjective understanding to accomplish institutional objectives (Brouwer et al., 2004; Firth, 2009; Kurhila, 2004; Mondada, 2004; Theodórsdóttir, 2011b). Even in the face of trouble stemming from L2 disfluencies, participants tend to seek resolutions that minimize disruption to the task at hand. While this needs not—and often does not—entail an orientation to language learning, L2 speakers are more likely to make language-related issues relevant in the local talk-in-interaction (Kurhila, 2004; Theodórsdóttir, 2011a). For example, Kurhila (2004) shows that L2 speakers sometimes flag trouble as linguistic in nature and thus publicly display awareness of their L2 status in order to implicitly claim their limited institutional competence. Likewise, Theodórsdóttir (2011a) observes that, even when intersubjective understanding has been restored following language-related trouble, L2 speakers insist on completing full turns while ignoring L1 speakers' attempts to resume the institutional activity. These studies suggest that L2 speakers may leverage language troubles as opportunities to learn even though the activity is inherently focused on accomplishing some institutional goal.

## Word searches and learning

The present study considers how L2 speakers deal with unfamiliar technical terms in workplace interaction and whether or not their strategies provide opportunities for learning new lexical items. Following other similar CA studies, the analytical focus here is on *word search sequences*, a type of forward-oriented repair in which a speaker delays a turn in progress in order to retrieve a lexical item (Schegloff, 1979). Though not a phenomenon specific to L2 speakers, these sequences often involve public displays of lexical gaps and the collaborative steps taken to resolve them. As such, they are a potential domain for revealing cognitive changes that might reflect learning (Brouwer, 2003; Mori, 2010).

Brouwer (2003), Jung (2004), and Mori (2010), in three CA studies of vocabulary learning in L1-L2 peer conversations, show that word searches are carried out by L2 speakers as opportunities to invite other-provided solutions, display uptake of those solutions, and orient to vocabulary learning. These studies identify at least five publicly evident social actions that may suggest learning is occurring: (a) the L2 speaker's self-initiated indication of trouble, (b) an invitation for another to provide a potential solution, (c) orientation to the potential trouble-solver as a "knowledgeable other" having the relative expertise necessary to provide a legitimate solution, (d) a candidate solution provided by the knowledgeable other, and (e) the L2 speaker's uptake or acceptance of the solution (see also Koshik & Seo, 2012; Reichert & Liebscher, 2012).

As Brouwer (2003) points out, however, while the presence of these elements is sufficient for showing that an *opportunity* for learning has presented itself, they do not prove long-term retention of the word. Thus, the fact that a word search has occurred does not necessarily indicate learning, particularly given the nature of institutional interaction. For instance, the onset of a word search is indicated with resources which place an ongoing turn on hold, allowing the speaker to search for a solution while maintaining the floor. This might be accomplished through hesitations, vowel lengthening, gazing away from the addressee, and so on (Greer, 2013; Hayashi, 2003). In multilingual workplaces, however, such speech perturbations do not always indicate lexical gaps, but could, for example, be the result of recalling technical details of an institutional task (Wagner & Firth, 1997). Furthermore, even when a word search is triggered, it is often concluded when enough understanding has been achieved to allow the work-related task in progress to continue, even if the underlying linguistic issue has not been solved (Kurhila, 2006).

It follows that evidence of a specific orientation toward a word search solution as a newly learned word is needed to claim that learning has occurred. One way this may be accomplished is to look for indications that the L2 speaker has *registered* the solution. Here, to register a term suggests a shift from a state of initial uncertainty to one of recognizing the meaning and function of a new term in a specific context (Kasper, 2006; Schegloff, 1999). Some ways this might be displayed in interaction include producing a change-of-state token (such as "Oh!") followed by a repetition of the potentially learned word, or explicitly confirming its meaning (Brouwer, 2003; Heritage, 1984). In this way, L2 speakers indicate acknowledgement of a solution, recognition of it as filling a lexical gap, and understanding of its meaning in context, all of which potentially suggests a cognitive change that may entail learning. Otherwise, the tight focus on completing work-related tasks may trump the opportunity for orienting to linguistic details sufficiently enough to encourage learning.

## The study: Learning technical terms while working

Building on prior work, which shows that participants in multilingual workplace interactions resolve language-related trouble in ways that minimally disturb progress toward institutional goals, the present study describes some of the conditions under which L2 speakers are able to find opportunities for learning in institutional settings. In this view, learning is embedded in social interactions that take place primarily to accomplish institutional goals.

The data are drawn from a larger ethnographically grounded observation of American college students participating in internships in Japan. Here, I focus on two interns, David and Ethan,[1] both mechanical engineering students who were employed at the same company but during separate summers (2012 and 2013). The internships took place in the headquarters of a large, international engineering firm near Tokyo where Japanese was the primary language spoken. Both interns lived in Japan for several years on previous, separate occasions, and spoke Japanese at an advanced level.

Audio recordings of the interns' interactions with their Japanese colleagues were made during two-day observations of each (4 days total), yielding roughly 30 hours of recordings. From these data, sequences in which the interns experienced trouble with technical terms were extracted, resulting in 32 interactions that were subsequently transcribed and analyzed. Transcripts were prepared by the author with the assistance of two native speakers of Japanese. As the company only allowed audio recordings, to compensate for a lack of visual information the author took detailed field notes during the observations. These notes were referenced when preparing transcripts in order to provide details of important non-verbal actions.

## Embedded learning at work

Consistent with prior work, analysis reveals that the interns and their colleagues tend to resolve word searches in ways that minimally disrupt progress toward accomplishing some work-related task. Despite the minimal disruption, however, the interns are often able to leverage these interactions as opportunities to learn. In the data, there are two types of word searches in which learning opportunities arise. The first collection (described in the first subsection below) includes sequences which are highly efficient in that participants are able to use linguistic and other semiotic resources in the workplace environment to quickly resume the primary task. Then, because the meaning and function of the technical term is contextualized by these same semiotic resources, in working to establish intersubjective understanding, the interns are able to simultaneously register previously unknown terms. The second collection (described in the second subsection below) includes searches which, for a number of reasons, involve lengthier discussion about the meaning of specific terms. In these sequences opportunities for learning are much more readily available, but come at the cost of reduced efficiency and increased diversion.

### Resuming the task while doing learning

Eighteen of the 32 sequences in which the interns flagged lexical problems can be collected together based on the presence of three common elements. First, the word that the intern experiences trouble with is central to describing the job task, and therefore, the trouble must be resolved in order for the work to continue. Second, the presence of semiotic resources specific to the workplace environment helps the word searches to be resolved quickly and with minimal disruption to the ongoing task at hand. Third, signals that the work activity can be resumed occur simultaneously with or immediately following public displays of cognitive changes, thus contributing to the efficiency of these institutionally situated word searches that embed learning.

In Excerpt 1, Ethan (abbreviated ET in the transcript) is working with a colleague, Miyazaki (MZ), while preparing a diagram when he experiences trouble producing the term *mufuka denryoku* 'no load power.'[2]

**Excerpt 1.** Mufuka denryoku

```
24   ET ai zero tte
        i  zero QT
25      ((studies diagram silently for 2.4 seconds))
26      do- (0.4) koko ni wa denai     desu    yone?
                  here in TP come out-NG COP-POL IP
```

```
27  →     ah- >to iu  ka<  mufuka::::=
          CS   QT say Q    no load
          I-O is... Wh- it's not in here, right? Ah, I mean, no load...

28  →MZ   =mufuka denryoku
           no load power
          No load power

29  →ET   mufuka denryoku  ka.
          no load power     Q
          Oh, it's "no load power."

30   MZ   nn.
          yeah
          Yeah.

31   ET   ah:: okay.
          CS

32        (4.2) ((Ethan writes the term in his notebook))

33   ET   de     (0.4) kono  ii shii wa,
          then         this  e  c    TP
          Ah, okay. And then this E.C.?

34   MZ   hai
          yes
          Yes.

35   ET   keisan     dekiru  mondai   janai yone
          calculate  do-POT  problem  CP-NG IP
          It is not something we can calculate, right?
```

Here, Ethan could not find an annotation on the diagram for a particular measurement (lines 24–26). He then realizes that it is recorded under a different label than he expected, producing a change of state token, *ah*, in line 27 followed by a rapid *to iu ka* 'I mean,' which marks the following utterance as a clarification of something stated previously (Makino & Tsutsui, 2008). Interactionally, *to iu ka* is used to initiate self-repair (Hosoda, 2000), which Ethan begins to do by saying the first part of *mufuka denryoku*. However, he struggles to recall the term, producing an extended vowel (*mufuka::::*) as he searches for the second part of the compound. Miyazaki then immediately volunteers a solution in line 28, which Ethan repeats in line 29. Miyazaki confirms in line 30, and Ethan displays understanding with another change-of-state marker, *ah::*, followed by *okay* in line 31.

This search is accomplished rather efficiently, requiring only five utterances: three by Ethan (lines 27, 29, and 31) and two minimal ones by Miyazaki (lines 28 and 30). When a speaker produces an extended vowel, as Ethan does in line 27, it often serves to hold the floor while attempting to recall a lexical item (Schegloff, Jefferson, & Sacks, 1977). Miyazaki, however, immediately interjects to signal that he has enough information for the task to continue. This is possible because the trouble source is highly contextualized as it both occurs in an interaction oriented to a specific work-related purpose and constitutes the first part of the compound. Moreover, Ethan has framed it by stating a concrete measurement in line 24, the participants are aware that the purpose of the conversation is to annotate measurements, and they have a visual clue (the diagram) in front of them. All of these semiotic resources help lighten Miyazaki's inferential load; there is no need to wait for Ethan to come up with the term in order for the ongoing task of annotating measurements to continue.

For Ethan, this appears to also provide an opportunity to address a linguistic issue. Initially, this sequence suggests trouble with recall rather than an actual lexical gap leading to learning: Ethan is able to produce the first part of the term and immediately recognizes Miyazaki's proposed solution, suggesting he has encountered the term *mufuka denryoku* before and maybe even knows it. However, after Miyazaki provides the solution, Ethan repeats it in line 29 followed by the question marker *ka* with falling intonation. The use of *ka* here particularly suggests an orientation to learning as it publicly displays Ethan's registering of the term, similar to saying "Oh, so it's *mufuka denryoku*" in English. Thus, his slow recall coupled with a public registering of the term suggests that even if he has encountered the term, he is nevertheless moving from a state of relative uncertainty to one of increased awareness of the term as used in a situated, work-related context. That Ethan uses this as an opportunity to learn is especially illustrated by noting that, after registering the term, he then takes the further public action of writing the term down in a notebook, a dedicated learning activity in which he records new terms for future reference (and which is something he did regularly during my observation).

Ethan's turns in lines 29, 31, and 32 appear to have dual consequences. First, in terms of their sequential placement, they complete the word search and are followed by *de* 'and then' in his next turn (line 33), which explicitly signals a topic shift back to work-related matters (see Hayashi, 2004). Second, as discussed above, line 29 indicates his registering of the term, and thus suggests he has experienced a cognitive change that could entail learning. In this way, Ethan is able to "do learning," and though the learning is peripheral to the primary institutional focus of the interaction, he is able to resume the ongoing work activity relatively quickly.

A second example, this one from David (DV), further shows that even though lexical trouble emerges within work-focused activities, opportunities for learning are available when the L2 speakers takes advantage of the trouble to orient to linguistic issues. While reading measurements on a computer display, David wants to change the measurement scale. The Japanese word for *scale*, however, which turns out to be the borrowed English word *sukeeru*, appears to ellude him. It is then provided by his colleague, Suzuki (SK).

**Excerpt 2.** Sukeeru

```
153 SK  de      mooikkai            oshite
        then    one more time       push-and
        Then push this one more time.

154→DV  ah-   (.)  so  kka  (0.4)  konna-  (0.2)
        CS         so  Q           this kind
155     moo    chotto sa  (.)  hyaku made  (.)  toka (0.8)
        more   little IP         100  until         for instance
156→    betsu-ni             ii     kka
        not particularly     okay   Q
        Ah, I see. But this… just a little more… Up to 100, or… It doesn't
        matter?

157     (1.2)

158     °nanka      kore°
         somewhat   this
        It's like, this…

159     (0.2)

160→SK  AH-   (.)  sukeeru  tte  koto?
        CS         scale    QT   thing
        Oh! Do you mean the "scale"?

161→DV  sukeeru.  (.)  sukeeru?  (0.4)  °sukeeru ka.°  (0.2)
        scale          scale            scale    Q
162     kantan-ni  kaerareru   kana
        simply     change-POT  Q
        Scale. Scale? It's 'scale,' huh. Can it be changed simply?

163 SK  iya   ↑demo  k-   (.)  kore wa  kore de  (.)  ii     yo.
        no    but                this TP  this PT       good   IP
        No, but, it's okay like this.
```

In contrast to Ethan's earlier example, here David struggles with an unknown word for a more extended period. His attempt to ask how to rescale the measurement units on the machine (lines 154–156) contains multiple hesitations, pauses, and other disfluencies, and in line 155 he appears to use an avoidance strategy (Wagner & Firth, 1997), saying *hyaku made* 'up to 100' to describe rescaling the measurement to units of 100, rather than, say, using the Japanese word for *scale*. When he is unsuccessful in formulating his question, David, in line 156, appears ready to give up on asking how to change the scale, suggesting that rescaling might not matter anyway.

Following a brief pause, however, David quietly states *nanka kore* 'It's like, this...' in a quiet, self-directed statement (line 158), indicating he is still internally puzzling over how to describe his (work-related) problem. *Nanka* 'somewhat' is often used to initiate a turn while flagging the upcoming statement as a rough approximation of something that is difficult to describe. Thus, it is possible David is preparing to reformulate and try again. A reformulation, however, if intended, is never produced. Instead, Suzuki steps in with a loud *AH-*, which displays a change-of-state in which he appears to suddenly realize what David is trying to do. Then, in a clarifying question (line 160), he provides a Japanese term for measurement scales, *sukeeru*, which turns out to be an English-based loanword and a convenient way to establish intersubjective understanding while resolving David's trouble.

In response, David repeats *sukeeru* three times, each with an apparently different function (line 161). First, he repeats it to display uptake. Next, after a micropause, he repeats it again with questioning intonation, indicating that he was previously unaware an English-based loanword would work to formulate his question.[3] Finally, he says it again with the question marker *ka* and falling intonation, which, as in Ethan's earlier interaction, indicates David is registering the term. This signals a cognitive shift from a state of not knowing the word to a state of recognizing its use in the present context. It thus appears David is learning the word. Then, as the trouble is resolved and intersubjective understanding is established, David immediately returns to the task in line 162, using *sukeeru* as the implied object of the verb *kaerareru* 'can change,' implicitly embedding it into the formulation of his previously aborted question.

While this word search is also quite efficient in that the resolution comes in just two utterances (lines 160 and 161), it followed a more lengthy display of trouble on the part of the learner than did the prior example. This seems to be a result of two factors. First, David does not indicate a specific word that is causing trouble, but rather is struggling with the formulation of an entire question. While Ethan produced the first part of the source compound, which helped identify the term he was seeking, David does not provide similar hints. Second, Ethan's trouble source was tied to a physical, visible resource (the diagram), whereas David's is with a procedure that is not as concretely evident (adjusting the display scale is not a required part of the activity of taking measurements). Indeed, Suzuki must work to infer a solution, as indicated when he provides his candidate solution in the form of a clarifying question (line 160) rather than stating it authoritatively.

Similar to Ethan's example, however, the public signal that a new term has been registered is followed by a resumption of the work activity. In this way, these instances of learning are occasioned by the need to produce a technical term in order to quickly return to the task at hand. Such word searches are efficient and the interaction is tightly focused on doing work, but they nevertheless appear to provide opportunities for learning.

### Digressing from work-related activities

In the next collection of interactions, the participants display clearer orientations to the meanings of specific terms although this comes at the cost of more extensively diverting the flow of the ongoing work activity. Here, I show two ways this is done. In the first instance (Excerpt 3), Ethan and Miyazaki allocate a little more time to focus on the meaning of a word. In the second instance (Excerpt 4), David and his colleagues completely divert the flow of a work meeting in order to pursue an explicit discussion of the meaning of a term for a rather extended period of time. While less frequent (8 of the 32 sequences) than the prior collection, these examples suggest that participants do, at times, attend more directly to linguistic issues, although these are also occasioned for work-related purposes.

Several hours after the sequence in Excerpt 1, but while working on a similar task (annotating a diagram), Ethan encounters the written word *yooryoo* 'capacity'[4] in a diagram, but is unable to read the Japanese script.

**Excerpt 3-1.** Yooryoo (word search)

```
73   ET   a- kore ((pointing at diagram)) kondensaa no:.
          CS this                          condenser LK
          Oh, this. The condenser...

74   MZ   nn:.
          yeah
          Yeah.

75  →ET   °>nan    desu    ka<° teikoo       desu     ka.
             what  CP-POL  Q    resistance   CP-POL   Q
          What is it? Is it "resistance"?

76  →MZ   kondensaa no    yo↑oryo↓o
          condenser LK    capacity
          Condenser capacity.
```

77  ET  **yooryoo?**
        *capacity*
        Capacity?

78  MZ  ano (1.5) i- (1.9) >impiidansu< (.) indakutansu
        *H                     impedance       inductance*
        Um, i- impedence. Inductance.

79  ET  kore  (0.1)  to    wa (0.9) ((points at diagram))
        *this         with  TP*
80      chigaimasu     ka?
        *different-POL Q*
        Is it different than this?

81  MZ  >ah kore no hoo da<       (.) un.
        *ah this LK way CP-PLN        yeah*
        Ah, this one. Yeah.

82  ET  wakarimashita.
        *understand-POL-PST*

83      (.)

84  ET  ja: kinyuu-suru toki wa koo
        *so  fill in     when TP this way*
85      deshou?
        *CP-probably-POL*
        I understand. So, when filling it in, I (write it) like this, right?

Here, we see a word search that involves more of a digression from the work activity. While looking at the diagram, Ethan locates a component called a *condenser*[5] and produces *condensaa no:,* ending with the genitive case-marker *no* and an elongated final vowel suggesting he is searching for the following term. He then explicitly signals an active word search in line 75 with *nan desu ka* 'what is it,' a phrase which often initiates self-repair and/or invites other-repair (e.g., Hayashi, 2003; Hosoda, 2000). Next, Ethan proffers *teikoo* 'resistance' as a potential solution, but this is repaired by Miyazaki (line 76), who says *condensaa no yooryoo* 'condenser capacity,' marking *yooryoo* as the correct term with a prosodic pattern of rising and falling intonation. Ethan repeats the item with rising intonation in line 77, indicating uncertainty regarding the word. In response, Miyazaki volunteers additional information by mentioning two other measures, impedance and inductance[6] (line 78). These terms all belong to the same set of standard measurements of condenser performance, and thus Miyazaki is indirectly defining *yooryoo* by listing contingent terms. This sort of strategy is a common way interlocutors resolve word searches in multilingual workplace conversations (Kurhila, 2006). Then, in lines 79 and 80, Ethan seeks further clarification of the term by asking if it is different than a label on the diagram to which he points. When Miyazaki confirms that Ethan has identified the correct term, Ethan explicitly claims understanding (line 82) and then produces *ja* 'so' to shift the topic back to the work activity of recording measurements on the diagram (line 84).

In contrast to prior examples where solutions are provided and registered relatively quickly so as to establish understanding and move on with the work, here the L1 speaker (Miyazaki) becomes more involved in an explicit discussion of the meaning of a word, specifically, by providing contingent terms from a similar collection of measurements. Here, understanding the exact term is more critical to the job task; that is, Ethan must match the correct measurements with the correct labels on the diagram. Thus, the orientation to meaning emerges because getting the term right is necessary for doing the task correctly. In this way, while discussing the meaning of the word provides opportunities for learning, such learning is again occasioned by the overarching goal of properly accomplishing institutional goals.

That Ethan has registered and indeed learned the word *yooryoo* 'capacity' is more clearly evidenced a short while later when he finds an opportunity to test it out.

**Excerpt 3-2.** Yooryoo (testing)

```
92   ET  koko ni  (.)  tatoeba      atsumi
         here in       for example  thickness
93       dewanakute (0.3)
         CP-NG-and
         Here. For example, not thickness, but...

94   MZ  nn.
         yeah
         Yeah.

95  →ET  yo↑oryo↓o
         capacity
         Capacity.

96       (0.7)

97   MZ  [↑nn?
         huh
         Huh?

98   ET  [.hh rei   ten   [sanjuusan
              zero  point  thirty three
         0.33
```

```
 99  MZ               [atsumi     wa  (0.8)  irete  oitte
                       thickness  TP         put in advance
                      Write in the thickness for now, and

100  ET  a-  soo   soo    soo   (0.3)  nanka  (.)  betsu     no:
         ah  right right  right               H         separate  LK
101      nanka koko ni  (0.3)  kondensaa  no
               H    here in          condenser  LK
102→     (0.7)  yooryoo  (0.4)
                capacity
103      rei   ten   sanjuusan   de
         zero point thirty three CP-and
         Ah, yeah, yeah, yeah. Like, a different one... Like, over here, the
         condenser... capacity... is 0.33, and

104  MZ  un.
         yes
         Yes.

105  ET  sonna      kanji   de
         that kind  feeling with
         Like that?

106  MZ  un.  >soo   soo<  sore  de
         yes  yeah   yeah  that  is
         Yes. Yeah, yeah, that'll do.
```

As the task progressed, Ethan found an occasion to test his knowledge of the word *yooryoo* 'capacity' by deploying it in two additional work-related turns. First, in line 92, he mentions a different measurement, *atsumi* 'thickness,' preceeded by *tatoeba* 'for example' and followed (line 93) by *dewanakute* 'not (thickness) but,' thereby setting up a contrast for *yooryoo* in line 95. Then when Ethan utters *yooryoo*, it is marked with rising intonation in the first syllable and falling intonation with additional stress in the second syllable, and set apart with pauses before and after (lines 93 and 96). This is similar to the practice of try-marking (Sacks & Schegloff, 1979), where a speaker will flag an item, usually with rising intonation, as a means of implicitly seeking confirmation that the item has been understood. In this way, Ethan appears to check Miyazaki's reaction to see if his use of the word was recognized or accepted.

When no verbal response is immediately forthcoming after 0.7 seconds, Ethan resumes his turn with an audible in-breath, but is interrupted by a sudden interjection from Miyazaki (*nn* with high pitch and sharp intonation). This indicates the onset of other-initiated repair (e.g., Hosoda, 2000), but when Miyazaki takes the floor he actually provides additional instruction rather than make a linguistic correction. In line 99, Miyazaki formulates a directive with the main verb *irete* 'put it' and auxiliary verb *oitte* 'in advance' (meaning something like "put it in for now"), instructing Ethan to record the *atsumi* measure. That is, although Ethan negates *atsumi* (lines 92–93) for the convenience of contrasting it with *yooryoo* as an apparent means to test lingusitic knowledge, Miyazaki interprets this action under an orientation to the task of recording measurements on a diagram and thus provides work-related instruction.

That Ethan is concerned with confirming his use of *yooryoo* can also be seen in his turn beginning in line 100. When Miyazaki provides work-related instruction, Ethan responds with *soo soo soo* 'right right right' and clarifies that he is asking about something else (*betsu no* 'a different one' followed by *koko ni* '[over] here'). This displays his institutional knowledge by claiming that he already knows he should record the *atsumi* measure and suggests he is primarily attending to his use of *yooryoo* (see Kurhila, 2004). He then produces *yooryoo* a second time with noticeable stress and set apart with two pauses (line 102). When Miyazaki does not indicate any trouble, Ethan moves on with the work, records the measurement, and asks Miyazaki if he has performed the task correctly. Both times, *yooryoo* is used within utterances ostensibly about a work-related activity.

Ethan's testing of *yooryoo* here is evidence that the prior word search (Excerpt 3-1) has indeed provided an opportunity for language learning. In this sequence, Ethan appears to be confirming that he is properly using a term that he registered earlier. Yet, even this opportunity for him to test the word emerges only to the extent that he is able to use it in order to accomplish work (which here is to ask questions about how to properly annotate the diagram). Therefore, we again see that learning in workplace interactions is occasioned due to work-related concerns.

The examples so far show that orientation to language learning can be seen even within primarily work-focused activities. A final example further demonstrates that there are times when language learning itself can take over as the main focus of an interaction. This is possible when participants are willing and able to put the primary task on hold in order to pursue further discussion of an unfamiliar term. The "interruptability" of an ongoing task consequently allows for a more direct orientation to linguistic issues, and therefore learning, even while it creates a larger disruption to the task in progress. Here, David is reporting during an informal team meeting, which includes Hayashi (HS) and Noda (ND) who also participate in the sequence. Immediately after taking the floor, he experiences trouble using the Japanese term for an "exploded-view diagram."[7]

**Excerpt 4-1.** Tenkaizu (initial trouble)

```
3    DV   e:tto.  (0.2)  konshuu      desu    ne:,  (0.4) ano:::
          H              this week    CP-POL  IP          H
4         Noda-san  to:  (0.3)  sono:  (0.4)  sanjigen  no  (0.6)
          Noda-AT   with        H             3-D       LK
5    →    uchuu:,  tenkaizu?
          space    expansion diagram
          Uh..., this week, well, uh..., (I worked) with Noda on the 3-D, uh...,
          space expanded-view diagram?

6         (1.2)

7    DV   to  °iimasu    ka  ne?°
          QT  say-POL    Q   IP
          Is that what it's called?

8    HS   °a::°
          ah
          Ah...

9   →DV   ats-  ano::  (.)  tsukue  ni  aru::   (.)  yatsu  TO:,
          H                 table   on  exists       thing  and
10        (0.7)  ano::  konshuu       kore  o  (0.4)  ano:  (0.3)
                 H      this week     this  O        H
11        tsukuri-dashimashita.  eh:
          make-put out-POL-PST   H
          Uh, the thing on the table and, uh, this one, uh, we made them, uh,
          this week. Uh...

12        (2.4)
```

David encounters trouble in line 5 when he attempts to describe a diagram with the term *uchuu tenkaizu* (which includes the erroneous term *uchuu*), displaying his uncertainty by try-marking it with rising intonation followed by a lengthy pause. When none of his colleagues respond, he makes his search explicit by saying *to iimasu ka* 'Is that what it's called?' followed by the interactional particle *ne*, which seeks mutual alignment and gives the listener the option of producing an acknowledgment (Ishida, 2009; Morita, 2005). When no solution is forthcoming, David then continues in line 9 in a manner that appears to avoid the term altogether, referring to a second, similar diagram as *tsukue ni aru yatsu* 'the thing on the table.'

Although in prior examples the Japanese co-workers volunteered solutions when the American interns encountered trouble, this is not the case here. One possible explanation may have to do with the setting: Ethan is reporting in a meeting. Meeting reports often take the form of monologues and it would violate turn-taking conventions for someone to volunteer a solution without a very explicit solicitation (see Yamada, 1990). Moreover, given that there are several diagrams physically available and which David makes reference to (for example, *tsukue ni aru yatsu* 'the thing on the table' in line 9 and *kore* 'this' in line 10), his co-workers probably need some time to work out exactly what he is referring to. Thus, despite his struggles as he reports (and thus has the floor allocated to him), David pushes forward with his report and his co-workers let him. That is, they "let it pass," a phenomenon wherein listeners do not correct a speaker if there is no immediate need to establish intersubjective understanding on a point (Firth, 1996). It is also possible that the co-workers could not immediately recall the correct term themselves. In fact, the actual diagram in question is probably most accurately called a *bunkaizu* 'exploded-view diagram' rather than a *tenkaizu* 'expanded-view diagram.' As Noda and Hayashi themselves use *tenkaizu* in Excerpt 4-2 below, they not only let it pass, but they also rely on a mutually understood (although technically incorrect) term to keep the interaction going.

As David attempts to continue his report, he is unable to get past his trouble. This leads him to more explicitly flag his trouble as linguistic in nature, as seen in Excerpt 4-2.

**Excerpt 4-2.** Tenkaizu (word search)

```
13   DV de    kore ga (0.3) ano (0.3) kore o (0.6) chotto
        then  this S         H        this O       a little
14      namae wa chotto  (0.3) fumei       desu    ne.
        name  TP a little       uncertain  CP-POL  IP
        Then this, um, this, well... I'm a little unsure, uh, about the name.

15      (0.2)

16 →DV  $nan  to yobeba   ii    ka$ (0.2)
        what  QT call-CND good  Q
17      chotto wakaranakatta    n desu   kedo
        little understand-NG-PST N CP-POL but
        I didn't know what I should call it, but...

18 →HS  nihongo  de?
        Japanese in
        In Japanese?

19 →DV  nihongo. (0.2) to   eigo:.
        Japanese       and  English
        Japanese and English.
```

```
20   HS  eigo?   (0.3)  eigo?
         English        English
         English? English?

21   DV  °koitsu      wa?°  ((points at diagram))
         this thing   TP
         This thing?

22  →HS  tenkaizu.
         expanded-view diagram
         Expanded-view diagram.

23  →DV  ah (.)  tenkaizu.              (.)  soo.
         CS      expanded-view diagram       I see
         Oh. expanded-view diagram. I see.
```

In line 13, David again encounters trouble describing the diagram right after saying *kore ga* 'this is,' and begins a word search in line 16 when he laughingly admits that he does not know the name for the diagram. As Kurhila (2004) points out, laughter when experiencing trouble is a way of signaling that the trouble is linguistic in nature rather than due to a deficiency in institutional knowledge. David is thus making his language struggles relevant, seemingly as a means of soliciting help. Hayashi finally joins the word search in line 18, but instead of providing a solution, his first move is to confirm that David is searching for the term in Japanese. In this way, Hayashi implicitly asks if the trouble is linguistic in nature, while also making David's identity as an L2 speaker relevant, to which David replies that he does not know the term in English either. It is not until David physically points to the diagram (line 21) that Hayashi provides a solution (line 22). Despite having initially used *tenkaizu* himself, David responds with a change-of-state token, *ah*, a repetition of the term, and *soo* (roughly 'I see'), indicating acknowledgement of Hayashi's proposed solution and resolving the search.

As David has now confirmed his understanding, he is able to continue with his report. Hayashi, however, perhaps taking David's mention of not knowing the word in Japanese or English as encouragement, extends the language-related discussion by playfully pursuing translations of *tenkaizu*, first in Chinese[8] and then in English.[9]

**Excerpt 4-3.** Tenkaizu (discussion)

```
26   HS  chuugokugo  >de iu   to<   (0.2)
         Chinese      in say  QT
27       bakuhaku-tu?  ((mispronounced Chinese))
         explosion diagram
         In Chinese, is it "explosion diagram?"
```

```
28         (0.4)

29   HS   °chigau      ka°
          different    Q
          Or maybe not?

30   DV   .hhhh (0.8)

31   HS   <bakuhaku>-tu?=   ((mispronounced Chinese))
          explosion diagram
          Explosion diagram?

32   ND   =bakuhatsu-zu
          explosion diagram
          Explosion diagram.

33  →HS   .hhh

34         (0.5)

35   HS   eigo     de  nan   to  iu   no?
          English  in  what  QT  say  Q
          What is it in English?

36   DV   $bakuhatsu?$ (0.5) (hhh)
          explosion
          Explosion?

37   ND   ekusupurojun,=
          explosion
          Explosion.

38   DV   =explosion.

39   HS   ekusplojun?
          explosion
          Explosion?

40  →DV   °tenkaizu                ka.°
          expanded-view diagram    Q
          Expanded-view diagram, huh.

41   HS   e:. (.) nihongo   wa.
          yes     Japanese  TP
          Yes, in Japanese.

42   DV   okay.
```

```
43          (0.6)

44          e::: .hhh (0.8) °okay°
            H
            Uh..., okay.

45          .hhhh hai.
                  okay
            Okay.

46          nde (0.2) sore igai  wa. (0.4) pii-tii-shii
            and so    that other TP              p  t  c
47          no koto: (0.6) .hh nakanaka susundenai  n desu
            LK matter          quite    progress-NG N CP-POL
48          (.) °ima no tokoro°
                now LK place
            And so, other than that, the PTC matter hasn't progressed much.
            At this point.
```

The playful sequence in lines 26 through 39 is clearly oriented toward a language-related issue and is tangential to the work activity of reporting in the meeting. Hayashi begins by searching for the Chinese term to refer to the exploded-view diagram (line 26), which he guesses is *bakuhaku-tu*, in a try-marked utterance. In Chinese orthography, this word is written as 爆発図 (literally, explosion diagram), but is actually pronounced *baofa-tu*. Although an equivalent reading of these characters in Japanese is *bakuhatsu-zu*, Hayashi is probably mispronouncing the Chinese by using a rough Japanese reading for the first two characters (*bakuhaku*) and the Chinese reading for the third (*tu*, rather than the Japanese *zu*). Noda, in line 32, also makes an attempt at the Chinese, but produces the Japanese reading, *bakuhatsu-zu,* which is not the usual term in Japanese, but does reflect the Japanese pronunciation of the Chinese characters. Then, after Hayashi and Noda have difficulty finding the Chinese word, Hayashi initiates a second search, this time for the English equivalent. In response, David takes a turn by repeating *bakuhatsu* 'explosion' laughingly in line 36, which grabs a turn in a way that shows he can answer the question. However, before David can provide an answer, Noda instead takes a turn and interjects the English word, explosion, in a Japanese pronunciation (line 37). David repairs this to its conventional English pronunciation (line 38), which Hayashi repeats in a Japanese pronunciation with questioning intonation (line 39).

Having established the English term for the diagram, David then relates it back to the Japanese. In line 40, he produces *tenkaizu* with the question marking particle *ka* and falling intonation, displaying that he is registering the term and publicly reorienting back to the original source of trouble. Hayashi follows this return to the original word search by acknowledging that David has understood the correct Japanese term (line 41), and David wraps up the search with "okay," thus concluding the word-search sequence. He then signals that he is resuming his report with *nde* 'and so' (line 46).

The extended discussion on a linguistic matter seen here seems to arise, at least in part, because David's report is "interruptable," since David, who is the participant with the rights to hold the floor during his own report, has explicitly opened the floor to participation from his co-workers. Then, as the participants digress into a playful discussion of translation equivalents of the focal term, the extended sequence provides David with more varied opportunities to reflect on the term that initially caused him trouble. Indeed, research on language play has shown that these sort of playful conversations support learning by allowing L2 speakers to experiment with various aspects of the target language on their own terms (Bushnell, 2009). Here, by relating the trouble source, the Japanese term for an 'exploded-view diagram,' to Chinese and English equivalents, the talk provides David with additional information regarding its meaning. This is indicated when he finally relates the ongoing talk back to his initial trouble by registering *tenkaizu* (that is, by repeating the word followed by *ka* with falling intonation), as in other examples, and then returning to his meeting report.

While the extended talk was pursued as a result of David's explicit solicitation of a linguistic item, David requires the item in order to complete his report during the meeting. In this sense, the learning opportunity is again occasioned by the larger work-related activity. In this case, however, because David controls the floor at the time the trouble is encountered and is thus able to ask a linguistic question, the work-related activity becomes diverted for a relatively longer period of time. The result is a clearer opportunity for learning, but a slower return to the institutional purpose of the original interaction.

## The interactional competence of learning at work

The word searches here reflect the participants' overall orientation to doing work. The interns only occasionally solicit help explicitly, instead showing a preference for making trouble public through the use of hesitations, vowel elongation on partial productions, pauses, try-marking, signals of uncertainty, attempts at self-repair, and statements of trouble. Then, detecting the trouble, others volunteer solutions so as to minimize disruption to the ongoing task. Once a solution has been provided, the interns register it with forms such as the question-marking particle *ka* with falling intonation, change-of-state tokens, other tokens of receipt (*okay, hai*), and explicit statements of understanding (e.g., *wakarimashita, soo*). However, if a solution is not immediately evident or forthcoming, and the term cannot be easily avoided while maintain a focus on the work-related task, then there may be occasions when the interaction digresses into a more explicit discussion of linguistic meaning.

The interactional competence displayed by the interns in these examples demonstrates how they navigate trouble with unfamiliar technical terms in ways that orient toward accomplishing work rather than learning language, seeking first to minimize disruption to the task at hand. This is similar to what has been found in other work on word searches in multilingual institutional talk. Kurhila (2006) and Wagner and Firth (1997), for example, show that word searches are concluded when enough intersubjective understanding has been established to allow the institutional talk to resume, even if source full resolution has not been realized. In these and other studies, however, learning is not always forthcoming. The tight focus on institutional goals often leads participants to forgo opportunities to orient to linguistic forms and meanings in ways that are conducive to learning (Brouwer et al., 2004; Kurhila, 2006; Theodórsdóttir, 2011a; Wagner & Firth, 1997).

The data considered here shed light on some conditions when L2 speakers in institutional settings are able to take advantage of word searches as opportunities for learning. In the first set of conversations (illustrated by Excerpts 1 and 2), trouble is resolved quickly, as is typical in institutional talk. The word searches are characterized by a focus on clearly defined work tasks and the presence of workplace resources (such as diagrams, computer screens, and so on), allowing the interns' colleagues to infer solutions without much effort. The interns are likewise able to easily relate the provided solutions to the source of their trouble with minimal effort by registering the term. Then, publicly displaying that they have registered it helps to smoothly and quickly resume the work activity.

The second, less frequent set of conversations shows that the institutional focus of workplace interactions at times may actually allow for deeper engagement with new technical terms. One way this happens is illustrated in Excerpt 3, where, after Miyazaki provides a solution which Ethan registers (Excerpt 3-1), an opportunity to use the same word emerges later as the collaborative work activity continues to unfold (Excerpt 3-2). Ethan leverages this as an opportunity to learn the word by orienting to language-related matters as he produces it with try-marking and other indications that he is doing learning. Another situation that allows for a greater variety of engagement with technical terms is illustrated in Excerpt 4, where the participants collectively and playfully pursue discussion of translation equivalents of the term.

These data, therefore, show that the interns are able to find opportunities for learning in otherwise work-focused interactions. At times, efficiency is sacrificed and the trouble source is pursued in more depth, though most frequently, the participants take advantage of the workplace environment to resolve the search quickly and move on with the task at hand. The interns, in collaboration with their colleagues, must therefore interactively balance the goals of doing work and discussing technical terms.

## Lost opportunities for learning

Although learning may occur in the examples discussed above, the interactions maintain a focus on doing work. In fact, the preference for maintaining an orientation to the work activity may, at times, override the opportunity for learning completely. In the data, in 6 out of the 32 sequences, the interns encounter what appears to be lexical trouble, but the focus on institutional activities prevents a resulting word search from providing opportunities for learning. One final example illustrates this. Here, David is asking Nakata (NT) how to remove a component called a "PTC," which is soldered onto a component called a "rotor." He experiences trouble, however, recalling the word for "melt," as in "to melt solder."[10]

**Excerpt 5.** Tokeru

```
10   DV  ima wa pii-tii-shii dake kaetai
         now TP  p  t   c     only want to change
11       n da kara (1.6)
         N CP so
         Right now, I just want to change the PTC, so...

12   NT  nn.
         yeah
         Yeah.

13  →DV  handa   o (1.0) e:: °>nan  to iu<° (.) nanka
         solder  O               H       what QT say         H
14       nanka tokete::, (0.9)
         H     melt-and
         The solder, um, what's it called, uh melt and...

15  →NT  hai.
         yeah
         Yeah.

16   DV  shoo-keesu eh- (.) pii-tii-shii dake:: (0.3)
         small case H       p  t  c       only
17       nukeru       kana (1.1) to omotte (.)
         remove-POT   Q           QT think-and
18       doo omoimasu ka?
         how think-POL Q
         The small case... I wonder if I can just remove the PTC? What do you
         think?

19       (.)
```

```
20  DV  <sore::  ni  suru::  ka>  (0.2)  atarashii  (0.4)
        that    PT  do      Q           new
21      rootaa ni suru ka (0.5)  docchi no hoo ga (0.4)
        rotor  PT do   Q         which  LK way  S
22      kookateki  deshoo              ka?
        effective  CP-probably-POL     Q
        Do that, or put on a new rotor? Which way is more effective?

23  NT  atarashii  rootaa  de  ii    n  janai   ka
        new        rotor   PT  good  N  CP-NG   Q
        A new rotor would do, wouldn't it?

24  DV  hhhhh  hai.
               okay
        Okay.

25      (0.7)

26      wakatta.
        understand-PST
        I understand.

27      (0.8)

28      yaru  shika   nai  n  desu    ne.
        do    except  NG   N  CP-POL  IP
        I just have to do it.
```

After explaining what he is trying to do, David attempts to ask Nakata if he should melt the solder in order to remove the PTC (lines 13–14). His mention of *handa* 'solder' is followed by the onset of a word search: a full second pause, the hesitation *e::*, and then a self-directed *nan to iu* 'what's it called.' Following another pause, David produces *tokete* 'melt and' with try-marking (an elongated final vowel, slight rising intonation, and followed by a pause), signaling his uncertainty about the word by also preceding it with two instances of *nanka*. Although David seems to display some uncertainty, the proposed solution *tokete* 'melt and' appears sufficient to conclude the word search. Nakata produces the acknowledgment token *hai* 'yes' in line 15, which generically aligns him to David's prior utterance and signals receipt. David then continues with a lengthy work-related question spanning lines 16 through 22.

In this instance, David's uncertainty was probably warranted. The verb *tokeru* 'melt' (which is conjugated as *tokete* 'melt and') is an intransitive verb (as in *handa ga toketa* 'the solder melted'). Here, however, David produces *handa* 'solder' with the accusative case marker, *o*, in the first part of line 13, suggesting a transitive structure, which would require the transitive verb *tokasu* 'to melt' (as in *handa o tokasu* '(I) melt the solder'). Despite this structural error, however, the core semantic meaning of his statement is unscathed. While David's utterance is technically incorrect and may even sound strange to an L1 speaker, Nakata treats it as acceptable. Intersubjective understanding for doing the work-related task is not compromised, and as such, the work may continue.

In this example, then, maintaining an orientation to the work means an opportunity for learning may have been lost. While David's try-marked utterance suggests he is not confident he is using the correct word, because this trouble does not impact the ability to talk about and do the work, neither participant pursues a correction; rather, they adhere to the practice of "let it pass" (Firth, 1996), and David does not ask about the meaning (unlike Excerpt 4 in which trouble is also initially overlooked, but David insists on getting the correct term anyway). In this way, the desire to minimize disruption to the ongoing task means there are times when opportunities to learn may not materialize.

## Conclusion

This study sheds light on the interactional competence of American interns in Japanese companies as they navigate the demands of doing work while interactionally dealing with unfamiliar technical terms. The analysis takes the perspective that learning is embedded in collaborative, social activities. Although the learning of unfamiliar technical terms may be peripheral to the primary purposes of work-related activities, L2 speakers make visible efforts to register and therefore learn words in their public actions during word searches. As in other CA work on institutional talk (Brouwer et al., 2004; Firth, 2009; Kurhila, 2004, 2006; Theodórsdóttir, 2011a, 2011b; Wagner & Firth, 1997), we see that when participants encounter troubles, they work to establish just enough understanding to allow the work task to resume. This study then shows how L2 speakers might leverage instances of lexical trouble as opportunities to learn language, and particularly explores the extent to which work-focused activities are diverted when doing so. The study finds that the easiest path back to the work-related activity is often to obtain a technical term as a solution to a word search. This is most likely to happen when the institutional environment and work-focused interaction contextualizes the solution in a way that makes it easy to infer. Then, in signaling that the term has been registered, the interns are able to end the word search and quickly resume the work activity.

However, the study also uncovers a potential tradeoff between efficiency (i.e., how little time participants devote to resolving trouble) and the depth of language-focused talk. Word searches are efficient when resources in the workplace environment provide clues (e.g., physical objects, contextualization of the topic of the intern's task, the intern's attempts to produce correct utterances) that help interlocutors quickly infer the interns' source of trouble and volunteer a solution. When resources in the work environment, however, are not sufficient to encourage quick resolutions, participants must work harder to achieve understanding, allowing the interns to more directly attend to the meaning and use of the term (such as by defining the term, providing related terms, comparing the term to other languages, or using the term in different contexts). In this way, more explicit discussion of linguistic meaning is likely held if and when the sequential environment allows for some diversion from the central work activity.

Finally, note that the division between learning a technical term and learning how to do work is not always clear, as technical terms are required for the kind of precise meaning-making that is needed to do work in specialized environments. By learning the *language* of their jobs, the interns are simultaneously learning how to *do* their jobs. Indeed, the nature of work in a specialized environment entails the proper use and understanding of the equipment, tools, and jargon that operate in that environment. The intersection between learning content as a new professional and learning language as an L2 speaker is thus an area for continued study. In addition to better understanding how L2 speakers manage learning on their own, this perspective challenges traditional, memorization-based approaches to teaching and learning technical terms by showing that even specialized, individual lexical items are perhaps best handled and learned in and through social interaction.

## Notes

1 All proper names are pseudonyms and reflect the typical practice in the company of referring to American interns by their first names and Japanese workers by their last names.
2 *Mufuka denryoku* 'no load power' is the amount of electrical energy consumed by a device when it is not active.
3 It seems that non-verbal resources are especially important here. If, for example, David looks at Suzuki while saying *sukeeru* with questioning intonation and Suzuki nods to confirm during the following pause, this would clearly indicate David is registering a new term. Unfortunately, as no video data exists, this cannot be said for certain.
4 *Yooryoo* 'capacity' is a reference to the ability of an item to store an electrical charge.
5 A condenser is a component which holds an electrical charge as measured by *yooryoo* 'capacity.'
6 The terms impedance and inductance are used as English loanwords in typical conversation at this company and refer to other measures of electrical performance.
7 An exploded-view diagram is a three-dimensional rendering showing the components of a complex mechanism in a disassembled state as if it had been pulled apart, allowing for analysis of the internal composition of a product. In

Japanese, this is referred to with the term *bunkaizu*. The term David uses, however, is *tenkaizu*, which is a different type that might be referred to as an "expanded-view diagram." The participants are indeed working on an exploded-view diagram, not an expanded-view one, so David's word choice is incorrect. The translations reflect his actual word choice, not his intended meaning.

8   Many workers traveled to the company's Chinese subsidiaries frequently and thus it was not uncommon for them to reference Chinese words, usually in playful ways.

9   Just prior to Excerpt 4-3, there were two lines which are largely incomprehensible due to background noise as several workers entered the meeting late, and thus lines 24 and 25 are not included.

10   In English, "to melt solder" usually refers to removing solder. When applying, it is common to use "solder" as a verb, as in "to solder two wires together." In Japanese, *handa o tokasu* 'to melt (=remove) solder' and *hanada-zuke (o) suru* 'to apply solder' are used.

## References

Azuma, S., & Sambongi, R. (2001). *Business Japanese*. Washington, DC: Georgetown University Press.

Brouwer, C. E. (2003). Word searches in NNS–NS interaction: Opportunities for language learning? *The Modern Language Journal, 87*(4), 534–545.

Brouwer, C. E., Rasmussen, G., & Wagner, J. (2004). Embedded corrections in second language talk. In R. Gardner & J. Wagner (Eds.), *Second language conversations* (pp. 75–92). London: Continuum.

Bushnell, C. (2009). 'Lego my keego!': An analysis of language play in a beginning Japanese as a foreign language classroom. *Applied Linguistics, 30*(1), 49–69.

Ellis, R. (1994). Factors in the incidental acquisition of second language vocabulary from oral input: A review essay. *Applied Language Learning, 5*(1), 1–32.

Firth, A. (1996). The discursive accomplishment of normality: On 'lingua franca' English and conversation analysis. *Journal of Pragmatics, 26*(2), 237–259.

Firth, A. (2009). Doing *not* being a foreign language learner: English as a *lingua franca* in the workplace and (some) implications for SLA. *IRAL, 47*, 127–156.

Gardner, R. (2008). Conversation analysis and orientation to learning. *Journal of Applied Linguistics, 5*(3), 229–244.

Greer, T. (2013). Word search sequences in bilingual interaction: Codeswitching and embodied orientation toward shifting participant constellations. *Journal of Pragmatics, 57*, 100–117.

Hayashi, M. (2003). Language and the body as resources for collaborative action: A study of word searches in Japanese conversation. *Research on Language and Social Interaction, 36*(2), 109–141.

Hayashi, M. (2004). Discourse within a sentence: An exploration of postpositions in Japanese as an interactional resource. *Language in Society, 33*(3), 343–376.

Heritage, J. (1984). A change-of state token and aspects of its sequential placement. In J. M. Atkinson & J. Heritage (Eds.), *Structure of social action* (pp. 299–345). Cambridge: Cambridge University Press.

Hosoda, Y. (2000). Other-repair in Japanese conversations between nonnative and native speakers. *Issues in Applied Linguistics, 11*(1), 39–63.

Huang, S., Willson, V., & Eslami, Z. (2012). The effects of task involvement load on L2 incidental vocabulary learning: A meta-analytic study. *The Modern Language Journal, 96*(4), 544–557.

Huckin, T., & Coady, J. (1999). Incidental vocabulary acquisition in a second language. *Studies in Second Language Acquisition, 21*(2), 181–193.

Ishida, M. (2009). Development of interactional competence: Changes in the use of *ne* in L2 Japanese during study abroad. In H. T. Nguyen & G. Kasper (Eds.), *Talk-in-interaction: Multilingual perspectives* (pp. 351–385). Honolulu, HI: University of Hawai'i, National Foreign Language Resource Center.

Jung, K. (2004). L2 vocabulary development through conversation: A conversation analysis. *Second Language Studies, 23*(1), 27–66.

Kasper, G. (2006). Beyond repair: Conversation analysis as an approach to SLA. *AILA Review, 19*(1), 83–99.

Koschmann, T. (2012). Conversation analysis and learning in interaction. In C. A. Chapelle (Ed.), *The encyclopedia of applied linguistics*. Hoboken, NJ: Blackwell.

Koshik, I., & Seo, M.-S. (2012). Word (and other) search sequences initiated by language learners. *Text & Talk, 32*(2), 167–189.

Kurhila, S. (2004). Clients or language learners: Being a second language speaker in institutional interaction. In R. Gardner & J. Wagner (Eds.), *Second language conversations* (pp. 58–74). London: Continuum.

Kurhila, S. (2006). *Second language interaction*. Philadelphia, PA: John Benjamins.

Makino, S., & Tsutsui, M. (2008). *A dictionary of advanced Japanese grammar*. Tokyo: Japan Times.

Mondada, L. (2004). Ways of 'doing being plurilingual' in international work meetings. In R. Gardner & J. Wagner (Eds.), *Second language conversations* (pp. 18–39). London: Continuum.

Mori, J. (2010). Learning language in real time: A case study of the Japanese demonstrative pronoun are in word-search sequences. In G. Kasper, H. T. Nguyen, D. Yoshimi & J. Yoshioka (Eds.), *Pragmatics and language learning* (Vol. 12, pp. 15–42). Honolulu, HI: University of Hawai'i, National Foreign Language Resource Center.

Mori, J., & Hasegawa, A. (2009). Doing being a foreign language learner in a classroom: Embodiment of cognitive states as social events. *International Review of Applied Linguistics in Language Teaching, 47*(1), 65–94.

Morita, E. (2005). *Negotiation of contingent talk: The Japanese interactional particles ne and sa*. Philadelphia, PA: John Benjamins.

Newton, J. (1995). Task-based interaction and incidental vocabulary learning: A case study. *Second Language Research, 11*(2), 159–176.
Newton, J. (2013). Incidental vocabulary learning in classroom communication tasks. *Language Teaching Research, 17*(2), 164–187.
Reichert, T., & Liebscher, G. (2012). Positioning the expert: Word searches, expertise, and learning opportunities in peer interaction. *The Modern Language Journal, 96*(4), 599–609.
Sacks, H., & Schegloff, E. A. (1979). Two preferences in the organization of reference to persons in conversation and their interaction. In G. Psathas (Ed.), *Everyday language: studies in ethnomethodology* (pp. 15–21). New York, NY: Irvington.
Schegloff, E. A. (1979). The relevance of repair in a syntax-for-conversation. In T. Givon (Ed.), *Discourse and syntax* (pp. 261–286). New York, NY: Academic Press.
Schegloff, E. A. (1991). Conversation analysis and socially shared cognition. In L. B. Resnick, J. M. Levine, & S. T. Teasley (Eds.) *Perspectives on socially shared cognition* (pp. 150–171). Washington, DC: American Psychological Association.
Schegloff, E. A. (1999). Discourse, pragmatics, conversation, analysis. *Discourse Studies, 1*(4), 405–435.
Schegloff, E. A., Jefferson, G., & Sacks, H. (1977). The preference for self-correction in the organization of repair in conversation. *Language, 53*, 361–382.
Seedhouse, P. (2004). *The interactional architecture of the language classroom: A conversation analysis perspective.* Oxford: Blackwell.
Suzuki, R., Hajikano, A., & Kataoka, S. (2006). *Business Japanese.* North Clarendon, VT: Tuttle.
Theodórsdóttir, G. (2011a). Language learning activities in real-life situations: Insisting on TCU completion in second language talk. In G. Pallotti & J. Wagner (Eds.), *L2 learning as social practice: Conversation-analytic perspectives* (pp. 185–208). Honolulu, HI: University of Hawai'i, National Foreign Language Resource Center.
Theodórsdóttir, G. (2011b). Second language interaction for business and learning. In J. K. Hall, J. Hellermann & S. P. Doehler (Eds.), *L2 interactional competence and development* (pp. 93–116). Bristol, UK: Multilingual Matters.
Wagner, J., & Firth, A. (1997). Communication strategies at work. In G. Kasper & E. Kellerman (Eds.), *Communication strategies: Psycholinguistic and sociolinguistic perspectives* (pp. 323–344). New York, NY: Longman.
Yamada, H. (1990). Topic management and turn distribution in business meetings: American versus Japanese strategies. *Text & Talk, 10*(3), 271–295.

# 4

# She who laughs first: Audience laughter and interactional competence at a *rakugo* performance for foreign students

Cade Bushnell
*University of Tsukuba*

## Introduction

From a common sense point of view, laughter may seem to be an uncontrollable reflex phenomenon, triggered by, for example, humor. As shown, however, by a number of studies examining the social organization of laughter in both humor related talk (Norrick, 2010; Sacks, 1989, 1992) and non-humor related talk (Jefferson, 1979, 1984; Jefferson, Sacks, & Schegloff, 1977, 1987), laughter can be a delicately organized interactional practice brought off by the participants through which an array of social actions, ranging from claiming epistemic stances to displaying (dis)affiliation (see Glenn, 2003 for an overview), are accomplished.

The present study examines data gathered from a live *rakugo* (i.e., story enactment by a single performer) performance for foreign students at a university in Japan. I use conversation analysis (CA) to describe when and how the audience members produce laughter. In so doing, I uncover the interactional competencies (IC) which underpin such audience participation. While there has been research examining the structure and accomplishment of humorous talk (Norrick, 2003) and the organization of humorous performances such as stand-up comedy (Furukawa, 2011; Katayama, 2009; Wells & Bull, 2007) and Japanese *manzai* 'team comedy' (Katayama, 2009; Tsutsumi, 2011), I am aware of only two studies looking at *rakugo* performance per se: One is a non-

CA study on the use of prosody in the organization of humor phenomena in *rakugo* (Kida, 2002) and the other is a CA study examining the ways in which a performer seems to make subtle adjustments to the story and its delivery, based on audience response, in order to pursue laughter from the audience (Bushnell, 2014). The present study seeks to provide further inroads to this little examined domain of social interaction.

Additionally, through examining the ways in which second language users of Japanese produce laughter in order to accomplish participation as audience members, this study contributes to our understanding of the interactional competencies of second language users, which underpin and facilitate their participation in social activities. While in recent years there has been significant research done from a CA perspective examining the interactional competencies of second language users—as evidenced, for example, in the edited volumes by Gardner and Wagner (2004), Nguyen and Kasper (2009), and Pallotti and Wagner (2011)—the interactional production and organization of laughter by second language users has not yet been given much consideration (see, however, Bushnell, 2009, 2014; Jacknick, 2013; Vöge, 2011). Thus, the present study builds upon and extends previous CA research on the interactional competencies of second language users.

In the following section, I review some key studies on laughter, with a focus on views of laughter as an interactional competency. Then, in order to contextualize the data for the unfamiliar reader, I make use of two subsections to first touch briefly on some characteristics of *rakugo* performance, and then upon the notions of *boke* 'goofiness' and *tsukkomi* 'straight response,' which figure prominently into many *rakugo* stories, including the one in my data. Following this, I describe the data of the present study and outline my research questions. I begin the analysis by first providing a gross description of the placement of laughter in the data. I then demonstrate how the participants orient to a format made visible by certain actions of the performer as indicating laughter-relevant positions within the performance, and how the participants use this format as a resource to organize their production of laughter. Finally, I consider the ways in which laughter might be related to real-time claims of understanding vis-à-vis laughable items being produced by the performer. I then conclude the chapter with a discussion of the findings of the analysis from the broader perspective of interactional competence and CA research on second language use.

## Laughter as an interactional competency

A considerable amount of research, done in fields ranging from psychology to evolutionary biology, has focused on the phenomenon of laughter—most often viewing laughter as one type of reflex response (see Glenn, 2003). As Glenn

(2003) argues, however, when viewed from a sociointeractional perspective, the interactional and communicative functions of laughter are thrown into relief.

Research on laughter done by Jefferson and her colleagues (i.e., Jefferson, 1979, 1984, 2004a; Jefferson et al., 1977, 1987) clearly demonstrates that laughter is one resource with which participants accomplish social action, and that the deployment and management of laughter is itself an interactional accomplishment of the participants. For instance, Jefferson (1979) demonstrates that laughter may function to invite laughter from a co-participant. Jefferson (1984) examines sequences of talk about mundane troubles (such as a family cat getting its whiskers singed off in a fire), and shows that participants may or may not deploy laughter in order to display "troubles-resistance" (i.e., showing that one is able to take the trouble in good spirit) and "troubles-receptiveness" (i.e., showing that one takes the speaker's trouble seriously). Jefferson et al. (1977, 1987) demonstrate that the production of laughter is organized by participants with an orientation to the same resources used to organize turns-at-talk, namely the turn-taking system (see Sacks, Schegloff, & Jefferson, 1974). Furthermore, researchers have noted that laughter can constitute both first- and second-pair parts in adjacency-pair sequences (e.g., Glenn, 2003; Jefferson et al., 1977; Schegloff, 2005).

According to Jefferson et al. (1977, p. 12), laughter may instantiate a "token of understanding," which can refer either backwards (e.g., to a joke that has just occurred) or forwards (i.e., indicating having seen the projected course of the talk). Furthermore, participants must deploy their laughter with precision timing, for as Sacks (1989, p. 348) notes:

> laughings are very locally responsive—if done on the completion of some utterance they affiliate to the last utterance and if done within some utterance they affiliate to its current state of development—the concern to have one's potential laugh locate what it is intendedly responsive to requires that it be done as rapidly as possible.

In this respect, in his analysis of the organization of laughter in joke telling in mundane conversation, Sacks (1989) maintains that jokes function as tests of understanding for the recipients. If the laughter is absent or occurs too late after the conclusion of the joke, Sacks argues, the producer may be heard as having not understood the joke. Norrick (2010, p. 90), on the other hand, notes that premature production of laughter, that is, prior to a punch line, presumably might also count as "failing the test and a potential loss of face [since such] laughter amounts to a disruption."[1] These studies by Sacks and Norrick demonstrate that timing is a critical factor in the deployment of laughter in interaction.

The research reviewed above clearly shows that, far from being a mere physical reflex, the timely production of laughter in social interaction constitutes an important interactional competency. As noted in the introduction, however, research on second language interaction has not yet considered laughter by second language users. The present study sheds light on some of these issues through an examination of when and how second language users produce laughter during a *rakugo* performance.

## Contextualizing information, data, and research questions

### *Rakugo*: A minimalist one (wo)man show

In this subsection, I provide a brief overview of some of the salient features of *rakugo* performance in order to make the data more accessible to the unfamiliar reader. *Rakugo* is one of the traditional oratory arts of Japan, and seems to have developed relatively independently and essentially simultaneously in the areas of Edo (now Tokyo) and western Japan, or *Kamigata* (esp., Kyoto and Osaka)[2] (Hayashiya, 2012). One of the most salient features of *rakugo* is that the performance is presented by a single performer, or *rakugoka*, who, rather than simply narrating the events, enacts the multiple characters of the story as if they were interacting with one another in a conversational format. In order to distinguish between which of the characters is being played at any given time, the *rakugoka* will use a variety of devices such as gaze direction, physical orientation and posture, pace and manner of speech, and so forth. Other salient features of *rakugo* performance are that costumes and special scenery are not used, props are kept to the bare minimum of only a folding fan and a handkerchief, and vocal mimicry (e.g., via the use of an overtly feminine voice) is avoided (Hayashiya, 2012). The *rakugoka* will rely on the imaginations of those in the audience as he or she[3] presents a minimalist performance, using the fan or handkerchief as stand-ins for various objects ranging from tobacco pipes and tools to account ledgers and comestibles. Many of the stories performed are comical in nature, but there are also many stories featuring frightening (i.e., *kaidan banashi*) or heartwarming (i.e., *ninjou banashi*) themes, as well as those offering moral teachings. The roots of *rakugo* are believed to extend back to sermons given by the Buddhist monk *Anrakuan Sakuden* (1554–1642), in which he would include comical or interesting elements in order to catch the attention of his listeners (Teruoka, 1959).

Classical *rakugo* stories are handed down through generations of *rakugoka* through a process of apprenticeship. Many *rakugoka*, however, make adaptations to the old stories (which range from minor changes, such as updating words, phrases, and locations, to major alterations of the storyline itself; Hayashiya, 2012, personal communication) in order to make them more accessible to contemporary audiences. Furthermore, although the text of the story is typically memorized and recited more or less verbatim by the *rakugoka*, real-time improvisation[4] may also occur based on, for instance, the reactions of the audience (Hayashiya, 2012, personal communication). Some *rakugoka* also create original stories, known as *shinsaku rakugo* 'newly created rakugo,' many of which have contemporary settings.

## A structural frame for humor in Japanese comedy

In western jokes, the humoristic element is commonly associated with a final punch line, which both indicates the conclusion of the joke and potentially makes relevant the production of laughter from the recipient(s) (Norrick, 2010; Sacks, 1989, 1992). Norrick (2003) (drawing on previous research) notes that the potential "humor" of a punch line seems to be related to how it induces a reinterpretation of the joke text preceding it via the use of a "script-switch trigger," or based on violations of Gricean maxims such as quantity and relation (see Grice, 1975). In *rakugo*, stories typically end with an *ochi* 'final pun,' which, according to Kida (2002), will also typically violate Gricean maxims.

As Kida notes, however, in *rakugo* a number of other devices are also intermittently used to invoke humor. Perhaps most salient of these, though not mentioned explicitly by Kida, are *boke* 'goofiness' and *tsukkomi* 'straight response' (Hayashiya, 2012), which also appear frequently in Japanese *manzai* team comedy (see Abe, 2006; Tsutsumi, 2011). According to Abe (2005a, 2005b), humor based on *boke* and *tsukkomi* seems to involve a contrast between two notions, which are linked to a shared condition (Figure 1).

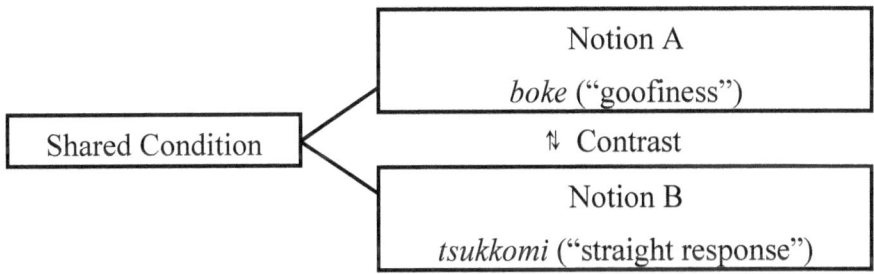

**Figure 1.** Boke and tsukkomi (Abe, 2005a, p. 49; translation by present author)

In Figure 1, an incongruity results from Notion A being submitted in the context of the Shared Condition. This incongruity is thrown into sharp relief by the presentation of Notion B. Below, a simple example of this format is taken from Tsutsumi (2011), who draws upon Abe (2005a) to analyze several Japanese *manzai* and American team comedy exchanges. In Excerpt 1, Fukuda (F) and Mashiko (M) are talking about going to the barber. Mashiko has a buzz cut. (I make note of the embodied actions of the participants as necessary in a line above the numbered first tier of the transcript. The positions of these actions are linked to the talk in the first tier through the use of a vertical line, i.e., "|." See the section below on data and transcriptions for other transcription conventions.)

**Excerpt 1.** (From Tsutsumi, 2011, p. 161–162; re-transcribed)

```
1    F:   hajimete    iku  tokoya  ttsu  no  wa   fuan
          first time  go   barber  QT    N   TP   uneasy
2         ssu yo ne.
          CP  IP IP
          It's unnerving to go to a barbershop for the first time, huh.

3    M:   fuan    da  yo ne: are ne:. nandaga   omoidoori  ni
          uneasy  CP  IP IP  that IP  somehow   my way     PT
                                |((rubbing shaven head))
4         nanne       n  |janee  ka  do  omodde,
          become-NG   N   CP-NG  Q   QT  think-and
5         sugee    kowagu   [nat-
          really   scared   become
          Yeah, really unnerving right. I worry that maybe it won't turn out
          how I want it to and get really scared

6    F:                    [boozu      da   kara
                            buzz cut   CP   so
7         kankee     nee    be yo!
          relation   none   IP IP
          It doesn't matter because you have a buzz cut!
```

As Tsutsumi (2011) notes, Mashiko's lines 3 through 5 create an incongruity in relation to the condition presented by Fukuda's lines 1 and 2, which suggests that people usually feel uneasy about going to a new barber. This incongruity results from the expectation that only people with hair long enough to style (i.e., longer than a military-style buzz cut) should be concerned with the results of a haircut. Though not overtly noted in Tsutsumi's analysis, the incongruency of Mashiko's turn is fully disclosed near the turn's conclusion through the delivery of a multimodal action, constituted both by Mashiko's talk and embodied action of rubbing the stubble on his head (line 4). These actions work to create a context wherein it becomes possible for Fukuda to sharply highlight this incongruity via the delivery of an explicit statement of the violated expectation in the next position (line 6). Here, Fukuda explicitly states the expectation violated by Mashiko's actions in lines 3 through 5.[5]

The *boke* and *tsukkomi* format shown in Excerpt 1 is assembled by two interactants who each supply one element of the format. As mentioned above, however, since *rakugo* involves a single performer enacting a conversational exchange between two or more participants, physically speaking the elements of both *boke* and *tsukkomi* are supplied by the performer as he or she performs different characters in the story.

## Data and transcripts

The data come from a two-day *rakugo* workshop event for foreign students at a university in eastern Japan. The event occurred in a medium-sized Japanese-style room in the University Hall. The *rakugo* performer was active in western Japan, and at the time of data collection had been performing *rakugo* professionally for over twenty years. One part of this event was his enactment of the classical *rakugo* story *Kohome* 'Praising Children.' This story portrays the antics of an absent minded man named Kiroku as he endeavors to obtain free *sake* 'rice wine' from various people. The performance of *Kohome* itself lasted for just over sixteen minutes.

The foreign student participants were graduate students conducting research and writing their theses in Japanese, and thus were all highly proficient in Japanese. In addition to the students, the audience also included the researcher, an assistant, and several university faculty members. The students were seated in the front rows, with the other audience members remaining in the back of the room. There were nineteen audience members in all. While some of the students were familiar with *rakugo*, this was their first experience with the story *Kohome*.

Data collection was done via audio- and video-recording. Written consent was obtained from all participants prior to recording. Video-recordings were made with two cameras operated by an assistant. One camera was placed facing the audience, and the other facing the performer. Audio-recordings were made via lapel microphones attached directly to the *rakugo* performer and to three audience members. The combination of the video-recordings and the audio data collected by these individually placed recording devices allowed the researcher to capture the laughter and other vocal response behavior of not only the participants on whom the devices were placed, but also those in the immediate vicinity. Audience members other than those seated in the first two rows are not considered in the analysis, as they were not clearly captured by the camera, nor were they audio-recorded.

Data analysis is done via CA (see ten Have, 2007). In preparing the transcripts, since *rakugo* performance involves a single performer enacting conversations between multiple characters, I have employed the following conventions in addition to the standard Jeffersonian conventions (see Jefferson, 2004b): (a) labeling each of the performer's utterances with a capital $P$ (i.e., performer) followed by a subscript initial for the name of the character being portrayed during that turn (e.g., $P_K$, $P_J$), and (b) using hash marks (i.e., #) to indicate a sharpness or roughness in tone.

## Research questions

I aim to describe how the participants (i.e., the performer and audience members) co-accomplish the orderly production of audience laughter during the *rakugo* performance. In order to achieve this goal, I pursue the following questions in the analyses:
1. How does the performer make visible laughter-relevant positions in the interaction?
2. How do the participants co-accomplish the production of audience laughter at laughter-relevant positions?
3. What kinds of competencies (interactional, linguistic, pragmatic, etc.) underpin the participants' temporally differentially produced laughter?

## Analysis: Laughter at the *rakugo* performance

### A preliminary analysis of whole audience laughter

A rough examination of Excerpt 2 reveals that audience laughter may be seen to occur at multiple points during a single scene of the story. Excerpt 2 shows a scene where Kiroku is importuning Jinbei for a cup of *sake*, which Kiroku had mistakenly heard Jinbei was distributing *gratis*. Jinbei informs Kiroku, however, that the *sake* is not *tada* 'free,' but rather is from relatives living in the Nada area of Osaka. In response, Kiroku demands to be served a cup, in spite of his mishearing. ($P_K$=Kiroku, $P_J$=Jinbei, Au=audience members.)

**Excerpt 2.** Kechinbo (transcript simplified)

```
1    P_K:   ippai    gurai  ogor[ii na:.  .hh kechinbo.
            one cup  about  treat   IP       stingy person
            At least treat me to one cup. You stinge.

2    Au:                         [heh heh heh °heh heh heh°

3    P_J:   n #dare ga ke[chinbo    ya.#
              who  S  stingy person CP
            Who are you calling stingy!

4    Au:                    [hah hah HAH HAH HAH HEH Heh
5           heh heh
```

If we apply Abe's (2005a) framework (Figure 1) to Excerpt 2, a Shared Condition is provided in the story-so-far, where it has been established that *Jinbei* is not distributing free *sake* and Kiroku has misheard in regard to Jinbei's newly acquired stock. *Kiroku* responds with a demand to be treated to *sake*.

The incongruency of this demand may be explained based on the following two points: (a) Kiroku supposes that he is being refused free *sake* as a result of his mishearing (i.e., rather than the fact that no free *sake* was available in the first place), and (b) Kiroku assesses Jinbei as having a miserly character based on the faulty logic of (a) and in spite of the fact that Kiroku himself is the one demanding free *sake*. In this way, Kiroku's actions recognizably constitute a Notion A move, according to Abe's (2005a) definition. On the other hand, Jinbei responds to Kiroku in each case by bringing the incongruency of Kiroku's actions into sharp relief, calling attention to the fact that it is Kiroku who might be appropriately assessed as being a cheapskate (i.e., by demanding to be served free *sake*). This function of highlighting an incongruency in Kiroku's prior utterance makes Jinbei's actions interpretable as an instantiation of Abe's (2005a) Notion B.

While Abe's (2005a) framework may enable an *ex post facto* identification of static instances of *boke* and *tsukkomi* in the script of a *rakugo* story, it does not provide an analyst with the tools necessary to understand how audience laughter is jointly accomplished during an actual *rakugo* performance, where audience members are faced with the ongoing task of developing an understanding of what actions are being assembled by the performer's utterances as they unfold in real time. For instance, in Excerpt 2, audience laughter appears in line 2 and lines 4 and 5, importantly, during (i.e., not following) Kiroku's demand to be treated to at least one cup of *sake* (line 1) and Jinbei's pointed response to this demand (line 3). To develop an understanding of how it is possible for the audience to produce such online laughter in an organized manner will require an examination of the concrete details of the *rakugo* performance as a social interaction. As mentioned above, according to Sacks (1989), laughter tends to get deployed in a manner sensitive to its local environment. Thus, we may assume that the audience laughter in line 2 and lines 4 and 5 is indexing and evaluating some feature of the preceding utterances (i.e., lines 1 and 3, respectively). Furthermore, in the case of *rakugo*, such an understanding must be developed in relation to both (a) the actions the performer him- or herself is assembling, and (b) the unfolding actions of the characters in the story. If the audience members are unfamiliar with the story, as is the case with the students in my data, they must carefully monitor and inspect each increment of action produced by the performer for its interpretability as making laughter relevant, or doing something else altogether. The analyses of the following two subsections bring the tools of CA to bear on these considerations in order to provide answers to my first two research questions about how laughter-relevant positions are made visible, and how audience laughter is accomplished at these positions.

## Demonstration by the performer of some features of laughter-relevant positions

The term *laughter-relevant position* is used to indicate structurally provided junctures in the talk wherein laughter might relevantly be submitted. This term contrasts with notions of humor or funniness in that it focuses exclusively on the sequential organization of the talk. In the analyses of the following subsections, I demonstrate how the audience displays an orientation to a particular action format assembled by the performer as they together accomplish the production of audience laughter at laughter-relevant positions. Prior to this, however, I first examine the performer's talk and actions just before he begins his telling of the story proper. As will be shown, through his prefatory talk and actions, the performer demonstrates some of the features by which this action format might become visible within the upcoming performance.

In the *makura* 'performance preface' of this performance of *Kohome*, the performer explains the concepts of *boke* 'goofiness' and *tsukkomi* 'straight response,' and announces that these are constitutive features of the upcoming main story.[6] As shown in Excerpt 3, he also provides an explanation of some of the characteristics of *boke* and *tsukkomi*, including a demonstration of some salient phonological and kinesic features of *tsukkomi* in particular.

**Excerpt 3.** Boke to tsukkomi

```
1    P:    boke  tte  yuu   no  wa,  (0.2)  un,  a-  baka    na
           goofy QT   say   N   TP         uhm  a-  stupid  LK
2          koto  o    yuu,  >kore ga boke< desu ne,
           thing O    say   this  S  goofy CP   IP
           Boke is, uhm, saying something foo- stupid, this is boke you see,

                                  |((turning to face opposite))
3          .h  sore ni  tsuite   |>#NANI  O   BAKA    NA  KOTO   O
           .h  that     about    what     O   stupid  LK  thing  O

                                          |((turning to face audience))
                                   |((shifts eyes to audience))
4          ITTERU  N  DA.#<  |(0.2)  |to  yuu  no  ga  tsukkomi
           saying  N  C                QT  say  N   S   ridicule
5          to  yuu  n  desu  keredomo,  .hhh
           QT  say  N  CP    but
           In regard to that, saying "What stupid thing are you saying!"
           is called tsukkomi but,
```

((lines omitted: 116.7 seconds during which the performer explains that in his experience audiences in western Japan laugh after the *tsukkomi*, and that it is only the appearance of a *tsukkomi* which can end the episode by putting the *boke* to rest))

```
6    P:    kono  boke  to   tsukkomi de dekiagatteru
           this goofy and  ridicule  by  constituted
7                to yuu ohanashi o  mazu  kiite      moraitai
                 QT say   story   O first listen   want to have
8                to omoimasu.
                 QT  think
           I'd first like to have you listen to a story that is made up of
           this boke and tsukkomi.
```

In line 1, the performer first topicalizes the term *boke*, and after a 0.2 second pause, defines it as "saying something foo- stupid" (*a- baka na koto o yuu*[7]). Then, in lines 3 through 5, he states that saying something like "What stupid thing are you saying!" (*nani o baka na koto o itteru n da*) constitutes a *tsukkomi*. It should be noted, however, that the performer does not simply provide a verbal explanation, as he did in regard to *boke*. In other words, rather than explaining *tsukkomi* as, for instance, "taking someone to task for their silliness," he provides the audience with a sample of an actual line that might be said in order to perform a *tsukkomi*. Furthermore, he produces this utterance at a pace faster than the surrounding speech, with a greater volume, and with a rough, harsh vocal quality (denoted by the hash marks). Such production features create a vivid contrast with the just prior utterance.

The embodied actions produced by the performer in conjunction with his utterance in line 3 also provide a physical demonstration of the types of bodily activities that might be associated with the production of a *tsukkomi*. A number of these features are considered in detail below.

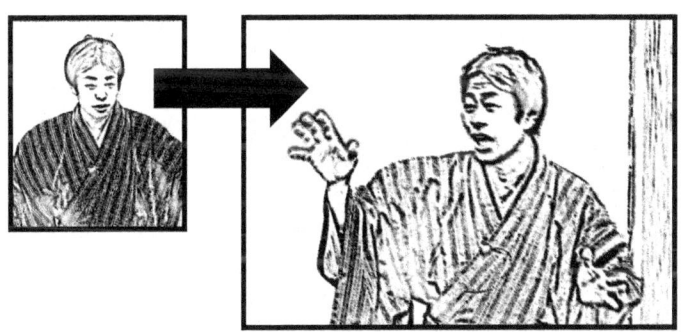

>#NANI O BAKA NA KOTO O ITTERU N DA.#<

**Figure 2.** Excerpt 3, lines 2 and 3

While first producing his explanation in regard to *boke*, the performer orients his body and gaze to directly face the audience. Following this, while uttering "what stupid thing are you saying!" (*nani o baka na koto o itteru n da*), he quickly turns his body and gaze to the side, and moves his hands as if to shove or strike something (Figure 2). In other words, by coordinating this utterance, produced in a manner so as to dramatically contrast with the just prior utterance, with the physical act of turning to face in the opposite direction while making a shoving gesture with his hands, and then subsequently labeling this constellation of actions as *tsukkomi* (lines 3–5), the performer seems to enact (rather than explain) the notion of *tsukkomi*.

Following this, in the omitted lines, the performer explains to the audience that, in his own experience, while Tokyo audiences tend to laugh immediately following the appearance of a *boke*, Osaka audiences save their laughter until after the appearance of the *tsukkomi*. He explains this by saying that Osaka people understand that a *boke* without a following *tsukkomi* is like a ghost floating around aimlessly, and that a *tsukkomi* functions to lay that ghost to rest. It may be noted that during this explanation, the performer provides two further brief enactments of *tsukkomi*. Then, in lines 6 through 8, he mentions that the story he is about to perform prominently features a *boke* and *tsukkomi* structure. After this, he immediately begins the story (not shown).

In this way, by providing vivid enactments accomplished through the deployment of delicately intercoordinated multimodal action, the performer makes salient a particular structural format which is bracketed at its end by a constellation of particular actions, including an abrupt change of gaze orientation and a dramatic change in the manner of utterance production. Furthermore, by labeling this format as *boke* and *tsukkomi*, the performer seems to underscore the utility of this format as a search frame whereby the audience members might locate laughter-relevant positions within the episodes of the story to be performed. Also, by relating information concerning when various audiences laugh in relation to the production status of this format, noting in particular that western Japanese audiences tend to laugh after the *tsukkomi* and that it is only the appearance of a *tsukkomi* that can finish the episode by "putting the *boke* to rest," he seems to suggest that laughter might be most relevantly produced after the appearance of a *tsukkomi*.

This demonstration by the performer highlights for the audience some of the key phonological and kinesic features characterizing an action format designed to make visible the arrival of a laughter-relevant position. It is interesting to note that the delivery of the punch line in American stand-up comedy also seems to be associated with similar prosodic and kinesic features, and to provide audience members with cues which facilitate the coordination of spontaneous and near simultaneous laughter production (E. D. Wrobbel, personal communication, May, 2015).

## Laughing at laughter-relevant positions in the *rakugo* performance

In the analyses of this subsection, I examine in detail how a laughter-relevant position is made visible, and how the participants (i.e., the performer and audience members) co-organize the production of audience laughter in relation to this position. Similar to the analyses of audience response during political oratory by Atkinson (1985) and Ikeda (2007, 2009), and of audience laughter by Wrobbel (personal communication), my analysis at this point treats the audience as a single unit. I examine the actions of individual audience members in a later section.

Let us return to the previous example (Excerpt 2) where Kiroku is demanding to be served *sake*. How are laughter-relevant positions made visible as such in this data, and how is audience laughter organized accordingly? ($P_K$=Kiroku, $P_J$=Jinbei, Au=audience members.)

**Excerpt 4.** Kechinbo (Excerpt 2 and its continuation)

```
1    P_K:  ippai    gurai ogor[ii na:.  .hh    kechinbo.
           one cup  about  treat   IP          stingy person
           At least treat me to one cup. You stinge.

2    Au:                             [heh heh heh °heh heh heh°

                 |((quickly turning to face opposite))
3    P_J:       |n #dare ga  ke[chinbo      ya.#[      (0.9)      ]
                    who  S   stingy person  CP
                Who are you calling stingy!

4    Au:                              [hah   hah   HAH  [HAH HAH HEH Heh]
5                 [heh heh

6    P_J:  [a:? sora   maa   washi to    omae no
           huh  that   well  me    and   you  LK
7          naka         ya kara na,
           friendship   CP so    IP
           Huh? Well of course we are friends so,
```

In line 1, Kiroku demands free *sake* from Jinbei, and follows this with an evaluation of Jinbei as "stingy" (*kechinbo*). To this, Jinbei retorts with "who are you calling stingy!" In line 2, the first instance of audience laughter appears just after the performer produces the first part of "treat me" (*ogorii na:*) (line 1). It may be noted that this is the moment when it becomes clear that Kiroku is in the process of making a demand for free *sake*, and thus seems to instantiate a "recognitional overlap" (Jefferson, 1983).[8] Furthermore, the laughter continues through and just past the performer's production of *kechinbo* (line 1). Thus, the audience laughter, through its delicately timed onset in relation to the performer's ongoing utterance, functions to pick out and evaluate certain elements of the performer's talk (i.e., *ogorii na:* and *kechinbo*) as being laughable—although, the relatively quiet manner in which this laughter is produced seems to simultaneously display an orientation to possible continuing talk from the performer. Then, in line 4, the audience initiates production of loud and unrestrained laughter once it is clear that the performer, qua Jinbei, is contesting being characterized as a "stingy person."

I now examine the interplay between the performer's actions and the audience's laughter in more detail.

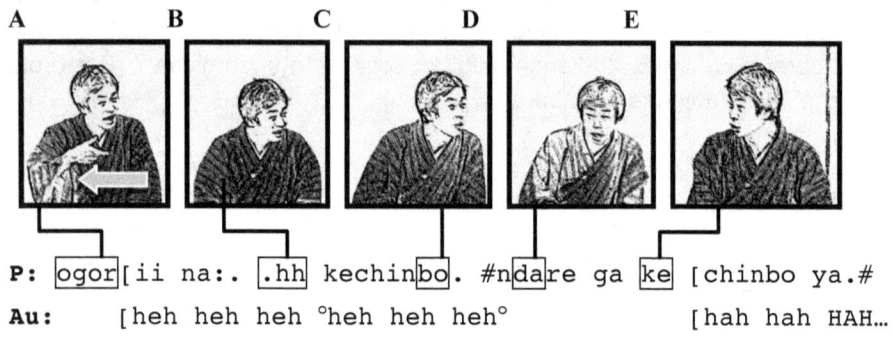

**Figure 3.** Excerpt 4, lines 1 through 4

In line 1, the performer-as-Kiroku produces "treat me" (*ogorii na:*) while motioning with his hand as if receiving a cup of *sake* (Figure 3A). It is at this point that the first occurrence of audience laughter begins. While certain features of the performer's talk around this point seem to indicate that more talk is forthcoming, for instance, that he begins to bring his hand down away from his face with his production of the interactional particle *na* and follows this with an inbreath taken with parted lips (Figure 3B), there is no feature of the production of his utterance that could be taken to indicate that he has already embarked on the production of a *boke* + *tsukkomi* format in particular. In fact, *ogorii na* is produced in a phonologically unmarked manner such that it blends seamlessly with the talk immediately preceding it. It therefore does not seem likely that the audience's laughter just after the sound *ogor* was informed by some overt phonological feature; his gesture of receiving a cup of *sake* is likewise not visible as being indicative that a *boke* is now underway as it is unmarked in relation to the stream of embodied action preceding it. In many cases (including that of Excerpt 4), if one were to rely solely on recognizing changes in the manner of action production by the performer as an indicator of laughter relevance, a *boke* would only become visible as such via a retro-specification through the subsequent production of the overt action format, *tsukkomi* (see Excerpt 3).[9]

So, how is it that the audience was able to undertake laughter production at this particular point in time? This seems to be facilitated by aspects of the talk not related to its manner of production per se, which come into play in making some bit of action visible in real time as being a *boke*. In particular, such visibility seems to depend on an understanding by the audience members of the portrayed actions of the characters in the story, rather than the actions of the performer per se in delivering the story (i.e., features such as changes in gaze, bodily orientation, pace, tone of speech production, etc.).[10]

In contrast to the performer's speech in line 1, that of line 3 is clearly marked by a change in manner of production. In particular, while quickly reorienting to face in the opposite direction (a *rakugo* convention used to indicate role change), the performer adopts a rough vocal quality, and an increased speed and volume throughout his production of *dare ga kechinbo ya* 'who are you calling stingy!' (Figures 3D and 3E). Importantly, these production features closely map onto those demonstrated earlier during the *makura* 'performance preface' (see Excerpt 3, above). Thus, in line 3, overt features of the production of the performer's utterance seem to indicate that the action format the performer has glossed as *tsukkomi* is underway. Furthermore, the potential completion of this *tsukkomi*, and thus of a *boke* + *tsukkomi* format itself, is projected by the onset of a clearly final intonational pattern, and then by the grammatical and pragmatic completion achieved by the production of the copula *ya*. Note that it is just prior to this point that the second instance of audience laughter begins. Importantly, the laughter this time occurs in an explosive and loud manner, climaxing around the performer's production of *ya* (Figure 3E)—a fact which seems to display an orientation to this point as being precisely laughter relevant. Furthermore, through delaying the progression of the story for 0.9 seconds, during which the audience clearly continues a round of robust laughter (lines 4–5), the performer also seems to treat this particular slot as being one relevantly filled with laughter from the audience.

Excerpt 5 provides an additional, slightly more complex example. Just prior to the excerpt, Kiroku had learned from Jinbei how to praise people (in order to get them to treat him to free *sake*), and has gone into town to try out his newly acquired skills. The excerpt starts just after Kiroku ($P_K$) has approached a man ($P_M$) on the street, greeting him by noting that the two have not seen each other in a while.

**Excerpt 5.** Narenareshii

```
1    P_K:   KONNICHI WA.   KONNICHI WA.  .HH  GOKIGENSAN
            today    TP    today    TP        how are you

2           DEGOZAIMASU  .HH NAGAI KOTO OMIKAKESHIMASEN
            CP-HON       .hh long  thing see-HUM¹¹-NG

3           na   n  da  NA:.
            CP   N  CP  IP
            Hello. Hello. How are you. I haven't seen you in
            a long time, huh!

                  |((staring blankly))
4    P_M:         |(1.1)

5    P_M:   °hai hai.°
            yes yes
            Yes yes.

6           (0.3)

7    Au:    heh heh

                  |((tilting head))
8    P_M:         |.ssss anta erai narenareshuu osshaimasu
                   .ssss you  very too  friendly  speak-HON
9           kedo ne: (0.5) dochirasan desu ka?
            but  IP        who-HON    CP   Q
            You're speaking in a very friendly way but who are you?

10          (0.4)

11   P_K:   are: (0.4) anta watashi no koto shirimasen ka?
            oh dear    you  I       LK thing know-POL-NG Q
            Oh dear! Don't you know who I am?

12   P_M:   s:a:: hajimete  mita yooni omoiman   nen kedo na.
            well  first time saw  like  think-POL IP  but  IP
            Well this seems to me like the first time I've ever laid eyes on you,
            you know.

13   P_K:   a sayoo ka: eheh .h >watai mo  anta no koto
            a that  Q           I     too you LK thing

                                         |((waiving hand in air))
14          shirimahen ne:n.< [.hh       |sainara=
            know-POL-NG IP                bye
            Oh is that right. I don't know who you are either. Bye.

15   Au:                        [heh heh heh heh
```

```
16    P_M:   =>#a  [na:n  ya    are    wa.#<[      (0.5)       ]
              a    what   CP    that   TP
             Ah what was that!

17    Au:          [ hah   hah   HAH   HAH    [HAH  HEH  HEH]

18                 [HEH  heh  heh

19    P_M:         [honma    e::   heh  heh
                    really   eh
                   Really eh! Heh heh.
```

The focus of the analysis is on the organization of the audience laughter in lines 15 and 17. In the lines leading up to this laughter, the performer portrays a scene where Kiroku extends a salutation to a man he has stopped on the street ("Man" below). Kiroku's talk in lines 1 through 3 is produced in a loud volume, and consists of four turn construction units (TCUs): a greeting (i.e., *konnichi wa*), a repetition of that greeting, a formulaic "how-are-you" (*gokigensan degozaimasu*), and a formulaic "long-time-no-see" element. The inhalations between the second and third TCUs and the third and fourth TCUs are each produced with a squeaky quality and a smile, which make them interpretable as inhaled laughter tokens. This, along with the loud volume with which this set of opening salutations is produced, functions to display an affective stance (Ochs, 1993) of great joy or excitement in relation to the reunion. It may be further noted that the end of the fourth and final TCU features the interactional particle *na*, which works to make relevant a confirming response from Man.

In line 4, however, Man allows a 1.1 second silence to develop prior to undertaking his response. It may also be noted that during this silence the performer, as Man, maintains a facial expression glossable as "a blank stare" (Figure 4, below). Then, when he does finally begin to respond, rather than displaying a recognition of Kiroku by reciprocating the greeting, or by providing an aligning response in regard to the length of time since their last meeting, Man treats Kiroku's talk in lines 1 through 3 as a summons by saying only *hai. hai.* 'yes. yes.' (line 5). Furthermore, he produces this at a near whisper volume, and with a deadpan face—features which contrast sharply with the loud volume and animated character of Kiroku's talk in lines 1 through 3. Taken as a whole, Man's behavior in lines 4 and 5 seems to make visible for the audience a hesitant and disaffiliative stance in response to Kiroku's course of action thus far—a stance acknowledged by the audience through a couple of small laughter particles in line 7.

P_M: .ssss

**Figure 4.** Line 4     **Figure 5.** Line 8

Then, Man continues on in line 8 to produce an inhalation characterized by an ingressive dental fricative sound, and accompanied by a cocked head and knitted brow (Figure 5, above). This constellation of actions is recognizable as a convention often used by Japanese speakers to claim that one is "thinking" or "puzzled." Man then continues on with an assessment of Kiroku's greeting as being "overly friendly" (*erai narenareshuu osshaimasu*). Then in line 9, following a 0.5 second silence during which he narrows his eyes and slightly tilts his head, Man formulates a question that makes relevant a self-identification from Kiroku. In this way, Man's difficulty in recognizing Kiroku is made an observable fact for the audience.

In line 10, however, rather than providing identifying information, Kiroku allows a 0.4 second silence to occur, after which he produces *are:* 'oh dear,' which functions here to claim surprise and puzzlement (line 11). Following an additional 0.4 second pause, Kiroku accounts for his puzzled response by formulating a question asking if Man does not know him (*anta watashi no koto shirimasen ka?*). To this, Man undertakes a reply in line 12 with *s:a::* 'well,' which, with its stretched out manner of production, projects a negative response. This is forthcoming with *hajimete mita yooni omoiman nen kedo na* 'this seems to me like the first time I ever laid eyes on you,' an utterance which claims no previous experience with Kiroku, while simultaneously maintaining an ambivalent epistemic stance allowing for the possibility of error. In such a sequential environment, the priority response (Bilmes, 1993, 1995) is for Kiroku to provide information or evidence concerning a previous encounter or relationship with Man. In other words, if such information or evidence is available to be brought forth, it is relevant that it be produced just now, following Man's talk in line 12. If not, the resulting implication is that no such evidence is available (Bilmes, 1993). This effectively places the burden of proof on Kiroku.

In line 13, Kiroku first receipts Man's line 12 utterance as news with a grinning *a sayoo ka:* 'oh is that right,' which, with the final sound stretch, is hearable as a claim that Man's talk in line 12 has provided Kiroku with a solution to the puzzle he (*Kiroku*) claimed to be struggling with in line 11, in that Man has now accounted for his disaffiliative stance by claiming to be unaware of having any prior experience with Kiroku. Then, rather than submitting any information or evidence regarding a prior relationship with Man, Kiroku continues to display a smile while producing a single aspirated laughter particle followed by an inbreath, and then provides *watai mo anta no koto shirimahen nen* 'I don't know who you are either.' He then bids a farewell to Man while waiving a hand in the air (line 14).

Concerning the audience laughter in line 15, the following points may be noted. First, in regard to the manner of production of the performer's lines 13 and 14, there is no change in verbal or embodied action which might function to alert the audience of an upcoming laughter-relevant position. Though the performer is grinning at the point of onset of audience laughter, he had been doing so intermittently from the beginning of the encounter in line 1. Furthermore, though the performer does produce phonological material hearable as a laugh (.*h*), this is hearable as a performed laugh, similar to those in lines 1 and 2. In other words, the laugh is not hearable as being one of mirth from the performer himself,[12] but rather as part of the lines of the character Kiroku at this point in the story. It may also be noted that the laugh consists only of single particle, and that it appears well before the onset of audience laughter, although it is possible that this laughter particle might function to signal the general humorous attitude of Kiroku, or to indicate embarrassment at admitting the truth about not knowing Man.[13] Thus, the audience laughter is not hearable as having been produced in response to an invitation to do laughing together (see Jefferson et al., 1987), for there is clearly no such invitation being extended at this point by the performer.

As mentioned above, Sacks (1989) states that "laughings are very locally responsive—if done on the completion of some utterance they affiliate to the last utterance and if done within some utterance they affiliate to its current state of development" (p. 348). Assuming this to be the case, we may inspect the laughter in line 15 to determine how its design exhibits a responsiveness to the utterance by the performer immediately preceding it in line 14. Notably, it is produced precisely following the completion of *shirimahen ne:n* 'I don't know.' The completion of this phrase results in the real-time unfolding for the audience of the incongruity of Kiroku's having behaved as if Man should know who he is, when in fact Kiroku himself knew all along that he and Man were mutual strangers. The following observations may be made about the performer's talk here: (a) both *shirimahen* and *nen* are produced under a single intonational contour, and (b) the TCU starting from *watai* is said quite rapidly within one breath unit (note the inbreath just after *nen*). Thus, although the incongruous nature of Kiroku's behavior is potentially visible at the point *shirima* of the word *shirimahen* 'don't know' has been produced,[14] it is possible that the smooth and rapid flow of the performer's talk led to a slight offset in the beginning of laughter production. When the audience laughter in line 15 does begin, it is just after

Kiroku's behavior had been revealed as being incongruous. In this way, the laughter functions to index Kiroku's goofy-behavior-so-revealed, and to assess this as being laughable. Thus, in a manner similar to Excerpt 4, laughter by the audience at the point of line 15 appears to turn on an understanding of the portrayed actions of the characters in the story—an understanding which hinges crucially on a grasp of the Japanese used by the performer rather than on the performer's manner of producing the utterances per se.[15] Also notable, the laughter is relatively low in volume (cf. Excerpt 4, line 2), a feature which seems to be designed with an orientation to possible further talk by the performer, and thus to possibly display an understanding that a *tsukkomi* might be forthcoming.

Then, in line 17, the audience engages in a round of loud and sustained laughter. The point of onset overlaps with the performer's talk in line 16 just after it is clear, via features of the manner in which the performer undertakes utterance production (such as quickly facing in the opposite direction, displaying a facial expression glossable as indignant or shocked, and changing the tone and pace of speech), that the talk-in-production is to be interpreted as a *tsukkomi*. With the occurrence of a *tsukkomi*, the audience is provided with the closing bracket of a *boke* + *tsukkomi* format, which signals the arrival of a possible laughter-relevant position; the audience members display a recognition of this position as such in and through their deployment of open and unrestrained laughter. The performer also orients to the relevance of audience laughter in this position by putting the production of further speech on hold for 0.5 seconds, by which time a number of robust laughter particles have clearly passed (lines 16–17).

In this section, I have demonstrated how the participants, inclusive of both the audience members and the performer, orient to the *boke* + *tsukkomi* format in order to jointly accomplish audience laughter at laughter-relevant positions within the story in progress. I have also argued that audience laughter affiliating to the *boke* component of this format hinges on an understanding of what the characters in the story are doing and what kind of situation is being portrayed; this kind of understanding is necessarily underpinned by a grasp of the Japanese being used by the performer. In the case of the Japanese second language audience members, this means that timely productions of laughter at such junctures instantiate possible displays of various linguistic and interactional competencies. In the following section, the analysis is taken to an even finer level of granularity in order to scrutinize the behaviors of individual audience members in this respect.

**She who laughs first: Claiming an understanding of the laughable item**
The analyses in the previous sections have mainly focused on how the participants are able to accomplish audience laughter as a whole. In this section, I sharpen the analysis to focus on examining the onset of laughter by individual audience members. As can be seen in Excerpt 6 (a detail of Excerpt

5, lines 13–17, with the laughter of individual audience members added), what might be seen *prima facie* as simultaneous laughter from the audience-as-a-group actually comes forth as a cascade of laughter from individual members of the audience. Importantly, as I discuss in greater detail below, each of these instances of laughter can be seen as "affiliating" (Sacks, 1989, p. 348) with some just prior element in the unfolding talk; this point has bearing on what kinds of epistemic stances are displayed in and through the laughter.

**Excerpt 6.** Narenareshii (detailed)

```
1    P_K:   a sayoo  ka:  eheh  .h  >watai  mo   anta  no  koto
            a that   Q                I    too   you   LK  thing
2           shirimahen ne:n.< [.hh sainara=
            know-POL-NG IP         bye
            Oh is that right. I don't know who you are either. Bye.

3    F:                           [heh  heh  heh  heh  heh=

4    J:                           [hihh  .hh  heh  heh  heh=

5    P_M:   =>#a  [na:n  ya   [are   [wa.#<
              a   what   CP   that    TP
            Ah what was that!

6    F:    =heh [ heh   HAH [HAH   [HAH   HAH   HEH

7    J:    =hah  [hah  hah  [ HAH [HAH   HAH   HAH

8    G:          [ heh  heh  [ HAH [HAH  HAH  heh  heh

9    C:                      [ heh [heh  HAH  HAH  HAH

10   E:                            [heh  [HAH  HAH  HAH

11   D:                                   [heh  HAH  HAH
```

The participants' visible actions from *ne:n* in line 2 through *na:n* in line 5 of Excerpt 6 are shown below in Figure 6. As the performer produces *ne:n* (line 2; Figure 6A), no audible laughter is being produced. Then, just after getting off *ne:n*, and as he begins to take an inbreath while raising a hand (line 2; Figure 6B), two participants, F and J begin to laugh (lines 3–4). While a number of other participants are visibly smiling (Figure 6A, B), this does not necessarily seem to instantiate "pre-laughter" in the sense of an initial and unobtrusive display of having identified something laughable in the performer's talk (see Glenn, 2003). In many instances in my data (and as in the present case) the participants appear to be maintaining a kind of "perma-grin" throughout the performer's telling. This grin exhibits the following characteristics, which are not done justice in the still images: (a) an apparent mirthlessness, (b) an "in-between-ness" resembling a smile paused prior to reaching its climax, and (c) relatively little movement or variation (note for instance the frozen expressions of participants A and B, who finally do not produce any laughter, compared to the expressions of C, E, F, G, and eventually even D across Figure 6A to 6D). Such a grin may provide a kind of stand-by state in between straight-facedness and vocal laughter production, and possibly a "safe-house" for those uncertain of whether or not the unfolding talk is of laughable quality.

Laughter by F and J continues in a restrained manner in overlap with the performer's inbreath and *sainara* (lines 2–4; Figure 6B, 6C). Then, when the performer abruptly changes the direction he is facing, along with the manner of his speech production (from a bright, bubbly quality to a harsh sharpness), and produces *na:n* (line 5; Figure 6D), participants F and J upgrade their laughter to an unrestrained level (lines 6–7). Participants G, C, E, and D also begin to produce loud and unrestrained laughter just after this point (lines 8–11).

**Figure 6.** Lines 2 through 5

Various competencies (interactional, linguistic, pragmatic, etc.) can be assumed to underpin the production of laughter by individual participants at just-that-moment in the interaction. I argue that such competencies are made visible by the participants through the epistemic stances they display in and through their laughter across various temporal points during the performer's unfolding telling of the story.

Sacks (1989) argues that recipients of jokes can claim an understanding of the joke through producing laughter after the punchline. He also notes, however, even when recipients are not able to understand the content of the joke per se, the structural features of the joke still provide a resource by which to produce laughter at an appropriate time (p. 345). Thus, Sacks maintains that in order for a claim of understanding to obtain as such there is a pressure for recipients of jokes to laugh "as soon as possible" in relation to the punchline, and prior to any other laughers (p. 350). By laughing "as soon as possible," recipients are able to claim that their laughter is based on an understanding of the content of the joke itself, rather than on simply having recognized a potentially laughter-relevant slot within the structural landscape of the joke. Furthermore, by laughing prior to other laughers, or indeed prior to being able to see "whether others will laugh at all" (p. 350), a recipient is able to claim that his or her laughter is not merely in response to an invitation to do laughing together (see Jefferson et al., 1987).

As noted in the analyses of the previous section, there are times when audience members laugh prior to the arrival of a laughter-relevant position. In other words, sometimes laughter occurs early, that is, in affiliation to the *boke* component of the format.[16] As has been shown, however, features of the performer's manner of production of the *boke* utterance do not provide a reliable cue as to whether or not production of a *boke* is underway; this is only visible in real time (as opposed to retrospect), based on an understanding of the situation of the story-so-far and of the portrayed actions of the characters. Crucially, such an understanding is necessarily underpinned by a grasp of the Japanese used by the performer. In the following excerpt (a reproduction of Excerpt 2 with the details of the laughter of individual audience members added), an audience member, C, begins laughing in line 2, in overlap with Kiroku's hearably incongruous utterance.

**Excerpt 7.** Kechinbo (detailed)

```
1    P_K:   ippai    gurai   ogor[ii  na:.  .hh ke[chinbo.=
            one cup  about   treat    IP        stingy person
            At least treat me to one cup. You stinge.

2    C:                              [heh heh heh   [°heh heh°

3    G:                                             [°heh heh heh°

4    F:     =°hih hih hih°

5    P_J:   n #dare ga
              who   S
6           ke [chi [n      [bo    [ya.#
            stingy person              CP
            Who are you calling stingy!

7    A:           [hah [hah
```

```
8    G:           [hhe  [h H  [AH   [HAH HAH HEH heh  heh
9    F:                 [he   [h H  [AH HAH HEH Heh  heh
10   C:                       [HAH  [HAH HAH HEH heh  heh
11   H:                             [hn HN [HN HN hn
12   B:                                    [heh heh heh
13   D:                                    [heh heh heh
```

The particular focus of the analysis here is on the differential claims of understanding, and displays of linguistic and interactional competence, accomplished by the laughter of individual audience members in lines 2, 3, 4, and 7 through 13. In line 1, just after Kiroku has produced the phonological material *ogor* of *ogorii na*, C begins to laugh quietly in line 2 (Figure 7, below). Importantly, as mentioned in the analysis of Excerpt 4 above, at this point in the performer's utterance, there seems to be no indication whatsoever in the manner of production that a laughable element is forthcoming. In this way, C's actions, by their early (i.e., in "recognitional overlap" [Jefferson, 1983] with the performer's turn-in-production, and prior to any overt indication of a forthcoming laughable) and independent appearance (i.e., not in response to laughter by other laughers), function to claim C's recognition of some laughable element in the performer's talk, and to publicly display her assessment of that element as laughable (see Sacks, 1989, p. 350).

**Figure 7.** Line 2

It bears emphasizing that, since no cues are made available in the performer's manner of utterance production, C's laughter in line 2 must turn on an understanding of the incongruent nature of Kiroku making a baseless demand to be served free *sake* at this particular stage in the development of the story (i.e., right after having been informed that there is no free *sake* being made available in the first place). It is important to further note that such an understanding hinges on competencies in Japanese phonology, morphology, lexicon, syntax, and pragmatics, as well as on a grasp of the socio-cultural implications of the situation, and of *Kiroku's* actions as part of that situation. In other words, in order to make sense out of the situation being portrayed in the story, and to be able to produce the laughter in line 2, C must be able to do the following: (a) parse the unfolding turn-in-progress, (b) grasp the meaning(s) of the words *ippai* 'one cup,' *gurai* 'at least,' and *ogoru* 'to treat,' (c) be aware that the word *ogoru* possibly instantiates the final predicate of the utterance, and that its arrival indicates that *Kiroku* is performing the action of demanding to be served *sake*, and (d) understand the socio-cultural implications of *Kiroku's* actions in the context of having just been informed that no free *sake* was available in the first place.

Additionally, C's laughter in line 2 also displays interactional competencies such as (a) an ability to recognize that the performer's TCU is nearing possible grammatical and pragmatic completion (see Hayashi, Mori, & Takagi, 2002; Tanaka, 1999; see also Ford, Fox & Thompson, 1996), (b) an orientation to producing laughter in reference to this point (see Jefferson et al., 1977, 1987), and (c) the ability to produce an assessment (via laughter) without disrupting the ongoing talk (see Goodwin & Goodwin, 1987; see also Norrick, 2010).

In line 3, G joins in with laughter of her own. While this laughter is clearly produced following and probably in partial reference to C's laughter, based on its placement just after the completion of *ogorii na*, G's laughter here also seems to display a grasp of the incongruity of Kiroku's demanding to be served free *sake*. Furthermore, the laughter by C, G, and F in lines 2 through 4 is very quiet, and thus displays an orientation to possible continuing talk from the performer (cf. the loud and unrestrained laughter they produce in lines 8 and 10 just as the performer produces the hearably final talk in line 6). In this way, this laughter functions to display, by virtue of its design, an interactional competence which underpins these participants' unproblematic participation as audience members at this particular point in the interaction.

In lines 5 and 6, as examined in detail in the analysis of Excerpt 4 above, the performer dramatically changes the orientation of his body and gaze, and the phonological characteristics of his speech. As noted, these actions provide a very explicit indication that a *tsukkomi* is under way, and thus that a laughter-relevant position is about to arrive. In lines 7 and 8, A and G display a recognition of this possible arrival through deploying laughter just after the performer has produced the first syllable of *kechinbo* 'stingy person.' Such a recognition is enabled only by an understanding of Japanese syntax (i.e., that a predicate is likely to follow the subject particle *ga*, and that *kechinbo* is a likely candidate component of this predicate based on its appearance in line 1), and may also be underpinned by and claim an understanding of the lexical item *kechinbo* 'stingy person' and the fact that Jinbei is assembling the action of protesting being assessed as a stingy person by Kiroku, who is himself demanding to be served free *sake*. In lines 9 through 11, F, C, and H join in the laughter at various points in the performer's emerging talk. The staggered onsets of laughter in each of these lines seem to display recognitions of the syntactic role of *kechinbo* as an initial component of the final predicate, and thus of an imminent possible conclusion of the TCU. Then, in lines 12 and 13, B and D submit a few particles of laughter. At this point, the performer has finished production of the copula *ya*, and brought off the utterance with a clear final falling intonation. Thus, the laughter here by B and D seems mainly to claim a recognition of the end of the TCU, and thus of the *tsukkomi*, and the arrival of a laughter-relevant position.

The analysis of Excerpt 7 has shown that differentially timed laughter by individual audience members may function to display a range of understandings regarding the content and current state of development of the performer's talk. In particular, early, independent laughter "affiliating" (Sacks, 1989, p. 348) to the *boke* component of a *boke* + *tsukkomi* format seems to claim an understanding of the portrayed situation and actions of the characters. I have argued that such an understanding necessarily hinges on interactional, linguistic, pragmatic, and other competencies, and that the laughter also functions as a display of such competencies. On the other hand, the laughter following that of the first laugher may be heard as being in partial reference to the first laughter. A careful examination of the onset of post-primary laughter, however, indicates that even such laughter also seems to be produced with an orientation to the current state of development of the performer's talk, and thus that it functions to display certain interactional and linguistic competencies.

## Summary of the analysis
The goals of the present study have been to describe 1) how the performer makes visible laughter-relevant positions, 2) how the participants co-accomplish the production of audience laughter at laughter-relevant positions, and 3) what kinds of competencies (interactional, linguistic, pragmatic, etc.) underpin the participants' temporally differentially produced laughter. In relation to the first two goals, I first showed how the performer explained the structure of the *boke* + *tsukkomi* 'goofiness + straight response' format to the audience. I then showed that laughter-relevant positions are made visible via such resources as embodied actions and voice quality during the unfolding of the story in real time via the *boke* + *tsukkomi* format. Then, I demonstrated how the audience members were able to produce relevant laughter in and through displaying orientations to this format. I showed in particular that the audience members orient themselves to the occurrence of *tsukkomi* as indicating the possible completion of a *boke* + *tsukkomi* format, and the concomitant arrival of a laughter-relevant position; I also showed the performer orienting to the position following a *tsukkomi* as a relevant slot for audience laughter in and through withholding further talk until the audience had got off a clear round of laughter.

In relation to the third goal, I further focused the analysis to account for the actions of individual audience members, whose audible activity was captured through the use of individually placed audio recording devices. In the analysis, I argued that, in the case of the data of the present study, early, independent laughter in affiliation to a *boke* functions to display an understanding of the content of the story-up-to-now, and that such an understanding hinges on a range of interactional and other competencies. Subsequent laughter "affiliating" (Sacks, 1989, p. 348) to a *boke* and laughter affiliating to a *tsukkomi* element may also function to display various competencies in relation to the talk-in-production. In general, it seems likely that *she-who-laughs-first* displays a multilevel understanding of both the development of the story (underpinned by interactional, linguistic, pragmatic, and socio-cultural competencies) and of the current state of the emerging talk by the performer, that is, whether or not a *boke* + *tsukkomi* format is under production, and if so, where the state of its production stands. On the other hand, *she-who-laughs-later* seems to chiefly display an understanding of the current state of the talk-in-production, that is, that a laughter-relevant position has occurred; secondary laughers may also be claiming an understanding in relation to the content of the story, although such a claim may stand in danger of being undercut by the hearability of such laughter as being in partial reference to prior laughter (see Sacks, 1989). Finally, *she-who-laughs-last* (i.e., after the appearance of the *tsukkomi*) displays an understanding that a *boke* + *tsukkomi* format has reached possible completion, and that a laughter-relevant position has arrived. Last laughers, however, may also be heard as laughing in response to prior laughter. Also, by the time last laughers undertake their laughter, first and second laughers have already gotten off a round of laughter, and the performer usually resumes enactment of the story shortly thereafter. Thus, last laughers usually do not "laugh longest," as the saying goes, at least in my data, since their laughter may need to be cut short as the performance moves forward to a next episode.

## Concluding discussion

As mentioned in the Introduction, while there are a growing number of studies looking at the interactional competencies of second language users (Gardner & Wagner, 2004; Nguyen & Kasper, 2009; Pallotti & Wagner, 2011), there are not many studies that have examined laughter in particular (see, however, Bushnell, 2009, 2014; Jacknick, 2013; Vöge, 2011). The analyses of the present study have looked at laughter as one type of responsive action during a live comedic performance.

Examining audience recipiency in conversational storytelling, Goodwin (1986) notes that an audience can be partitioned based on the differential competencies of the audience members in the domain of the current topic-at-talk. For instance, in Goodwin's study, during a story about a fight at a car race, one participant (Curt) displayed a competence in the discourse domain of car racing, while another (Gary) seemed to show a lack of such competence. Importantly, as Goodwin argues, the competencies of these audience members were publicly displayed in and through their respective responsive actions. Curt, for example, was able to display a knowledge of the people involved in the altercation by producing talk in overlap with the storyteller's utterance just after the storyteller had begun to mention the names of the people. The timing of the onset of Curt's talk in this case is crucial, for as Goodwin argues, the overlap functions to "claim independent access" (p. 288) to knowledge pertaining to the protagonists of the story, and to car racing.

In the case of my data, since the interaction is not conversational, but rather a semi-formal performance, the audience members do not typically have the interactional latitude to produce talk in overlap with that of the performer. Such behavior would likely be seen as an interruption and treated as problematic. This does not mean, however, that the audience must sit silently through the performance. Rather, the audience members produce various types of response behaviors, ranging from embodied actions, such as facial expressions and bodily movements, to vocal expressions, such as laughter. While responsive actions such as audience laughter may seem at first to be rather homogenous and even trivial in comparison to the types of behaviors examined by Goodwin (1986), the present study has shown that laughter by the audience members also worked to make visible differential knowledge and competencies.[17]

It is important to note that the kinds of knowledge and competencies claimed by the participants in Goodwin's study are based in prior experience with a specific domain of activity (that is, car racing), and with ways of talking about this activity. In the present study, the understandings claimed by the audience members' laughter, and the concomitant knowledge and competencies, are not related to any previous experience with *rakugo* or prior knowledge of that discourse domain, or even of the storyline itself; this was all a first-time experience for the audience members. Thus, the knowledge and competencies claimed in this case were those such as linguistic competence, pragmatic competence, and so forth, and as such were more closely intertwined with the practical activity of accomplishing participation as audience members at the *rakugo* performance itself. In both Goodwin's study and the present study, however, the delicate timing of action onset was seen to be a crucial factor for displaying independent access to knowledge. In other words, such access was displayed through early onset in relation to the possible completion of the unfolding talk by the storyteller or performer. Such an ability to produce precisely timed actions meshing with the ongoing flow of another participant's talk-in-production constitutes one important aspect of interactional competence within the domains of turn-taking and sequence organization.

## Notes

1 This does not mean however, as Norrick shows in his analyses, that laughter may not relevantly occur prior to the punch line; it may also occur as, e.g., laughter about issues in the performance of the joke, laughter in response to multiple punchlines, laughing at jab lines, laughter in response to the preface of a joke, laughter in response to the joke introduction, pre-punch line laughter with commentary, and laughter at a potential punch line.
2 *Kamigata* refers to the area of the domicile of the emperor. During the formative years of *rakugo*, this was Kyoto, and, more generally, the neighboring areas of Osaka, Kobe, Nara, and so forth. The term has remained in use to refer to *rakugo* from the Kansai area.
3 *Rakugo* has been traditionally performed by only men, though there are also a small number of women who have gained acceptance and even seniority as *rakugoka*. A good example is Sandaime Katsura Ayame (i.e., Katsura Ayame III), a woman who is officially recognized as the third generation heir to the tradition of the original (1891–1958) and second (1930–2005) Katsura Ayame, who were both men.
4 For instance, the *rakugoka* may, in an impromptu manner, try to escalate the laughter of a receptive audience or warm up a cold audience with material that is not officially part of the story text; depending on factors such as audience reception, these alterations may then become sedimented into the story text and repeated during subsequent performances (see Bushnell, 2014).
5 This dynamic contrasts with (American) "comic+straight man" jokes, for instance, in that with these it is the final punchline of the joke which typically reveals the incongruency:
Example (Tsutsumi, 2011, p. 157)
((Rossi, R, is playing the part of an interviewer and Allen, A, the part of a boxer))
R: What's your trickiest punch?
A: Left hook.
R: What's so tricky about that?
A: I use my right hand.
While "left hook" in line 2 might be said to create an incongruity in relation to "what's your trickiest punch?" in line 1, it does so in an obscured manner. In other words, it is not clear at this point how a left hook, a standard move in boxing, could be considered "a tricky punch." This fact is made clear by Rossi in line 3, where he requests a clarification as to which aspect of a left hook might be regarded as tricky, upon which Allen provides a response in line 4 that fully discloses the incongruency—that is, as Tsutsumi notes, it is not physically possible to deliver a left hook with one's right hand.

6   An interview with the present performer revealed that, in his case at least, an explanation of *boke* and *tsukkkomi* is not typically undertaken in the *makura*. The performer further suggested that he offered such an explanation on this occasion in orientation to the fact that most of the audience members were second language users of Japanese, and he wanted to make sure that they were aware of the concepts of *boke* and *tsukkkomi*, as they are a salient feature of *Kohome*.

7   The *a-* is most likely the beginning of the western Japanese *ahoo* 'foolish,' which is similar in meaning to the eastern Japanese *baka* 'stupid.'

8   One reviewer noted that since *ogorii na* is a dialect form (specifically, of Kansai), it must presumably be unfamiliar to many of the Japanese as a second language audience members. It is important to stress, however, that even if the audience members were unfamiliar with this particular form, as highly proficient users of standard Japanese, they would no doubt have known the standard form *ogorinasai* 'treat me" (imperative mood) and its abbreviated version, *ogorina*. Although I was not able to ask the audience members about this, it is possible that for some audience members the initial material of *ogorii na* was hearable as the beginning of the standard *ogorinasai* or *ogorina*. This fact, along with the material preceding this element, that is, *ippai gurai* 'at least one cup,' is sufficient to provide for the visibility of Kiroku's action as demanding to be served *sake* at the point of the onset of laughter in line 2.

9   Once the performer starts into the production of *kechinbo*, however, he begins to shift his body to the right of the frame, and slightly sticks out his lips and drops his head in coordination with the production of the sound *bo* (Figure 3C). These features may also potentially work to make his actions up to this point visible as having been a "tease," which may in turn offer some grounds for the audience to interpret those actions as being a possible *boke*, and to expect that a corresponding *tsukkomi* might be forthcoming—notably, the laughing audience members drop the volume of their laughter at this point, possibly in preparation to receive further talk from the performer.

10   I discuss the participants' displayed understandings in more detail in the following section.

11   I.e., "humble form."

12   I have seen occasions, though not in my data, when the *rakugo* performer actually laughs genuinely *as him- or herself* prior to or along with the audience. Here, however, the performer laughs *as Kiroku*.

13   Thanks are due to one of the editors for pointing out this additional possibility.

14   While *shirimahen* itself is a dialect form, some of the audience may have achieved an understanding of the talk here based on their knowledge of the standard *shirimasen*. It may also be noted that Kansai dialects are very common on television and in other media, so many of the audience members are likely to have heard *shirimahen* before.

15   I discuss this in more detail in the following section.

16  In some sense, as was pointed out by one of the editors, "post-*boke*" might be considered to instantiate an additional laughter-relevant position. As may be recalled, in his prefatory comments to the story, the performer did mention to the audience that in his experience audiences from the Tokyo area tend to laugh after the *boke*, while Osaka audiences tend to laugh only after the *tsukkomi*. It is relevant to note, however, that in my data (a) the performer does not seem to provide a temporal space wherein the audience might produce laughter after a *boke*, although the analysis has demonstrated that he does do so following a *tsukkomi*; and (b) as has been shown, while the appearance of a *tsukkomi* is made overtly observable for the audience through a number of features in the manner of the performer's production of talk and embodied action, the appearance of a *boke* is usually only visible via an understanding of the characters' actions portrayed against a backdrop of the development of the story to that point, and the trajectory of the forthcoming story. Structually speaking, a *boke* is made observable retrospectively through the occurance of a *tsukkomi*.

17  As one of the editors pointed out, it is possible that this might also be related to a differential orientation to what is laughable. While it is not possible to rule out that the individual senses of humor of the audience members may have been involved with when or if they produced laughter, I hope to have demonstrated in the analysis some regular organizational features of their laughter production which suggest a structural rather than (or in addition to) a psychological basis for the details of the participants' laughter.

## References

Abe, T. (2005a). Manzai ni okeru "boke" no shitsuteki tokuchou to keitaiteki tokuchou [Qualitative and formal characteristics of "goofiness" in Japanese team comedy]. *Waseda Nihongo Kenkyu, 13*, 61–72.

Abe, T. (2005b). Manzai ni okeru "tsukkomi" no ruikei to sono hyougen kouka [Types and expressional effects of "straightness" in Japanese team comedy]. *Kokugogaku Kenkyu to Shiryo, 28*, 48–60.

Abe, T. (2006). Manzai ni okeru "furi" "boke" "tsukkomi" no dainamizumu [The dynamics of "set up," "goofiness," and "straightness" in Japanese team comedy]. *Bulletin of the Graduate Division of Letters, Arts, and Sciences of Waseda University, 51*, 51–69.

Atkinson, J. M. (1985). Public speaking and audience responses: Some techniques for inviting applause. In J. M. Atkinson & J. Heritage (Eds.), *Structures of social action* (pp. 370–410). Cambridge: Cambridge University Press.

Bilmes, J. (1993). Ethnomethodology, culture, and implicature: Toward an empirical pragmatics. *Pragmatics, 3*, 387–409.

Bilmes, J. (1995). Negotiation and compromise. In A. Firth (Ed.), *The discourse of negotiation: Studies of language in the workplace* (pp. 61–81). Oxford: Pergamon Press Oxford.

Bushnell, C. (2009). "Lego my keego!": An analysis of language play in a beginning Japanese as a foreign language classroom. *Applied Linguistics, 30*(1), 49–69.

Bushnell, C. (2014). Warai no tsuikyuu: Ryuugakusei mukeno rakugokai niokeru warai o fukumu sougokoui nitsuite [Pursuing laughter: A look at interactional processes including laughter at a rakugo performance for foreign students]. *University of Tsukuba Journal of Japanese Language Teaching, 29*, 19–41.

Ford, C. E., Fox, B. A., & Thompson, S. A. (1996). Practices in the construction of turns: The TCU revisited. *Pragmatics, 6*(3), 427–454.

Furukawa, T. (2011). *Humor-ing the local: Multivocal performance in stand-up comedy in Hawai'i* (Doctoral dissertation). Retrieved from ProQuest Dissertations and Theses database. (UMI No. 3472243)

Gardner, R., & Wagner, J. (Eds.). (2004). *Second language conversations*. London: Continuum.

Glenn, P. J. (2003). *Laughter in interaction*. Cambridge: Cambridge University Press.

Goodwin, C. (1986). Audience diversity, participation and interpretation. *Text, 6*, 283–316.

Goodwin, C., & Goodwin, M. H. (1987). Concurrent operations on talk: Notes on the interactive organization of assessments. *IPrA Papers in Pragmatics, 1*(1), 1–54.

Grice, H.P. (1975). Logic and conversation. In P. Cole and J. L. Morgan (Eds.), *Speech acts* (pp. 41–58). New York: Academic Press.

Hayashi, M., Mori, J., & Takagi, T. (2002). Contingent achievement of co-tellership in a Japanese conversation: An analysis of talk, gaze, and gesture. In C. Ford, B. Fox, & S. Thompson (Eds.), *The language of turn and sequence* (pp. 81–122). Oxford: Oxford University Press.

Hayashiya, S. (2012, August 18). *Ukeru, ukesaseru [To get it, to make them get it]*. Presentation at the International Conference on Japanese Language Education (ICJLE), University of Nagoya, Japan.

Ikeda, K. (2007). *Audience presence and Japanese political oratory: A case study of a municipal assembly candidate* (Doctoral dissertation). Retrieved from ProQuest Dissertations and Theses database. (UMI No. 3264855)

Ikeda, K. (2009). Audience participation through interjection: Japanese municipal council sessions. *Journal of Language and Politics, 8*(1), 52–71.

Jacknick, C. (2013). "Cause the textbook says...": Laughter and student challenges in the ESL classroom. In P. Glenn & E. Holt (Eds.), *Studies of laughter in interaction* (pp. 185–200). New York, NY: Bloomsbury.

Jefferson, G. (1979). A technique for inviting laughter and its subsequent acceptance/declination. In G. Psathas (Ed.), *Everyday language: Studies in ethnomethodology* (pp. 79–96). New York, NY: Irvington Publishers.

Jefferson, G. (1983). Notes on some orderliness of overlap onset. *Tilburg Papers in Language and Literature, 28,* 1–28.

Jefferson, G. (1984). On the organization of laughter in talk about troubles. In J. M. Atkinson & J. Heritage (Eds.), *Structures of social action: Studies in conversation analysis* (pp. 346–369). Cambridge: Cambridge University Press.

Jefferson, G. (2004a). A note on laughter in "male-female" interaction. *Discourse Studies, 6*(1), 117–131.

Jefferson, G. (2004b). Glossary of transcript symbols with an introduction. In G. H. Lerner (Ed.), *Conversation analysis: Studies from the first generation* (pp. 13–31). Amsterdam: John Benjamins.

Jefferson, G., Sacks, H., & Schegloff, E. A. (1977). Preliminary notes on the sequential organization of laughter. *Pragmatics Microfiche, 1*(Fiche 8), A2–D9.

Jefferson, G., Sacks, H., & Schegloff, E. A. (1987). Notes on laughter in the pursuit of intimacy. In G. Button & J. R. E. Lee (Eds.), *Talk and social organisation* (pp. 152–205). Clevedon, UK: Multilingual Matters.

Katayama, H. (2009). A cross-cultural analysis of humor in stand-up comedy in the United States and Japan. *JoLIE, 2*(2), 125–142.

Kida, T. (2002). Prosody – a laughing matter?: A crosscultural comparison of a humour phenomenon (rakugo) in France, Tokyo, and Osaka. Paper presented at Speech Prosody 2002. Retrieved from http://www.isca-speech.org/archive_open/sp2002/sp02_427.pdf

Nguyen, H. T., & Kasper, G. (Eds.). (2009). *Talk-in-interaction: Multilingual perspectives.* Honolulu, HI: University of Hawai'i, National Foreign Language Resource Center.

Norrick, N. (2003). Issues in conversational joking. *Journal of Pragmatics, 35*(9), 1333–1359.

Norrick, N. (2010). Laughter before the punch line during the performance of narrative jokes in conversation. *Text, 30*(1), 75–95.

Ochs, E. (1993). Constructing social identity: A language socialization perspective. *Research on Language and Social Interaction, 26*(3), 287–306.

Pallotti, G., & Wagner, J. (Eds.). (2011). *L2 learning as social practice: Conversation-analytic perspectives.* Honolulu, HI: University of Hawai'i, National Foreign Language Resource Center.

Sacks, H. (1989). An analysis of the course of a joke's telling in conversation. In R. Bauman & J. F. Sherzer (Eds.), *Explorations in the ethnography of speaking* (pp. 337–353). Cambridge: Cambridge University Press.

Sacks, H. (1992). *Lectures on conversation* (Vols. 1-2). Oxford: Blackwell.

Sacks, H., Schegloff, E. A., & Jefferson, G. (1974). A simplest systematics for the organization of turn-taking for conversation. *Language, 50*(4), 696–735.

Schegloff, E. A. (2005). On complainability. *Social Problems, 52*(4), 449–476.

Tanaka, H. (1999). *Turn-taking in Japanese conversation: A study in grammar and interaction.* Amsterdam: John Benjamins.

ten Have, P. (2007). *Doing conversation analysis* (2nd ed.). Boston, MA: Sage.

Teruoka, Y. (1959). *Shomin no goraku: Rakugo no rekishi* [Entertainment for the masses: A history of rakugo]. Tokyo: Bonjinsha.

Tsutsumi, H. (2011). Conversation analysis of boke-tsukkomi exchange in Japanese comedy. In M. Karlsson (Ed.), *New voices* (Vol. 5, pp. 147–173). Sydney: The Japan Foundation.

Vöge, M. (2010). Local identity processes in business meetings displayed through laughter in complaint sequences. *Journal of Pragmatics, 42*(6), 1556–1576.

Wells, P., & Bull, P. (2007). From politics to comedy. *Journal of Language and Social Psychology, 26*(4), 321–342.

# 5 Co-construction of an L2 speaker's Interactional Competence: Recipient Responses in an Interview Activity[1]

Mari Yamamoto
*Kwansei Gakuin University*

Tomoharu Yanagimachi
*Hokusei Gakuen University*

## Introduction

Using data in which a second language (L2) speaker of Japanese interviews a Japanese researcher, this paper will describe from a conversation analytic point of view the way in which the L2 speaker acts as a competent interviewer, and accomplishes the task of conducting an interview. When speakers try to show that they have understood their interlocutor's talk, it is not enough to simply use receipt tokens such as *hai* 'yes' and *un* 'yeah.' Recipients have to pay attention to the information conveyed, anticipate the development of the talk, decide when to initiate embodied actions such as nodding or starting to laugh, and adjust their actions accordingly as capable interlocutors.

For L2 speakers of Japanese to accomplish these things, understanding the grammar and vocabulary of the target language and comprehending what they hear does not suffice. They also need to make their understanding public and observable to the speaker through the use of various semiotic resources, including appropriately timed responses and embodied actions.

In order to delineate this type of interactional competence (IC), researchers must observe and describe what is actually happening in naturally occurring conversations, because unlike linguistic or lexical competence, IC can be judged only as a result of collaborative work with others. Young (2011), for example, comparing communicative competence and IC, writes:

> [T]he fundamental difference between communicative competence and IC is that an individual's knowledge and employment of these resources is contingent on what other participants do; that is, IC is distributed across participants and varies in different interactional practices. (p. 430)

If we apply these context-dependent and emergent views of IC to our discussion of the present data, the competence of the interviewer (an L2 speaker of Japanese) can be considered contingent on what the interviewer and interviewee actually do moment by moment and what they accomplish during the course of the interview. Based on an analysis of data collected from ESL writing conferences between a Vietnamese learner and his American tutor, Young and Miller (2004) describe how the way the tutor participated in their interaction itself changed over time:

> It appears that the student is the one whose participation is most dramatically transformed, but the instructor is a co-learner, and her participation develops in a way that complements the student's learning. In fact, the effectiveness of the instructor is precisely in how she manages a division of participation that allows for growth on the part of the student. (p. 533)

It is thus crucial to examine what is going on in conversational data through the observation of not just what the L2 speaker is doing individually, but also what is being accomplished through the interaction with the interlocutor. As earlier studies on this topic, such as those by Kramsch (1987), Hall (1995), and Young (1999), have suggested, L2 speakers' IC is influenced by the interlocutor's actions as well as changes in the context concerning the purpose of the interaction.

## Recipient role in interviewing and recipient responses

In the field of Japanese as a second language (JSL) teaching in the 1990s, *aizuchi* 'back-channeling' and recipient behaviors were discussed as forms of communication strategies (e.g., N. Mizutani, 1983; O. Mizutani, 1992). In Ozaki (1993), for example, repetition (or "asking back") was analyzed according to a taxonomy which included "request for repetition," "confirmation request for comprehending," "request for explanation," and "confirmation request for understanding." Horiguchi (1990, 1997) also focused on recipients' repetition and the subsequent development of conversation. These aspects of active recipient participation in interactions, however, had not received enough attention in previous studies and thus did not have a major influence on the field of JSL at that time. Ozaki (1992) and Kinoshita Thomson (1994) also looked at how L2 speakers used repetition, and the findings of such studies led to practical suggestions about how repetition should be presented and taught in Japanese language textbooks in order to avoid problems often found in the language production of novice-level learners. More recently, Hatasa (2007) looked at the types of *aizuchi* that JSL learners receive and produce in the language classroom, and reported that the frequency and functions of *aizuchi* used in formal settings were limited compared to those in face-to-face conversations.

These studies, however, often described L2 speaker behaviors as something that could be attributed simply to individual speakers' language competence. In other words, these studies assumed that L2 speakers' ability to behave appropriately in interaction with others was dependent on the speaker's listening comprehension ability or how effectively he or she could use communication strategies. The problem with these studies is that they failed to look at the L2 speaker's competence as a recipient from a socio-constructionist perspective. The studies mentioned above did not incorporate elements other than the L2 speaker's verbal production: such as how the L2 speaker's actions were influenced by the interlocutor's participation in the interaction, embodied resources, how the L2 speaker's response and embodied actions were produced and received by the other participants, or how these all led to the subsequent development of the interaction. CA studies have demonstrated that speakers contribute to the development of the talk as recipients and that their competence as recipients is not something that resides in their head, but is instead co-constructed within the talk, not only in conversations among L1 speakers of English (e.g., Gardner, 1998; Goodwin, 1980; Jefferson, 1984), but also in conversations involving L2 speakers and in other languages (e.g., Firth, 1996; Firth & Wagner, 1997).

Interviewers' actions as recipients are further investigated in a number of CA studies (e.g., Clayman, 2013; Richards, 2011). Unlike ordinary conversations, interactions in interviews often include adjacency pairs in which the interviewer asks a question and the interviewee responds to it. In this particular context of exchange, one of the interviewer's tasks is to ask questions which will draw out adequate answers from the interviewee. In this process, the interviewer is also expected not just to ask questions, but also to give various positive responses in order to elicit adequate information from the interviewee and actively and collaboratively construct the interviewee's talk while continuing to display recipiency. Many previous CA studies on interviews (e.g., Clayman, 2013) look at TV news programs and job interviews where the interviewers are people in news media or a particular industry. On the other hand, Richards (2011) looks at over 40 research interviews and shows how less knowledgeable interviewers can contribute to the development of the interviews through their use of receipt tokens. In one interview, the interviewer used *mm* as a neutral 'continuer' (Schegloff, 1982), but at one point switched to *yeah* and repeated it two more times. Richards argues that such a switch by the recipient was not done randomly, but was instead designed to align with the interviewer and prompt a subsequent elaboration. Moreover, to our knowledge, Mori (2002) and Ikeda (2004) are the only studies that look at the actions of an interviewer who is an L2 speaker of Japanese. In her study, Ikeda shows that L2 interviewers perform various actions to accomplish their interviews, including making preliminary remarks prior to their questions and making subjective comments on interviewees' answers to show their active involvement in the interview.

## Data

In the present data, an L2 speaker of Japanese assumes the role of interviewer and asks questions of a Japanese researcher. The data are taken from a video-recording of the interview, which was conducted at a major research university in Japan. The interview was implemented as part of a project-based course designed for international students by instructors in the science and technology communication department. In the course, four different groups of international students each visited a different laboratory, each of which focused on a particular field of natural science, video-taped an interview with one of the researchers there, and then posted the interview on the Internet. One of the purposes of the project was to increase the general public's knowledge of the university's research activities and their recent findings. One factor that might have affected the development of interviews was that the instructors of the course were not Japanese language teachers, but scholars in the natural sciences who specialized in scientific and technical communication, and did not orient primarily to the linguistic skills of the L2 speakers. Thus, the instructors, researchers, and interviewers all shared the same goal of creating an interview which was rich in content, rather than focusing on the linguistic forms used in their interaction.

The present data extract comes from one of the four interviews conducted during this project. In the extract, two international students visit a veterinary science laboratory and interview a male researcher who is a specialist in kidney diseases. The four participants in the interview are shown in the picture below (Figure 1): Dr. Aida (A) is the researcher, Betty (B) and Cathy (C) are the international students, and Mr. Doi (D) is a specialist in scientific and technical communication who shoots the video of the interview. Before the interview, the L2 speakers observed the laboratory mice used for experiments and asked Aida questions about them. They then returned to Aida's office and talked with him about his research for approximately an hour.

## Analysis

This section describes in detail a segment in which one of the L2 speakers, Cathy, interacts as an interviewer and asks Aida questions. Although she frequently uses just *hai* 'yes' to demonstrate recipiency, there are also places where she uses different responses to present herself as a recipient. Each of the following three subsections focuses on one of the three types of recipient response Cathy produces as Aida answers her questions. The term 'recipient response' is used in this chapter to include not only receipt tokens such as *mm*, *hm*, and *yeah*, but also other recipient linguistic and embodied actions. The three focal recipient responses are (a) repeating what the researcher has just said, (b) using the "change-of-state" token *aa* 'oh' (Heritage, 1984; Ikeda, 2007; Tanaka, 1999), and (c) reformulating (Clayman, 1993) an expression the researcher has just used in his explanation. The use of these recipient responses, as discussed below, can be seen as evidence of Cathy's IC, which enables her to participate in the interaction as a capable interviewer. Our analysis investigates features of the production, formulation, and sequential positioning of these recipient responses. These descriptions make it clear that the L2 speaker's responses are produced not just due to changes in her cognitive state, but also through close attention to the interlocutor's utterances and non-verbal resources.

**Figure 1.** Seating arrangement at the interview

### Other-repetition
Prior to Excerpt 1, shown below, Cathy (C) refers to Aida's (A) long-time engagement in his research. As the excerpt starts, Cathy asks Aida about the qualities of good researchers and if he has any advice for future researchers.

**Excerpt 1.**

```
04  C:   ket-  kagaku  ↑ken↑kyuu ni  taishite  .h etto
         res-  science  research  to  about        H
05       jibun    no  keiken ↑kara .hh etto yoi kenkyuusha:
         oneself LK  experience from   H   good researcher
06       ga motsu $shishi-$ shishitsu to wa .hh tto nani
          S  have  qual-     quality   QT TP   H   what
07       ka .hh tto: moshikuwa: etto:  kouhai     e  no
         Q   H        or        H     junior person for LK
08       (0.7)etto: ataerareru adobaisu:(0.6)etto:(0.6)
                H   can give     advice           H
09       yoona mono (0.7) tto: attara(.) tto nanika
         like thing        H   exist-CND  H  something
```
About scientific research, um, based on your own experience, um, what are some qualities good researchers have, um, or, um, if there is something like advice you can give to junior researchers, um, something.

((Lines omitted, in which Aida says that he will talk about researchers other than himself because he himself is not a very good researcher.))

```
17  A:   ii    kenkyuusha no mo[tsu] shishitsu tte
         good researcher   S  have    quality   QT
18  C:                        [.hh]
19  A:   no wa: tabun (0.4) nankoka atte (.)
         N  TP  probably    several exist-and
20       maa  hitotsu wa (ma/mo)
         well one     TP  (well)
21       |gan|bareru|°hito°. (.)
         |((bends the thumb of his left hand))
             |((nods slightly several times))
                  |((looking at C))
         work hard-POT person
```
With regard to the qualities good researchers have, there are probably several of them and, well, one is, well, to be a person who is able to work hard.

```
22       [|doryoku.
          |((still nodding))
         effort
```
Effort.

```
23  C:   [|hai
          |((nods and smiles while looking at A))
         Yes.
```

```
24         (0.6)/((A looks down at a note² while nodding))

25  A:   jibun ga koo      da to omou kasetsu    o
         onself S this way CP QT think hypothesis O
26       shinjite:, tsukisusumeru       ka doo ka
         believe-and move forward-POT   or not
         Whether or not one can have faith in his or her hypothesis
         and can move forward.

27  C:   hai
         Yes.

28  A:   °te yuu°(.)|tokoro?
                    |((looking at C))
         QT say      point
         That sort of point.

29       (0.5)/((A drops his gaze to his hands and
                 C nods))

30  A:   de, (0.3) moo hitotsu wa:
         and       another    TP
31       ano  |↑ME       ga    |ii |koto
              |((looks at C))|((points to eye))(Figure 2)
                                   |((nods twice))
         well eyes S          good N
         And, another thing is having a good eye

32       (0.5)/((A and C maintain eye contact))

33→ C:   |me ga ii.
         |((leans forward))
          eye S good
         Have a good eye.

34  A:   me ga ii   t[te no wa]: (0.6)
         eye S good QT   N  TP
         What 'having a good eye' means is...

35  C:              [ hai     ]
                      Yes.

36  A:   ano: ijoo_³(0.6) na koto ga wakaranai to
         H    abnormal       thing S find-NEG  CND
         um, if you can't find abnormalities,
```

To answer Cathy's question, Aida explains each quality one by one. He makes an initial comment that he is not a good researcher himself, and in line 17 starts to talk about his view of the qualities that good researchers should possess. Here, he makes it clear that there is more than one quality by using the word *nankoka* 'several' in line 19. The combination of the lexical item and the connective *–te* suggests that extended explanation talk over multiple turns will follow. By going on to use *hitotsu wa* 'one is' in line 20 and bending the thumb of his left hand in line 21, Aida shows that he is now talking about the first of several qualities.

He starts his explanation with *maa* 'well' (line 20), which implies that the quality he is about to give Cathy is not a particularly special one. He then mentions *ganbareru* 'can work hard,' as the first quality a good researcher. It is also important to pay attention to how this quality is formulated. With the formulation *ganbareru hito* 'a person who is able to work hard,' Aida presents the first quality without offering details. This is similar to what Goodwin (1996) calls a 'prospective indexical' in the sense that it projects extended subsequent talk and encourages the recipient to find out exactly what the indexical refers to. Here Aida tries to ensure that Cathy receives this prospective indexical by nodding slightly several times while saying *ganbareru* 'able to work hard,' and looking at her in line 21. Cathy then acknowledges this first quality by smiling and saying *hai* 'yes' in line 23. Her acknowledgement overlaps with *doryoku* 'effort,' which Aida is likely using to reformulate *ganbareru* 'can work hard.'

In the interview, when Cathy listens to Aida's explanation, she mostly acknowledges it with *hai* 'yes' or a nod, or with both (e.g., lines 23, 27, 29, and 35). This *hai* seems to be used as a "continuer" (Schegloff, 1982) to indicate to Aida that up to that point she has understood him and urges him to continue talking. Aida acknowledges Cathy's receipt tokens, and continues to provide further information.

After a 0.6-second gap of silence in line 24, Aida looks down at a note in front of him, and goes on to provide a detailed explanation, in lines 25 and 26, of exactly what he meant by saying 'can work hard' and 'effort.' Cathy then again indicates her understanding by producing *hai* 'yes' in line 27 when Aida's turn approaches a possible boundary at the end of *tsukisusumeru ka doo ka* 'whether (one) can push forward or not.' The fact that Cathy was able to produce *hai* at this particular position, the point where Aida's action becomes recognizable as an explanation of one quality needed to be a researcher, suggests Cathy's competence as an interviewer. In line 28, Aida extends his turn by saying *te yuu tokoro* 'That sort of point,' and clearly indicates that the explanation of the first quality has come to an end by looking at Cathy as well as producing the end of the turn with a rising intonation. Cathy then nods during the 0.5-second gap of silence in line 29.

In line 30, Aida begins his turn with *de moo hitotsu wa* 'and another one is,' thus announcing that he is now moving to the second quality. He then presents a new prospective indexical in the form of a noun phrase, *me ga ii koto* 'having a good eye.' Here, Aida again uses a prospective indexical for the introduction of a quality. During a 0.5-second gap of silence in line 32, he maintains eye contact with Cathy while still pointing at his right eye with his right index finger. Cathy then repeats part of the phrase, *me ga ii* 'have a good eye,' with a falling intonation and her torso bent forward. Cathy's response shows she is treating this prospective indexical in a different way from the first one; she has no problem hearing the phrase, but has some trouble understanding what exactly the prospective indexical means as a quality of a good researcher. In fact, in line 34, by saying *me ga ii tte no wa* 'what "having a good eye" means is,' Aida shows his understanding that some additional explanation is now necessary, and he moves on to a detailed account of this second quality.

Cathy's repetition here can be regarded not as a display of understanding, but instead as an other-initiated repair (Hayashi, Raymond, & Sidnell, 2013; Kitzinger, 2013; Schegloff, 2007; Schegloff, Sacks, & Jefferson, 1977) if we look at the position and construction of the utterance and the way it is presented to Aida. First, we should take notice that the repetition is started after a 0.5-second gap. Svennevig (2004) and Greer, Bussinguer, Butterfield, and Mischinger (2009) suggest that when a recipient repeats a key element in the next turn, the repetition is produced without a hesitation or gap. This manner of showing understanding is "a way of displaying listenership that is more specific than just 'uhuh' or 'mm' (Greer et al., 2009, p. 15). In contrast, as Schegloff et al. (1977) illustrate, "other-initiations regularly are withheld a bit PAST the possible completion of trouble-source turn" and "other-initiations occur after a slight gap" (p. 374, emphasis in original). This provides "an 'extra' opportunity...for [the] speaker of [the] trouble source to self-initiate repair" (p. 374).

Second, attention should be paid to how the repetition is constructed and delivered. Cathy repeats only the key element *me ga ii* 'have a good eye,' rather than copying the whole phrase Aida produced, *me ga ii koto* 'having a good eye.' Cathy also does the repetition with her upper body leaning forward. Aida's displayed understanding of Cathy's repetition as a repair initiation is made possible through the timing and formation of the repetition as well as the way it is delivered.

As will be shown in Excerpt 2, Cathy's repetition of the prospective indexical can be seen as evidence of IC, which enables her to act as a capable interviewer. In this interview context, Cathy is designing her participation in such a way that she can draw additional explanation from Aida in order to move the interview forward. This excerpt overlaps the transcript shown in Excerpt 1.

**Excerpt 2.** (Fragment taken from Excerpt 1)

```
30  A:   de,  (0.3)  moo hitotsu wa:
         and         another     TP
31       ano  |↑ME       ga    |ii |koto
              |((looks at C))|((points to eye))(Figure 2)
                             |((nods twice))
         well    eyes    S          good  N
         And, another thing is having a good eye

32            (0.5)/((A and C maintain eye contact))

33→C:    |me  ga  ii.
         |((leans forward))
           eye  S  good.
         Have a good eye.
```

**Figure 2.** Aida points at his eye while saying *me ga ii koto* 'having a good eye' (line 31).

Through an examination of how Aida presents the prospective indexical *ME ga ii koto* 'having a good eye' in line 31, it can be seen that there are at least three notable features in his turn. First, Aida indicates, through the lengthening of the final vowel of *moo hitotsu wa:* 'the other one is' and the use of the hesitation marker *ano*, that the item he is about to explain is potentially problematic. This is different from *ma: hitotsu wa* 'well, one is' in line 20 in Excerpt 1, which was produced when he presented the first quality, *doryoku* 'effort.' Second, Aida pronounces the word *ME* 'eye' in *ME ga ii koto* in a high pitch with stress on it, and he says *ii koto* 'to be good' while pointing at his right eye with the index finger of his right hand (Figure 2). In addition, he begins to twist his torso to Cathy while doing the pointing gesture, and at the end of *ME ga ii koto* he shifts his upper body to his left so that his right eye is positioned just in front of Cathy. These parts of Aida's talk and non-verbal actions strongly suggest that *ME* 'eyes' in *ME ga ii koto* is something worthy of emphasis and he is designing his talk accordingly. Third and final, in his turn, Aida begins to look at Cathy, and nods twice with the turn-final *koto* 'thing', a possible completion point. Aoki (2011) points out three places where head nods by the speaker are observed, and argues that "in each position, speaker head nods are employed to mark the points where recipients' differentiated actions are relevant, and such a move by speakers prompts recipient responses" (p. 102). The fact that the speaker, Aida, nods while securing the eye gaze of the recipient at this particular point suggests that this is a place where Aida is expecting a different response from the recipient, Cathy.

These three features of Aida's turn in lines 30 and 31 thus work to lead Cathy to produce a recipient response that is more than just acknowledging by simply saying *hai* or nodding as in the previous cases. In addition, Aida presents only the prospective indexical of the item, here *ME ga ii koto* 'having a good eye,' just as he did in the introduction of the first quality. This formulation works to prepare an interactional environment in which more detailed explanations from Aida can be projected.

The design of Aida's turn thus makes it relevant for Cathy to solicit further talk on what *me ga ii* 'have a good eye' means. In this sense, Cathy's recipient response in line 33 can be described as 'being invited' by Aida. In fact, Cathy also adopts the format that Aida used: She accepts the 'invitation' and repeats the prospective indexical with a falling intonation (line 33). Cathy produces her response with her upper body leaning over the desk, and repeats not the entire phrase *me ga ii koto,* but just part of it, *me ga ii*. This suggests that she understands the point that Aida emphasized with the phrase. Cathy's recipiency in line 33 now provides a 'space' where he can elaborate on what exactly having good eyes means.

Cook's (2006) analysis on the use of 'naked,' plain forms of verbs and adjectives in interaction is relevant to the present discussion. Examining a conversation between a professor and a graduate student at a Japanese university, Cook shows that the student's use of a plain form appears at a point "where the professor may end his turn" and that "the plain form grammatically fits the co-construction of the joint utterance" (p. 280). According to Cook, the student's use of the plain form toward the professor does not necessarily result in indicating rudeness. Rather, the form "becomes embedded in the professor's utterance in the unfolding of the talk" and therefore constitutes "a resource for the co-construction of the idea with the professor" (p. 281). Cathy's utterance *me ga ii* 'have a good eye' in the plain form in the present data can be analyzed in line with Cook's argument that the plain form indexes Cathy's finely-tuned alignment with the content and progression of Aida's talk.

To summarize, Aida was designing *ME ga ii koto* 'having a good eye' in line 31 as a prospective indexical, which the recipient might not be able to understand immediately, and in this way it becomes appropriate for the recipient to repeat it, which prompts the interviewee to explain its meaning. Cathy paid attention to the verbal and non-verbal features which accompanied Aida's talk and formulated a response to his invitation in an appropriate manner and at the right sequential slot. This recipient response (line 33) by the L2 speaking interviewer should thus be seen not as an initiation of a repair sequence at the expense of blocking the progressivity of talk-in-interaction, but as an elicitor to invite the interlocutor's elaboration, an elicitor which was finely tuned to the design of the interlocutor's talk. This can be seen as a manifestation of the L2 speaker's IC as accomplished through collaborative work with her interactant.

**Use of change-of-state tokens**
In this section, we look at Cathy's use of *aa*, a Japanese change-of-state token similar to *oh* in English (Heritage, 1984). Our analysis focuses particularly on this token in relation to her competence in participating in the interaction. In the ongoing interview (Excerpt 3 below), in line 34, Aida begins to elaborate on what he means by *me ga ii* 'have a good eye.' At this point, he says *ijoona koto ga wakaranai to kenkyuu tte susumerarenai* 'if you can't find abnormalities, you cannot advance your research,' and in doing so posits a specific ability required for good scientific researchers. Cathy then deploys her default recipient token, *hai* 'yes', in line 41.

**Excerpt 3.** (Continues on from Excerpt 2)

```
34  A:   me ga ii tte [no wa]:  (0.6)
         eye S  good QT  N  TP
         What 'having a good eye' means is...

35  C:                 [ hai ]
                        Yes.

36  A:   ano: ijoo_(0.6) na koto ga wakaranai to
         H    abnormal      thing S  find-NEG  CND
         well, if you can't find abnormalities,

37  C:   hai
         Yes.

38       (0.4)

39  A:   kenkyuu tte susu- deki- susumerarenai
         research QT  advan- can-  advance-POT-NEG
40       n desu yo
         N Cop  IP
         You adv-, can-, cannot advance your research.
```

```
41  C:   hai
         Yes.

42  A:   >tsumari<  <|ijoo      ni>
                     |((points at right eye))
         that is     abonormal to
43       >|kizukana kya< °ikenai° n su  yo ne
          |((repeats pointing))
            notice-NEG-CND not good N CP IP IP
         That is, you must take notice of abnormalities, you know.
```

**Figure 3.**  *Ijoo ni* '(take notice) of abnormalities' (line 42)

```
44  C:   |aa=
         |((moves head upward))
          CS
         Oh.

45  A:   =demo:  |me ga warui hito tte [me ga]
                 |((pointing at his right eye))
          but    eye S bad    people QT  eye S
         But, people who have bad eyes, eyes...

46  C:                                     [ hai ]
                                             Yes.

47  A:   tsumari ano: shiryoku no mondai ja nakute:
         that is  H   vision    LK problem CP NEG and
         that is, well, not a vision problem but...

48  C:   hai
         Yes.
```

```
49  A:   kizuku ka  kizukanai  ka
         notice or  notice-NEG Q
50       [tte yuu imi]      [de me ga i]i  ka warui ka?
         QT  say meaning    PT eye S good  or bad    Q
         whether their eyes are good or bad
         in the sense of whether or not they notice things.

51  C:   [ |↑a a:     ]    [    hai    ]
           |((moves head upward))
             CS                  yes

         Oh, yes.

52       hai
         Yes.
```

After Cathy uses a receipt token *hai* 'yes' as a continuer in line 41, Aida uses *tsumari* 'that is to say' and then slowly says *ijoo ni* 'to abnormality' in line 42. This turn by Aida suggests he is trying to reformulate what he wants to tell Cathy—that good researchers must be able to detect abnormality—and that his explanation on the second quality will come to its conclusion. At this point, Cathy replies not with her default recipient token *hai*, but with *aa*, which indicates a change in her cognitive state. It should also be noted that her change-of-state token is produced with an upward head movement in a clearly differentiated way from the downward movement that accompanied her previous receipt tokens. By designing her receipt tokens in this manner with precise timing, i.e., immediately at the end of a TCU (turn construction unit), Cathy successfully indicates to Aida that she has now reached an understanding of what he meant by *me ga ii* 'have a good eye'.

Cathy's use of the change-of-state token in line 44 is partly guided by the formulation of Aida's talk (lines 42–43), which is introduced by *tsumari* 'that is' and followed by *ijoo ni kizukanakya ikenai* 'must take notice of abnormalities,' a reformulation of the quality needed for good researchers he worded earlier as *ijoo na koto ga wakaranai to* 'if you can't find abnormalities" in line 36. It should be noted here that the change-of-state token is also guided by Aida's embodied action. When he pronounces *ijoo ni* 'to abnormality' in line 42, he delivers it slowly and points to his right eye with the index finger of this right hand (Figure 3), just as he did with *ME ga ii* 'have a good eye' in line 31. Employing the same gesture, used previously when they achieved better understanding, allows Aida to signal to Cathy that the key point of his explanation has just been delivered. This creates the slot where Cathy's change-of-state token *aa* is used as an indication of the understanding that she has just reached.

Aida's explanation, however, does not stop here. In line 45, he continues his talk with *demo* 'but,' and in this way displays that his explanation has not finished. He again points at his right eye when he delivers the word *me* 'eyes' in *me ga warui hito tte* 'people who have bad eyes,' an expression that formulates a contrast to the topic of the ongoing segment of their conversation, *me ga ii* 'have a good eye.' The introduction of this contrasting description implies that Aida treats Cathy's change-of-state token *aa* in line 44 as not enough to demonstrate her understanding, as he goes on to provide another comment from a different perspective.

Cathy then provides the continuer *hai* 'yes' in line 48 after she hears Aida's account in line 47, *shiryoku no mondai ja nakute* 'not a vision problem but.' The use of the *te* form suggests the continuation of talk by Aida. When Aida's explanation reaches the end of the phrase *kizuku ka kizukanai ka* 'whether or not they notice things' in line 49, Cathy responds with *aa:* in line 51 with the lengthening of the vowel and in a higher pitch than when she produced the same token in line 44. She accompanies the display of change in her cognitive state with an upward head movement as soon as the main point of Aida's account is delivered. How Aida treats this token by Cathy will be discussed in the following section.

## Rephrasing of an expression used by the interviewee

The third type of recipient response which will be discussed in this section is the rephrasing of an expression previously used by the interviewee. This is illustrated in Excerpt 4.

**Excerpt 4.** (Overlap and continuation of Excerpt 3)

```
49  A:  kizuku ka kizukanai  ka
        notice or notice-NEG Q
50      [tte yuu imi]    [de me ga i]i  ka warui ka?
        QT  say meaning PT  eye S good or bad    Q
        whether their eyes are good or bad
        in the sense of whether or not they notice things.

51  C:  [ |↑a a: ]      [    hai    ]
        |((moves head upward))
              CS                 yes
        Oh, yes.

52          hai
            Yes.

53  A:  °sono° <kantei> suru nooryoku ga
            H    judgement do ability   S
54          aru ka nai [ka
            have or not Q
        Um, whether or not one has the ability to judge
```

55  C:                    [hai
         Yes.

56  A:  tte yuu no de,   nai        hito   tte no wa
        QT  say  N CP-and have-NEG  people QT  N  TP
        this is what I mean, and, people who don't have such ability...

57  C:  hai
        Yes.

58  A:  kizukenai       n desu yo ijoo         ni
        notice-POT-NEG  N Cop  IP abnormality  to
        can't notice, I tell you, the abnormalities.

59  C:  hai
        Yes.

60      (0.5)

61  A:  dakara: boku ga omou
        so      I    S  think
62      ii   kenkyuusha tte >yuu< no wa:(.)
        good researcher  OT  say   N  Top
63      sono: (0.7) kanteisuru nooryoku me o-
        H                to judge  ability  eye O
64      ii   me  o mot[teru]
        good eye o have
        So, good researchers I think are- um,
        have the ability to judge, eyes-, have good eyes.

65→C:                    [hai ]kansatsuryoku.
                          yes  ability to observe
        Yes, the ability to observe.

66  A:  soo, kansatsuryo[ku       ga] ii.
        right, ability to observe S   good
        Right, their ability to observe is good.

In lines 49 to 50, Aida tells Cathy that *me ga warui* 'having bad eyes' does not mean a vision problem, but means that one cannot notice things. Cathy's use of the change-of-state token *aa* in line 51 shows that she has reached a good understanding of Aida's explanation, which prompts him to elaborate further on the topic of people who have bad eyes. In lines 53 to 54, Aida rephrases his previously used phrase *kizuku ka kizukanai ka* 'whether or not they notice things' with another, *kantei suru nooryoku ga aru ka nai ka* 'whether or not one has the ability to judge,' and then in line 56 says *nai hito tte no wa* 'people who don't have such ability.' With these he continues his explanation and Cathy produces *hai* once in line 57.

Aida uses the expression *kanteisuru nooryoku* 'ability to judge' in lines 53 and 63. Cathy does not repeat the expression used in his explanation, but instead, in line 65 uses another expression with a similar meaning, *kansatsuryoku* 'ability to observe', to show her candidate understanding of the explanation he provided. Aida's acceptance of Cathy's rephrasing with his *soo* (Kushida, 2011) and later utilization of her word in line 66 suggests Cathy's IC as a recipient in the interview.

Cathy's rephrasing, however, should not be discussed only in terms of the vocabulary knowledge she possesses as an individual. Rather, the talk should be closely observed to see how this use of another expression for the demonstration of understanding is realized differently from the case of recipient tokens *hai* or *aa*. In the analysis which follows, we will discuss how the interviewer employs a new expression to acknowledge the information provided by the interviewee, and how the occurrence of such a recipient action is made possible by the participants' close attention to the details of interaction and collaborative work.

In line 53, Aida, who had previously used the expressions *me ga ii* 'have a good eye' and *ijoona koto ni kizukeru* 'can notice abnormalities,' introduces a similar expression *kanteisuru nooryoku* 'ability to judge.' At least three observations can be made about this turn. First, Aida's explanation of ME ga *ii koto* (line 31) was originally started as an answer to Cathy's initial question, introduced in lines 4 through 9, and in this turn he uses a phrase which includes the word *nooryoku* 'ability,' implying that one of the important qualities (*shishitsu*, line 6) of good researchers is being presented here. Second, by saying *kanteisuru nooryoku* 'ability to judge' slowly, Aida suggests to Cathy that an important piece of information is now being presented. A similar procedure occurred in lines 42 and 43 when he pronounced *ijoo ni* 'of abnormalities' slowly and said *kizukanakya ikenai* 'must take notice' with stress, prosodic features with which he successfully elicited Cathy's *aa* response. In this excerpt, however, Cathy uses the default recipient token *hai*. Third, the expression *kanteisuru nooryoku ga aru ka nai ka* 'whether or not one has the ability to judge' in lines 53 and 54 includes the form *ka nai ka* 'X or not,' which Aida also used in his previous expressions: *kizuku ka kizukanai ka* 'whether or not they notice things' (line 49) and *me ga ii ka warui ka* 'their eyes are good or bad' (line 50). Aida's recycling of the same formulation makes it observable to Cathy that the expression being used here is a developed form of the previous ones and that this phrase is another elaboration of *me ga ii*.

In line 56, Aida begins to present his main point with *nai hito tte no wa* 'people who do not have such ability'—bringing up an opposite concept of *me ga ii* 'have a good eye' once again, just like *me ga warui hito tte* 'people who have bad eyes' in line 45—and tells Cathy where the problem lies. Cathy acknowledges this with her default receipt token *hai* in line 59. Aida has designed the turn, as we can see in the use of the interactional particle *yo* 'I tell you,' as something hearable as the conclusion of his explanation (Hayano, 2011). Cathy, however, does not indicate an understanding that the utterance carries an important piece of information worth replying to with a recipient token other than the usual *hai*. In this situation, Aida, having received no special acknowledgement from Cathy, faces the task of reiterating his main point. In the following excerpt, we look at the ways which Aida responds to Cathy's paraphrasing of *kansatsuryoku* 'ability to observe' in line 65, summarizes the second quality he introduced with *me ga ii*, and brings up the next quality.

**Excerpt 5.** (Overlap and continuation of Excerpt 4)

```
61  A:   dakara: boku ga omou
         so     I    S  think
62       ii  kenkyuusha tte >yuu< no wa:(.)
         good researcher OT  say   N  Top
63       sono:(0.7) kanteisuru nooryoku me o-
         H          to judge  ability  eye O
64       ii   me  o mot[teru]
         good eye o have
         So, good researchers I think are-- um,
         have the ability to judge, eyes- have good eyes.

65→ C:                [hai ]kansatsuryoku.
                       yes   ability to observe
         Yes, the ability to observe.

66  A:   soo, kansatsuryo[ ku       ga ] ii.
         right,ability to observe   S  good
         Right, their ability to observe is good.

67  C:                      [to yuu (ko-)]
                              QT say (ko-)
         I see, that's the point.

68  A:   [soo] desu ne
          right Cop IP
         That's right.

69  C:   [|hai]
         |((looks down at memo))
         Yes.

70       (0.3)/((C keeps looking at memo))
```

```
71   C:      ha[i
             Yes.

72   A:         [tte yuu koto to:,  (0.9)
                 QT  say  thing and
73           kansatsusuru (0.4) genba o: chanto
             observe              site  O  properly
74           mo-(1.0) genba kara hanarenai?
             hav-      site from  leave-NEG
             That point, and to properly hav- a lab to observe...
             to never leave the lab.
```

The topic of the talk between Aida and Cathy in the current segment, *ii kenkyuusha* 'good researcher,' was previously introduced in Cathy's initial question (lines 5–6), which Aida announced he would answer by saying *ii kenkyuusha ga motsu shishitsu tte no wa* 'the qualities good researchers have' (lines 17 and 19). In line 61, by starting his turn with *dakara* 'so,' an expression used to summarize what has been discussed, and using the same formulation of *ii kenkyuusha* plus *tte (yuu) no wa*, Aida shows that he is wrapping up his explanation of the second quality that good researchers have.

Although this point previously received no particular uptake from Cathy, in the continuation of his turn, Aida reintroduces *kanteisuru nooryoku* 'ability to judge' in a careful manner with the hedge *sono:* 'um' and a 0.7-second pause. He not only approaches the task of reintroducing the phrase cautiously, but also immediately rephrases the expression with *ii me o motteru* 'have a good eye'[4] in line 64, a notion previously acknowledged twice by Cathy with the change-of-state token *aa* in lines 44 and 51. It seems clear here that Aida, after not having received the uptake he expected from Cathy at the right moment, is now reformulating his talk while paying careful attention to Cathy's reaction. Through his multiple, finely tuned attempts at eliciting Cathy's claim of understanding, Aida scaffolds her participation in the interaction and therefore adjusts his turn construction to his changing assumptions of her IC. This shows that IC is not an attribute of an individual participant (Young, 2013), but is instead co-constructed by all participants.

Cathy's recipient response in line 65 is worth noting. She has so far used *hai* 'yes' as a default display of recipiency and *aa* 'oh' in circumstances where she shows she has reached an understanding. Here, however, Cathy acknowledges Aida's explanation with *hai* at the point where his explanation sequence reaches its conclusion, and then adds *kansatsuryoku* 'ability to observe,' which is a rewording of Aida's *kanteisuru nooryoku* 'ability to judge' from line 63.

It seems that Cathy successfully accomplishes two things through this reformulating of Aida's words. First, considering the position of Cathy's production of *kansatsuryoku* 'ability to observe,' it can be seen that she started this recipient response at the earliest possible point where Aida's self-initiated repair (*me o- ii me* 'eyes-, good eyes', lines 63–64) regarding *kanteisuru nooryoku* 'ability to judge' was completed. Recall that Aida originally designed this self-repair so that Cathy could better understand his talk. Through her use of the recipient token *hai* and by its placement (Yamamoto, 2016), Cathy demonstrates her understanding that there is a possibility Aida's restart of his explanation was designed to help her understand the words. Cathy then rephrases Aida's explanation with her own choice of words in order to demonstrate her understanding (Sacks, 1992).

Cathy's recipient response in line 65 is produced at a sequential position where Aida's explanation of the meaning of *me ga ii* 'have a good eye' is being wrapped up. This observation is made possible, as discussed above, in that Aida commenced his turn in line 61 with *dakara* 'so' and in that the topical part of his explanation, *boku ga omou ii kenkyuusha tte no wa* 'the researchers I consider good,' enables Cathy to anticipate that the completion point of his explanation is approaching. Cathy's entrance at this point demonstrates her understanding that Aida's conclusion is under way and the process will be completed by supplying a candidate understanding.

Second, although the expression Cathy used in her rephrasing, *kansatsuryoku* 'ability to observe,' may not be semantically the same as Aida's original phrase, *kanteisuru nooryoku* 'ability to judge,' her new choice is treated by Aida as a better one in that he repeats it with *soo* 'right' in line 66. As similarly illustrated in Schegloff's (1996) discussion of "confirming an allusion," Aida confirms not only Cathy's understanding of his explanation but also that this is what he was conveying in his prior talk in lines 61 through 64. He then incorporates the repeated expression into his own explanation in line 66 to introduce another quality of a good researcher.

Kushida (2011) points out that there are two types of confirmation tokens in Japanese, *un* 'yes' and *soo* 'right,' and that they work differently in talk-in-interaction. When a person who produced a trouble source uses *soo* 'right' in response to an interactant's offer of a candidate understanding, the response token *soo* not only confirms understanding but also confirms the contribution of reformulating the trouble source. In the current data, Cathy's offer of candidate understanding, *kansatsuryoku* 'ability to observe', shows her understanding of Aida's message and contributes to a better flow of the interview through the rephrasing of his production (lines 62–63).[5]

Cathy's rephrasing in line 65 has thus been done with her full understanding that Aida's words, *me ga ii* 'have a good eye,' do not simply mean one has good eyesight. The fact that Cathy could provide a phrase which best describes the focal point of the second quality, however, should not be reduced only to an issue of the speaker's linguistic repertoire or competence. Rather, it should be examined and discussed based on how her participation in the interview was coordinated through collaborative work with her interlocutor.

## Summary of analysis

Through this micro-analysis of interview data between an L2 speaking interviewer and an L1 speaking interviewee, the following points have been illustrated. First, the L2 speaker was not supplying recipient responses randomly, but was instead doing so by paying close attention to the design of the interviewee's talk. It was also shown that the L2 speaker's recipient responses (e.g., *hai* 'yes,' *aa* 'oh,' repetitions, and rephrasing) were employed not only to indicate that she was listening to the interviewee, but also to publicly show that she was getting the gist of his talk and to facilitate their joint participation and the progressivity of the interview. More importantly, from the perspective of second language studies, the L2 speaker's three types of recipient responses (as the primary recipient in the interview)—the repetition of an expression used in the interviewee's prior turn, the use of a change-of-state token, and the rephrasing of the expression used by the interviewee—were not derived from her communicative competence as an individual, but were co-realized through both interlocutors' finely-tuned participation in the interaction.

## Discussion and conclusion

Based on a single case analysis, this chapter used CA to explicate how an L2 interviewer and her L1 interviewee align with each other, and thus demonstrated how the interviewer's IC is co-constructed. Analysis illustrated that such L2 speaker competence can be understood not as a construct detached from the context in which the speakers and their activity were embedded, but as the product of collaborative work between the interlocutors. Pointing out that L2 speakers are given the role of interviewee more often than the role of interviewer, Mori (2008) discusses how the competence L2 learners exercise in "question, answer, and response to the answer" sequences is not fully exerted in classroom activities (p. 13). She also argues that the contributions L2 speakers can make to interaction, without letting their non-native status surface, offer image of L2 speakers that contrasts with what has been created in second language acquisition studies—an image of speakers who are inferior to native speakers or are missing something and incomplete (see also Firth & Wagner, 1997). The case of the L2 speaker examined in the present study offers an effective example of an interactionally competent L2 speaker similar to the ones Mori, and Firth and Wagner have discussed.

In Excerpt 3 of the present study, Cathy used *hai* 'yes' as her default recipient response, but also occasionally employed a different token to acknowledge Aida's answer, indicating her finely-tuned alignment with the progress of his talk. This shows that Cathy responded to her interviewee's talk in the same way as the L1 interviewer in Richards' (2011) study discussed above.

Moreover, our analysis has shown that Cathy's other repetition and rephrasing of Aida's expression are more than just displays of recipiency; they are employed to demonstrate her temporal understanding of Aida's talk. We have also observed that Cathy's repetitions are produced with proper timing and with appropriate forms and embodied actions, which work to prompt Aida's subsequent elaboration. Our analysis thus illustrates how an L2 interviewer can contribute to an interviewee's talk, as discussed in Ikeda (2005), through being an attentive recipient and actively participating in the co-construction of the interviewee's talk.

It is also important to examine how the competence of an L2 speaker is displayed in the context of a particular interaction—an interview context in the present data. The L2 speaker undertook an interview task in which she interviewed a researcher in his laboratory and posted a video of the interview on the Internet. The interview was recorded by staff (from the science and technology communication department of the institution) who accompanied the L2 speaker to the laboratory. The video recording was to be edited and posted on the Internet as part of the university's public relations activities. This situation made it impossible for the L2 interviewer to ask the staff member for language-related help or to block the progressivity of the interaction during the interview. One of the primary aims of both the L2-speaking interviewer and the L1-speaking interviewee was to create a natural and spontaneous interview. The interviewee thus treated his interlocutor not as an L2-speaking international student but as an interviewer, while the L2 speaker tried to produce appropriate responses. It is reasonable to assume that the nature of this interview task worked to elicit speakers' natural responses, in contrast to the factitious activities often designed and practiced in language classrooms. As Gardner and Wagner (2004) note, the consequences of authentic interaction affect the real lives of participants. The authenticity and context of the interview thus contributed to creating an environment where the realization of such interaction was possible.

Historically, in the field of second language acquisition much discussion of L2 competence has centered around students' individual and static abilities detached from the contexts of actual interaction. What the present study illustrates is that the L2 speaking interviewer constructs her responses according to the design of the interviewee's talk and that his finely-tuned attempts at inviting the interviewer's display of understanding lead her participation in the interaction. The interviewer's IC thus emerges from the actual course of exchanges with her interviewee, and is embedded in the interviewing activity in which the interactants are engaged. Interactions are resources through which people organize their activities. People exchange information, as in the interview in the current study, through activities embedded in a larger social context. The IC of L2 speakers, thus, can be most typically demonstrated and observed in the various activities in which they engage.

Very little investigation has been done from a CA perspective to find out how L2 Japanese speakers produce recipient responses. The present study has endeavored to account for the ways in which one L2 interviewer responded to the answers of her L1-Japanese interviewee. An analysis of recipient actions other than the three types of responses discussed above, however, was beyond the scope of this single case study. In order to see how the sort of IC realized and distributed between the participants in the present data can be extended to other interactional contexts, we need to examine more cases of recipient responses in L1-L2 data in other situations as well.

## Notes

1. This research was supported by Grant-in-Aid for Young Scientists (B) (15K21447) awarded to Mari Yamamoto by Japan Society for the Promotion of Science.
2. The note, which was given to the interviewee prior to the interview, lists a set of possible questions the interviewer might ask.
3. An underscore indicates that the word-final intonation is being kept flat.
4. A note on difference in the meaning of *kanteisuru nooryoku* 'ability to judge' and of *ii me* 'good eyes' is due here. The former usually refers to someone's ability to examine and judge the authenticity of antiques. Aida is using this expression to refer to one of the qualities researchers should have as professionals in a particular field. The latter is an idiomatic phrase and its meaning overlaps with that of the former. It, however, also refers to people's ability to judge the value of things correctly in a broad sense. The former is made up with words of Chinese origin and thus sounds more formal than the latter, which consists of common words. This could indicate Aida's consideration of Cathy's possible comprehension problem.
5. In fact, Cathy's choice of phrase, *kansatsuryoku* 'ability to observe,' suggests the ability to notice that something might be wrong with laboratory mice in everyday situations, whereas Aida's choice of words implies the ability to evaluate the condition of the mice on specific occasions and does not imply a continuous attention to them in laboratory work.

## References

Aoki, H. (2011). Some functions of speaker head nods. In J. Streeck, C. Goodwin, & C. LeBaron (Eds.), *Embodied interaction: Language and body in the material world* (pp. 93–105). Cambridge: Cambridge University Press.

Clayman, S. (1993). Reformulating the question: A device for answering/not answering questions in news interviews and press conferences. *Text 13*, 159–188.

Clayman, S. (2013). Conversation analysis in the news interview. In J. Sidnell & T. Stivers (Eds.), *The handbook of conversation analysis* (pp. 630–656). Oxford: Wiley-Blackwell.

Cook, H. M. (2006). Japanese politeness as an interactional achievement: Academic consultation sessions in Japanese universities. *Multilingua, 25*(3). 269–291.

Firth, A. (1996). The discursive accomplishment of normality: On Conversation Analysis and 'Lingua Franca' English. *Journal of Pragmatics, 26*(2), 237–259.

Firth, A., & Wagner, J. (1997). On discourse, communication and (some) fundamental concepts in SLA research. *Modern Language Journal, 81*, 285–300.

Gardner, R. (1998). Between speaking and listening: The vocalisation of understandings. *Applied Linguistics, 19*(2), 204–224.

Gardner, R., & Wagner, J. (2004). Introduction. In R. Gardner & J. Wagner (Eds.), *Second language conversations* (pp. 1–17). London: Continuum.

Goodwin, C. (1980). Restarts, pauses, and the achievement of a state of mutual gaze at turn beginning. *Sociological Inquiry, 50*, 272–302.

Goodwin, C. (1996). Transparent vision. In E. Ochs, E. A. Schegloff, & S. A. Thompson (Eds.), *Interaction and grammar* (pp. 370–404). Cambridge: Cambridge University Press.

Greer, T., Bussinguer, V., Butterfield, J., & Mischinger, A. (2009). Receipt through repetition. *JALT Journal, 31*(1), 5–34.

Hall, J. K. (1995). (Re)creating our worlds with words: A sociohistorical perspective of face-to-face interaction. *Applied Linguistics, 16*(2), 206–232.

Hatasa, Y. (2007). Aizuchi responses in JFL classrooms: Teacher input and learner use. In D. Yoshimi & H. Wang (Eds.), *Selected papers from pragmatics in the CJK classroom: The state of the art* (pp. 80–96). Honolulu, HI: University of Hawai'i, National Foreign Language Resource Center. Available from http://nflrc.hawaii.edu/CJKProceedings

Hayano, K. (2011). Claiming epistemic primacy: Yo-marked assessments in Japanese. In T. Stivers, L. Mondada, & J. Steensig (Eds.), *The morality of knowledge in conversation* (pp. 58–81). Cambridge: Cambridge University Press.

Hayashi, M., Raymond, G., & Sidnell, J. (2013). Conversational repair and human understanding: An introduction. In M. Hayashi, G. Raymond, & J. Sidnell (Eds.), *Conversational repair and human understanding* (pp. 1–40). Cambridge: Cambridge University Press.

Heritage, J. (1984). A change of state token and aspects of its sequential placement. In J. M. Atkinson & J. Heritage (Eds.), *Structures of social action* (pp. 299–345). Cambridge: Cambridge University Press.

Horiguchi, S. (1988). Komyunikeeshon ni okeru kikite no gengokoodoo [Listener's language behavior in communication]. *Nihongo Kyooiku* [Journal of Japanese Language Education], *64*, 13–25.

Horiguchi, S. (1990). Jyookyuu nihongo gakushuusha no taiwa ni okeru kikite toshite no gengokoodoo [Language behavior as a listener in advanced Japanese learners' conversation]. *Nihongo Kyooiku* [Journal of Japanese Language Education], *71*, 16–32.

Horiguchi, S. (1997). *Nihongo kyooiku to kaiwabunseki* [Japanese language teaching and conversation analysis]. Tokyo: Kuroshio Shuppan.

Ikeda, K. (2004). Listenership in Japanese: An examination of overlapping listener response. *NFLRC NetWork, 32.* Honolulu, HI: University of Hawai'i, Second Language Teaching and Curriculum Center. Available from http://www.nflrc.hawaii.edu/networks/NW32.pdf

Ikeda, K. (2005). Intaaakushon gengo unyoo nooryoku no koojoo o mezashite: Intabyuu toyuu tasuku no saikoo [A communicative task reconsidered: Interview for L2 interactional competence development]. *ICU Studies in Japanese Language Education, 1,* 45–58.

Ikeda, K. (2007). The change-of-state token *a* in Japanese language proficiency interviews. In T. Newfields, I. Gledall, P. Wanner, & M. Kawate-Mierzejewska (Eds.), *Second Language Acquisition—Theory and Pedagogy: Proceedings of the 6th Annual JALT Pan-SIG Conference* (pp. 56–64). Sendai, Japan: JALT. Retrieved from https://jalt.org/pansig/2007/HTML/Ikeda.htm

Jefferson, G. (1984). Notes on a systematic deployment of the acknowledgement tokens "yeah" and "mm hm." *Papers in Linguistics, 17*(2), 197–216.

Kinoshita Thomson, C. K. (1994). Shokyuu nihongo kyookasho to 'kikikaeshi' no sutoratejii [Communication strategies in elementary Japanese language textbooks: A strategy of "asking back"]. *Japanese-Language Education around the Globe, 4,* 31–43.

Kitzinger, C. (2013). Repair. In J. Sidnell & T. Stivers (Eds.), *The handbook of conversation analysis* (pp. 229–256). Hoboken, NJ: Wiley-Blackwell.

Kramsch, C. (1987). From language proficiency to interactional competence. *Modern Language Journal, 70*(4), 366–372.

Kushida, S. (2011). Confirming understanding and acknowledging assistance: Managing trouble responsibility in response to understanding check in Japanese talk-in-interaction. *Journal of Pragmatics, 43*(11), 2716–2739.

Mizutani, N. (1983). Aizuchi to ootoo [Backchanneling and response]. In O. Mizutani (Ed.), *Hanashikotoba no hyoogen* [Expressions in spoken language] (pp. 37–-44). Tokyo: Chikuma Shoboo.

Mizutani, O. (1992). *Hanashikotoba to nihonjin: Nihongo no seitai* [Japanese: The spoken language in Japanese life]. Tokyo: Sootakusha.

Mori, J. (2002). Task design, plan, and development of talk-in-interaction: An analysis of a small group activity in a Japanese language classroom. *Applied Linguistics, 23*(3), 323–347.

Mori, J. (2008). Kyooshitsugai deno kaiwa ni mirareru dainigengo washa no nooryoku to aidentitii: "Shirooto" no hyooka kara manabu koto [Second language speakers' competence and identity found in conversation outside the classroom: What we can learn from "lay people"]. *Proceedings of the 19th Conference of JASLA,* 10–16.

Ozaki, A. (1992). 'Kikikaeshi' no sutoratejii to nihongo kyooiku ['Asking back' strategy and Japanese language teaching]. In H. C. Quackenbush, A. Ozaki, T. Kashima, M.

Fujiwara, & Y. Momiyama. (Eds.), *Nihongo kenkyuu to Nihongo kyooiku* [Japanese language studies and Japanese language teaching] (pp. 251–263). Nagoya, Japan: Nagoya University Press.

Ozaki, A. (1993). Sesshoku bamen no teisei sutoratejii: "Kikikaeshi" no hatsuwa kookan o megutte [Correction strategy in contact situation: On the exchange of "asking-back" utterances]. *Nihongo Kyooiku* [Journal of Japanese Language Education], *81*, 19–30.

Richards, K. (2011). Using micro-analysis in interviewer training: 'Continuers' and interviewer positioning. *Applied Linguistics, 32*, 95–112.

Schegloff, E. A. (1982). Discourse as an interactional achievement: Some uses of 'uh huh' and other things that come between sentences. In D. Tannen (Ed.), *Analyzing discourse: Text and talk. Georgetown University Roundtable on Languages and Linguistics 1981* (pp. 71–93). Washington, DC: Georgetown University Press.

Schegloff, E. A. (1996). Confirming allusions: Toward an empirical account of action. *American Journal of Sociology, 104*, 161–216.

Schegloff, E. A. (2007). *Sequence organization in interaction: A primer in conversation analysis* (Vol. 1). Cambridge: Cambridge University Press.

Schegloff, E. A., Sacks, H., & Jefferson, G. (1977). The preference for self-correction in the organization of repair in conversation. *Language, 53*, 361–382.

Svennevig, J. (2004). Other-repetition as display of hearing, understanding and emotional stance. *Discourse Studies, 6*, 489–516.

Tanaka, H. (1999). *Turn-taking in Japanese conversation: A study in grammar and interaction.* Amsterdam: John Benjamins.

Yamamoto, M. (2016). Differences in interactive usage of Japanese recipient response tokens *un* and *hai*. *NINJAL Research Papers, 10*, 297–313.

Young, R. (1999). Sociolinguistic approaches to SLA. *Annual Review of Applied Linguistics, 19*, 105–132.

Young, R. F. (2011). Interactional competence in language learning, teaching, and testing. In E. Hinkel (Ed.), *Handbook of research in second language teaching and learning* (Vol. 2, pp. 426–443). London: Routledge.

Young, R. F. (2013). Learning to talk the talk and walk the walk: Interactional competence in academic spoken English. *Ibérica, 25*, 15–38.

Young, R. F., & Miller, E. R. (2004). Learning as changing participation: Discourse roles in ESL writing conferences. *The Modern Language Journal, 88*(4), 519–535.

# 6
# Multimodal Interactional Competence in the Use of Technology in L2 Japanese Classrooms

Keiko Ikeda
*Kansai University*

Don Bysouth
*Osaka University*

## Introduction

This chapter explores a dimension of interactional competence (IC) that involves the use of technology, particularly information technology (IT), in multiparty contexts.[1] Commonly utilized IT tools include devices such as personal computers (i.e., desktop or notebook computers), tablets (e.g., iPads), or smart phones (e.g., iPhones), and smart boards (such as BIGPADs, see Figure 1), and it is likely that over the next decade there will be further development and adoption of a range of IT tools that explicitly aim to enhance collaborative work. The ubiquitous use of these digital tools as mediators of contemporary human social interaction may invite closer examinations of IC as it has been traditionally conceptualized: for example, how entire architectures of social interaction may require participants to develop new practices which are otherwise not relevant in traditional face-to-face, everyday interactions that occur between physically co-present interactants in the absence of technological mediation.

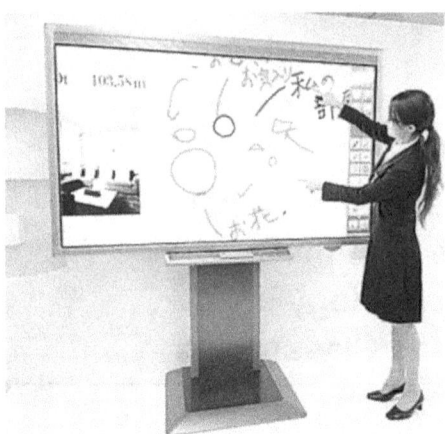

**Figure 1.** BIGPAD (a smart board).

In accordance with a growing body of contemporary literature on IT use in human communication in the fields of computer supported cooperative work (CSCW) and computer-human interaction (CHI), our broad interest is in how people adapt their communicative practices in response to constraints and affordances of communication that are enabled by particular tools in technologically-mediated environments. More specifically, we are interested in how people employ various multimodal practices, such as the use of bodily conduct (e.g., gestures or pointing) and other non-verbal methods of communication, to embed such tool use into social interaction.[2] Moreover, our study aims to illustrate IC for communication in contexts in which IT tools are accessible by both primary users (i.e., operators) and secondary users (i.e., other participants who do not warrantably have primary operational control of the IT tool). Such interaction entails that participants make a systematic use of these tools and other repertoires of semiotic resources for interaction (Goodwin, 2011), and as pointed to in previous studies on embodied interactions, that these media mutually elaborate each other (Nevile, Haddington, Heinemann, & Rauniomaa, 2014; Streeck, Goodwin, & LeBaron, 2011). Reflecting on this dynamic nature we use the term "multimodal interactional competence in the use of technology" (MICT) as one dimension of IC.

The use of multimodal practices is also of particular relevance when we consider the range of contexts in which second language (L2) learning and acquisition are matters of significant concern. This study regards multimodal interactional practices as an essential element of IC and indeed as equally important as linguistic practices. The authors of this study are exposed routinely to L2 speakers who are situated in a host community (i.e., users of Japanese as an L2), on a daily basis, and we strongly feel that there is a growing trend towards the promotion and deployment of information and communication technologies (ICT), regardless of grade or level of study in Japan. For example, in Japan there is currently a nation-wide push by the Japanese Ministry of Education to transform traditional classroom designs into Web 2.0 generation settings (Ministry of Education, Culture, Sports, Science, and Technology in Japan).[3] Such initiatives have entailed increasing governmental investment in renovations of educational environments in both public and private institutions by installing ICT devices (e.g., iPads for all students, WiFi-environments, smart board devices) in an increasing number of classrooms.

From a global perspective, it is important to note the almost ubiquitous availability of and access to a diverse range of IT tools may feature as relevant matters in the performance of various social interactions. This is particularly relevant when one considers that many IT devices are now readily mobile. They can be present at home, at school, or in a specific space for learning (e.g., a lab). This implies that IT objects can be made relevant as semiotic resources (Goodwin, 2011) for growing numbers of users, in increasingly varied settings and contexts, and increasingly by L2 speakers.

Given our interest in MICT and the differential roles that may be adopted by primary versus secondary users of IT devices in various settings, it is useful here to make a further clarification with regard to what our conceptualization of IC entails. Our formulation assumes that users possess pragmatic knowledge on how to use IT devices, as opposed to sophisticated technical understandings. Furthermore, such knowledge needs to be crafted into participants' communities and their practices in each context to make the devices relevant as semiotic resources for interaction. For example, consider an interaction in which one participant operates a smartphone while conversing with another participant who is unfamiliar with smartphone operation. The smartphone user might engage in a range of actions (e.g., glancing at the screen, reading out text, holding the smartphone screen towards their interlocutor) with some degree of competence, but such technical competence alone will not determine the relative smoothness of the social interaction with a technically non-proficient interlocutor. In more general terms, here we suggest that the competence to manage IT tools in interaction may need to be regarded as comprising an essential element of MICT.[4]

In this regard, we seek to investigate how L2 speakers of Japanese manage themselves in a group interaction during a class in which they are routinely required to use various IT tools. Consider that for L2 speakers of Japanese, effective management of technology in situated talk (such as in a classroom) can enable them to effectively undertake participation roles that can serve to achieve various institutional aims and objectives (e.g., completion of group learning tasks). More specifically, we explore cases involving the use of three different tools: an iPad, a desktop PC, and a BIGPAD. In our examinations of the interactional data, we seek to highlight how linguistic resources (i.e., Japanese,

English, or other languages available to the participants) are used as one of the multiplex non-verbal modalities for their interaction. The L2 speaking participants we observe vary in their L2 proficiency level, based on the Japanese Language Proficiency Test (JLPT) and Oral Proficiency Interview (OPI). Employing an ethnomethodologically informed conversation analysis and the application of a multimodal analysis, we demonstrate how participants, both L1 and L2 speakers, manage their interactional conduct in each target context.

Returning to the concept of IC, scholars have suggested that such competence (involving a range of knowledge, skills, abilities, and situated resources) is about using communicative resources to collaboratively accomplish context-specific goals (Kramsch, 1986; Young, 2011). Clearly, any interactional resources that might be available for participants to co-construct understandings (intersubjectivity) and accomplish particular social goals will vary according to each situation. The point we would like to make here is that when technology features as a relevant component in an interactional setting, the particular technology (as with any other media serving as a semiotic resource) can often be understood as being embedded within a range of embodied multimodal activities.

By way of clarification, consider that Pekarek Doehler and Pochon-Berger (2011) argue that (L2) IC includes an adaptation to the local contingencies of the talk, which implies sensitivity to the local context and diversification of interactional practices (see also Hall, Hellermann, & Pekarek Doehler, 2011). To manage communication, speakers need to monitor both the linguistic details of their interlocutors and the socio-pragmatic actions taking place, with such communication performed across a range of multimodal channels. For L2 speakers too, the ability to project upcoming actions enables them to participate more fully in talk-in-interaction (Pekarek Doehler & Pochon-Berger, 2011). Consider then that classroom contexts which involve IT tools may naturally bring students together to co-construct a multiparty social interactional setting, and participants in such contexts may embed the use of various IT tools (technology) while they proceed with their social action. In this case, the analytic interest is to find out how multiparty, multimodal social interactions get done, given that students' indigenous IT practices are deeply embedded within them. In short, participants do not communicate *through* technology, as one would typically imagine in a CMC context (e.g., online chat), rather they are engaged in a face-to-face interpersonal interaction in which technology serves as an interactional resource.

# Literature review

**Computer-supported cooperative work and computer human interaction**
The two fields of computer-supported cooperative work (CSCW) and computer human interaction (CHI) are identifiable research fields which have focused on understanding characteristics of interdependent group work with the objective of designing adequate computer-based technology to support such cooperative work. The bulk of the extant literature on these fields show how human participants work cooperatively through technology. Although smaller in size and scope compared to mainstream CSCW or CHI studies, there does exist a rich seam of literature (e.g., Greatbatch, Luff, Heath, & Campion, 1993; Heath & Luff, 1992, 2000; Hughes, Randall, & Shapiro, 1993) that provides detailed empirical examinations of technology in institutional interactions by adopting CA and ethnomethodology.

Heath and Luff (1992) examine understandings of the organization of video-mediated interaction, particularly how people handle audio-visual technology. Their findings suggest technology introduces certain asymmetries into interpersonal communication, and they imply that IT may transform the impact of visual and vocal conduct. These asymmetries are due to the design of audio-visual infrastructures, and thus changes in the design may involve changes in interactional dynamic natureHughes et al. (1993) document a project by a team consisting of sociologists and engineers working in the domain of air traffic control systems. When a new system (an electronic display of flight strip information) was about to be installed, an in-depth ethnographic description of the activities performed by controllers during the installation was undertaken, applying an ethnomethodological analysis. Their work highlighted the degree to which the social interactions of the users (in this case the controllers) with the technology revealed important elements relating to how systems are actually used, which may often be overlooked or disregarded by engineers and system developers.

As Dourish and Button (1998) have pointed out, however, within CHI and CSCW fields, ethnomethodology is often poorly understood or misapplied, and such studies tend to highlight the research importance of identifying the specific nature of any technology present in a given setting, often with an eye toward providing analysis of how the technology is utilized (or misused) by participants (i.e., as evaluations of ergonomic or human factors). Despite the domain of the research being very relevant, there is a paucity of studies that explicitly attend to providing analyses of detailed *socio-interactional* aspects of the communication, that is, how human participants in the setting interact with each other, along with the technology. We would argue that a greater focus needs to be directed to investigating the practical purposes to which technological tools and their apparatuses are deployed by human participants, appreciating a very diverse range of unexpected and unanticipated affordances for social interaction.

**Technology as a semiotic resource in multimodal interaction**
Ethnomethodologically speaking, technology can be regarded as just one of many kinds of *objects* employed in social interaction. For example, such technology objects could include (as a non-exhaustive list) tools, devices, appliances, equipment, instruments, goods, products, vehicles, toys, clothing, materials, food, containers, utensils, weapons, gifts, and papers (Nevile et al., 2014, p. 5). There are a growing number of studies on embodied interaction involving objects (e.g., Goodwin, 2000; Haddington, Keisanen, Mondada, & Nevile, 2014; Mondada, 2014; Nevile et al., 2014) that draw upon ethnomethodology (Garfinkel, 1967) and conversation analysis (Sacks, Schegloff, & Jefferson, 1974). These studies highlight the importance of conceptualizing social interaction as involving multifaceted "complex multimodal gestalts" (Mondada, 2014), and that studies of social interaction must show how multimodal resources are integrated in a holistic way. Moreover, these studies emphasize that serious consideration be given to the plurality of modalities, as they are constitutively intertwined and made use of simultaneously.

One recent example of analysis of technology-as-objects is a study by Aaltonen, Arminen, and Raudaskoski (2014), who examined the use of digital cameras and digital photography as augmentative and alternative communication methods featuring in interaction between aphasic and non-aphasic speakers. For example, they detail how an aphasic participant undertakes meaningful participation in an interaction featuring discussion of a bird-watching experience by showing photos of birds taken on that occasion. The camera alters the contextual configuration by constructing a new semiotic field that allows the aphasic participant a way to respond to another participant's question such as "what have you taken photographs of?" The aphasic speaker hands the camera (with the photo projected on the camera display) to the recipient and says "here" to the addressee—and in so doing effectively constructs a multimodal sequence of actions (i.e., using both verbal and non-verbal resources together). Use of the digital camera in this way can be seen to comprise part of the aphasic speaker's IC. It enables the speaker to manifest his or her knowledge by participating in various interactional moves, for example by initiating a turn, or replying to an inquiry. The authors suggest that affordances provided by the camera serve to facilitate interaction in multiple ways. Physical passing and receiving of the camera among participants can act as a resource to support the sequential organization of the social activity. Accessibility of the photographs projected on the camera display add a further semiotic resource that help progress the talk.

In another example which more explicitly features a focus on IT use in interaction, Nielsen (2014) analyzed medical consultations in which a doctor uses a computer to check a patient's record of previous visits. Doctors recurrently orient toward their computer (observing digital records) as they listen to patients sharing their symptoms. A patient's medical history presented in the record may guide the on-going talk and play an important constitutive role for the interaction. Nielsen examined the moment when the doctors turn to the computer in the consultations—thus disengaging from the patient's eye gaze (a patient-centered participation format)—in order to look at the screen. Nielsen provides analysis of this moment as a significant interactional phase where a computer is elevated with regard to its participation status—when a general class of object becomes a specific object that is essential for the completion of medical business (p. 82). Crucially, participants treat such computer use as relevant to the tasks at hand, and thus treat it as a momentary but relevant departure from a patient-doctor (person-to-person) interactional framework.

Following in this tradition, we seek to explore the use of a range of IT tools in interaction with an analytic focus applied to how such IT tools are handled as objects in interaction, and how participants' gestures and bodily conduct orient to such tools accordingly. Our broad interest in the common approach employed by studies such as these is to explore how objects (specifically IT tools) reveal something of how participants act socially and meaningfully to construct and interpret practical activities and objects. The analytic approach in the studies reviewed here, and the orientation of the current study, seeks to examine how people shape, design, and orient to IT tools as part of their on-going interaction to establish Intersubjectivity, or shared understandings, of what is happening (e.g., Hanks, 1990; Heritage, 1984). More specific to our interest with regard to MICT, such orientations might provide for significant advances in the empirical investigation of language learning domains, particularly given the growing and sustained focus directed towards investigations of IC.

## Context of the study

The present data corpus comprises video-recorded interactional data extracted from two sets of class recordings collected during 2013 and 2014. The first dataset comes from a course entitled "Study Skills." This class was offered to both international students (L2 speakers of Japanese) and local Japanese students (L1 speakers) at a private university in Japan. Students were divided into groups of 3 to 4 people to carry out several project-based tasks throughout a 15-week long term. Analyses feature examinations of selected interactions drawn from approximately 450 minutes of video data in total. The selected interactional sets were chosen because they are illustrative of how L2 speakers participate in an on-going task with Japanese peers when some kind of IT device is being used as a research engine or note-taking tool. The examples we consider involve tasks in which progressivity cannot be achieved unless the given IT tool is employed in some capacity.

The second dataset comprises occasional Japanese tutorial sessions, which were conducted at the same private university, for international students learning Japanese, and held three times. Each session was approximately 50 minutes long, and the multiparty interactions were video recorded. In each session, L2 speaking students were paired up with an L1 speaker of Japanese and were provided with a specific learning task (e.g., to come up with a list of destinations in Japan to recommend to a visitor from a different country). Each task to be done in a Japanese language tutorial session was provided by the instructor (the first author) of the class.[5] In undertaking each task, students were provided with an IT device for their convenience, either (a) an iPad (utilizing the online browsing application Safari) to get information for the task, or (b) a smart board (e.g., BIGPAD) which they used to digitally take notes on the discussion. The participating students chose a device depending on the task they were assigned.

At this particular university (a private comprehensive university in Japan), the Japanese language program had recently adopted a new IT-room with a mobile laptop available for each student, in addition to work desks that could be moved and arranged for various group work purposes. The university also provided a classroom with a BIGPAD and iPads ready to be used by any classroom users. In the university affiliated Japanese language school for international students preparing to enter a Japanese university (known as a *bekka* in Japanese), an e-portfolio system was used for daily quizzes, lecture notes, and submission of homework and other assignments in each class. As a normal part of classroom routine, many classes began with students logging into their own LMS (learning management system, a web-based platform) and checking their own e-portfolio site. The students made use of their smart phones or computers to manage these transactions for their language learning. Therefore, IT use in the language learning setting for learners of Japanese was not an uncommon occurrence for the L2 participants in this study.

In the following three subsections, we examine three different classroom settings each featuring a different IT tool. The first case in the first subsection shows a moment in which participants engage in a new action (the pointing out of a mistake and suggestion to redress the course of action by someone else in the group) through their interactions with the desktop PC. In the second subsection, the examples show how the development of a shared practice in their community, featuring the use of a shared iPad, enables participants to co-construct their "utterance" (Kendon, 2004) that co-occurs with various non-verbal visual actions using the iPad device. In the third subsection, we provide examples illustrative of the use of another technology (BIGPAD), which serves to constrain all four participants' engagement in joint attention to what the current speaker is doing visually, and how this provides affordances for the participants to manage next-speaker selection (Lerner, 2002). In these examples, we also see participants' orientations towards the current speaker's management of the technology and how this plays an important role in shaping relevant next actions by other participants.

**Semiotic agency mediated by the use of personal computer**

Before turning to a consideration of the first extracts, it will be useful to first briefly outline the concept of "semiotic agency" as articulated by Goodwin (2011). Semiotic agency incorporates how interactants can initiate a course of action through systematic sign use. Goodwin's illustrative example was how an aphasic patient's use of pointing gestures and orientation to physical materials (such as a plate on a table or a cup) are made relevant for action-projection. In our example detailed here, a primary medium which serves to mediate systematic sign use for participants is personal computers, either desktops or laptops. In our first dataset, there are three participants in Excerpts 1 and 2. Aline (from Germany) and Net (from Thailand) are L2 speakers of Japanese, both at the JLPT N2 level in their Japanese proficiency.[6] Their teammate is Taka, a 4th year Japanese male undergraduate student. They are working together to build an online survey to share with an American university as a task given during class (Figure 2).[7]

**Figure 2.** Participants' seating arrangement.

Here, it is important to provide some background details for the following two excerpts in order to assist in developing an account of the main course of action being undertaken in them. The topic areas for the survey questions have been suggested by the instructor of the class on a university LMS (learning management system) page called CEAS (see Figure 3). All students have log-in access to CEAS, but this particular topic assignment page is available only to Net and Aline (international students) and is not available to Taka (Japanese student). The three students do find out that they have different information access in their CEAS pages until in Excerpt 2, and this is what causes Net's challenge towards Taka for redressing a track of action as a group.

In order to generate a survey form, they are instructed to use a free online application called "SurveyMonkey" (see Figure 4).

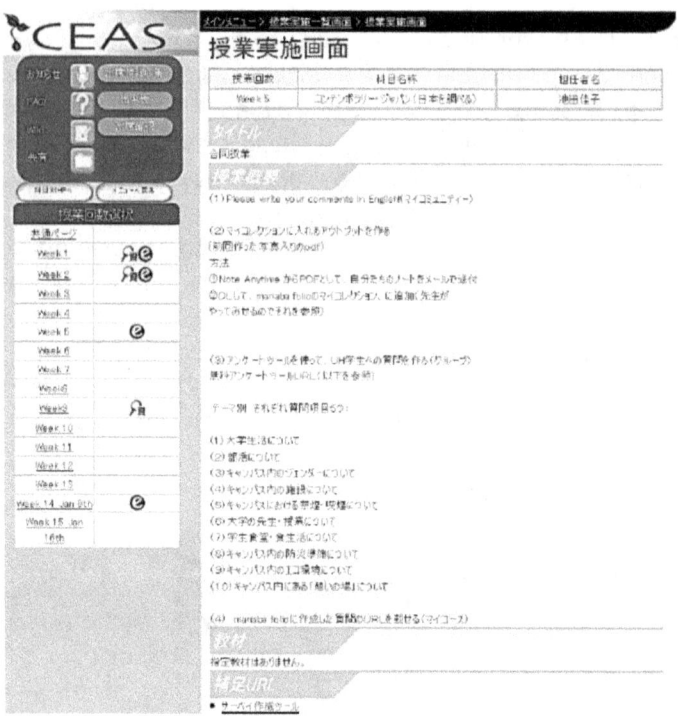

**Figure 3.** CEAS (LMS) page accessible to Net and Aline (Question 10 reads kyanpasu nai ni aru ikoi no ba ni tsuite '(write) about relaxation spots within (your) campus'.)

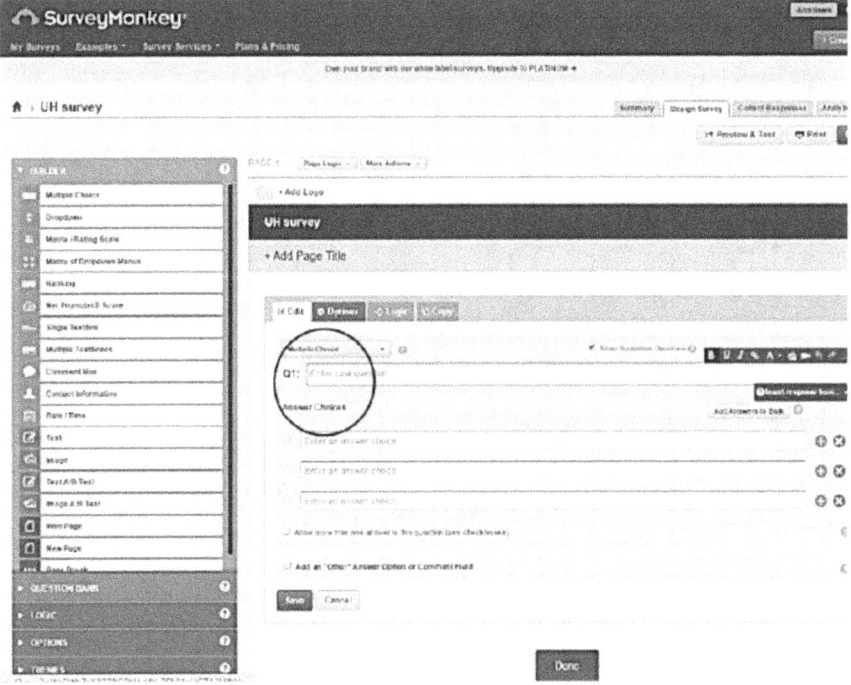

**Figure 4.** Online survey tool (SurveyMonkey), as shown on Taka's screen

In the beginning of Excerpt 1, following the task direction, Taka has opened the SurveyMonkey page. The students have logged in to the SurveyMonkey site and are ready to generate ten questions as requested. Excerpt 1 captures a moment when the students encounter a problem in proceeding in their survey construction. Net, seated beside Taka (see Figure 2), notices that the information on the CEAS page could not be viewed by him. In line 1, Net uses a hesitation marker to summon attention from Taka, who is notably gazing at his screen (Figure 4).

**Excerpt 1.** (Aline=A, Net=N, Taka=T)

```
1 N: ano::
     uhm
     Uhm

2    (0.5)

3 T: hmm
     hmm
     Yeah?
```

Image*1

```
 4 N:   |CEAS (.) no.*¹
         CEAS    LK
        |((Net points to T's PC screen))
         In CEAS's

 5 T:   un
        yeah
        Yeah.

 6 N:   juu::
        ten::
        Ten

 7      (2.0)/((Taka logs into his CEAS page))

 8 N:   |a iie.    (0.5) juuban   wa,  juuban  no  shitsumon.
         oh no           ten-no.  TP   ten-no. LK  question
        Oh, no. For No. 10, Question No.10.
        |((T brings his right hand down to the desk))
        |((N gestures swiping twice))*²

 9 T:   un
        yeah
        Yeah.
```

Image*2

```
10 N:   a. ky- |kyanpasu no  nai [:
        uh ca-  campus   LK  inside
        Uh inside of the campus
                |((T looks at N))
11 T:                          [a:  ano (.) are ne? um.
                                oh   H      that one IP yeah
                               Oh. Uh, that one, right? Yeah.
```

In line 4, Net points to the SurveyMonkey questionnaire item "Q1" (circled in Figure 4) and says *CEAS no* 'In CEAS.' Upon receiving a minimal receipt from Taka in line 5, Net goes on to say *juu:* 'ten:::.' At this point in line 7, Taka types on his keyboard and logs into his own CEAS page, reacting to Net's mentioning of CEAS. Observing his reaction, Net says up front *a iie* 'oh no,' and re-starts her utterance from line 4.[8] Here, Net displays alertness to Taka's next action in line 7. She has detected what Taka is about to do, and immediately provides a response *a iie* 'oh no' without its first pair part. This serves to adjust his attention back to her continuation of the turn. Net then says *juuban wa juuban no shitsumon* 'for No.10, Question No.10,' meaning that in order for them to generate a question here, it has to refer to No.10, the topic that was previously provided in the CEAS instruction. While Net is telling Taka about this, she brings her right hand to the desk and gestures with her thumb and index fingers (as shown in Image*2), swiping from left to right two times, as she says 'Question No.10.' What she has done here through the gesture is to indicate that the instruction for each question (here she uses No.10 as an illustration) for SurveyMonkey is already provided in the CEAS page (Figure 3), so they will need to refer to it. The swiping gesture on the desk serves as an iconic construction of a different location from what is now being projected on Taka's computer monitor. Note that while making this iconic gesture, Net keeps her gaze towards Taka's face, not the monitor. Taka, however, still gazes at the monitor.

Upon this suggestion, Taka provides another minimal response *un* 'yeah,' which functions as a continuer (Schegloff, 1982)—it does not, however, appear to constitute a sufficient display of understanding of Net's point. Then in line 10, Net undertakes some elaboration on the topic given for question No.10 in the CEAS instruction[9], saying, *kyanpasu no nai*[10] 'inside the campus...' In line 11, Taka this time responds with a more solid confirmation, *are ne? um* 'that one, right? Yeah,' that serves to clearly display that he understands Net's reference (i.e., the set of questions listed on the LMS page). At this point, Taka shifts his gaze from the monitor and looks towards Net.

Considering that Net is trying to explain the missing information required for their task, which Taka does not have tangible access to in front of him, this is a rather complex communication task for an L2 speaker of Japanese. In this instance, Net has a JLPT N3 level with an approximate OPI Intermediate-Low level for her L2 linguistic proficiency. Given these constraints, her prime timing of pointing to the trouble source on the screen and producing iconic gesturing on the desk can be regarded as an efficient method by which to resolve the interactional trouble.

Net's turn in line 10 is evidently effective in terms of generating a gaze shift (for Taka) from the monitor to the speaker of the turn. In many contexts that feature embedded use of IT devices in complex multiparty social interaction, users routinely fixate their gaze towards the devices, mostly because the reference of their talk tends to be projected on the devices. During a repair sequence in interaction (as we have seen in this excerpt), however, participants may have to shift their attention away from the device and engage in a human-to-human turn-taking sequence (i.e., shift gaze towards Taka, instead of the monitor). Net's employment of bodily conduct is most effective in generating a personal engagement away from the PC screen.

Through this sequence of actions, Net denotes that a response is being requested from Taka upon her inquiry (i.e., whether Taka can retrieve the list of task questions from his LMS account page). The action which Net performs in this particular interactional segment, suggesting to revise the way to proceed with the task, incorporates highly complex semiotic agency (Goodwin, 2011) which obviates the limitation that she may not have been able to perform successfully if this were to be done by employing verbal resources alone.

We now turn to analysis of another excerpt, drawn from recordings of the same group. In this excerpt, which immediately follows the interaction detailed in Excerpt 1, Taka brings up a CEAS page (on the computer, in his account) for their class. This was the action that was called to a halt in line 8 by Net. After having produced a clear display of understanding of Net's turn in line 10, Taka returned to his previous action of bringing up his CEAS page. As we have pointed out, his account page does not show the same information, thus there is no instruction for the questionnaire for Taka. In Excerpt 2 below, Taka explains this to the other two group mates.

**Excerpt 2.**

```
15 T:   koo |yuu yatsu?
        this like one
        Like this one, right?
            |((T clicks on the URL link on the screen and
                projects his LMS page on PC with his account))

16      (0.5)

17 N: a. soo soo. |(daimee)    ni shi[ta::    ]
        oh right right title    O  made
        Oh, right, it has a title::
                    |((N points to T's screen))

18 T:                                [kore ne] nai   no yo.
                                      this  IP none  NE IP

19         |ore kono gamen wa
            I   this page  TP
            This, I (don't have) this page.
            |((T points to A's PC*[1]))
```

Image*1

```
20      ryuugakusee : ano [Net| chan toka:]Aline chan toka no=
        Int. students H   Net   AT   etc.  Aline AT   etc. LK
                          |((T points with his right
                          hand open*²))
```

Image*2

```
21 N:                     [ |ah : : :        ]
                            CS
                            Oh::::::
                          |((N shifts gaze away from T
                          and then towards A's PC))
                          |((A sits up in her chair))

22 T:  =yatsu |to   chigau    no yo. so   so   so   so.
        one    from different N  IP  right right right right
       (Mine) is different from Int'll students' page like yours. Right right right.
                  |((A types on her keyboard to log
                  into her CEAS page))
```

23      (3.0)*³ /((T and N both gaze towards
        A's PC screen))

Image*3

In line 15, Taka clicks (on his screen) on another page in his CEAS account to display the same page (but without the instructions), saying "(you mean) like this one?" Net views Taka's page in LMS (logged into with Taka's account), saying *soo soo* 'right right,' showing that this is the right page. She then starts to elaborate further in line 17 on what they should do next: use the title given in the instruction.

Overlapping with her turn, Taka cuts her off and starts his turn by saying *kore ne nai no yo* '(I) don't have this.' By first denoting that he does not have the affordance to show the requested instruction part on his page. Taka then continues to undertake an elaboration of why he does not have the access. In lines 18 to 19, he says that his page does not have it, suggesting that the international students do. In projecting this turn, Taka points to Aline's monitor while saying *ore kono gamen wa* 'I (don't have) this screen' (Image*1), which then leads to what is to come next. He follows this utterance by saying in lines 20 and 22 *ryuugakusee: ano Net chan toka: Aline chan toka no yatsu to chigau no yo.* '(mine) is different from international students' page like yours'. Upon hearing this, Net and Aline provide differential responses. Net, in line 21, displays an epistemic change of state marker *ah::::* 'oh::::', accompanied by the production of a visible frowning expression on her face. Then she shifts her gaze away from Taka's screen and looks towards Aline's monitor (though, at this point the monitor does not project her LMS page). Aline, when she hears *Aline chan toka* 'like Aline' in line 20 by Taka, sits up in her chair from her relaxed seating position. In line 22, while Taka is coming to a turn-construction unit (TCU) by saying *yatsu to chigau no yo* 'different from those ones,' Aline pulls her keyboard drawer towards her torso and starts typing in her ID to log into the CEAS site. Note here that Taka and Net observe Aline's action, then direct their gaze towards Aline's screen (Image*3). Across a three second duration, Net has both her hands on her lap, and Taka rests on his left elbow with his torso facing away from his own monitor.

What we wish to highlight with this excerpt is the manner by which each participant contributes to this particular transitional moment in interaction through his or her orientation to the available technology. The bodily conduct they employ, such as gaze towards the computer or pointing towards it, serve to index a normatively understood possible next action. These displays of interactional affordance can be conceptualized as autochthonous in that participants display and demonstrate understandings of the significance of these actions in the production and recognition of the particular tasks from within the specific setting. For example, consider how Aline's sitting up on her chair can serve to project expanded availability to other participants—an action that likely entails more than the doing of just an observation (Nevile et al., 2014). Consider also Taka's resting position in line 23, and how this serves as a display to the other participants that his role in the on-going interaction has now changed. Throughout the interactional sequence we can discern how participants actively work to incorporate relevant and specific features of their environment, particularly their relation with the computer. With Taka and Aline's bodily adjustment relative to the computer, the participants create a distinctive form of co-operative sociality (Goodwin, 2013) through joint attention to the same target.

### Use of an iPad in a routinized peer activity

The next excerpt comes from the second dataset, in which an iPad was shared between two users, an L2 speaker, Maria (from the UK, JLPT N2 level, OPI Intermediate-Mid level), and an L1 speaker, Shun, during their tutorial sessions. They are using an iPad to search for a photo depicting a place in Japan that they can use in constructing an introduction for a new visitor to the country. While they were given a handout that describes the task details there was no supervisor present to monitor their work progress. In line 1, Shun takes the initiative by starting a conversation, asking Maria what to look for.

**Excerpt 3.** (Maria=M, Shun=S)

```
1 S: ii   toko  iroiro|arimasu ne: (1.0)
     good place various  exist    IP
                  |((S holds a pen in his left hand,
                     gets ready to tap on the iPad with
                     his right hand; gazing at iPad))

2     nani ga ii   desu ka?*[1]
      what S  good CP   Q
      There are lots of good places, yeah. What should we choose?
```

Image*1

```
3 M:    |rainbow bridge?
        |((M looks at S, while S gazes at the iPad))
         Rainbow Bridge?

4 S:    rainbow |bridge,(.) desu [ka.
        rainbow  bridge        CP   Q
        Rainbow Bridge, huh.
                       |((M's right hand moves towards the iPad))
                       |((S taps one letter on the keyboard.
                          S and M both gaze toward the iPad))

5 M:                              [hmm.
                                   hmm
                                   Hmm.

6 S:    rainbou burijji. (0.5)|Tookyoo desu ne:
        rainbow  bridge        Tokyo   CP   IP
        Rainbow Bridge. It is in Tokyo, right?
                              |((S taps on the iPad and types
                                 "rainbow bridge" in English*²))
```

Image*2

```
7 M:   |soo.
        right
        Right.
       |((M sits up in her seat*3,
           still gazing towards the iPad))
```

Image*3

```
8       (0.5)  / ((S re-types "rainboo burijji" using
           Japanese characters))
9 S:    rai- (.) bo (1.0) reinboo burijji nara
        rain       bow     rainbow bridge   if
10     | deteki[mashita
         appear-PST
       |((S taps the iPad twice))
        (Pictures on the search) showed up for rainboo burijji.
11 M:              [hmm.
                    hmm
                    Hmm.
```

Here, note that during Shun's production of the utterance *nani ga ii desu ka* 'what should we choose?,' his bodily conduct also serves as a display to Maria that he is willing to tap in keywords on the iPad for them. Observing this as a possible projection for a next action, Maria gazes towards Shun and suggests "rainbow bridge?" in line 4. After that, Shun first types "rainbow bridge" in a search engine while typing aloud in line 6. In line 6, while he is typing, with his gaze still fixated on the iPad, Shun says *Tookyoo desu ne* 'It's in Tokyo, right?' to Maria. In response, Maria provides a clear ratification *soo* 'right' while adjusting her sitting posture and maintaining her eye gaze towards the iPad (line 7). Here, note how Shun first types "rainbow bridge" utilizing an English spelling, but then re-types it using the Japanese orthography (レインボーブリッジ). During this part, Maria sits up in her chair, positioning her right elbow and arm on the desk. In lines 9 to 10 Shun says '(pictures on the search) showed up for *reinboo burijji,*' pronouncing the word in Japanese. Upon this, and while still gazing towards the iPad, Maria provides a quiet minimal receipt token in line 11 (*hmm*).

This extract details an interactional sequence in which Maria and Shun perform the first action of searching for images with a new keyword. We can observe that Maria adopts a rather remote bodily posture towards the iPad whereas Shun maintains his direct access to it across the sequence. Both Shun and Maria have their gaze directed towards the iPad screen, with both participants displaying alertness to what appears on it. Maria's change of seated posture takes place while Shun is in the process of handling the iPad search, aiming the precise timing to coordinate her actions with the main on-going task activity.

The interaction between the two across lines 1 to 10 takes place without the participants engaging in any mutual eye gaze, yet each participant is clearly addressing the other as the primary recipient of the conversation. The participants thus form an instrumental F-formation (Kendon, 1990) together with the iPad, and their behaviors with regard to an orientation to the iPad are seen and treated as relevant for their interaction. For instance, we see in this excerpt that tapping on the iPad (e.g., lines 4 and 8) is treated as a confirming act upon Maria's proposal for a search. While Shun is typing and focused on the iPad screen, Maria sits up with her gaze still fixated towards the iPad screen along with Shun. Their orienting to the iPad as the primary target for joint attention is the core element for generating this F-formation into a collaborative work site.

Excerpt 4 begins after Shun and Maria have found various images of Rainbow Bridge. In this excerpt too, we can observe how Shun and Maria both orient to the iPad as a resource for engaging in the pursuit of a common task together.

**Excerpt 4.**

```
12 S: nani ga aru kana.   kore kiree desu ne*¹
      what  S  have IP    this pretty CP    IP
      What do we have here? This one is pretty, isn't it?

13 M: a! |kiree. (soo). ironna iro. (.)
      oh pretty  right  various colors
      Oh pretty. Yes. Many colors.
         |((S taps on the image to
            enlarge it))
```

Image *1

```
14 S:  |kore wa mita koto arimasu ka.=
        this TP  saw  N    have     Q
       Have you see this before?
       |((S points the projected images on the iPad
           screen with the pen in his right hand))

15 M:  =hai.
        yes
       Yes.

16 S:   koko       ni shimasu ka.
        this place to select   Q
       Should we decide on this place?

17 M:  |hmm hai.
        hmm yes
       Uh yes.
       |((M sits up and turns her head towards
          her handout to write))

18     (2.0)/((S takes a screen capture*² with the
              iPad for the screen capture (iPad) function))

19     (0.5)/((S clicks on his ball point pen))
```

Image *2

```
20 S: reinboo| bu[rijji:
      rainbow bridge
      Rainbow Bridge:
              |((S starts writing on his handout/
                 M also continues to write her handout))
```

21  M:         [°hmm  °*³
               hmm
               Hmm.

Image *3

In line 12, Shun points to one of the pictures displayed on the iPad screen (Image*1). Here, Maria gazes at the screen just as Shun provides a positive assessment, 'This one is pretty,' which is immediately followed with a tag question, 'isn't it?.' Maria receives this with an immediate confirmatory assessment, 'Oh, pretty. Yes.' (line 13). At this point, Shun taps on the small image to enlarge it, as Maria displays her orientation to the same target, expanding her initial positive assessment with 'Many colors.'

Shun and Maria decide to use this picture to answer a question in the given handout, which asks for a particular location they like the most in Japan (here, Rainbow Bridge). In line 16, Shun suggests *koko ni shimasu ka* 'Should we decide on this place?' to Maria, who provides agreement in line 17. Of interest here is how her utterance co-occurs with her embodied actions of sitting up in her chair once again and turning of her head and upper torso to orient towards the handout on the desk. While Shun does not project any verbal response in line 18, he uses both of his hands to make a screen capture of the image displayed on the iPad, which was required as a part of the instructions. After performing the screen capture (which involves pressing the power button and bottom tab simultaneously, and producing a shutter noise of the camera) in line 18, Shun clicks on his ballpoint pen to start writing on his own handout (line 19). Shun sounds out "Rainbow Bridge" as he writes it on the handout (line 20), to which Maria produces a minimal receipt-token "*hmm*" (line 21) while she also fills out her assignment handout.

Here, it is worth exploring in more detail how the participants dealt with the last transaction, which involved taking a screen capture on the iPad. Shun's next action after their mutual decision on a particular picture is to save it with an iPad screen capture. Both participants knew that such a practice makes a noise, which serves to indicate the capture was successful. Shun's next action is to work on his own handout, and the sound from the pen and his utterance, "rainbow bridge," serve to inform Maria of his current action. The successful production of a "task" is sensitive to the *emergent activities* of colleagues within the local milieu (Heath & Luff, 2000). Indigenous practices and reasoning from the practices carried out with the iPad here plays an important role for their collaborative work.

Consider that as Shun works on this action, Maria continues writing her answer on the handout and does not orient or gaze directly towards Shun nor the iPad. Without making use of visual resources, Maria produces a recipient token in line 21 that serves as an acknowledgement of what Shun is doing at the time. What the participants demonstrate here is what could be described as a good acquisition of "indigenous practices and reasoning" (Heath & Luff, 2000, p. 117) relevant for the use of the iPad as technology, with various interactional practices being made use of as resources for the on-going interaction (rather than as trivial epiphenomena).

**Meaning-making in a technologically laminated environment**
In the final excerpt, we turn to an examination of a multiparty group interaction where two L2 speakers (Ron from the US and James from the UK, both at a JLPT N3 level of proficiency) and two L1 speakers (Kanako and Shun) work on a task together using a smart board (here, BIGPAD). The participants have been assigned the task of discussing and summarizing their ideas on the topic of "the features of a good class." In the classroom, a BIGPAD replaced the whiteboard about six months prior, and the participants have decided to use it.[11] A BIGPAD allows the users to directly write onto the screen either with a hand or a touch pen. One person at a time can draw onto the screen, similarly to the touch panels of other devices. It also digitally saves what has been written on the screen.

As shown in Image*1 below, all participants first stand in front of the BIGPAD screen and start to work out how they should manage the task they have been given. A clear difference of the BIGPAD from the other IT tools discussed in this paper so far is its visual affordance to the present participants. While an iPad or a PC monitor generates a smaller range of F-formations with a few participants, a BIGPAD allows all four participants to face it, and any actions done on the tool are made visible to them. This particular multimedia related technological affordance (Gaver, 1991; Heath & Luff, 1991, 1992) is made of use in the following interaction as a locally relevant semiotic field that the participants demonstrably orient to (Goodwin, 2000).

Consider that right at the beginning of Excerpt 5 below, we can observe Shun holding a touch pen, which is used to write on the BIGPAD. In line 1, one of the L2 speakers, Ron, says *kore ni shiyoo* 'let's do this' while taking the touch pen from Shun.

**Excerpt 5.** (Ron=R, Shun=S, Kanako=K, James=J)

```
1 R: kore ni |shiyoo, (1.0)
     this to do
     Let's do this
               |*1-----------|*2--------------|
     ((*1 R takes the touch pen from S))
     ((*2 R turns towards the menu icons on the right
          side of the BIGPAD))
```

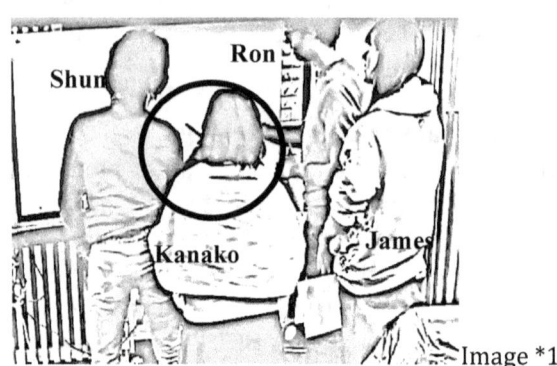
Image *1

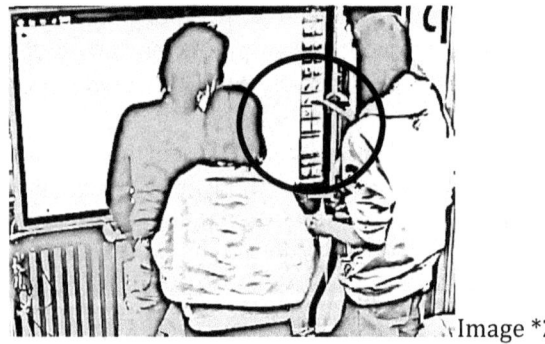
Image *2

```
2 R: |hmmm. (1.5)
     Hmm
     hmm
     |*3----------------------------------|
     ((*3 R selects one of the colors for the pen,
          moves it to the center of the BIGPAD))

3    kore ni shiyoo, |(2.0)
     this to do
     Let's do this,
                     |*4------------------|
     ((*4 R draws a dotted line, about 10 cm long))
```

*Use of Technology in L2 Japanese Classrooms  165*

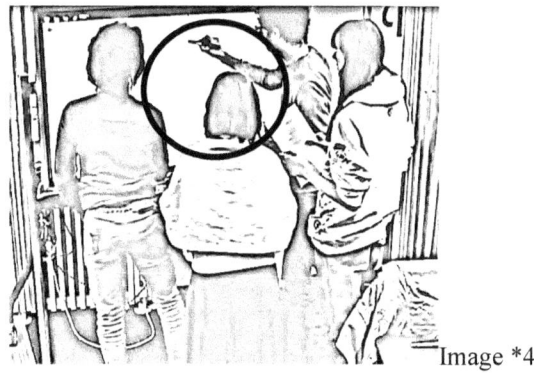
Image *4

```
4 S:                                              |*5 ------|
   ((*5 S takes the pen from R and starts to draw a
    dotted line))
```

Image*5

```
5 R:  |nanka. kore sen. (.) kaite, (0.5)
       H     this line      write
      Like, this line. Write it.
      |*6----------------------------
      ((*6 R gestures with his right hand up and down to
         show where a line should go up to))

6 K:  hmm. (0.5)
      hmm
      Hmm
```

Image *6

```
7 J:   a [:  a: naruhodo.]
       CS    CS  I see
       Oh:: oh: I see.
       |*7----------------|
       ((*7 R, smiling briefly, looks at J then turns
       back to the BIGPAD))
```

Image*7

```
8 K:    [a:::      wa ]kete.[kaku   n desu ka?
        Oh         separate-and  write N CP   Q
        Oh, separately. We should write it, you mean?
                               |*8----------------
        ((*8 R's right hand pointing at the BIGPAD
        while he looks at K))
```

Image *8

```
9  R:            [|anata(tachi) no bun,| a:(0.5)
                   your(s)         LK part H
                 Your part, and uh:

                                   |((Shun
                 starts to complete the line
                 on the BIGPAD))

10 J: okke.
      okay
      Okay.
```

As shown, we can observe that across the first several lines Ron forms his preface to the next immediate action. In line 1, Ron takes the pen from Shun (displaying self-selection for the next action), clicks on the icon for drawing on the right side of the BIGPAD while he utters *hmm* (holding the floor), and then attempts to initiate drawing a line after verbalizing 'let's do this' (line 3).

Ron's action here is observed by the other participants, and is thus relevant for the next action. Shun in line 4 takes the touch pen from Ron, and then continues to complete what Ron has initiated (i.e., writing a dotted line). In line 5, while Shun works on the actual drawing on the BIGPAD, Ron provides a gesture of drawing a line and says *nanka kore sen kaite* 'Like, this line. Write (it)'. Since only one user at a time can input information, Ron only shows what to do—it is Shun that undertakes the actual drawing production. Consider that while no verbal agreement is produced, Shun's collaborative work with Ron here can be seen as a form of well-established intersubjectivity.[12]

Upon seeing this happening, Kanako produces the minimal acknowledgement token "hmm." in line 6, which, with a down contour, is hearable as a display of minimal understanding. Following a brief gap of silence, the other L2 speaker, James, says *a:: naruhodo* 'oh I see' (line 7), using the epistemic change of state token 'oh' (Heritage, 2012) which serves to clearly display that, regardless of Kanako's understanding, James now claims to understand the action in progress. Ron, with a smile on his face, then turns towards James, who is still gazing towards the BIGPAD. Ron turns back towards the BIGPAD, establishing a joint attention towards the IT device.

As Shun finishes drawing the line on the BIGPAD, Kanako says in line 8 *a::: wakete. kaku n desu ka?* 'Oh:: separately. (We should) write it, you mean?,' which serves as a more direct articulation of the previous 'hmm' and a clear display of her epistemic status with regard to the collaborative task at hand. In line 9, Ron follows up by saying in a partial overlap *anata(tachi) no bun, a:* 'your part, and uh:,' confirming to Kanako that her interpretation is congruent (or at least compatible) with his own.

In addition to the delicate epistemic work being done in this sequence, we can also observe how a variety of modalities are of significant interactional importance to the collaborative task, particularly when examining how Ron constructs and performs a number of relevant social actions. For example, note that Ron first prefaces his turn with a verbal projection ("Let's do this"), and then uses the BIGPAD to actually show to the rest of the group what the "this" refers to (i.e., Ron starts to draw a line to suggest that they divide into smaller groups and use separate spaces on the BIGPAD for their memos). Further, Ron does not complete the main task action by himself from beginning to the end, but instead allows another participant to complete the latter half of the action by lending the BIGPAD pen to Shun. Shun does not utter a word, but instead takes the pen from Ron and displays his understanding by simply carrying out what Ron had started to do on the screen.

Ron includes the remaining participants James and Kanako into the on-going interaction, inviting them to display their understandings of his attempt. Taken together, these observations show that Ron was able to make a suggestion of how to go about the task in the group. With the available semiotic field created by the particular IT device, Ron was able to utilize the semantics afforded to take an active part in the multiparty talk. Meaning-making efforts observed in this particular excerpt are specific to the technological affordance of the BIGPAD. The other participants in the talk also take into account this specific technology-enhanced lamination of the environment (Goodwin, 2014) to make sense of Ron's gestures (see also Goodwin, 2007).

## Discussion and conclusion

Sacks et al. (1974) show that turn-taking in conversation can be conceptualized as an economy that allocates a resource and turns of talk among participants. While this definitely comprises a core element of our formulation of IC, consider also that a range of visible (i.e., witnessable, accountable) actions may be as important as (if not more than) single discursive utterances for interactants in pursuing specific kinds of social actions in a range of settings and contexts (Kendon, 2004). In short, we may miss or overlook a range of significant interactional practices relating to IC with examinations that focus solely on speech exchange. More to the point, we would argue that examinations such as the one presented here can serve to illustrate the complexity of a range of IC dimensions, with our formulation of MICT being offered as one in which we can analyze IT tools and their usage, not as separate or discrete elements that are essentially grafted into interactional episodes, but as being embedded in-and-as ongoing sequences of action.

This paper examined three different settings that featured the use of IT tools, including personal computers, an iPad, and a BIGPAD (smart board). A multimodal analysis of participant interactions highlighted participants' involvement in the interaction through the use of IT tools as mediated signs (Goodwin, 2011). For the participants in the examples investigated here, orienting to these tools was a relevant and critical action for managing their on-going actions. For each different tool, there were different practices shared and understood by the users of them. Given that such practices are treated as a part of the complex ecology of the setting, various kinds of semiotic resources (Goodwin, 2013) such as language, visual displays, other bodily conduct, and actions towards the IT device become intelligible to participants. Making use of these resources, including actions and conduct that have to do with each technology, is an essential part of identifying a particular dimension of IC— which we gloss as MICT. Moreover, for both L1 and L2 speakers, this particular dimension of IC may be an important element to consider when designing or implementing formal language training programs given the growing utilization of IT tools in language education.

**Notes**

1 Technology refers to the branch of knowledge that deals with the creation and use of technical means and their interrelation with life, society, and the environment. While any products such as a mechanical pencil or a vacuum cleaner can be labeled as technology, information technology (IT) refers to the use of any computers, storage, networking, and other physical devices, and infrastructure and processes to create, process, store, secure, and exchange all forms of electronic data.
2 Multimodal practice in interaction highlights that participants constantly establish intersubjectivity in a multimodal way: participants manifest to each other their current understanding in their gesture, gaze, facial expression, body position, and so forth (Mondada, 2011).
3 http://www.mext.go.jp/a_menu/koutou/itaku/1347642.htm (last accessed February 16, 2016)
4 Within CA for SLA research, there has developed a sub-field called CA for computer assisted language learning (CALL), which explores the use of technology

in language learning contexts (for an extensive review see González-Lloret, 2015). CALL may appear to be essentially a tool that helps teachers to facilitate the language learning process, yet it also allows participants of such a class to develop an IC which works to suit its situation. It can be used to reinforce what has already been learned in the classroom, or as a remedial tool to help learners who require additional support. Scholars interested in CALL studies have delivered CA work revealing otherwise unnoticed features of ICT-mediated virtual interaction (computer mediated communication or CMC) as a site of communication practice for L2 learners. The core focus in this vein of research thus far has been to explore how the structure of interaction is different from face-to-face interaction. The purpose of many CALL studies is to identify how the IT tool or CMC aids language learning, and thus differences between the two contexts (virtual vs. in-person) are highly important findings.

5   The tutorial sessions were held approximately once a month on campus. The pairs or group sessions (one L2 speaker and one L1 speaker for the pair, and even number of L2/L1 speakers for the group sessions) were randomly arranged each time.

6   The Japanese-Language Proficiency Test (JLPT) has been offered by the Japan Foundation and Japan Educational Exchanges and Services (formerly Association of International Education, Japan) as a reliable means of evaluating and certifying the Japanese proficiency of non-native speakers. It is widely used in many higher education level institutions. At the N2 level, one is able to read clearly materials written on a variety of topics, such as articles and commentaries in newspapers and magazines as well as simple critiques, and comprehend their contents. One is also able to follow and comprehend orally presented materials, such as coherent conversations and news reports, spoken at nearly natural speed in everyday situations as well as in a variety of settings.

7   This class at the present university and a class at an American state university worked on what is called COIL (Collaborative Online International Learning), in which they communicate virtually as well as synchronously as they work on a project together. The task assigned to the students in Japan is to construct an online survey which the American students will take, in order to compare and contrast their own answers and those of the American students on various aspects.

8   We do not have a recording of what the PC monitor was showing at this moment when Net says *a iie* 'oh no'. Since Taka's CEAS page, however, does not have the same information as Net's page, we can speculate that Net is responding to that gap. This is, nonetheless, not grounded in any evidence.

9   The full instruction on the CEAS page reads *kyanpasu nai ni aru ikoi no ba ni tsuite* "(write) about relaxation spots within (your) campus."

10  This is a grammatical error. The correct form should be *kyanpasu nai no* 'inside the campus.'

11  There are various merits for using a BIGPAD instead of a whiteboard. It can digitally save what has been written on the screen, and users can get online to send the

file to themselves immediately or save it to the hard drive. Users can also use an internet browser to search for information on the big screen and on the spot when they need to know something. They can also retrieve other files and documents from a memory stick or a SD card just as they can with a personal computer.

12  Koschmann (2011) suggests that collaboration represents a kind of understanding. It is a way of organizing an activity as if the participants share a goal or task orientation. We align with Koschmann in that we have no way of truly determining (either as participants or as analysts) whether or not the students are actually pursuing the same goal in the absence of what we can observe empirically from their embodied actions. Our knowledge is only of what they actually do (i.e., as witnessable and accountable social actions) to organize their interaction. What we have observed in this study is a variety of methods by which participants establish and maintain intersubjectivity (i.e., understandings) and how each participant provides displays of such understandings through the use of technology. Each must, in a sense, discover the affordability of behavior and conduct accorded to particular IT tools in-and-through interaction, rather than coming to each new interaction with a rigid framework of action.

## References

Aaltonen, T., Arminen, I., & Raudaskoski, S. (2014). Photo sharing as a joint activity between an aphasic speaker and others to our download area. In M. Nevile, P. Haddington, T. Heinemann, & M. Rauniomaa (Eds.), *Interacting with objects: Language, materiality, and social activity* (pp. 125–144). Philadelphia, PA: John Benjamins.

Dourish, P., & Button, G. (1998). On "technomethodology": Foundational relationships between ethnomethodology and system design. *Human-Computer Interaction, 13*(4), 395–432.

Garfinkel, H. (1967). *Studies in ethnomethodology.* Englewood Cliffs, NJ: Prentice-Hall.

Gaver, W. W. (1991). Technology affordances. In S. P. Robertson, G. M. Olson, & J. S. Olson (Eds.), *Proceedings of the ACM CHI 91 Human Factors in Computing Systems Conference* (pp. 79–84). New York, NY: ACM Press.

Goodwin, C. (2000). Action and embodiment within situated human interaction. *Journal of Pragmatics, 32*(10), 1489–1522.

Goodwin, C. (2007). Environmentally-coupled gestures. In S. D. Duncan, J. Cassell, & E. T. Levy (Eds.), *Gesture and the dynamic nature of language: Essays in honor of David McNeill* (pp. 195–212). Philadelphia, PA: John Benjamins.

Goodwin, C. (2011). Contextures of action. In J. Streeck, C. Goodwin, & C. D. LeBaron (Eds.), *Embodied interaction: Language and body in the material world* (pp. 182–193). New York, NY: Cambridge University Press.

Goodwin, C. (2013). The co-operative, transformative organization of human action and knowledge. *Journal of Pragmatics, 46*(1), 8–23.
Goodwin, C. (2014). The intelligibility of gesture within a framework of co-operative action. In M. Seyfeddinipur & M. Gullberg (Eds.), *From gesture in conversation to visible action as utterance: Essays in honor of Adam Kendon* (pp. 199–216). Philadelphia, PA: John Benjamins.
González-Lloret, M. (2015). Conversation analysis in computer-assisted language learning. *CALICO Journal, 32*(3), 569–594.
Greatbatch, D., Luff, P., Heath, C., & Campion, P. (1993). Interpersonal communication and human-computer interaction: An examination of the use of computers in medical consultations. *Interacting with Computers, 5*(2), 193–216.
Haddington, P., Keisanen, T., Mondada, L., & Nevile, M. (2014). *Beyond multitasking: Multiactivity in social interaction*. Amsterdam: John Benjamins.
Hall, J. K., Hellermann, J., & Pekarek Doehler, S. (Eds.). (2011). *L2 interactional competence and development*. Clevedon, UK: Multilingual Matters.
Hanks, W. (1990). *Referential practice: Language and lived space among the Maya*. Chicago, IL: University of Chicago Press.
Heath, C., & Luff, P. (1991). Disembodied conduct: Communication through video in a multi-media office environment. In S. P. Robertson, G. M. Olson, & J. S. Olson (Eds.), *Proceedings of the ACM CHI 91 Human Factors in Computing Systems Conference*, (pp. 99–103). New York, NY: ACM Press.
Heath, C., & Luff, P. (1992). Media space and communicative asymmetries: Preliminary observations of video-mediated interaction. *Human-Computer Interaction, 7*(3), 315–346.
Heath, C., & Luff, P. (2000). *Technology in action*. Cambridge: Cambridge University Press.
Heritage, J. (1984). *Garfinkel and ethnomethodology*. Cambridge: Polity Press.
Heritage, J. (2012). Epistemics in action: Action formation and territories of knowledge. *Research on Language and Social Interaction, 45*(1), 1–29.
Hughes, J., Randall, D., & Shapiro, D. (1993). From ethnographic record to system design: Some experiences from the field. *Computer Supported Cooperative Work, 1*(3), 123–141.
Kendon, A. (1990). *Conducting interaction: Patterns of behavior in focused encounters*. Cambridge: Cambridge University Press.
Kendon, A. (2004). *Gesture: Visible action as utterance*. Cambridge: Cambridge University Press.
Kramsch, C. (1986). From language proficiency to interactional competence. *The Modern Language Journal, 70*, 366–372.
Koschmann, T. (2011). Understanding understanding in action. *Journal of Pragmatics, 43*(2), 435–437.
Lave, J., & Wenger, E. (1991). *Situated learning: Legitimate peripheral participation*. Cambridge, UK: Cambridge University Press.

Lerner, G. (2002). Turn-sharing: The choral co-production of talk-in-interaction. In C. Ford, B. Fox, & S. Thompson (Eds.), *The language of turn and sequence* (pp. 225–256). Oxford: Oxford University Press.

Mondada, L. (2011). Understanding as an embodied, situated, and sequential achievement in interaction. *Journal of Pragmatics, 43*(2), 542–552.

Mondada, L. (2014). Pointing, talk, and the bodies: Reference and joint attention as embodied interactional achievements. In M. Seyfeddinipur & M. Gullberg (Eds.), *From gesture in conversation to visible action as utterance: Essays in honor of Adam Kendon* (pp. 95–124). Philadelphia, PA: John Benjamins.

Neville, M., Haddington, P., Heinemann, T., & Rauniomaa, M. (2014). On the interactional ecology of objects. In M. Neville, P. Haddington, T. Heinemann, & M. Rauniomaa (Eds.), *Interacting with objects: Language, materiality, and social activity (pp. 3–26)*. Philadelphia, PA: John Benjamins.

Nielsen, S. (2014). Medical record keeping as interactional accomplishment. *Pragmatics & Society, 5*(2), 221–242.

Pekarek Doehler, S. & Pochon-Berger, E. (2011). Developing 'methods' for interaction: A cross-sectional study of disagreement in French L2. In J. K. Hall, J. Hellermann, & S. Pekarek Doehler (Eds.), *L2 interactional competence and development* (pp. 206–243). Clevedon, UK: Multilingual Matters.

Sacks, H., Schegloff, E., & Jefferson, G. (1974). A simplest systematics for the organization of turn-taking for conversation. *Language, 50*(4), 696–735.

Schegloff, E. (1982). Discourse as an interactional achievement: Some uses of 'uh huh' and other things that come between sentences. In D. Tannen (Ed.), *Analyzing discourse: Text and talk* (pp. 71–93). Washington, DC: Georgetown University Press.

Streeck, J., Goodwin, C., & LeBaron, C. D. (Eds.). (2011). *Embodied interaction: Language and body in the material world*. New York, NY: Cambridge University Press.

Young, R. F. (2011). Interactional competence in language learning, teaching and testing. In E. Hinkel (Ed.), *Handbook of research in second language teaching and learning* (Vol. 2, pp. 426–443). New York, NY: Routledge.

# 7 Collaborative Orientation to the 'Search for What-to-Say' in Pair Work Interactions

Atsushi Hasegawa
*University of Kentucky*

## Introduction

Language proficiency has traditionally been conceptualized as individual competence with regard to "how to say something," including grammatical accuracy, fluency, cultural appropriateness, and so forth (e.g., Ellis & Shintani, 2014; Hadley, 2001). In such pedagogical discourse, it is also presumed that other elements of interaction such as topics, messages, and meanings—namely, what-to-say—also exist in the individual mind. From an interactional competence (IC) perspective, however, these elements are viewed fundamentally as co-constructed by all participants in an episode of interaction (Hall, Hellermann, & Pekarek Doehler, 2011; Lee, 2006; Young, 1999, 2011, 2013). A speaker does not produce talk irrespective of others present. Instead, talk is *recipient-designed* for a particular addressee, and the addressed recipient understands the produced talk as such (Sacks, Schegloff, & Jefferson, 1974). When it comes to L2 speakers, who often work with limited linguistic resources, coming up with what-to-say can be a considerable burden when participating in interaction.

This chapter explores how students in beginning L2 Japanese classrooms conduct searches for what-to-say during pair work activities and how their engagement in this type of search activity can be understood as a component of the students' IC. This type of search sequence is frequently[1] found in my collection of pair work cases, yet has rarely been discussed in previous research. Similar to a word search, a search for what-to-say[2] is an instance of forward-oriented repair (Schegloff, 1979) in which the speaker halts an ongoing turn at talk while conducting a search. Unlike word searches, however, objects of searches for what-to-say are not simply lexical items, but can be extended to involve a larger chunk of talk, such as turn construction units (TCUs). Essentially, coming up with what-to-say is a process prevalent in any type of talk-in-interaction, whether instructional or institutional talk or mundane conversation. When it is done explicitly, however, by halting the ongoing turn-in-progress and thus catalyzing the observable activity of searching for what-to-say, it becomes a public matter that needs to be dealt with by the participants in the interaction, much like a word search.

## Word search and other search activities

Word searching, or, for that matter, any search activity, is a common practice speakers undertake when one of the participants experiences trouble in accessing an item due next in the midst of a turn at talk. According to Schegloff (1979), a word search is essentially a repair activity characterized as forward-oriented, as opposed to the backward-oriented repair associated with already-produced talk. When a solitary search is taking place, it is typically signaled by various methods of marking (Schegloff, Jefferson, & Sacks, 1977). One explicit way of indicating a solitary search is with speech perturbations, such as sound stretches, vowel elongations, and hesitation markers. Disfluencies in speech can indicate a problem in the progression of the ongoing turn. Systematic deployment of nonverbal resources, such as gaze (upward or middle distance) and facial expressions (e.g., thinking face), can also indicate the onset of a word search (Goodwin, 1980, 1987).

On the one hand, word search sequences display the speaker's cognitive process, since he or she is attempting to retrieve information from memory storage. On the other hand, the word search also manifests itself as a social event because it unveils the speaker's lack of memory or knowledge in a public sphere (i.e., interaction). Previous CA research has examined how other participants orient to the speaker's facial expressions and gaze shifts when the speaker is searching for a word. Accordingly, even solitary word searches inevitably entail interactional consequences. That is to say, because a word search delays turn progression, even when it is intended as a solitary activity, the recipient attends to the event. For example, as Goodwin (1980, 1987) notes, when a search is initiated, the recipient typically directs their gaze to the speaker and watches him or her while the search is underway. If a solitary search fails, the speaker may use gaze shifts to call on the recipient to join the search, or the recipient may voluntarily jump in to help with the search. As such, the recipient is always included as a participant in a (potentially joint) search activity.

There are various ways in which a searched-for item is made recognizable to the recipient so that he or she can help find it. The most explicit method is for the speaker to ask specifically about the item in question, such as "what was her name?" (Schegloff et al., 1977). This explicit handling relies on both the speaker and the recipient sharing knowledge of the searched-for item. At times, the speaker repeats a part of the searched-for item, such as "B, Bobby?," which may provide a hint to the recipient as to what is being looked for. More frequently than not, the projectability of the turn-so-far, both syntactically and semantically, may enable the recipient to access the searched-for item (Lerner, 1996).

While word search sequences are prevalent in any talk-in-interaction, they hold particular significance for L2 research, which, in recent years, has led many applied linguistics researchers to investigate this topic (e.g., Brouwer, 2003, 2004; Funayama, 2002; Greer, 2013; Hosoda, 2006; Kurhila, 2006; Mori & Hasegawa, 2009; Park, 2007; Sasuga & Greer, 2014). In interactions involving L2 speakers, word searches have been discussed in relation to the issue of language expertise (see Brouwer, 2003; Carroll, 2005; Hosoda, 2006). For example, Park (2007) investigated instances of word searches involving L1 and L2 speakers of English within the institutional context of a writing conference. In her data, word searches were manifested in the following proto-typical sequence of actions: (a) initiation, (b) request for help and display of resources, (c) proposal of candidate, (d) acceptance/rejection, and (e) celebratory ending. As Park pointed out, when a nonnative speaker (NNS) invites a native speaker (NS) to engage in a joint word search, knowledge of language and content is complementarily distributed across the NNS and NS (Table 1).

Table 1. Complementarily distributed knowledge (from Park, 2007)

|  | Speaker (NNS) | Recipient (NS) |
|---|---|---|
| **Content** | Knowing | Unknowing |
| **Language** | Unknowing | Knowing |

That is, the speaker (NNS) knows what he or she wants to say, but without the language resource to express it, whereas the recipient (NS) may have a large vocabulary in the language, but does not have access to what the speaker is trying to say. Consequently, successful word searches require collaboration between the NNS and NS. This finding also points to the tendency for word search sequences that are triggered by L2 speakers' trouble finding the right word to be more likely attributable to the unknowing of an item, rather than the forgetting of it. Funayama (2002) reported a similar finding in his examination of word searches carried out by Japanese speakers of Mandarin Chinese, presenting cases in which the acceptance-rejection sequence was completely absent from joint word search sequences. The L2 speakers in his study apparently accepted any candidate items provided by the L1 speakers without acknowledging them, which suggested that there was no way for these learners to scrutinize whether the word offered was correct or not.

When it comes to the language classroom context, where all participants (except the teacher in some cases) are L2 speakers, the procedures of a word search may look different. For example, Mori and Hasegawa (2009) examined pair work interactions in a beginning-level Japanese language classroom and reported various ways of searching for lexical items to which neither student had access. The students frequently took advantage of the textbook glossary and the list of new vocabulary in each chapter. They skillfully navigated these resources depending on the types of words they were searching for (e.g., formerly introduced vs. newly introduced). The students also made creative use of *katakana* words (English-based loan words) and rephrasing strategies when they could not come up with the items in question. As such, the students' lack of linguistic resources was compensated by various semiotic resources available to them.

Originally, research on search practices by L1 speakers focused primarily on lexical items, but when L2 data were examined, diverse items were found to be target objects of search activities. With limited language resources, L2 speakers are prone to encounter more frequent and diverse troubles, and search activities are a common solution to such troubles. More specifically, when L2 speakers have trouble producing an utterance, the objects of their search activities are not only limited to lexical items: Other linguistic forms, such as pronunciation and conjugation, are also frequently observed (e.g., Brouwer, 2004; Carroll, 2005; Hasegawa, 2010; Kurhila, 2006). For example, Brouwer (2004) reported on instances of "doing pronunciation," in which L2 speakers searched for correct pronunciations. Similarly, Hasegawa (2010) discussed cases of "conjugation search" found in the Japanese classroom. These search activities are, by and large, concerned with formal aspects of language that are less likely to be an issue among adult first language users who have already acquired these skills.

While various objects were found to be the target of search activities, past research was primarily concerned with the circumstances in which the speaker knew what they wanted to say, but could not retrieve it for various reasons (e.g., they had forgotten it; they lacked the knowledge). In examining pair work cases in my dataset, however, I found quite a few cases in which the speaker apparently did not know what they wanted to say and conducted a search. Although no studies, to my knowledge, have formerly focused on this type of search, previous research has indeed presented a similar activity in their data. For example, Prior (2015) presented instances of interview interaction in which

L2 interviewees attempted to remember and searched for materials or topics to talk about in order to tell stories to an interviewer.

Likewise, Greer (2013) also discussed a case in which a speaker (Gino) of a bilingual focus group discussion conducted a search for an example as solicited by the discussion moderator, as shown below.

**Excerpt 1.** (From Greer [2013])

```
01 Mod:    For example?

02         (1.8)

03 Gino:   For example=

04 Mod:    =mm=

05 Gino:   =Yeah um (.)              nanka (.)
                ↑                    ↑ something
                                       like
           ((Gino looking at Mod))   ((Gino looks to the right))

06         ↑ my way of thinking is=
           ((Gino looks back at Mod))

07         =(.)[diff]er[ent=
```

In response to the moderator's question, a long gap follows in line 2. This silence by itself indicates Gino's thinking and searching process for his answer, and the hesitation markers (*um* and *nanka*) and micropauses in line 5 also suggest that Gino is still showing his struggle with his answer. Moreover, a gaze away from the moderator is indicative of the presence of a solitary search (Goodwin, 1987).

In a setting where opinion is sought, the speaker halting his or her turn to ponder and organize his or her thoughts, as in this example, is probably a common occurrence. When it comes to L2 speakers, who need to work with limited linguistic resources, the activity of coming up with what-to-say is probably done more frequently and markedly. Therefore, it is important to examine the use of resources that enable L2 speakers to conduct successful searches for what-to-say. As I will discuss in the data analysis section below, the classroom activities examined in the current study frequently make use of written activity prompts, typically displayed on the front screen, that partially prescribe sequences of turns. Such a pedagogical setup may or may not provide additional resources for students to make use of in accomplishing their searches.

The goals of this chapter are three-fold. First, as an initial attempt to investigate the activities of searching for what-to-say [3], this study will examine the procedural characteristics of this interactional practice, with a special focus on collaborative cases. Second, by describing moment-by-moment conduct, I will discuss how students make use of various resources and how their engagement in searches for what-to-say relates to their IC. The third goal of this chapter is to examine the relationship between the search for what-to-say and the pedagogical norms of these classes, which are mediated by activity prompts and which are reflexively constructed by the students' conduct.

## Data

The data for this study come from a larger corpus that consists of 160 pair work activities[4] video-recorded during a second-semester Japanese language course at a U.S. university. The 15-week course met for eight 50-minute sessions per week, consisting of three lecture sessions taught by a professor and five discussion sessions taught by graduate teaching assistants. While all students met together in a large lecture hall for the lecture sessions, they were split into smaller classes for the discussion sessions. Data were collected during these smaller discussion sessions. Each discussion class consisted of approximately 14 to 20 students.

According to the course syllabus, the main objective of the course was continuous development of the four basic skills of communication:

(a) the ability to listen to and understand everyday conversation;
(b) the ability to communicate everyday needs and uncomplicated ideas in common conversational situations;
(c) the ability to read and understand simple essays and stories; and
(d) the ability to write simple memos, letters, and essays.

Although the skills of communication were certainly emphasized in the course design, the curriculum was largely organized around grammar components with communicative add-ons, as is typically the case in university Japanese-as-a-foreign-language (JFL) instruction in the United States (Fujita, 1997; Mori, 2005; Ohta, 2001).

A mixed-syllabus (i.e., grammatical-topical-functional) textbook, *Genki II* (Banno, Ohno, Sakane, Shinagawa, & Tokashiki, 1999), was used as the primary course material, and the course curriculum was organized around the 11 chapters of the textbook. The oral practice activities provided in each chapter (including pair work) did not always conform to the topic of the chapter, but were instead aimed at exercises on discrete grammar items introduced in the chapter. Based on the textbook, a typical lesson for a discussion session was made up of some or all of the following components:

(a) review of grammar items introduced in the lecture session;
(b) (oral) grammar practice drawn from the textbook or created by the teacher;
(c) dialogue practice, including recitation and application; and
(d) integrative activities, such as topic-based conversations and role plays.

Pair work was an integral part of these discussion classes, but most of the pair work activities were highly controlled, often with an activity prompt projected on the front screen via an overhead projector. That is, the written prompts prescribed, to differing degrees, a sequence of turns in a conversational style, with or without linguistic cues, and students were supposed to follow the sequence accordingly. This type of pair work was presumably aimed at the practice of discrete grammar items, even though it was conducted in an ostensibly interactive format.

Communicative language teaching utilizes a type of activity called "social interaction" in which students are asked to engage in a topic conversation or a debate (Richards & Rodgers, 2001). The activities examined in this study seem to share some characteristics of this type (e.g., question-answer exchanges), but a striking difference lies in the form-orientedness of the activities. According to Ellis (2003), this format is called a cue-card activity and it does not constitute a communicative task.

I visited each discussion class multiple times over the semester (35 class sessions in total) and video-recorded the entire classroom interaction, which typically included a few cases of pair work activities. External microphones were set in front of focal participants,[5] so that audio quality could be ensured. In addition to the video recordings, I also conducted follow-up interviews with the focal students, using a retrospective protocol, in order to collect information about parts of interactions that were inaudible or unintelligible. During the interviews, I also obtained information from the students regarding their background knowledge, such as their learning histories and their knowledge of each other. I additionally collected as many teaching and course materials as possible, such as the course syllabus, textbook, and overhead transparencies. These ethnographic data were collected in order to complement a CA analysis of the video-recorded data. While the use of information external to video- and audio-recorded data is not common in the CA approach, Maynard (2003) considers ethnography (including interviews and documents) as an "ineluctable resource for analysis" (p. 65). Maynard does, however, still caution that the use of such resources should be restricted, characterizing the relationship between CA and ethnography as "limited affinity" (p. 65). Accordingly, the ethnographic data were referred to in this study only when participants' visible conduct indexed the presence of such information (see also Moerman, 1988).

## Data analysis

This section is organized around the three goals explained in the literature review section. First, I will describe how searches for what-to-say surface in the pair work activities and what observable conduct signals the presence of an ongoing search. In so doing, I will discuss how difficult it is to pinpoint the target of a search for what-to-say, which can involve not only ideas for the utterance but also the formulation of the utterance. Second, I will examine the resources that the students make use of in order to accomplish searches for what-to-say and discuss how engagement in such activities is indicative of underlying IC. Finally, I will discuss the relationship between searches for what-to-say and the particular pedagogical context.

### Embodied procedure of search for what-to-say

As described above, the pair work activities assigned in these classrooms are highly structured, with sequences of turns written on activity prompts. These prompts vary in type and length, but most of them consist of turns with written cues as well as blank segments that need to be filled in by the students. These design features of the activity prompts, especially the position and the length of blanks, create a particular pattern of participation, most notably, in regard to the point at which students are prone to engage in search activities. For example, when a blank is targeted at a verb conjugation, the students may engage in a search for the verb conjugation at the exact location of the blank (Hasegawa, 2010). In other cases, blanks in the prompt require the students to formulate longer and more extensive utterances, encompassing a TCU. When this type of prompt is assigned, the students are expected to come up with appropriate utterances that fit the ongoing sequence. Therefore, most cases of a search for what-to-say found in the current dataset are regarded as reflexive constructions of pedagogical foci embedded in the activity prompts.

For example, the following case (Figure 1) presents the relationship between the activity prompt and the occurrence of a search activity. In this unit, the class was practicing the grammar item *tara* (*if*-conditional). For pair work, the following activity prompt was displayed on the front screen via an overhead projector.

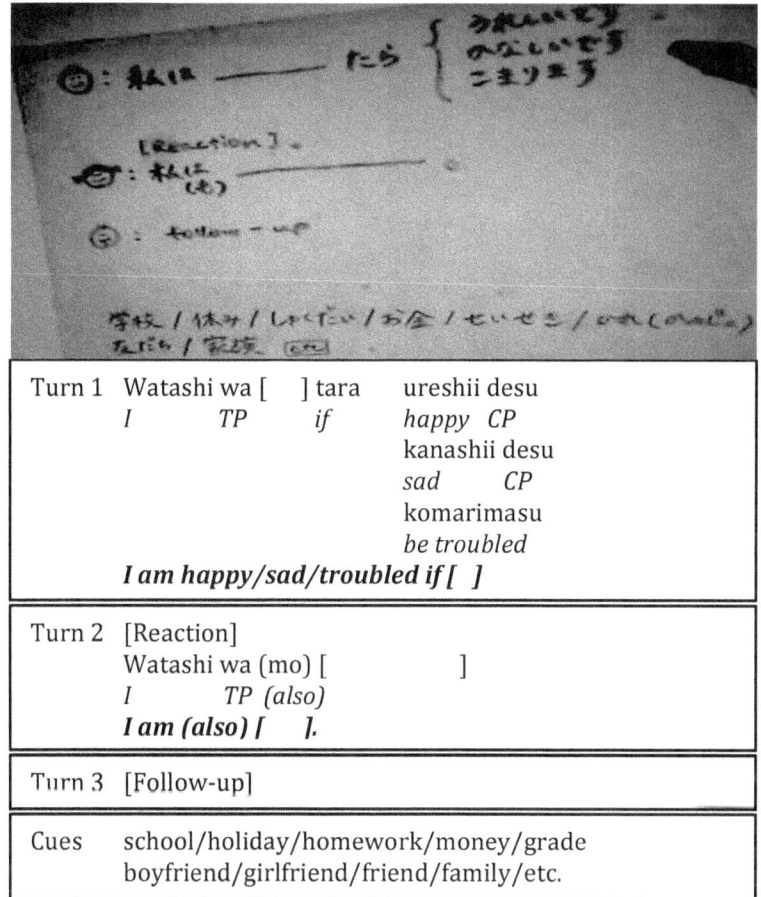

**Figure 1.** Activity prompt for Excerpt 2

By following this three-turn sequence, the students were supposed to practice the target grammar item in an interactive format. A search was observed at the very first turn, as shown in Excerpt 2 below.[6] In this excerpt, Bob is trying to fill in the blank in the activity cue presented above in a pair work activity with Kurt, who is sitting on his right side. For the purpose of the present analysis, the elements of the utterance that were written on the prompt are enclosed in boxes. In other words, non-enclosed parts are utterances that cannot be simply read from the prompt.

**Excerpt 2.** Searching for what-to-say in the first turn

```
1    Bob:    hai  (0.8)  u:n:  eeto:  (2.5)  uh::  (4.5)
             yes         H     H             H
                  ↓
             ((looking at middle-distance))
2            u:n  (1.0)  uh::  (2.5)  uh:  oishii       tabemono::
             H           H           H    delicious    food
3            (0.8)  uh::  ga  (0.3)  at tara:  (.)  ureshii  desu.
                    H     S          exist-if       happy    CP
                                                  ↓
                                          ((Bob looks to his co-participant))
             Uhm, well, uh, uhm, uh, uh, if I have, uh, good food,
             I'm happy.
```

In this example, Bob's apparent trouble is signaled by the presence of numerous non-lexical speech perturbations, such as intra-turn pauses and hesitation markers (*eeto, u:n,* etc.), prior to the onset of a TCU. On initial examination, these speech perturbations may appear to point to a search for the first lexical item of the TCU, *oishii* 'delicious.' However, his persistent gaze directed to the middle-distance from the beginning of line 1 and the subsequent gaze shift to Kurt observed at the end of the if-clause are indicative of this search being not simply a search for a single lexical item, but an extended search for the entire utterance. As a case in point, Bob's perturbations (vowel elongations, pauses, and the hesitation markers) continue until the if-clause is complete. Figure 2 below shows the change in his gaze direction from during the search (lines 1–3) on the left to after the search has completed (at the micropause in line 3) on the right. As shown here, his middle-distance gaze is maintained until the end of the non-scripted part, and it is precisely at this point that he directs his gaze toward Kurt.

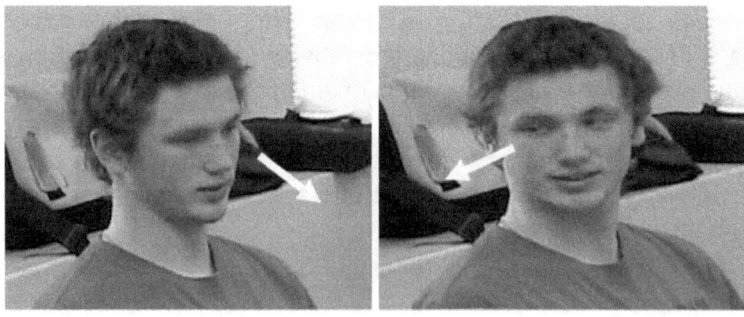

**Figure 2.** Bob's gaze direction during (left) and after (right) the search

Now, what exactly is Bob looking for in this segment? This is a difficult question to answer, at least, in this particular case. He may be looking for ideas to fill in the blank, but it could also be lexical items, verb conjugations, or grammatical markers such as particles. Or possibly, he could be looking for a combination of all of these. At any rate, pinpointing the source of the trouble is a tricky matter and not always straightforward. Nonetheless, what we can indisputably observe here is the precise coordination of the speaker's perturbations and his gaze shifts with the non-scripted parts of the utterance, where he needs to come up with what-to-say on his own. As we will see in the next case, when the speaker tries to retrieve a specific item—such as a conjugation—from memory in the midst of a search for what-to-say, he marks the attempt at retrieval explicitly by shifting his gaze upward from a middle-distance gaze or showing a noticeably thinking face. In this segment, Bob does not show any of these features, which suggests that this search is not so much concerned with specific linguistic items per se.

Let us consider the next example. This pair work task, conducted by the same students, took place after the previous activity. It is a question-answer practice based on given cues and a sequence of turns. Four turns are specified on the activity prompt, as shown in Figure 3. In addition to the sequence of turns that the students are required to follow, clausal cues, to be used in the first turn, are also provided. For example, with the cue *takarakuji ni ataru* 'to win the lottery,' the first turn may look like *[name] san wa takarakuji ni atattara doo shimasu ka?* 'If you won the lottery, what would you do?.' In formulating an answer to the question, the students need to make the appropriate verb conjugation (i.e., one that fits the if-morpheme *tara*), which is the assumed instructional focus of this pair work activity.

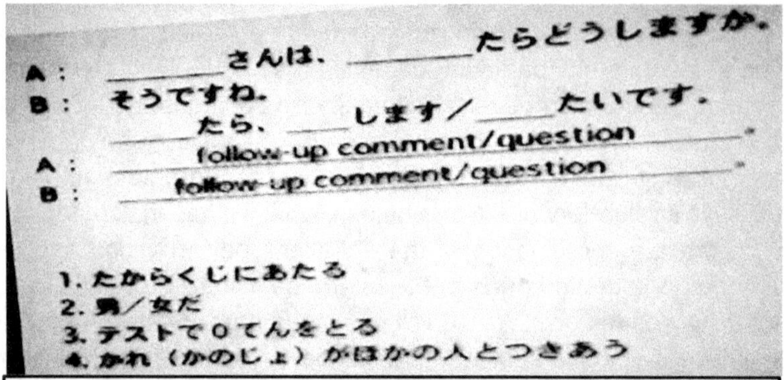

A: _____ さんは、_____ たらどうしますか。
B: そうですね。
   _____ たら、_____ します／_____ たいです。
A: follow-up comment/question
B: follow-up comment/question

1. たからくじにあたる
2. 男／女だ
3. テストで０てんをとる
4. かれ（かのじょ）がほかの人とつきあう

| Turn 1 | [ ] san wa [ ] tara, doo shimasu ka? <br>    Mr. TP   if   how do   Q <br> **Mr. [ ], if [ ], what would you do?** |
|---|---|
| Turn 2 | Soo desu ne. [ ] tara, [ ] shimasu/tai desu <br>   so CP IP   if   do   want CP <br> **Let's see, if I [ ], I will/want to do [ ].** |
| Turn 3 | [Follow-up comment/question] |
| Turn 4 | [Follow-up comment/question] |
| Cues | (1) *Takarakuji ni ataru* (win the lottery) <br> (2) *Otoko/onna da* (be a man/woman) <br> (3) *Tesuto de reeten o toru* (get 0 on the test) <br> (4) *Kare (kanojo) ga hoka no hito to tsukiau* <br>     (boyfriend/girlfriend dates someone else) |

**Figure 3.** Activity prompt for Excerpt 3

Excerpt 3 shows a sequence of talk in which Bob provides his answer to the question, *takarakuji ni atattara doo shimasu ka*? 'What would you do if you won the lottery?'

**Excerpt 3.** Searching for an answer to 'What would you do if you won the lottery?'

```
1    Bob:   uh:: (0.4) eeto:: (0.3) khh. (0.3) tch
            H          H                       ↓
            ↳((Bob looks down))        ((Bob looks to the screen))
2           takarakuji ni atattara: (1.0) uh:: (0.5) tch
            lottery    PT win-if ↓         H
                               ((Bob looks at the middle-distance))
3           (0.3) atarashii chi: (0.6) o: (1.4) n:: (0.8)
                  new       (house)    o         uhm
                           ↳((Kurt looks to the screen))
4           kai (1.7) >°I don't know°< (0.3) ka- (1.2)
            buy                               (buy)
            ↳((Bob looks up))
5           kau tsumori desu?
            buy intend   CP
            Uhm, well, if I won the lottery, uh, I'll b-,
            I don't know, intend to buy, uh, a new house?
```

Prior to line 1, Bob's partner, Kurt, has asked him the question, *takarakuji ni atattara doo shimasu ka*? 'What would you do if you won the lottery?,' as specified on the prompt. It is obvious that Bob has trouble producing the answer, evidenced by numerous instances of speech perturbations. Note that these speech perturbations are observed before he actually starts producing his answer in line 2. According to Figure 4 below, he looks down and directs his gaze toward the middle-distance as early as the beginning of line 1, indicating the initiation of a search at the onset of his turn.

While his search for an answer was initiated in line 1, Bob shifts his gaze to the front screen (Figure 5) and reads off the first component of the compound TCU, *takarakuji ni ata*, written on the prompt, followed by the correct conjugation of the verb *ataru* 'to win.'

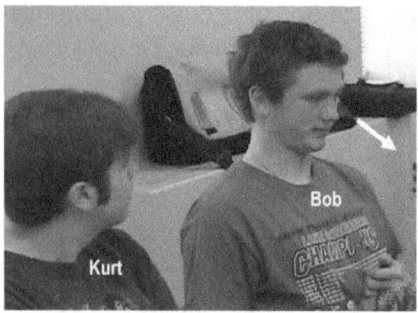 

**Figure 4.**   Gaze at uh:: (line 1)   **Figure 5.**   Gaze at tch (line 1)

After reading the script, some speech perturbations follow, suggesting that Bob is still having trouble. Given the precise timing of his gaze withdrawal from the prompt (Figure 6), it is clear that his trouble, observable from the very beginning, originates in the non-written portion of his answer (the second component of "if-X, then-Y").

**Figure 6.**   Gaze at tara: (line 2)

At line 3, Bob finally starts his answer by saying *atarashii chi:* 'new (house)', which is soon followed by more perturbations. This is the same pattern we saw in Excerpt 2: The speaker displays he is undertaking a solitary search even before the onset of his answer, and the search remains throughout the utterance. After a series of pauses, he then engages in a conjugation search, looking for the correct way to use the verb *kau* 'to buy,' as evidenced by the presence of self-repair at *ka-*, and a lack-of-knowledge claim, >°*I don't know*°<, in line 4. Note that there is a clear gaze shift from middle-distance to upward at the initiation of self-repair, *kai* (Figure 7).

**Figure 7.** Gaze at kai (line 4)

As discussed in Hasegawa (2010), the search for a conjugation often occurs at the exact moments where blank segments on a prompt are targeted. In this excerpt, the blank slot targets an utterance unit larger than a verb phrase, so the conjugation search itself is embedded in the search for what-to-say. According to Goodwin (1987), a middle-distance gaze itself indicates an ongoing solitary search for a forgotten item (i.e., word). In the current example, Bob is already engaged in a search for his answer, and the shift to upward gazing from a middle-distance gaze at the beginning of line 4 is indicative of a different type of search being underway, namely, retrieval of the correct conjugation. On the one hand, Bob is undertaking an extended search for a chunk of talk, including ideas to express, as indicated by his middle-distance gaze. On the other hand, when a specific problem arises, such as the conjugation, he handles it by bringing his gaze upward. In this regard, we can observe here an embodied process of the speaker's cognition involved in interaction (see Kasper, 2009). It is noteworthy that the students are not necessarily treating their engagement in these searches as particularly problematic, but rather, it seems that these searches are seen as a normative practice. I will elaborate on this issue later in relation to pedagogical expectations.

**Resources used to accomplish searches for what-to-say**
Thus far, I have focused primarily on when the speaker is conducting a solitary search. This does not mean, however, that these searches are individualistic activities. As is the case with word search sequences, searches for what-to-say are also a socially visible activity that halts the progression of turn-taking. For example, during Bob's seemingly disfluent talk in the above example, Kurt keeps his eyes directed at him, but right after Bob starts producing the non-prompt utterance, *atarashii:* 'new,' Kurt withdraws gaze from Bob (Figure 8).

**Figure 8.**  Gaze shift at atarashii: (line 3)

This gaze shift suggests Kurt's recognition of the termination of Bob's solitary search. As discussed in Goodwin (1987), a solitary word search is normally watched closely by the recipient, which allows the recipient to join the search upon request. Even in a solitary search like this, Kurt, the recipient, is demonstrating his understanding of the ongoing search by monitoring the speaker's conduct closely. Thus, it is not only that the speaker is engaged in a search for what-to-say, but also that the involvement of the recipient is a critical part of the interaction.

Occasionally, the recipient is significantly involved in helping to provide a solution to the search in progress. Excerpt 4, a segment extracted from the same pair work activity as in Excerpt 3, presents such a case. Bob is now asking the second question written on the prompt, *onna dattara doo shimasu ka?* 'What would you do if you were a woman?.'

**Excerpt 4.**  Searching for an answer to 'What would you do if you were a woman?'

```
1    Bob:      uh: kurt san:, (.) uh: (0.7) onna ttara: (.)
               H    Kurt Mr.       H         woman  if
2              doo shimasu ka?=
               how do       Q
               Kurt, uh, what would you do if you were a woman?

3    Kurt:     =hmhmhm huh um

4              (1.8)
```

```
5  Kurt:   °zenzen°    (.) shir(h)im(hh)as(h)en(h). °so°
           not at all      know-NG
6                   (0.4) uh: (1.9) onna    dattara  (0.9) uh:
                     H              female  CP-if           H
7                   (2.5) °da-°=dattara: (2.3) uh: (0.9)
                           CP   CP-if            H
```
              ((Kurt shakes his head))    ((Kurt looks to Bob repetitively))

```
8          ata[rashii-
           new
```
           I have no idea (laughter). If I were a woman,
           uh, w- were a woman, uh, new-

```
9  Bob:       [baazu ni: (.) >erh< baazu de (1.0) uh
               bars  to         H   bars   at        H
10         takusan free [drinks o:
           many              O
```
           To bars, erh, at bars, many free drinks,

```
11 Kurt:                [o(h)h(h) y(h)eah(h), hahahahah

12 Bob:    [HHh hhh

13 Kurt:   [baa de (.) takusan free drinku o (.) mora-
            bar at     many         drink   O     get
14         moraimasu.
           get
```
           I would get many free drinks at bars.

In lines 1 and 2, Bob formulates the question as indicated on the prompt. In response, Kurt at first produces a lack-of-knowledge (or more precisely a lack-of-ideas) claim, with laughter particles inserted throughout it (line 5). Nonetheless, he proceeds with the if-clause in line 6. Note that he repeats *dattara* in line 7. While this repetition looks like a self-repair, the second production of *dattara* simply redoes the first *dattara* in line 6, which was the correct conjugation. Considering that Kurt already made an explicit lack-of-knowledge claim and now shakes his head while producing the second *dattara*, his trouble here is not the conjugation, but the need for an idea to fill in the second component of the TCU. By redoing the ending of the first component ("if-X"), he is displaying his ongoing uncertainty about the second component ("then-Y"). During the pauses that follow in line 7, Kurt invites Bob's collaboration by repetitively shifting his gaze to Bob (Figure 9). Bob is likewise gazing at Kurt.

**Figure 9.** Gaze during a 2.3-second gap of silence (line 7)

By this point, Kurt has made use of three methods for displaying his lack of knowledge and seeking help from Bob: (a) stating that he has no idea about what to say as an answer to the question, (b) redoing the ending of the first-TCU, and (c) repeatedly shifting his gaze to Bob. After exhausting these means of appealing for assistance, Kurt finally starts producing the remainder of his answer, *atarashii* (line 8), which is then overlapped by Bob's provision of an alternative candidate idea. It is noteworthy that even though Kurt has already started formulating his utterance, he yields his turn to Bob and lets him finish with his candidate idea. Note that Bob recycles and repeats the overlapped portion of his utterance of *baazu* so that it is produced in the clear[7]—a common overlap management technique (see Sacks et al., 1974; Schegloff, 2000). As soon as Kurt hears *baazu de takusan free* 'at bars, many free,' he approves the candidate idea by saying *oh yeah*, as well as by inserting laughter particles. Heritage (1998) maintains that *oh* signals "a marked shift of attention" on the part of respondent (p. 294). By using *oh*, Kurt shows his realization of the idea suggested by Bob. The laughter particles inserted into the utterance of *oh yeah* index both his assessment of Bob's candidate item as laughable and his affiliative stance toward the assessed (see Glenn, 2003). At the same time, by providing the assessment, Kurt is demonstrating his access to the assessed referent (Pomerantz, 1984), namely, getting free drinks at bars.

Note that Kurt's response (lines 13–14) shows that he is not simply copying what Bob has offered, but instead, is re-formulating his idea using his own words. This is seen in the contrasting ways Bob and Kurt use loanwords. Bob uses *zu* in *baazu* to mark the plural (-s for 'bars') whereas Kurt uses a more common Japanese way of referring to bars (*baa*) by not adding any plural marker. Japanese does not normally make a distinction between singular and plural, and loanwords are imported mostly in singular form. Therefore, *baa* is more accurate than *baazu* in Japanese. Here, Kurt is demonstrating his knowledge of this by changing *baazu* to *baa*. Likewise, Bob uses the English word *drinks*, plural, with the English pronunciation, but Kurt uses a more Japanized pronunciation *drinku*, which also displays his sensitivity to the accurate production of this utterance. He then completes his turn with the verb *moraimasu* 'to get' without a problem. These pieces of information show that Kurt has no problem with the formulation of this utterance. Rather, his trouble in lines 3 through 7 has mainly been about generating an idea for his response to the initial question.

The fact that the answerer can seek help for an idea from the questioner—and that the questioner can provide an idea for the answer slot on behalf of the answerer—seems to defy the whole business of question-answer exchange. Unlike the provision of candidate items based on the projectability of a turn-in-progress, as in "anticipatory completion" (Lerner, 1996), the original questioner giving a candidate answer is indeed idiosyncratic.[8] Bob and Kurt are apparently not adhering to their original interactional roles of questioner and answerer here, especially given that Kurt has already started formulating his answer in line 8. Both Bob and Kurt are, instead, orienting to the collaborative search for the answer slot, and in this case, it looks as if both students are taking on the role of answerer. On the one hand, this seemingly contradictory process points to the students' treatment of the current event as primarily and simply the practice of the focal grammar item prescribed by the prompt (i.e., "if-X, then-Y"). It looks as if the ideas exchanged thereby bear little relevance to these students because the linguistic forms specified on the prompt remain the focal point. On the other hand, the laughter particles inserted into Kurt's agreement token show that he is doing more than simply acknowledging the candidate idea suggested by Bob. Kurt is providing an affiliative stance toward Bob's idea, in this case, judging it as funny. By collaboratively working on the answer slot, Bob and Kurt are still orienting to the exchange of a "funny" idea. Therefore, although the students largely maintain the instructional focus on linguistic forms, they are simultaneously orienting to, or even valuing, the meanings expressed in this exchange.

Notice also that Kurt understands the candidate idea as soon as Bob says the word *free* of *free drinks* (line 10), recognizing the candidate item before the turn is fully produced. Providing an assessable candidate and making it accessible to his co-participant requires Bob's careful attention. In fact, Kurt chooses Bob's candidate response over his own idea (*atarashii-*), which he had already started in line 8. It seems that the candidate idea proffered by Bob is not a random item, but rather, is designed to be relevant to—or to be shared by—Kurt. Retrospectively, Kurt's laugh particles in his initial lack-of-knowledge claim (line 5) may have framed this topical talk itself as laughable, which then led Bob to suggest a laughable idea.[9] In any case, Bob's candidate idea is clearly tailored for this particular occasion—an omnipresent practice of interaction known as recipient design (Sacks et al., 1974). The next example will explore this issue further.

Excerpt 4 above showed an instance in which the first speaker accepts and adopts a candidate idea, but this is not always the case. Sometimes the speaker rejects a candidate item suggested by the recipient. Consider the following case. In this activity Carl, Rick, and Bob[10] are discussing the question *donna hito ni naritai desu ka?* 'What kind of person do you want to be?,' as shown on the activity prompt (Figure 10).

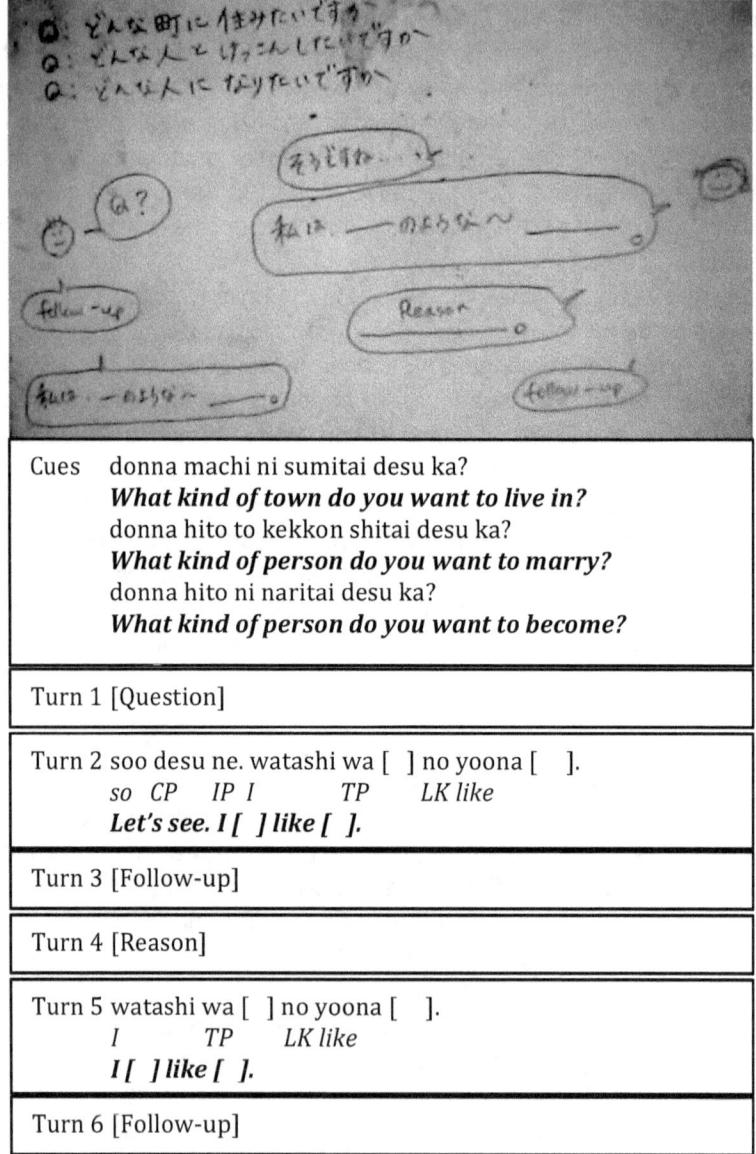

| Cues | donna machi ni sumitai desu ka?<br>***What kind of town do you want to live in?***<br>donna hito to kekkon shitai desu ka?<br>***What kind of person do you want to marry?***<br>donna hito ni naritai desu ka?<br>***What kind of person do you want to become?*** |
|---|---|

| Turn 1 [Question] |
|---|

| Turn 2 soo desu ne. watashi wa [ ] no yoona [ ].<br>so   CP    IP  I           TP        LK like<br>***Let's see. I [ ] like [ ].*** |
|---|

| Turn 3 [Follow-up] |
|---|

| Turn 4 [Reason] |
|---|

| Turn 5 watashi wa [ ] no yoona [ ].<br>I          TP       LK like<br>***I [ ] like [ ].*** |
|---|

| Turn 6 [Follow-up] |
|---|

**Figure 10.** Activity prompt for Excerpt 5

The target grammar in this activity is *yoona* 'like,' as in *[noun] no yoona hito ni naritai desu* 'I want to be a person like [noun].'

**Excerpt 5.** Searching for an answer to 'What kind of person do you want to become?'

```
1    Carl:   donna      hito::   (0.8) ni: (.) naritai
             what kind  person         PT      become-want
2            desu ka?
             CP   Q
             What kind of person do you want to become?

3            (0.4)

4    Rick:   uh::   (6.1)  [uh: uh:
              ↓             ↳((Rick shakes his head and smiles))
             ((Rick looks down))
5    Bob:                  [christian bale no yoona:=
                            christian bale LK like
                            Like Christian Bale

6    Rick:   =<chi(.)chi>,  (0.4) °ya°  (1.5)
              father              and
              father and

7    Carl:   astronooto no yoo:
             astronaut  LK like
             Like an astronaut

8            (3.5)
              ↳((Rick smiles))
9    Rick:   >chichi no yoona hito  ni naritai   desu.<
              father LK like  person PT become-want CP
              I want to become a person like my father.
```

Carl asks Rick the question in line 1, but the following lines show Rick's apparent trouble with his answer. The 6.1-second pause in line 4 is particularly noteworthy. Rick engages in a search for what-to-say at this point, as evidenced by his gaze shift down to middle-distance, followed by head shaking during the pause, which indicates he does not have an answer to produce at the moment. Additionally, while shaking his head, he also smiles, which is associable with the occasion of "production difficulties" as discussed by Ohta (2008).[11] Seemingly recognizing Rick's struggle, Carl reciprocates with a smile (Figure 11).

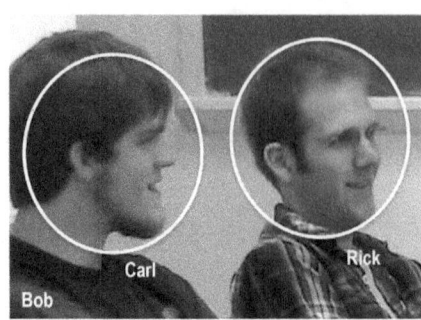

**Figure 11.** Smile during a 6.1 gap of silence (line 4)

In observing the trouble that Rick is displaying, it is Bob who first proffers a candidate response for the answer slot (line 5). It is important to note that this candidate item is produced without Rick's active appeal for assistance or the projection of the turn-so-far. In other words, Bob is treating Rick's struggle at that moment to be a struggle to come up with ideas for his answer. However, this candidate idea is in overlap with Rick's *uh: uh:* in line 4, which makes Bob's turn less noticeable, meaning Rick might not have heard it. In fact, without acknowledging Bob's contribution, Rick starts uttering <*chi(.)chi*> 'father,' producing it in a slower, uncertain tone and following it with a quiet °*ya*°. *Ya* is a particle used to list items non-exhaustively ('and so forth'). Thus, even though Rick has uttered the item *chichi* 'father,' he is apparently looking for one more item to add. The following pause shows his ongoing struggle with the turn, which, this time, prompts Carl to proffer his candidate idea (line 7). Again, Carl's offering of a candidate idea even without the projection of Rick's turn-so-far or an explicit appeal for assistance (e.g., What else should I say?) signals Carl's understanding of this search to be for an idea rather than for a lexical item per se. Rick acknowledges Carl's idea by smiling (Figure 12). However, Rick dismisses the candidate item and, without adding another item to *chichi* 'father,' completes his answer. Note that this utterance, >*chichi no yoona hito ni naritai desu*<, is produced smoothly, and at a faster rate without signs of production difficulty.

**Figure 12.** Smile during a 3.5-second gap of silence (line 8)

Although Rick persists with his own idea without taking in any of the candidate ideas offered by his classmates, the rejected candidate items are not necessarily randomly-produced items. On the contrary, these items are carefully considered and designed for Rick, or more accurately, for this particular occasion, just as in the previous case (Excerpt 4). First, note that Christian Bale is an English actor, known for his portrayal of *Batman* in recent films. Prior to this activity, these students were assigned another one, a sentence-making exercise using the grammar item *no yooni* 'like.' They together created sentences such as *chuck norris no yooni keremasu* 'I can kick like Chuck Norris,' *clint eastwood no yooni uma ni noremasu* 'I can ride a horse like Clint Eastwood,' *superman no yooni tobimasu* 'I fly like Superman,' making reference to heroic film characters. Among those sentences, Rick made *batman no yooni doroboo to kenka dekimasu* 'I can fight with robbers like Batman.' In Excerpt 5, Bob's candidate item *Christian Bale* is therefore specifically indexing this previous episode shared between them. In other words, Bob tailored his candidate item so that it is made relevant to Rick.

Sacks et al. (1974) described recipient design as "a multitude of respects in which the talk by a party in a conversation is constructed or designed in ways which display an orientation and sensitivity to the particular other(s) who are the co-participants" (p. 727). Among other items, it encompasses "word selection, topic selection, admissibility and ordering of sequences" (p. 727). In the example above, Bob's idea selection for Rick's answer slot is designed specifically for Rick, which is considered admissible and suitable in this particular occasion (but probably not on other occasions). Moreover, Carl's selection of the candidate idea *astronaut* may also be indicative of his past relationship with Rick. According to the follow-up interview conducted after the class, Rick and Carl have known each other since high school, where they took the same Japanese class. In this college Japanese class, they still work together as partners for pair work activities all the time and often bring up topics related to their mutual interests, such as mechanical engineering (their major) and science fiction movies.[12] The candidate item *astronaut* therefore seems to be brought up in line with their mutual interests that come to light through their previous experiences (i.e., of pair-work and of being friends). This is also evidenced by Rick's treatment of Carl's candidate idea. Instead of expressing his dissent with the idea, Rick simply smiles as if saying, "I know what you mean."

This example (Excerpt 5), as well as the preceding one (Excerpt 4), demonstrates the many resources that are used to accomplish joint searches for what-to-say. First, when a solitary search is seemingly unsuccessful, the present co-participants jump in to help the troubled speaker. This can be done voluntarily, as in the case of Bob and Carl in Excerpt 5, or upon the speaker's request through gaze shift, as seen in Bob's candidate response in Excerpt 4. Second, to signal trouble, Kurt, in Excerpt 4, uses various verbal and non-verbal resources, such as a lack-of-knowledge claim, gaze, and partial repetition of the preceding utterance. Collectively, these multimodal operations work to seek collaboration in the search for what-to-say. Third, candidate ideas are carefully tailored to the recipient and the occasion, as seen in both cases. In Excerpt 4, Bob makes use of a shared understanding of "getting free drinks at bars" as an amusing thing to say for Kurt's answer slot, whereas Carl and Bob in Excerpt 5 make reference to their shared history (i.e., previous pair-work activity) and their shared background knowledge of each other's interests. Finally, these search activities are built on the students' understanding and deployment of fundamental interactional routines, such as turn-taking (including overlap management technique), which all constitute fundamental aspects of IC.

**The reflexive relationship between the searches and pedagogical norms**
As with other interactional practices, search activities may reflexively index the context in which they are occasioned. As we have seen in the above examples, searches for what-to-say are occasioned in close relation to the blank sections of the activity prompts. That is, there is a robust tendency for the students to conduct searches precisely at these blanks. This, however, does not mean that the teachers designed these activities so as to encourage these searches. As far as I can understand, based on the information collected from the instructors, there was no explicit mention of, or attention to, search activities as an instructional goal when they designed these activities. Nonetheless, via the presence of activity prompts, the current pedagogical setting indirectly and implicitly encourages the students to engage in searches for what-to-say.

The evidence for such a reflexive relationship can be found in Excerpts 4 and 5. In Excerpt 4, even after the display of his lack-of-knowledge claim in line 5, *zenzen shirimasen* 'I have no idea,' Kurt was still committed to providing an answer on his own. Such commitment is evidenced by his repetitive gaze shifts to Bob (Figure 9), through which he is even seeking assistance from Bob, the questioner, who should not normatively have an answer to provide. By the same token, after Kurt had already started saying something in line 8, Bob took over the turn to produce a candidate idea. The collaborative orientation to fulfilling the answer slot was clearly observed in this case. The same orientation was evident in Excerpt 5, in which Bob and Carl both offered their candidate ideas even though Rick was not actively appealing for such offers. This student orientation, of collaboratively exploring possible ideas to produce an answer, points to the pedagogical context in which these students are situated. To be precise, the activity prompts—designed to target the production of a larger chunk of talk that restricts a response type (i.e., target grammar) without specifying ideas to fill in—apparently orient the students to the production of conceivable ideas for these slots. Note again that the ideas they came up with are not just random items: The students, in fact, attempted to recipient design their utterances for each other.

To illustrate my point clearly, I present a case in which a search for what-to-say is aborted midway. In this pair work task, Katy and Billy are assigned to work on a question-answer exchange, with the initial questions displayed on the front screen (Figure 13). The target grammar item for this activity is *[verb]-yasui* 'easy to [verb]' and *[verb]-nikui* 'hard to [verb].' Students are also expected to ask follow-up questions, so this activity moves beyond simple two-turn exchanges.

200 Atsushi Hasegawa

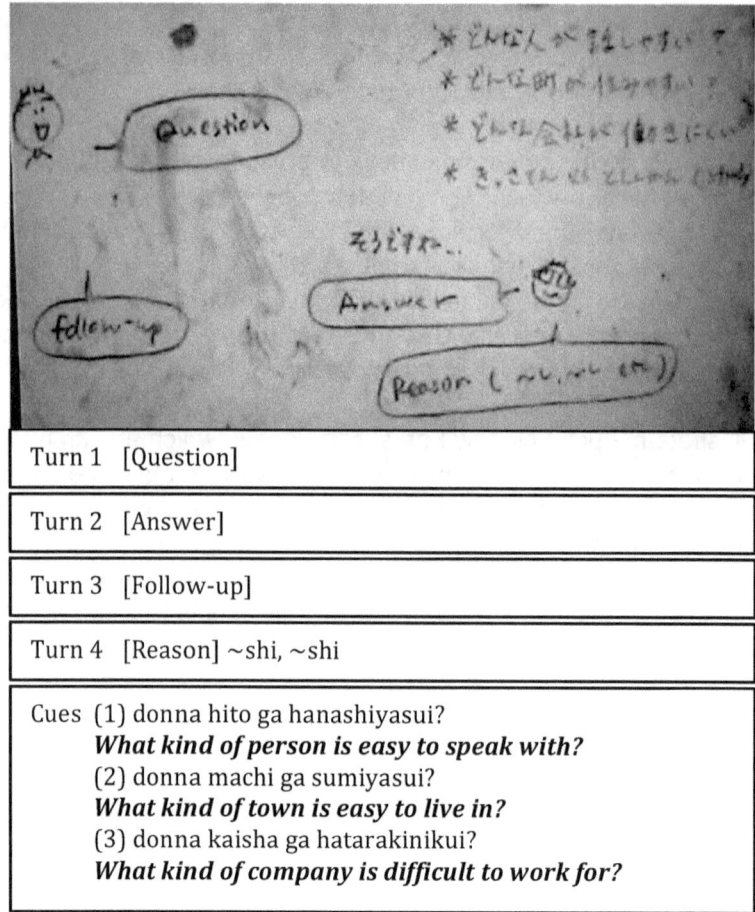

| Turn 1 [Question] |
| Turn 2 [Answer] |
| Turn 3 [Follow-up] |
| Turn 4 [Reason] ~shi, ~shi |
| Cues (1) donna hito ga hanashiyasui?<br>***What kind of person is easy to speak with?***<br>(2) donna machi ga sumiyasui?<br>***What kind of town is easy to live in?***<br>(3) donna kaisha ga hatarakinikui?<br>***What kind of company is difficult to work for?*** |

**Figure 13.** Activity prompt for Excerpt 6

Prior to the focal segment, Katy and Billy exchange several turns by following the prompt. In order to clearly illustrate what takes place up to the focal segment, I show an abbreviated and simplified transcript in Excerpt 6-1.

**Excerpt 6-1.**

1   Katy: *Donna machi ga sumiyasui desu ka?*
        'What kind of city is easy to live in?'
2   Billy: *Ookii no ga sumiyasui desu.*
        'Big ones are easy to live in.'
3   Katy: *Dooshite desu ka?*
        'Why is that?'

| | | |
|---|---|---|
| 4 | Billy: | *Ookii machi de takusan mono ga arimasu.* |
| | | 'There are many things in big cities.' |
| 5 | Katy: | *Marion wa ookii desu ka?* |
| | | 'Is Marion big?' |
| 6 | Billy: | *Marion wa chotto ookii desu. demo daijoobu desu.* |
| | | 'Marion is a little big. But, it's all right.' |
| 7 | Katy: | *Un.* |
| | | 'Yeah' |

Katy and Billy successfully complete the required sequence by line 4, and engage in an extra question-answer sequence in lines 5 and 6. Katy's provision of *un* 'yeah', a type of sequence-closing third (Schegloff, 2007), at the end of this segment may signal a move to the next round of the prescribed sequence. Interestingly, however, Billy chooses to further elaborate on the topic. The focal segment, Excerpt 6-2, shows a detailed transcript of the exchange that takes place after Excerpt 6-1.

**Excerpt 6-2.** Searching for an answer to 'Why is that?'

```
8   Billy:  jaa,  (1.0)  ookisugiru: (1.0)  ookisugiru:  machi
            so           too  big           too  big     town
9           ga: (0.5) uh (1.0) °sukinai° (0.3) sukinai desu.
            S         H        like-NG         like-NG CP
            So, I, uh, not like, not like cities that are
            too big, too big.

10          (0.4)

11  Katy:   huhm

12  Billy:  [suki janai.
             like CP-NG
            I don't like them

13  Katy:   [dooshite desu ka?
             why       CP   Q
            Why is that?

14          (4.0)
              ↳((Billy looks to the middle-distance))

15  Billy:  jaa, (.) ooki:sugi: sugi- (0.3) ookisugi:
            so       too  big   too          too big
16          (0.3) sugiru: machi wa: (0.3) ga: sukina(h)i(h)
                  too     town  TP        S   like-NG
```

```
17            >I don't kno(h)w<=
              So, I don't like cities that are too-,
              too big, too big. I don't know.

18  Katy:     =huhuhuhuh

19  Billy:    I just don't like'em, (0.3) towns °that° are
20            too big

21  Katy:     ((nods))
```

In lines 8 and 9, Billy makes another utterance, *ooki sugiru: (1.0) ooki sugiru: machi ga: (0.5) uh (1.0) °sukinai° (0.3) sukinai desu.* 'I don't like cities that are too big.' It seems that he is trying to clarify what he said previously. That is, he likes big cities, but he also likes Marion,[13] which he considers to be "a little" big (Excerpt 6-1, line 6). By producing this additional utterance, he clarifies that he likes moderately big cities, but not huge cities. This utterance—backward-looking in the sense that it is produced as a clarification of a prior utterance—can potentially mark the end of the prior sequence. Yet, Katy opts to further ask *dooshite desu ka?* 'why is that?'—the same question format she used in a prior turn (Excerpt 6-1, line 3). Mori (2005) discusses the pedagogical advantage of asking *dooshite* in the third-turn position over other *wh*-question words, such as *nani* 'what,' *itsu* 'when,' and *doko* 'where,' because "respondents need to supply not only simple words or phrases, but also original content providing reasons or explanations and the appropriate structures to express them" (p. 258). Billy's subsequent conduct points precisely to this nature of *dooshite* used in the third-turn position. After Katy has asked the question, a long silence (4.0 seconds) ensues. Now the second pair part is due, and Billy is undertaking a search for his answer (Figure 14).

**Figure 14.** Gaze during a 4.0-second gap of silence (line 14)

Billy's next utterance (lines 15–16) after the long silence repeats his previous one.[14] This redoing indicates that his search has somewhat failed, because he could not come up with a timely reason for not liking towns that are too big. The additional >*I don't kno(h)w*< in English also demonstrates his epistemic state (a lack-of-knowledge claim) and indicates that he has aborted his search for what-to-say in the end. Of particular note here is the insertion of laughter particles. These laughter particles are indicative of the production difficulty that he is facing (Ohta, 2008). Katy does not offer help to Billy or pursue the topic by rephrasing the question differently (yes-no questions or other *wh*-questions). Instead, she merely reciprocates the laughter (line 18) and lets it pass, signaling that this question-answer round may have ended. Billy then goes on to produce another utterance in English, *I just don't like'em, (0.3) towns °that° are too big*, in lines 19 and 20. Although this turn may look like an English translation of the previous utterance, with the addition of *just*, it is hearable as an account for not being able to provide a reason. It is similar to the sense of "just because" used as an account in place of a more substantial explanation.

Note that Billy's search is occasioned after the required pair work sequence has ended. In contrast to the previous cases (e.g., Excerpts 4 and 5), in which searches were carried out in order to fill in the blank slots in the activity prompts, his answer constitutes an additional turn, which is seemingly related to his abandonment of the search for what-to-say and Katy's acceptance of it with the laughter. Katy's orientation here is contrastive to Bob's and Carl's in Excerpts 4 and 5. Moreover, Billy resorts to English in the end in order to say what he wants to say. Many applied linguists have previously pointed out the fundamental dilemma regarding the feasibility of the classroom for promoting real-life interactions (e.g., Bannink, 2002; Mori, 2002). In a foreign language context, where students share their L1, spontaneous interactions tend to occur mostly in the L1 (Hancock, 1997). Billy's codeswitch to English may indicate his treatment of this part in such a way. In sum, the students' orientation to the collaborative construction of ideas is more strongly shown in the fulfillment of blank slots, while such an orientation is less obvious in other parts of pair work.

## Discussion

As one of the first attempts to examine closely the search for what-to-say, this chapter has discussed several characteristics. The presence of a search for what-to-say at the individual's level is marked largely by middle-distance gazing and persistent speech perturbations from the onset of a turn. Searches for what-to-say often appear vague, and the identification of the actual item being searched for is not straightforward. Nonetheless, when a word search or a conjugation search is occasioned in the midst of a search for what-to-say, it is clearly marked by upward gazing or with a thinking face.

In addition, I have closely analyzed how the students use multimodal resources to accomplish searches as collaborative activities. For example, the speaker's deployment of non-verbal conduct—gaze, smile, and laughter—signals the ongoing search activity to the co-participants, who in turn can use these cues to provide appropriate help as needed. When a solitary search fails, the speaker uses gaze shifts to the present co-participant (Excerpt 4). Sometimes, verbal resources, such as *shirimasen* 'I don't know,' can trigger a collaborative search (Excerpt 4). While Mori and Hasegawa (2009) reported on cases in which students (of the same beginning level) skillfully used the textbook to organize their word search activities, interestingly, I found no instance in my dataset in which the students refer to the textbook to complete their search for what-to-say. As seen by the presence of smiles and laughter (Excerpts 4 and 5), these students often orient to funny and enjoyable utterances (see also Bushnell, 2008, p. 64 on "task-as-play" in JFL pair work). This orientation may have contributed to the tendency not to consult the textbook, which only supplies official and unoriginal ideas. Importantly, when the co-participants provide help for the speaker searching for an idea (e.g., Bob in Excerpt 4; Carl and Bob in Excerpt 5), they design their candidate ideas so that they are relevant to the speaker and the context. Being able to accomplish successful recipient-design is an essential element of IC, and the current cases of searches for what-to-say expose this integral interactional process in a noticeable way. In recipient-designing their candidate ideas, these students evoke their shared experiences and knowledge of each other. To put it differently, the students "relied upon mutually assumed knowledge of one another's biography" (Maynard & Zimmerman, 1984, p. 303). If successful collaboration for a search for what-to-say may benefit from familiarity with each other, it is probably rare to observe joint search activities between strangers or people who do not have much in common. As Greer notes in this volume, the emergent familiarity of participants alters the process of interaction in a noticeable way. In this respect, the classroom setting, where people develop familiarity with one another through constant opportunities for interaction, may contribute to the success of joint searches.

I have also discussed how these search sequences reflexively index the pedagogical norms mediated by activity prompts. The students orient to the collaborative production of ideas in order to complete the prescribed sequence of turns in the prompts. Ostensibly, the pair work activities examined in this study look highly structured, with grammar items as exclusive learning objects. The students, however, orient not only to linguistic form, but also to finding something to say that fits the prescribed turn sequence. In discussing the nature of the language classroom, Schegloff (in Wong & Olsher, 2000) rightly stated that students are assigned with "an interactionally impossible task, which is to make talk when they have nothing to talk to one another about..." (p. 121). This statement is relevant to the pair work interactions examined in this chapter, because the students were at a loss with the provided topics (e.g., 'What would you do if you were a woman?'). The students were asked to provide answers to questions that they might never have thought about, and their frequent engagement in searches for what-to-say points to this tendency. In real world communication, it is probably uncommon to see a speaker and a recipient working collaboratively to come up with an idea for the answer in a question-answer sequence (see Pomerantz, 1988, endnote 8 for a discussion on "candidate answers"). Indeed, as seen in Excerpt 6-2, novice L2 speakers might frequently resort to a strategy of "avoidance" and simply get by with *I don't know*. It should be pointed out, however, that avoidance/reduction strategies are known to be less conducive to the development of communicative resources (e.g., Færch & Kasper, 1980). In this regard, even though form-oriented exercises, like the ones I have examined in this chapter, look unrealistic and unnatural, they seem to provide, at least, important practice opportunities for students to broaden their repertoires of produce-able ideas vis-à-vis available linguistic resources.

As a non-longitudinal study, this chapter does not delve into the issues of development. Nonetheless, the present analysis offers further insight for the design of instructional activities that take into account students' IC. Pekarek Doehler and Pochon-Berger (2015) state that one indication of L2 learners' development of IC is the diversification of techniques or interactional methods. Therefore, if students are to be encouraged to conduct various types of searches and broaden their repertoires of interactional resources, then classroom activities should also be sensitive to and reflect such variations. However, most cases of searching for what-to-say examined in this chapter (except for Excerpt 2), and in the entire dataset, are occasioned in the answer slot. The overwhelming focus of these activities is on responses to given questions (question-answer practice). What is missing here is a focus on the sequence-onset turn (first pair part), such as questions. The practice of initiating a sequence is especially important in light of topic management (Button & Casey, 1984, 1985; Maynard & Zimmerman, 1984; Schegloff, 1990, 2007; Schegloff & Sacks, 1973; Svennevig, 1999). In this volume, for example, Mori and Matsunaga present cases in which the focal learner, Michael, manages to successfully provide a new topic and carry on the topical talk at a dinner table conversation. Before proffering a new topic, he conducts a search in an attempt to come up with what-to-say. As activity prompts such as those examined in the present study seem to have a significant impact on students' conduct, more diversified foci in these activities may enable beginning students to practice and potentially develop their IC. This aspect of activity design should be emphasized more in discussions of pedagogical design.

## Acknowledgments
I am deeply grateful to the volume editors and the anonymous reviewers for their valuable suggestions and helpful insights on the earlier versions of my manuscript.

## Notes
1. "Frequently" in this chapter does not mean rigorous quantification of cases. It is based on "informal quantification," as suggested by Schegloff (1993).
2. Elsewhere (Hasegawa, 2010), I called this type of search sequence "content search". With much consideration of what it is and what it can entail, as well as the feedback I received from the reviewers and editors, I opt to instead use "search for what-to-say.".
3. Although it was first noted in Hasegawa (2010), this study aims to further investigate this type of search activity.
4. The 160 cases were all the pair and small group work activities recorded in the focal classes.
5. Participants were solicited at the beginning of the semester, and the selection of focal participants (52 in total) at each video-recording was contingent upon who was present on each day.
6. Arrows in excerpts indicate the onset of embodied action, which is noted in double parentheses.
7. Note this is also a self-repair of the particle *ni* 'to' to *de* 'at.'
8. Pomerantz (1988) discusses cases of candidate answers offered by a questioner. The candidate answers in Pomerantz's study were incorporated in and produced as questions, which is different from my cases.
9. Or else, as one of the editors pointed out, the assigned question itself (i.e., what would you do if you were a woman?) frames this exchange as potentially laughable talk.
10. Bob, Carl, and Rick worked together for this class period because Bob's usual partner was absent.
11. In the case Ohta (2008) documents, "laughter works to complete his troubled turn and show that the speaker has given up" (p. 227). The smile in the present data is also indicative of a similar phenomenon.
12. During other pair work episodes in the same class, Carl has mentioned *Star Wars*, indicating his (and possibly shared) interest in space.
13. Marion is the city where the present university is located.
14. As one of the editors pointed out, Billy may have started to formulate the reason up until *wa*, but aborted the search midway and in the end produced the same utterance.

# References

Bannink, A. (2002). Negotiating the paradoxes of spontaneous talk in advanced L2 classes. In C. Kramsch (Ed.), *Language acquisition and language socialization* (pp. 266–288). New York, NY: Continuum.

Banno, E., Ohno, Y., Sakane, Y., Shinagawa, C., & Tokashiki, K. (1999). *Genki II: An integrated course in elementary Japanese*. Tokyo: The Japan Times.

Brouwer, C. (2003). Word searches in NNS–NS interaction: Opportunities for language learning? *The Modern Language Journal, 87*, 534–545.

Brouwer, C. (2004). Doing pronunciation: A specific type of repair sequence. In R. Gardner & J. Wagner (Eds.), *Second language conversations* (pp. 93–113). New York, NY: Continuum.

Bushnell, C. (2008). 'Lego my keego!': An analysis of language play in a beginning Japanese as a foreign language classroom. *Applied Linguistics, 30*, 49–69.

Button, G., & Casey, N. (1984). Generating topic: The use of topic initial elicitors. In J. Atkinson & J. Heritage (Eds.), *Structures of social action: Studies in conversation analysis* (pp. 167–190). New York, NY: Cambridge University Press.

Button, G., & Casey, N. (1985). Topic nomination and topic pursuit. *Human Studies, 8*, 3–55.

Carroll, D. (2005). Vowel-marking as an interactional resource in Japanese novice ESL conversation. In K. Richards & P. Seedhouse (Eds.), *Applying conversation analysis* (pp. 214–234). London: Palgrave-MacMillan.

Ellis, R. (2003). *Task-based language learning and teaching*. New York, NY: Oxford University Press.

Ellis, R. & Shintani, N. (2014). *Exploring language pedagogy through second language acquisition research*. New York, NY: Routledge.

Færch, C., & Kasper, G. (1980). Processes and strategies in foreign language learning and communication. *Interlanguage Studies Bulletin, 4*, 47–118.

Fujita, N. (1997). Situation-driven or structure-driven?: Teaching Japanese at the college level in the United States. In H. M. Cook, K. Hijirida, & M. Tahara (Eds.), *New trends and issues in teaching Japanese language and culture* (pp. 119–132). Honolulu, HI: University of Hawai'i, Second Language Teaching and Curriculum Center.

Funayama, I. (2002). Word searches in cross-linguistic settings: Teaching-learning collaboration between native and non-native speakers. *Crossroads of Language, Interaction, and Culture, 4*, 33–57.

Glenn, P. (2003). *Laughter in interaction*. Cambridge, MA: Cambridge University Press.

Goodwin, C. (1980). Restarts, pauses, and the achievement of mutual gaze at turn-beginning. *Sociological Inquiry, 50*, 272–302.

Goodwin, C. (1987). Forgetfulness as an interactive resource. *Social Psychology Quarterly, 50*(2), 115–131.

Greer, T. (2013). Word search sequences in bilingual interaction: Code switching and embodied orientation toward shifting participant constellations. *Journal of Pragmatics, 57*, 100–117.

Hadley, O. A. (2001). *Teaching language in context* (3rd ed.). Boston, MA: Heinle & Heinle.

Hall, J. K., Hellermann, J., & Pekarek Doehler, S. (Eds.). (2011). *L2 interactional competence and development.* Bristol, UK: Multilingual Matters.

Hancock, M. (1997). Behind classroom code switching: Layering and language choice in L2 learner interaction. *TESOL Quarterly, 31*(2), 217–235.

Hasegawa, A. (2010). *Learner construction of task-in-process: A conversation-analytic study of semiscripted pair work interaction.* (Doctoral dissertation). Available from ProQuest Dissertations and Theses database. (UMI No. 3424233)

Heritage, J. (1998). Oh-prefaced responses to inquiry. *Language in Society, 27,* 291–334.

Hosoda, Y. (2006). Repair and relevance of differential language expertise in second language conversations. *Applied Linguistics, 27*(1), 25–50.

Kurhila, S. (2006). *Second language interaction.* Amsterdam: John Benjamins.

Kasper, G. (2009). Locating cognition in second language interaction and learning: Inside the skull or in public view? *International Review of Applied Linguistics in Language Teaching, 47,* 11–36.

Lee, Y. (2006). Towards respecification of communicative competence: Condition of L2 instruction or its objective? *Applied Linguistics, 27*(3), 349–376.

Lerner, G. H. (1996). On the "semi-permeable" character of grammatical units in conversation: Conditional entry into the turn space of another speaker. In E. Ochs, E. A. Schegloff & S. A. Thompson. (Eds.), *Interaction and grammar* (pp. 238–276). Cambridge: Cambridge University Press.

Maynard, D. (2003). *Bad news, good news: Conversational order in everyday talk and clinical settings.* Chicago, IL: University of Chicago Press.

Maynard, D. W., & Zimmerman, D. H. (1984). Topical talk, ritual, and the social organization of relationships. *Social Psychology Quarterly, 47*(4), 301–316.

Moerman, M. (1988). *Talking culture: Ethnography and conversation analysis.* Philadelphia, PA: University of Pennsylvania.

Mori, J. (2002). Task design, plan, and development of talk-in-interaction: An analysis of a small group activity in a Japanese language classroom. *Applied Linguistics, 23*(3), 323–347.

Mori, J. (2005). Why not why? The teaching of grammar, discourse, sociolinguistic, and cross-cultural perspectives. *Japanese Language and Literature, 39*(2), 255–289.

Mori, J., & Hasegawa, A. (2009). Doing being a foreign language learner in a classroom: Embodiment of cognitive states as social events. *International Review of Applied Linguistics in Language Teaching, 47,* 65–94.

Ohta, A. S. (2001). *Second language acquisition processes in the classroom: Learning Japanese.* Mahwah, NJ: Lawrence Erlbaum.

Ohta, A. S. (2008). Laughter and second language acquisition: A study of Japanese foreign language classes. In J. Mori & A. S. Ohta (Eds.), *Japanese applied linguistics: Discourse and social perspectives* (pp. 213–242). New York, NY: Continuum.

Park, I. (2007). Co-construction of word search activities in native and non-native speaker interaction. *Teachers College, Columbia University, Working Papers in TESOL & Applied Linguistics, 7*(2), 1–23.

Pekarek Doehler, S., & Pochon-Berger, E. (2015). The development of L2 interactional competence: Evidence from turn-taking organization, sequence organization, repair organization and preference organization. In T. Cadierno & S. Eskildsen (Eds.), *Usage-based perspectives on second language learning* (pp. 233–268). Berlin: Mouton De Gruyter.

Prior, M. T. (2015). *Emotion and discourse in L2 narrative research*. Bristol, UK: Multilingual Matters.

Pomerantz, A. (1984). Agreeing and disagreeing with assessments: Some features of preferred/dispreferred turn shapes. In J. M. Atkinson & J. Heritage. (Eds.), *Structures of social action: Studies in conversation analysis* (pp. 57–101). Cambridge: Cambridge University Press.

Pomerantz, A. (1988). Offering a candidate answer: An information seeking strategy. *Communication Monographs, 55*, 360–373.

Richards, J. C., & Rodgers, T. S. (2001). *Approaches and methods in language teaching* (2nd ed.). New York, NY: Cambridge University Press.

Sacks, H., Schegloff, E., & Jefferson, G. (1974). A simplest systematics for the organization of turn-taking in conversation. *Language, 50*, 696–735.

Sasuga, M., & Greer, T. (2014). Forward-oriented medium repair in Japanese/English bilingual interaction. *Japan Journal of Multilingualism and Multiculturalism, 20*, 1–16.

Schegloff, E. A. (1979). The relevance of repair to syntax-for-conversation. In T. Givón. (Ed.), *Syntax and semantics 12: Discourse and syntax* (pp. 261–286). New York, NY: Academic Press.

Schegloff, E. A. (1990). On the organization of sequences as a source of "coherence" in talk-in-interaction. In B. Dorval (Ed.), *Conversational organization and its development* (pp. 51–77). Norwood, NJ: Ablex.

Schegloff, E. A. (1993). Reflections on quantification in the study of conversation. *Research on Language and Social Interaction, 26*, 99–128.

Schegloff, E. A. (2000). Overlapping talk and the organization of turn-taking for conversation. *Language in Society, 29*(1), 1–63.

Schegloff, E. A. (2007). *Sequence organization in interaction: A primer in conversation analysis*. Cambridge: Cambridge University Press.

Schegloff, E. A., & Sacks, H. (1973). Opening up closing. *Semiotica, 8*(4), 289–327.

Schegloff, E. A., Jefferson, G., & Sacks, H. (1977). The preference for self-correction in the organization of repair in conversation. *Language, 53*, 361–382.

Svennevig, J. (1999). *Getting acquainted in conversation. A study of initial interactions*. Amsterdam: John Benjamins.

Wong, J., & Olsher, D. (2000). Reflections on conversation analysis and nonnative speaker talk: An interview with Emanuel A. Schegloff. *Issues in Applied Linguistics, 11*, 111–128.

Young, R. F. (1999). Sociolinguistic approaches to SLA. *Annual Review of Applied Linguistics, 19*, 105–132.

Young, R. F. (2011). Interactional competence in language learning, teaching, and testing. In E. Hinkel (Ed.), *Handbook of research in second language teaching and learning* (Vol. 2, pp. 426–443). London: Routledge.

Young, R. F. (2013). Learning to talk the talk and walk the walk: Interactional competence in academic spoken English. *Ibérica, 25*, 15–38.

# 8 Assessing Interactional Competence: Storytelling in the Japanese Oral Proficiency Interview

Waka Tominaga
*Kapiʻolani Community College*

## Introduction

The continued prominence of the *ACTFL Proficiency Guidelines* (hereafter, the Guidelines) and the *ACTFL Oral Proficiency Interview* (hereafter, the OPI) is evidenced by their prevalent use in the field of foreign language teaching and assessment in the United States today. The Guidelines are widely used for curriculum development and classroom instruction in foreign language programs in universities and secondary schools, and the OPI, in which a candidate's performance is rated according to the proficiency levels described in the Guidelines, is used for various assessment purposes in academic and professional contexts, including program admission, academic placement, exit requirements, program evaluation, hiring, promotion, and teacher certification (ACTFL, 2012a; Chambless, 2012; Houston, 2005; Kagan & Friedman, 2003; Kondo-Brown, 2012; Rifkin, 2003). As the Guidelines and the OPI have a great influence on how foreign languages are taught, learned, and evaluated, it is extremely important to ensure their validity. Among the many aspects of competence assessed in the OPI, the present study focuses on the assessment of storytelling since the ability to tell a story is an important aspect of interactional competence (IC).

The OPI currently tests for the four major levels of Novice, Intermediate, Advanced, and Superior. The first three levels are further divided into Low, Mid, and High sublevels (e.g., Intermediate-Low, Intermediate-Mid, Intermediate-High). The rating criteria of the OPI are organized into four categories: global tasks and functions, context/content, accuracy, and text type. The text type criterion, which refers to "the type of oral text or discourse the speaker is capable of producing" (ACTFL, 2012a, p. 6), is the focus of interest for this study. The text types of the four major levels are described as follows: "individual words and phrases" (Novice), "discrete sentences" (Intermediate), "paragraphs" (Advanced), and "extended discourse" (Superior) (ACTFL, 2012a, p. 6).

It has long been noted that the Guidelines and the OPI, despite their widespread use, were not developed based on adequate theory or empirical research on spoken interaction (Bachman, 1988; Bachman & Savignon, 1986; Lantolf & Frawley, 1988; Raffaldini, 1988; Savignon, 1985). The use of units of analysis for writing (e.g., sentences, paragraphs) to describe the levels of oral proficiency seems particularly problematic. For instance, the use of the term "paragraph" in the OPI rating criteria gives the impression that the candidates are expected to produce discourse that resembles a written text of paragraph length, which would be unnatural if produced in spontaneous spoken interaction. Barnwell (1993) criticizes the OPI for this reason, stating that "exhibition of what is called 'paragraph length' discourse is required at Advanced level. Yet people do not speak in paragraphs" (p. 206). Previous studies have shown how spoken interaction is organized differently than written language, for instance, in the following ways: the density of information packing, syntactic complexity, vocabulary, functions, and the presence of fillers, incomplete utterances, pauses, and repetitions (Brown & Yule, 1983a, 1983b); turn construction and the sequential organization of turns (Sacks, Schegloff, & Jefferson, 1974; Schegloff, 2007; Schegloff & Sacks, 1973); the speaker's monitoring of the recipient's participation (Goodwin, 1980, 1984); the use of discourse markers (Schiffrin, 1987); and the importance of prosody in the accomplishment of coherence (Gumperz, Kaltman, & O'Connor, 1984).

In the past few decades, a number of conversation analytic and discourse analytic studies have been conducted on OPIs. Many of these studies examined the interviewer–candidate interaction and interviewer behavior in *non*-ACTFL OPIs (e.g., Brown, 2003; Johnson, 2001; Kasper, 2006b, 2013; Kasper & Ross, 2003, 2007; Lazaraton, 2002; Okada, 2010; Okada & Greer, 2013; Ross, 2007; Ross & Berwick, 1992; Seedhouse, 2013; Young & He, 1998; Young & Milanovic, 1992). Some studies have also investigated the relationship between candidates' performances and the resulting ratings on ACTFL and non-ACTFL OPIs (Lazaraton, 2002; Lee, Park, & Sohn, 2011; Liskin-Gasparro, 1996a, 1996b; Ross & O'Connell, 2013; Tominaga, 2013; Watanabe, 2003). Yet, there is little empirical evidence to support or refute the text type criterion of the ACTFL OPI. In an attempt to fill this gap, this study will investigate the appropriateness of this criterion by examining how candidates produce stories in extended turns in the Japanese OPI.[1]

## Approach to interactional competence

Since it is claimed that "the OPI assesses language proficiency in terms of a speaker's ability to use the language effectively and appropriately in real-life situations" (ACTFL, 2012a, p. 4), the rating criteria must include adequate descriptions of candidates' interactional ability in the target language. In relation to the text type criterion, it is important to examine how candidates produce short utterances (e.g., answers to simple background questions) and extended turns (e.g., storytelling) in the interaction, and to what extent their performance matches the level characterizations in the Guidelines. For this purpose, I adopt the notion of IC (Hall & Pekarek Doehler, 2011; He & Young, 1998; Kasper, 2006a), which I consider as the ability to effectively participate in an interaction by producing and understanding social actions in ways appropriate to the particular context. IC is locally co-constructed by all participants and cannot be attributed to individuals (He & Young, 1998). In producing and understanding actions, participants draw on relevant resources and put them together in contextually appropriate ways. These resources, including linguistic and sociolinguistic knowledge, non-vocal semiotic resources, cultural practices, and understandings of interactional organizations, are shared, partly created, maintained, and modified in the interaction. While McNamara (2000) notes the challenge of "isolating the contribution of a single individual (the candidate) in a joint communicative activity" (p. 84), I suggest that raters can make *inferences* about a candidate's individual competence based on evidence found in the co-constructed performance in the OPI. Kasper and Ross (2013) also suggest that "the portability of resources between practices may enable valid inferences from test performance to performance in the target domain if comparative analysis of both practices identifies essential commonalities" (p. 14).

Since conversation analysis (CA) has been shown to be an optimal approach to investigate IC, I draw on CA as an analytical framework. CA studies on second language (L2) talk have documented various aspects of L2 speakers' IC (e.g., Carroll, 2004; Hall, Hellermann, & Pekarek Doehler, 2011; Hauser, 2009; Hellermann, 2008; Ishida, 2006, 2009, 2011; Kim, 2009; Lee, 2006; Ohta, 2001; Young & Miller, 2004). Kasper (2006a) notes that IC serves as both *resource* and *object* in L2 learning. As adult L2 learners are already interactionally competent in their first language, their fully developed understanding of interactional organization helps them participate in L2 interaction. Furthermore, Lee (2006) argues that students' current IC ("communicative competence" in Lee's terms) to participate in classroom activities serves as a resource for L2 teaching and learning. Similarly, in the OPI, while a candidate's IC can be seen as the object of measurement, it also serves as a resource for the OPI interaction to take place. A candidate's ability to attend to the moment-by-moment development of the interaction, analyze the sequential environment, and produce an appropriate next action enables the interviewer and the candidate to jointly construct the activity of the OPI (Okada, 2010; Tominaga, 2013; van Compernolle, 2011).

CA has identified various aspects of interactional organizations that ordinary speakers orient to in the production and interpretation of utterances in an interaction, such as adjacency pairs (Schegloff & Sacks, 1973), turn-taking (Sacks et al., 1974), repair (Schegloff, Jefferson, & Sacks, 1977), and preference organization (Pomerantz, 1984). The literature on turn-taking is particularly relevant to the purpose of this study because whether an OPI candidate's response turn will be a short utterance or an extended turn largely depends on how the candidate projects (and the interviewer understands) the continuation and completion of a turn-in-progress. In their seminal paper, Sacks et al. (1974) proposed that turns are built out of *turn-constructional units* (TCUs), which include words, phrases, clauses, and sentences, and that speaker change may occur at a *transition-relevance place* (TRP), i.e., the possible completion point of a TCU. Ford and Thompson (1996) found that turn completion is not only shaped by syntax, but is also formed by pragmatics and intonation. They compared the three potential indicators of turn completion (i.e., syntax, intonation, and pragmatics) and found that the points where all three completion types coincided, rather than the points where syntactic completion alone occurred, recurrently formed TRPs. Schegloff (1982, 1996, 2007) discusses how extended turns are methodically and interactionally achieved by participants in conversation. He points out that the speaker often uses devices such as discourse markers, story prefaces, and preliminaries to preliminaries (e.g., "can I ask you a question?") in order to project the production of an extended turn. Moreover, at a possible TRP, the speaker may "rush through" the juncture and start another TCU, thereby preventing a potential next speaker from starting a new turn. As noted by Schegloff (1982), however, extended turns are collaborative achievements by all participants, not just the speaker. For instance, the hearer can make contributions to the achievement of extended turns by providing continuers (e.g., "uh huh") and withholding from taking full turns, thus letting the speaker continue.

Storytelling is a type of extended turn that has been extensively discussed in CA literature. Liddicoat (2011) suggests that stories are often initiated by the speaker in ordinary conversation, rather than solicited by the recipient. Jefferson (1978) notes that the speaker introduces a story because it is relevant to the current talk and appropriate for the recipient. In order to initiate a story, the speaker must secure the interactional space for an extended turn, temporarily suspending regular turn-taking. The speaker may indicate that a story is forthcoming by using devices such as a story-preface question-answer sequence, disjunctive markers, embedded repetition, and temporal markers. Jefferson further shows that storytelling is sequentially implicative, creating a context for subsequent interaction. For instance, the recipient often produces an assessment of the story at its completion point, and may introduce a second story that is deemed relevant. The ability to use these resources is one of the aspects of IC, and I will examine how they are used by the OPI participants in the current study.

## The study

Among the many previous studies on OPIs, the one most relevant to the present research is Watanabe's (2003) non-CA study, which investigated the text-type criterion of the ACTFL OPI in relation to cohesion and coherence strategies. By examining 15 Japanese OPIs evaluated at proficiency levels ranging from Intermediate-High to Superior, Watanabe gauged the candidates' overall use of linguistic resources that contributed to the achievement of extended discourse. She found that the use of embedded predicates expanded as the proficiency level went up, as relatively proficient speakers incorporated more embedded clauses per response unit. She also observed that speakers at higher proficiency levels employed more post-predicate elements (e.g., connective particles, sentence-final particles) while speakers at lower proficiency levels tended to produce the bare form of predicates. While the present study has a similar focus to Watanabe's, it is different in the following ways: I specifically focus on the candidates' storytelling in the OPI, I use CA as an analytical approach, and I examine the performance of candidates whose proficiency levels were lower than those of the participants in Watanabe's study. In this way, the present study will complement Watanabe's findings.

As mentioned earlier, according to the text type rating criterion of the ACTFL OPI, Intermediate speakers typically respond with short utterances while Advanced speakers are capable of producing extended turns, which involve the production of multiple utterances within a turn and the use of connectors and discourse organization. This study closely examines the candidates' storytelling in the OPI, and investigates how the candidates achieve an extended turn and employ connectors[2], discourse organization, and other interactional resources. I further describe the candidates' IC as observed in the OPI interactions, and discuss implications for the OPI and the Guidelines.

The OPIs analyzed in this study were conducted as part of a larger program assessment project at an American university. In this research program, undergraduate students majoring in modern foreign languages were invited to participate, on a voluntary basis, in the OPI during the semester in which they were graduating. Between Spring 2011 and Spring 2013, a total of 57 students majoring in Japanese participated. With the participants' permission, these Japanese OPIs were audio- and video-recorded. They were conducted face-to-face by the present author,[3] an ACTFL-certified tester, in an office on the university campus, following the standard format of the OPI. Each OPI was initially rated by the author/interviewer, and then audio-recordings were sent to Language Testing International (LTI), the testing agency for the ACTFL OPI, for official ratings and certification. From the pool of 57 Japanese OPI recordings, 15 (three for each of the five levels from Intermediate-Low to Advanced-Mid) were randomly selected and transcribed using CA transcription conventions. In this study, I focus on the narration task performed by two of the Intermediate candidates, George (Intermediate-Low) and Emily (Intermediate-Mid).[4] Short extracts from the Guidelines are given below to describe George's and Emily's proficiency levels (ACTFL, 2012b, pp. 7–8).

**Intermediate-Low**
Intermediate-Low speakers express personal meaning by combining and recombining what they know and what they hear from their interlocutors into short statements and discrete sentences. Their responses are often filled with hesitancy and inaccuracies as they search for appropriate linguistic forms and vocabulary while attempting to give form to the message.

**Intermediate-Mid**
Intermediate-Mid speakers are able to express personal meaning by creating with the language, in part by combining and recombining known elements and conversational input to produce responses typically consisting of sentences and strings of sentences. Their speech may contain pauses, reformulations, and self-corrections as they search for adequate vocabulary and appropriate language forms to express themselves.

The narration task is one of the major Advanced-level tasks in the OPI. An interviewer introduces the task when they estimate a candidate's proficiency level at Intermediate or higher during the interview. In the Japanese OPI, the target story for the narration task can be a personal narrative or the retelling of a novel, movie, or other such text (Makino et al., 2001).

## George's story retelling and personal narrative

In this section, I present both the retelling of a short story and a personal narrative from George's OPI (Intermediate-Low). George produced these two types of stories in his OPI, and his stories illustrate the possible difference in difficulty between these two narration tasks: It appeared he was overwhelmed by the task of retelling a short story, but was able to tell a personal narrative more fully and competently.

**Retelling of a short story**

Excerpts 1.1 and 1.2 show George's retelling of a short story. Prior to Excerpt 1.1, George (G) mentioned that he had read *Chinmoku* "The Silence," a short story by Haruki Murakami, in his Japanese literature class. In lines 1 through 4, the interviewer (IR) asks if he would retell the story.[5]

**Excerpt 1.1** The Silence

```
1   IR: jaa   sono sutoor(hh)ii o,
        then  that story       O
2       chotto oshiete kuremasen ka?
        little tell    give-NG  Q
        So, would you please tell me that story?

3       (0.5)
        ((George shifts his gaze slightly upward))

4   IR: wakaru toko dake de ii   node.
        know   part only PT good because
        Just the part(s) you know would be fine.

5   G:  ano: (1.7) e: (1.8) sutoorii wa, etto (3.3)
        H          H        story    TP  H
        ((leans forward slightly, and then
        leans back and gazes upward))
6       e: (1.2) neru- a: (2.4) neruta, no, ano:
        H            H          Neruta  LK  H
        ((straightens up))      ((gazes down))
7       (3.1) a: hheh (1.7) hheh (.) hhuh: a: (1.2)
              H                                 H
              ((puts his right hand on his chin))
        Uh um the story is, uh Neru- um Neruta's um uh

8   IR: °a hai hai.°
        Oh, uh huh

9       (1.3)

10  G:  b(hhh)o- hheh bokushing(hh)u hheh hheh
                      boxing
        Bo- boxing
```

In Excerpt 1.1, the interviewer's request to describe the story (lines 1–2) is followed by a brief gap of silence. Orienting to this delay of response as a sign of interactional trouble, the interviewer modifies the request by making it potentially easier for George to respond (*wakaru toko dake de ii node* 'just the part(s) you know would be fine,' line 4). After some hesitation, George begins the story retelling by topicalizing the story (*sutoorii wa* 'the story is,' line 5), and then produces a fragmented utterance that contains what appears to be the name of the character (*neruta*, line 6). George exhibits much difficulty in formulating the utterance, evidenced by a number of long pauses and the use of hesitation markers (lines 5–7). His laughter (line 7) also indexes interactional trouble. His intention and effort to continue his turn, however, is evident in his use of hesitation markers and a "thinking" pose (here, putting his hand on his chin). In line 8, the interviewer provides continuers, encouraging him to say more. After a gap of silence, George resumes his turn, uttering *bokushing(hh)u* 'boxing' (line 10). Excerpt 1.2 shows the subsequent part of the interaction.

**Excerpt 1.2** The Silence (cont.)

```
10 G:    b(hhh)o- hheh bokushing(hh)u hheh hheh
                          boxing
         Bo- boxing

11 IR:   bokushingu no hanashi.
         boxing     LK story
         A story about boxing.

12 G:    hai.
         yes
         ((nods))
         Yes.

13 IR:   hai hai.
         Uh huh.

14 G:    ano: (1.7) neruta no, ano: (0.5) ano
         H          Neruta LK  H          H
15       hoka  no hito, etto (.) e (0.6) aoki san?
         other LK person H         H     Aoki AT
         Uh Neruta's, uh um the other person, uh Mr. Aoki?

16 IR:   hai [hai.
         Uh huh.

17 G:        [to ano (0.8) wa, ano (.) bokushingu
              PT H           TP  H             boxing
```

```
18         suru koto (.) ano (0.6) a: shiteimasu.
           do   thing       H            H   do-CONT
           Uh they are um doing, um uh doing um boxing.

19  IR:    [hai hai.
           Uh huh.

20  G:     [soshite, ano (0.7) a: (1.3)
            and      H          H
21         a: ne- (.) neruta wa ano: (1.1)
           H          Neruta TP   H
22         i- (.) itsumo ano: (.) a: ayamashi? (.)
                  always H        H  jealous*
                                        ((gazes at IR))
23         a (0.5) jealous, (.) a:
           H       jealous      H
           And uh um Ne- Neruta is um a- always uh um jealous? Uh jealous uh

24  IR:    hai.
           Uh huh.

25         (0.9)

26  G:     kono hito    no: ano: (1.5) e:: (1.9)
           this person  LK  H           H
27         e: (1.2) seikaku:    toka:
           H        personality etc.
           this person's uh um um personality, for instance

28  IR:    hai [hai.
           Uh huh.

29  G:         [ano: (1.1) e: (1.5) dekiru koto, ano
                H           H       can-do thing H
30         (0.5) sonna kanj(hh)i
                 that  like
           Uh um ability. Uh It's kinda like that.

31  IR:    hu:n aa [soo desu ka:.
           ah   oh  so  CP   Q
           Oh I see.

32  G:             [hai.
           Yes.
```

```
33  IR:  aa:  soo  desu  ka.
         Oh   so   CP    Q
34       omoshiroi    desu  ka?  sutoorii  wa.
         interesting  CP    Q    story     TP
         Oh I see. Is that story interesting?
```

In Excerpt 1.2, after producing a few utterances to describe the story, George somewhat suddenly concludes his retelling by producing a wrap-up utterance *sonna kanj(hh)i* 'it's kinda like that' (line 30). In response, the interviewer provides acknowledgements (lines 31, 33) and then asks a question to elicit an assessment of the story (line 34). By looking at this segment, one might consider that George is not quite able to tell a story in Japanese yet. His utterances are filled with lengthy pauses and hesitation markers, and are often fragmented and difficult to understand. In terms of narrative structure (Labov, 1972), the story only contains an orientation (i.e., the introduction of characters and setting), as George does not describe what happened throughout and at the end of the story. It should be noted, however, that despite the difficulty he exhibited, George still organizes his retelling in a logical manner, by first introducing the characters and their activity (lines 14–18) and then describing their problematic relationship (lines 20–29), which could have developed into a complication in the story. In addition, his retelling has a clear opening (the topicalization of the story) and closing (the wrap-up utterance), and his utterances are linked by the use of the connective *soshite* 'and' (line 20). These features indicate his ability to organize his discourse and connect utterances with a limited range of linguistic resources. At the same time, it is important to note that his competence in retelling the story is interactionally co-constructed with the interviewer, who constantly monitors George's actions and provides support in various ways (e.g., providing continuers and claiming understanding). It is also interesting to see how George tries to achieve a mutual understanding with the interviewer on his potentially problematic utterance in line 22: When he utters the non-target-like Japanese word *ayamashi* (meant as *urayamashii* 'jealous'), he try-marks it with rising intonation, flagging the formulation as marked (Firth, 2009), and gazes at the interviewer to check its recognizability. When the interviewer does not show any sign of recognition, he produces the English equivalent word, *jealous* (line 23), which is accepted by the interviewer. This indicates that George is aware of a potential problem in his utterance, and that he makes an effort to achieve intersubjectivity with the interviewer by using available resources in a context-sensitive manner—first try-marking the Japanese word and then codeswitching to English.

George's IC is also observable in his responses to the interviewer's various interactional moves. For instance, when the interviewer displays her understanding of his prior utterance (line 11), George promptly confirms it verbally and nonverbally (line 12). Also, he properly responds to the interviewer's continuers *hai* (*hai*) 'uh huh,' which appear in various sequential environments and function slightly differently: First, with the continuers in line 13, the interviewer implicitly closes the prior confirmation sequence (lines 11–12) and suggests that George resume his retelling; second, *hai hai* in line 16 is a response to George's preceding try-marked utterance (*aoki san?* 'Mr. Aoki?' line 15), indicating the interviewer's recognition; third, the tokens in line 19 follow a TCU completion, and display the interviewer's analysis that George's current turn would continue beyond the possible TRP; fourth, *hai* in line 24 is placed where George exhibits uncertainty about a Japanese word and codeswitches to English (lines 22–23), as the interviewer urges George to continue his retelling, without offering help with the word search; and finally, the continuers in line 28 are a response to George's prolonged word search and its outcome (lines 26–27), indicating the interviewer's hearing and understanding. In each case, George appropriately responds to the continuers by continuing his turn in the next sequential slot (in overlap in some cases). In addition, George collaboratively closes the request-response sequence with the interviewer, as she goes on to produce acknowledgement tokens in line 31. The acknowledgement turn in the OPI can be considered what Schegloff (2007) calls a *sequence-closing third*, which proposes to close the sequence. While the acknowledgement indicates receipt of information, it also displays the interviewer's interpretation that George's response turn has been completed. George ratifies the interpretation by producing a minimal response (line 32), aligning with the interviewer's interactional move to close the sequence.[6]

**Personal narrative**
Excerpts 2.1 and 2.2 are taken from the same OPI as Excerpts 1.1 and 1.2, and present George's production of a personal narrative. It is evident that, compared to his retelling of the short story, George demonstrates his competence in telling a story more fully in this personal narrative, though his utterances still contain many pauses, hesitation markers, self-corrections, grammatically incomplete utterances, non-target-like word choices, and occasional codeswitches to English. Prior to Excerpt 2.1, George said that he had traveled to Japan to visit his friends a few years ago. The interviewer prompts him to talk more about his trip (lines 1–3), and the topical talk eventually leads to his initiation of a personal narrative on his first experience with *onsen*, Japanese-style hot springs baths, at a traditional Japanese inn.

**Excerpt 2.1** Hot springs baths

```
1  IR: jaa   chotto sono toki no, nihon no ryokoo
       then  little that time  LK  Japan LK travel
2      ni tsuite chotto moo   chotto kuwashiku
       PT about  little more  little in-detail
3      oshiete kuremasen ka?
       tell    give-NG   Q
       So, would you please tell me about your trip to Japan
       in more detail?
```

((Transcript of the following 60 seconds omitted: George describes his trip to Japan, saying that his friends lived in Japan at that time, and that he and his friends visited several cities such as Kobe, Kyoto, and Osaka; he also mentions that they went to Fukui and stayed in a *ryokan*, a Japanese-style inn.))

```
4  IR: dooshite fukui made itta n desu ka?
       why      Fukui to   went N CP   Q
       Why did you go to Fukui?

5  G:  ano: (.) tomodachi wa: ano: (.)
       H        friend    TP  H
6      watashi o ano: (1.3) a: (0.8)
       me      O H          H
7      ryokan no koto  o oshie(.)ta(katta)
       ryokan LK thing O wanted-to-teach
       Uh my friends um wanted to show uh me uh a ryokan.

8  IR: hai hai.
       Uh huh.

9  G:  a: (1.5) a:
       H        H
       ((gazes at IR and nods slightly))

10 IR: jaa  fukui ni ii   ryokan ga atta n desu ka?
       then Fukui in good ryokan S  had  N CP   Q
       So, was there a good ryokan in Fukui?

11 G:  fukui wa: (.) inaka desu kedo, ano:
       Fukui TP      rural CP   but   H
12     ryokan wa (0.6) yokatta  desu.
       ryokan TP       good-PST CP
       Fukui is rural, but uh the ryokan was good.
```

## Storytelling in the Japanese Oral Proficiency Interview

```
13 IR:  aa: soo [desu ka.
        oh  so    CP   Q
        Oh I see.

14 G:           [ano:
                 H

15 IR:  ee ee
        Uh huh.

16      (0.8)

17 G:   etto: (.) sore wa: (.) onsen      no:
         H         that  TP    hot-spring LK
18      (.) a: (0.5) (ha-) (.) haji- (.) a (.)
             H                              H
19      (e?) (.) hajime- (.) e? hajimeta koto?
         H                        H      started  thing
        Uh that was uh my f- fir- um first time? in an onsen.

20 IR:  hai hai.
        Uh huh.

21      (0.7)
        ((George and IR gaze at each other))

22 IR:  [aa
         Oh

23 G:   [ano:
         H

24 IR:  ee ee.
        Uh huh.

25      (0.9)

26 G:   soshite, ano: (1.7) e: i- (1.3) a: (0.8)
        and       H         H           H
27      °what is it° (.) i- (.) ippaku:    e: (1.3)
                                one-night   H
28      °I can't° hheh
        ((shakes his head slightly))
        And, uh um what is it? One, one night, uh I can't.
```

```
29  IR:  hai hai. ip[paku?
         yes yes  one-night
         Uh huh. One night?

30  G:              [a:
                     H

31  IR:  hai.
         Uh huh.

32  G:   ano: (0.7) e (0.5) hajime no: yoru  wa,
          H          H      first   LK night TP
33       ano: (1.1) etto: (0.8) a: (3.3) ano:
          H          H           H        H
34       (0.9) oto- (.) otoko no tomodachi to:
                         male  LK  friend  with

35  IR:  hai [hai
         Uh huh.

36  G:       [etto: (0.5) on- (.) e: onsen ni:
              H                   H  onsen in
37       ano: (.) hairimashita.
          H        enter-POL-PST
```

Uh um on the first night, uh um um I uh went in uh the *onsen* with my ma- male friend.

```
38  IR:  [ee ee.
         Uh huh.

39  G:   [ano: (.) demo: e: (.) tsugi no: (1.1)
          H         but   H     next  LK
40       tsugi no: ano: ichi wa,
         next  LK  H    day* TP

41  IR:  hai.
         Uh huh.

42  G:   etto: (0.6) a: watashi wa: hayaku:
          H           H  I       TP  early
43       (.) okita.
             wake-up-PLN-PST
```

Uh but uh the next, the next uh day, uh um I woke up early.

```
44         a- ano:  soshite
           H       and

45   IR:   ee ee.
           Uh huh.

46   G:    etto: (1.2) a: on- (.) onsen- (.) e?
           H           H       H    onsen      H
47         (.) onsen ni hairu toki, [ano: (0.7)
               onsen in enter time   H

           Uh and uh um when I went into the on- onsen- uh onsen,

48   IR:                                   [hai hai.
                                            Uh huh.

49   G:    ano: (1.1) e (.) a: (.) minna:     ano:
           H          H     H      everyone    H
50         (.) nanimo: (.) inakatta.
               nothing*     be-NG-PST-PLN
           Uh um there was uh nobody.

51   IR:   hai hai.
           Uh huh.
```

Excerpt 2.1 shows how George spontaneously initiates a personal narrative during a series of question–answer sequences in the OPI. After a few exchanges about his trip to Fukui (lines 4–12), the interviewer produces an acknowledgement (line 13), taking a step toward closing the current question–answer sequence. It is at this point that George self-selects to initiate storytelling: Instead of providing a minimal response (e.g., *hai* 'yes') to align with the interviewer's move to close the sequence, he produces in an overlap a hesitation marker *ano:* 'um,' which projects more talk (line 14). In response, the interviewer utters the continuers *ee ee* 'uh huh' (line 15) and yields the floor. The interviewer's yielding the floor here is quite important for George's story initiation as it provides a sequential slot for it to happen. It should be noted that the interviewer does not necessarily always refrain from starting a new turn in response to the candidate's production of hesitation markers. Other interactional resources such as sequential environments, timings, and embodied actions also play a crucial role in determining a relevant next action. For instance, in line 10, the interviewer moves on to a next question after George's short vocalizations. The hesitation markers in line 9 can be seen as somewhat "pushed out" by the interviewer's prior continuers (line 8) when he had nothing to say (as indicated by his gaze direction and nodding). In contrast, the hesitation marker in line 14 is located immediately after the interviewer's acknowledgement (in a partial overlap), i.e., a sequential slot where he was not obligated to talk, which clearly indicates his intention to talk more.

After securing the interactional space for story initiation, George locates the relevance of the upcoming story to the current topical talk (lines 17–19), a common method for introducing a story in ordinary conversation (Jefferson, 1978). George anaphorically refers to his stay at the *ryokan* (traditional Japanese inn) in Fukui, the topic of the talk-so-far, as *sore* 'that,' and states that that was his first time in an *onsen*. By doing so, he effectively brings in the main topic of his story, *onsen*, while identifying how it is related to the topic of the ongoing talk. While the segment illustrates his IC to introduce a story in an orderly manner, it also shows how he overcame lexical problems before launching the story proper. In lines 18 and 19, after repeated self-corrections, he utters *hajimeta koto?* 'what I began?' (probably meant as *hajimete (no koto)* 'the first time'). The try-marked intonation elicits the interviewer's response, *hai hai* 'uh huh', by which she claims understanding and encourages George to continue (line 20). Then, in lines 26 through 28, as George provides background information to his story, he struggles again to find a word, codeswitches to English to produce self-directed speech (°what is it°), utters the Japanese expression *ippaku* 'one night,' and codeswitches to English again to claim his inability (°I can't°). In response, the interviewer provides continuers *hai hai* 'uh huh' and displays her hearing (*ippaku?* 'one night?,' line 29). In this interaction, the interviewer uses both *hai hai* and *ee ee* as continuers, but she only uses *hai hai* to respond to George's try-marked utterances and codeswitches. That is, when lexical problems arise, the interviewer employs *hai hai* (rather than *ee ee*) as a device to let George move the talk forward.

In line 32, George starts describing a series of events in chronological order. As he does so, he explicitly indicates the time of the events using adverbial phrases (e.g., *hajime no: yoru wa* 'on the first night,' line 32; *tsugi no: ano: ichi[7] wa* 'next day,' line 40) and a relative clause, the dependent noun *toki* 'at the time when' (Makino & Tsutsui, 1986) (*onsen ni hairu toki* 'when I went into the *onsen*,' line 47). In addition, his utterances are linked to each other by connectives, which are used as discourse markers: *demo* 'but' in line 39 indicates a contrastive transition between the events, and *soshite* 'and' in line 44 shows the continuation of the storyline. These linguistic features help George to produce coherent discourse rather than a series of isolated utterances. On the other hand, most of his utterances are relatively short, as he does not employ clause-final connective expressions to combine clauses (e.g., the *te*-form of the predicate, connective particles). He typically completes clauses with the bare final-form of the predicate, marked with a falling intonation (e.g., *hairimashita* 'went in,' line 37; *okita* 'woke up,' line 43; *inakatta* 'there was not,' line 50). While these utterances do not project turn-continuation in terms of grammar or intonation, they do not cause problems in turn-taking in this segment: As George's story is building toward the climax, the semantic content of the utterances projects more talk, and the interviewer keeps producing continuers at the end of TCUs (as well as at phrasal boundaries). Excerpt 2.2 presents the subsequent part of George's personal narrative.

**Excerpt 2.2** Hot springs baths (cont.)

```
51  IR:  hai hai.
         Uh huh.

52  G:   etto (0.7)  soshite  ano:  (0.9)  e
         H           and      H            H
53       modoru toki,  [ano (1.0)  e: (1.3)
         return time    H          H
         Uh and uh on my return, uh um

54  IR:                [hai.
                       Uh huh.

55  G:   °how do I say like° changing room?

56  IR:  hai hai. [(  )
         Uh huh.

57  G:            [ni iku to:
                   to go when
         when I went to (the changing room),

58  IR:  [ee.
         Uh huh.

59  G:   [ano:  (0.9)  josei no  tomodachi  ga  ita.
          H            female LK friend     S   be-PST-PLN
         Uh my female friend was there.

60  IR:  aa soo! hhuh
         oh so
         Oh I see!

61  G:   ano: [(.) t(hh)omodachi kara ano:  (.)
         H         friend        from H
         Uh according to my friend, uh

62  IR:       [hhuh hhuh hhuh hhuh

63  G:   chott(hh)o,
         little
```

```
64  IR:  ee.
         Uh huh.

65  G:   ano: (.) otoko no: (.) e?
         H       male   LK    H
66       otoko no onsen to  onna   no onsen ga,
         male  LK onsen and female LK onsen  S

         Uh the male um the male onsen and female onsen were,

67  IR:  a [hai.
         Uh huh.

68  G:    [ano: chotto (1.0) switch(hh)?
          H     little       switch
              ((crosses his hands a few times))
         Um switched?

69  IR:  aa! soo.
         oh  so
         Oh! I see.

70  G:   un. wakarimasendeshit(hh)a.
         yes understand-NG-PST-POL
71       hheh hheh hheh hheh
         Yeah. I didn't know.

72  IR:  aa s(hh)oo d(hh)esu ka.
         oh so      CP       Q
         Oh I see.

73  G:   omoshirokatta    desu.
         interesting-PST  CP
         It was funny.

74       [hheh hheh hheh hheh hheh hheh hheh

75  IR:  [hhuh hhuh hhuh hhuh
76       aa demo daremo inakute,
         oh but  nobody be-PST-NG-and
77       yokatta  desu ne:.
         good-PST CP   IP
         Oh but it was good that nobody was there.

78  G:   h(hh)ai. hheh hheh hheh
         Yeah.

79  IR:  aa hhuh s(hh)oo desu ka:.
            oh   so      CP   Q
```

```
80        hhuh hhuh .hheh omoshiroi,
                         interesting
81        [omoshiroi  [keeken       deshita ne:..
           interesting experience  CP-PST   IP
          Oh I see. That was a funny experience, wasn't it?

82 G:     [.hh            [hai.
          Yeah.
```

Excerpt 2.2 shows how George's personal narrative was concluded. The climax of the story appears in lines 52 to 59, where George describes an unexpected event. In this utterance, he effectively employs the connective particle *to* 'when/if,' which "marks a condition that brings about an uncontrollable event or state" (Makino & Tsutsui, 1986, p. 480) (*changing room? ni iku to: ano: (0.9) josei no tomodachi ga ita* 'When I went to the changing room, my female friend was there,' lines 55–59). The interviewer's exclamatory response with laughter (line 60) also shows that George successfully constructed the surprise and funniness of this event. Then he explains why this happened,[8] and concludes his story with a sequence-closing assessment (*omoshirokatta desu* 'It was funny,' line 73). In response, the interviewer expresses her stance toward the story. Her reciprocated laughter and reciprocated assessments (*omoshiroi, omoshiroi keeken deshita ne:* 'That was an interesting experience, wasn't it?,' lines 80–81) indicate that George successfully engaged the interviewer in his storytelling and got the gist of the story across.

As in the previous segments, George occasionally codeswitches to English in this excerpt. When using English words, he marks them with a try-marked intonation to check their recognizability and acceptability (°*how do I say like*° *changing room?*, line 55; *switch(hh)?*, line 68). His (observable) word searches prior to the codeswitches and the try-marked intonation indicate that these code-switches are not the product of carelessness, but a deliberate attempt to achieve mutual understanding on the subject matter when he cannot find the Japanese equivalent. As such, the interviewer does not ask for Japanese expressions or circumlocution,[9] but lets the problem pass, responding with recipient tokens. At the same time, she refrains from offering assistance with word searches, which shows her orientation toward her role as a tester. These strategies from both parties work to keep George's storytelling going. For instance, in line 55, when George codeswitches to English in the middle of a TCU, his try-marked intonation (*changing room?*) elicits an interviewer response, in this case, continuers (line 56), which then allow George to continue the (temporarily suspended) TCU in a coherent manner (line 57).

Another notable aspect of this interaction is that George's predominant use of the bare final-form of predicate might have prevented the interviewer from predicting the exact completion point of his storytelling. Since most of George's utterances do not project turn-continuation in terms of grammar or intonation, the interviewer would need to rely on other indicators of turn-continuation and turn-completion, such as the semantic content of utterances, to locate a possible turn-completion point. This was not a problem when George's story was building toward the climax (Excerpt 2.1). Once the story reaches the climax (line 59), however, the interviewer starts providing acknowledgements at the end of TCUs (lines 60, 69, 72) even though George's turn still continues beyond these points. It seems that, after the climax, the semantic content of the utterances no longer clearly projects turn-continuation (since the story could finish at any time), and without clues, the interviewer repeatedly displays her analysis that George's turn was possibly completed at the end of each TCU. The analysis is denied by George each time in the next sequential slot as he continues his turn. The interviewer also first uses the shorter, plain-form version of acknowledgement *aa soo* 'Oh I see' (lines 60, 69), which seems to indicate a tentativeness about her analysis.[10] As George's storytelling progresses toward its completion, she switches to the longer, *masu*-form version *aa soo desu ka* 'Oh I see' (line 72), possibly showing more confidence in closing the sequence. While this interaction illustrates how George and the interviewer managed the continuation and completion of George's turn, it also shows a possible weakness in George's use of linguistic forms.

The two stories George produced in his OPI both show his competence in producing sequentially relevant actions (i.e., story retelling as a second pair part of an adjacency pair; and a personal narrative spontaneously initiated in relation to the ongoing topical talk). In both cases, George achieves an extended turn, organizes his discourse in a logical order, links utterances using a few connective expressions, and effectively responds to the interviewer's various interactional moves. His personal narrative, however, which included orientation, complication, resolution, and evaluation (Labov, 1972), was told more fully than the short story retelling, which contained only an orientation. The retelling task seems to have overwhelmed George, preventing him from fully demonstrating his storytelling abilities. This suggests that interviewers and raters need to be aware of the varying linguistic and cognitive demands that the two types of narration tasks may pose for candidates. The above segments also show two different ways in which stories were produced in the OPI interaction: a direct elicitation through the interviewer's request, and a spontaneous initiation by the candidate. As stories are commonly initiated by the speaker (rather than elicited by the recipient) in ordinary conversation (Jefferson, 1978; Liddicoat, 2011), George's personal narrative can be considered a good indicator of his storytelling competence in conversation. His production of a narrative suggests that stories may be produced in a spontaneous manner in the OPI as the talk expands on a topic familiar to the candidate. Such an indirect way of eliciting stories may be worth further consideration as an interviewer technique that might enable the OPI to more effectively assess a candidate's storytelling skills in real-life situations.

## Emily's story retelling

Excerpts 3.1 and 3.2 are taken from Emily's OPI (Intermediate-Mid) and present her performance in the narration task. She retells the story of *Natsume Yuujinchoo* 'Natsume's Book of Friends,' a Japanese anime series based on the manga by Yuki Midorikawa. Prior to Excerpt 3.1, the interviewer brought up the topic of anime, one of Emily's hobbies mentioned earlier in the interview. In response to the interviewer's prompt, Emily (E) said that she recently had watched *Natsume Yuujinchoo*. After a few exchanges about the anime, the interviewer asks Emily to retell the story (lines 1–2). (In this excerpt, all the interviewer's nods are included in order to discuss how they function in the interaction.)

**Excerpt 3.1** Natsume's Book of Friends

```
1   IR:  chotto sutoorii ga donna      sutoorii
         little  story    S what-kind  story
2        datta   ka, chotto oshiete kuremasen ka
         CP-PST Q/N little  tell    give-NG   Q
         Would you please tell me what kind of story it was?

3   E:   etto: (0.7) natsume wa: ano:
         H           Natsume TP   H
4        (2.5) yookai  (.) [ga] mieru
               spirits       O   can see

5   IR:                     [((nods))]
6        |hai.
         |((nods))
         Uh huh.

7   E:   ano shoonen de, [(.)
         H   boy         CP-and
```

Uh Natsume is uh a boy who can see uh spirits, and

```
8   IR:                  [((nods))

9   E:   ano (.) ju- (.) juugosai, gurai?
         H               fifteen   about
10       [ (.) ]   no shoonen de,
                   LK boy     CP-and
```

Uh he is a boy about fif- fifteen years old, and

```
11  IR:  [((nods))]
12       |hai.
         |((nods))
         Uh huh.

13  E:   etto (1.9) ano (0.9) henni [(0.7)
          H          H         strangely

14  IR:                                [((nods))

15  E:   mieru k(h)ar(h)a [(.)
         looks   because
         
         Um uh because he looks strange

16  IR:                      [((nods))

17  E:   ano (1.4) n:[:] (1.6) natsume no [(.)
          H          H          Natsume LK

18  IR:              [((nods))]          [((nods))

19  E:   ano (.) oya      ga [(.)
          H       parents  S

20  IR:                      [((nods))

21  E:   in(h)ai to omoimasu?
         be-NG   QT  think
         
         Uh um I think Natsume doesn't have uh parents.

22  IR:  |hai.=
         |((nods))
         Uh huh.

23  E:   =etto (0.6) .hh [(1.2)
           H

24  IR:                    [((nods))

25  E:   shin:seki: [(0.7)
         relative

26  IR:              [((nods))

27  E:   iroirona shinseki ga [(.)
         various  relative  S
```

```
28  IR:                    [((nods))

29  E:   ano: natsume o sewashita    n  desu ga,
         H    Natsume O take-care-PST N  CP   but

         Um his relatives, various relatives uh took care of him, but

30  IR:  |hai.
         |((nods))
         Uh huh.

31  E:   etto (2.2) °eh:° [ano: (.)
         H                H    H

32  IR:                   [((nods))

33  E:   yookai  wa [(.)] hito: toshit(h)e
         spirits TP       human as

34  IR:             [((nods))]

35  E:   miru n (.) desu kara [(0.9)
         see  N     CP   because

36  IR:                       [((nods))

         Um eh uh because he sees spirits as human,

37  E:   ano (2.5) sono shinseki ga [(.)
         H         that relative  S

38  IR:                             [((nods))

39  E:   natsume o (.) ano sewa o shitakunai
         Natsume O     H   care O want-to-do-NG

40  IR:  |°hu::n.°
         | ((nods))
         Ah.

41  E:   desu.
         CP

         Uh the relatives uh don't want to take care of Natsume.

42       ano [ (.) ] ((a cough)) demo [(.)
         H                       but
```

```
43 IR:        [((nods))]              [((nods))

44 E:    yatto [(.)] ano (2.2) sewa o shitai (.)
         finally      H            care O want-to-do

45 IR:        [((nods))]

46 E:    [ano:] shinseki ga [(0.5)] ano (.) atte,
           H    relative  S          H       be-and
```
Uh but finally, uh there are um relatives uh who want to take care of him, and
```
47 IR:   [((nods))]            [((nods))]
48       |hai.
         |((nods))
```
Uh huh.
```
49 E:    etto (1.2) n: inaka   no dokoka    de hheh
          H             H country LK somewhere at
```
Um somewhere in the countryside
```
50 IR:   |hai hai.
         |((nods))
```
Uh huh.
```
51 E:    ano (0.5) s: sorede [(.)]  ano: (3.2)
          H            then          H

52 IR:                        [((nods))]

53 E:    ano (.) natsume no [oba]asan    ga
          H      Natsume LK grandmother  S

54 IR:                        [((nods))]
55       |hai.
         |((nods))
```
Uh huh.
```
56 E:    ano (0.8) yuujinchoo to yuu mo- (.)
          H        book-of-friends QT say

57       ano [hon] o          [(1.2)
          H   book O

58 IR:        [((nods))]    [((nods))
```

```
59 E:    ano (.) natsume o (.) agete,
         H       Natsume O*     give-and
```

Uh and then, uh um his grandmother gives uh Natsume um
a book called uh the Book of Friends, and

```
60 IR:  |hai.
        |((nods))
```
Uh huh.

In Excerpt 3.1, in response to the interviewer's request, Emily starts retelling the story of *Natsume Yuujinchoo* in line 3. After a moment of hesitation, she first introduces the main character, and then presents a number of story events in chronological order while supplying relevant background information and reasons. She often exhibits difficulty in formulating utterances, and her speech contains many hesitation markers, long pauses, and self-corrections. Despite frequent word searches, however, she eventually finds Japanese words in each case and does not codeswitch to English (in contrast to George's case). Emily employs hesitation markers as an interactional resource, and lengthy pauses in her turn are almost always prefaced by a hesitation marker. This allows the interviewer to see that Emily is engaged in word searches and to cooperate with her by refraining from starting a new turn or making interventions during long pauses. Emily's word searches and production of utterances are also tacitly supported by the interviewer's frequent nodding. For instance, when Emily engages in prolonged word searches (e.g., line 17, 23, 31), the interviewer gives nods even before Emily produces any content words (e.g., lines 18, 24, 32). By doing so, the interviewer displays her continued listenership, encouraging Emily to continue her word search and to speak. Then, when Emily produces content words, the interviewer often acknowledges them by nodding, almost on a word-by-word basis at times, especially when the production of words is preceded by a word search (e.g., lines 13–22). While some of her nods occur with vocal continuers, they are more often produced silently. Vocal continuers tend to appear at clausal boundaries (lines 12, 22, 30, 48, 60), where the interviewer passes the opportunity to take a turn and aligns with the ongoing storytelling activity (Schegloff, 1982). On the other hand, silent nods frequently occur while a TCU is still in progress. Stivers (2008) suggests that nods are used by the story recipient to display affiliation with the teller's stance toward the events reported. In this interaction, however, the interviewer seems to use nods to provide affective support for Emily when she displays difficulty in formulating utterances. Such use of nods may be specific to interaction towards speakers of limited proficiency. At any rate, the above features illustrate how Emily and the interviewer collaboratively constructed the interaction as Emily performs the linguistically demanding task of retelling: Emily constantly and overtly indicates her current engagement in word searches and enables the interviewer to cooperate while the interviewer continually monitors and supports Emily's turn-in-progress with nods and continuers.

As for linguistic features in her retelling, Emily tends to produce relatively long, multi-clause utterances by grammatically connecting clauses with the *te*-form of the predicate and connective particles. The *te*-form of the predicate here is used to present the states and events that construct the main line of the story. For instance, the first two clauses in her retelling, which describe the main character, are marked with the *te*-form of the predicate (the copula *de*, lines 7, 10). Also, several story events are connected with the *te*-form of the predicate as successive occurrences (*atte* 'have,' line 46; *agete* 'give,' line 59). In addition, Emily employs connective particles to provide information subordinate to the main line of the story: The causal marker *kara* 'because' (lines 15, 35) is used to present reasons for the story events, and the contrastive marker *ga* 'but' (line 29) is used to provide background information against which the main event is contrasted. Since these clause-final connective expressions grammatically project the production of a next clause, they also function as turn-holding devices. Furthermore, Emily utilizes connectives as discourse markers to indicate transition points in her telling: *demo* 'but' shows a contrastive transition between events (line 42), and *sorede* 'and then' presents a sequential transition between events (line 51). These features indicate Emily's ability to use various linguistic resources to organize her telling in the interaction.

Although many of the connective expressions are appropriately used in Emily's retelling, at times there seems to be a problem in the backgrounding and foregrounding of information (Yoshimi, 2001). For instance, in lines 17 to 21, in order to provide the background information necessary for the recipient to understand an upcoming event (that relatives took care of Natsume), Emily says *natsume no (.) ano (.) oya ga (.) in(h)ai to omoimasu?* 'I think Natsume doesn't have parents.' Although this is a piece of background information to be fitted into the telling, it is presented more like a stand-alone utterance. It is linguistically unconnected to the next clause and somewhat foregrounded due to the use of the final-form of the predicate. If a connective particle (such as *kara* 'because') were employed to mark this clause (e.g., *natsume wa oya ga inai kara* 'because Natsume doesn't have parents'), the information would have been more adequately integrated into the story, and the clause would have been suitably connected to the next clause (as reason and result). Excerpt 3.2 presents the subsequent part of Emily's retelling.

**Excerpt 3.2** Natsume's Book of Friends (cont.)

```
60 IR:   |hai.
         |((nods))
         Uh huh.

61 E:    etto (1.4) yuujinchoo         w(hh)a [(.)
         H          book-of-friends    TP

62 IR:                                        [((nods))

63 E:    to wa (.) ano (1.7) obaasan      ga [(.)
         QT TP     H         grandmother  S

64 IR:                                       [((nods))

65 E:    ano taoshita   [(0.7)
         H   defeat-PST

66 IR:                  [((nods))

67 E:    yookai no [namae] ga atte,
         spirit LK name    S  have-and

         Um the Book of Friends, has the names of the spirits
         uh (his) grandmother uh defeated, and

68 IR:              [((nods))]
69       |hai.
         |((nods))
         Uh huh.

70 E:    etto, natsume wa yasashii ko (.) na node
         H     Natsume TP kind     child   CP because
         Um because Natsume is a kind kid,

71 IR:   |hai.
         |((nods))
         Uh huh.

72 E:    sono: namae o (.) kaeshitai       n desu.
         that  name  O    want-to-return   N CP
         he wants to return the names.

73       (0.5)/((IR and Emily gaze at each other.))

74 E:    [etto] (.) sorede [(.)] anime wa, [(1.4)
          H        then           anime TP
```

```
75  IR:  [((nods))]         [((nods))]         [((nods))

76  E:   etto: [(1.4)
         H

77  IR:          [((nods))

78  E:   namae o (.) kaeshita, kaesu, [ano
         name  O     returned  return  H

79  IR:                                    [((nods))

80  E:   (1.5) to yuu h(hh)anashi desu.
               QT say   story    CP

         Um and then, the anime is uh a story where he returned, returns
         uh the names.

81  IR:  namae o kaesu  tte yuu  to
         name  O return QT  say  when
         What do you mean by "return the names"?

82  E:   hai. ano (1.1) namae ga: (.) areba,
         yes  H         name  S       have-if
         Yes. Uh if you have the names,

83  IR:  [|hai.
          |((nods))
         Uh huh.

84  E:   [ano (.) sono yookai no chikara
          H       that spirit LK power
85       ga [ (.) ]    [arimasu.
         S                have
         Uh you have the power of the spirits.

86  IR:       [((nods)) [°hu:n°
         Ah.

87       (1.2)/((IR nods))

88  E:   ano (1.4) meeree(.)shitara [(0.7)
         H         order    do-if
         Uh if you give them orders,

89  IR:                                 [((nods))
```

```
 90 E:   ano: (1.7) shitaga: (.) shitaga-
         H          obey         obey
 91      shitagae- [(0.9)
         obey
         Uh they mus- mus- must o-

 92 IR:            [((nods))

 93 E:   ((coughs))
 94      suimasen.
         Sorry.

 95 IR:  ie ie.
         no no
         No problem.

 96      (1.2)/((IR nods))

 97 E:   ano: shitagawa(.)nakerebanaranai desu.
         H    obey-must                   CP
         Uh they must obey.

 98 IR:  |aa: soo desu ka. hee:.
          oh  so  CP   Q   wow
         |((nods several times))
         Oh I see. Wow.

 99      jaa   obaasan     ga sono: (.) namae o
         then  grandmother S  that      name  O
100      totteshimatta, tte yuu koto desu ka?
         took           QT  say thing CP   Q
         So, the grandmother took their names away?

101 E:   hai.
         Yes.

102 IR:  aa:    soo desu ka. wakarimashita:.
         oh     so  CP   Q   understand-PST
         ((nods))
         Oh I see. I understand.

103      .h eeto: soo desu ne:, soredewa etto mata
            H     so  CP   IP   then     H    again
104      chotto hanashi ga kawatteshimaimasu ga
         little talk    S  change              but
         Let's see. Well then, ((we'll)) change topics again, but
```

Excerpt 3.2 shows the ending part of Emily's retelling as well as the subsequent interaction between the participants. In lines 74 to 80, Emily wraps up the retelling with an utterance hearable as a completion point of her turn (in terms of grammar, intonation, and semantic content). The interviewer takes it as such, but instead of providing an acknowledgement, she initiates a repair on Emily's utterance, locating a trouble source in the previous turn and asking a follow-up question (*namae o kaesu tte yuu to* 'What do you mean by "return the names"?,' line 81). Her trouble in understanding the phrase *namae o kaesu* 'return the names' was already indicated earlier in line 73, where she did not respond to Emily's utterance that contained the first appearance of the phrase (line 72). Considering the frequency of nods and continuers she usually provides, it is noteworthy that she does not show any sign of hearing or understanding during the 0.5-second silence even though Emily had just completed an utterance. While this was the first available opportunity for the interviewer to initiate repair, she passes the opportunity, and as soon as Emily resumes her retelling (line 74), she starts nodding to encourage Emily to talk more (line 75). When Emily repeats the same expression ('return the names') and completes her retelling, however, the interviewer initiates repair (line 81). This delayed repair initiation indicates the interviewer's orientation toward her role as a tester and the purpose of the OPI (i.e., in order to collect ratable speech samples an interviewer should not interrupt a candidate's talk).

The subsequent interaction shows how the participants work together to achieve mutual understanding regarding the trouble source. In response to the interviewer's repair initiation, Emily first provides an explanation in a multi-clausal utterance (lines 82–85). Then, when the interviewer silently nods at the possible TRP (line 87), Emily interprets the embodied action as an invitation to continue, and produces another utterance to elaborate (lines 88–97). As Emily struggles with verb conjugation and coughs in the middle of her utterance, she immediately initiates an apology-minimization sequence, but after a gap of silence, resumes and completes her utterance, which gets acknowledged by the interviewer (line 98). Subsequently, the interviewer displays her interpretation and asks for confirmation (lines 99–100). Upon Emily's confirmation, the interviewer claims understanding and moves on to a next topic. The above interaction indicates that Emily's explanation in response to the interviewer's repair initiation, as well as the interviewer's display of her interpretation and Emily's confirmation of it, enabled them to achieve mutual understanding.

Overall, in my OPI data some general differences related to proficiency level were observed in the degree of completeness and comprehensibility of the stories retold by the candidates. When the Intermediate-Low candidates were asked to retell a story from a movie, novel, or other text, their utterances were often fragmented with pauses and hesitation markers and sometimes difficult to understand due to lexical limitations, though they organized the stories in a canonical order and made effort to achieve intersubjectivity with the interviewer. (It should be also noted that these candidates too were able to talk about their own experiences more effectively.) The Intermediate-Mid candidates' utterances were mostly comprehensible in the story retelling task, but their retellings were treated as somewhat unsatisfactory by the interviewer at initial completion points: Upon completion of these candidates' turns, the interviewer delayed acknowledgement and either initiated repair on an utterance (as in Emily's case), asked what happened next in the story, or waited to see if the candidate would continue the turn. Such responses by the interviewer seemed to point to possible problems in Intermediate-Mid candidates' story retelling, such as insufficient explanation or a sudden jump in the storyline. On the other hand, as discussed elsewhere (Tominaga, 2014), the Intermediate-High and Advanced candidates' retellings were done well enough so that, in each case, the interviewer was able to provide an acknowledgement without delay upon completion of the candidate's turn.

## Discussion and conclusion

The purpose of this study was to examine how Intermediate candidates produce stories in the Japanese OPI and investigate to what extent their performances match the text type criterion of the ACTFL OPI and the related parts of the level descriptions in the Guidelines. The findings of the study provide evidence to support the overall adequacy of the assignment of proficiency levels and the effectiveness of the narration task in generating differential performance from candidates. In my data, candidates at the higher proficiency levels generally demonstrate a superior ability in using connective expressions and managing their telling, whereas candidates at the lower proficiency levels tend to rely on a limited variety of connective expressions. This finding appears to be consistent with findings from previous studies that have observed increased use and control of a broader range of expressions by candidates at higher proficiency levels in OPIs (Lazaraton, 2002; Lee, Park, & Sohn, 2011; Watanabe, 2003).

This being said, the findings of the present study also suggest that the level descriptions concerning the text type rating criterion of the OPI do not necessarily match the candidates' actual performance in my data. In particular, the descriptors of "sentences" and "paragraphs" appear problematic since what the candidates produced in storytelling (and other tasks) did not resemble written sentences or paragraphs. Rather, the candidates and the interviewer worked together to construct the interaction, carefully monitoring each other's interactional moves and producing sequentially appropriate actions on a moment-by-moment basis. In addition, even the Intermediate-Low and Intermediate-Mid candidates, whose responses are characterized as "sentences" in the

Guidelines, were able to produce stories in an extended turn with the cooperation and support of the interviewer. Although they showed some signs of weakness in using appropriate linguistic forms, they were capable of maintaining a turn to produce multiple utterances, organizing the telling in a logical and canonical manner, and linking utterances with (a limited range of) connective expressions. Therefore, the sentence/paragraph distinction in the OPI rating criteria does not seem to adequately capture level differences, and I argue that this text type rating criterion needs reconsideration from an interactional perspective. From my observation, whether candidates' response turns are short or extended often depends on the extent of the information required to answer the interviewer's questions. What is different across the proficiency levels, then, is the degree to which the candidates are able to draw on linguistic resources to manage their tellings. In addition, lexical knowledge, fluency, and smoothness of speech, and the overall comprehensibility of the tellings appear to have a good deal of weight in the rating. Utterances containing many hesitation markers, long pauses, self-corrections, lexical searches, grammatical and lexical errors, and codeswitching to English are likely to affect the resulting ratings negatively.

The problem concerning the level descriptions of Intermediate-Low and Intermediate-Mid speakers seems to reside in the Guidelines' failure to adequately recognize lower-proficiency-level candidates' IC, including their abilities and tendencies to produce sequentially appropriate actions in interaction (including extended turns), to organize their turns in an orderly manner, and to use available resources to achieve coherent and cohesive discourse. As competent speakers of their first languages, adult L2 speakers have a good understanding of interactional organization, which they can use as a resource when they participate in L2 interaction (Kasper, 2006a), often regardless of their current L2 proficiency level. As shown above, George's (Intermediate-Low) two instances of storytelling demonstrated his IC in using extended turns despite his linguistic limitations. While he had much difficulty in performing the story retelling task, he still managed to make a clear opening and closing in his discourse, to organize the retelling in a logical order, and to link his utterances with *soshite* 'and.' In his personal narrative, he more fully demonstrated his storytelling ability, initiating a story spontaneously, describing a number of events in chronological order, indicating the time of the events, and linking utterances using a few connective expressions. He competently shared an interesting story with the interviewer, evidenced by reciprocated laughter and assessments around the completion point of his story. Emily (Intermediate-Mid) also demonstrated her IC in telling a story in an extended turn, with a greater ability to use linguistic resources. In her retelling of an anime series, she presented a number of story events in a chronological order and provided relevant background information and reasons to facilitate the interviewer's understanding of the story. She employed several connective expressions to link utterances, though her backgrounding and foregrounding of information was not always effective. The analysis also showed that both candidates appropriately responded to the interviewer's various interactional moves (e.g., requests, continuers, nodding, acknowledgement, repair initiation). In addition, they were able to use available interactional resources, such as hesitation markers, try-marked intonations, and codeswitching, to solve problems in formulating utterances. While these features do not necessarily contribute to the achievement of a higher rating in the OPI, they certainly indicate the candidates' competence to participate in interaction in real-life situations.

Since the ACTFL OPI and Guidelines are highly influential in the field of foreign language teaching and assessment, it is very important that they describe proficiency levels accurately and clearly so that test takers, teachers, administrators, employers, and policy makers can appropriately interpret OPI ratings and use them to make proper decisions. For instance, the OPI certificates, which candidates are awarded and may use when applying for jobs or academic programs, include the level descriptions from the Guidelines. If the Guidelines do not adequately describe what the candidate can do with the target language, this could lead to unfair judgments of the candidate's speaking proficiency. In addition, since the Guidelines are widely used for curriculum design and materials development in foreign language programs in universities and secondary schools, if the Guidelines incorrectly characterize proficiency levels, this could have an unwarranted or even damaging influence on foreign language teaching and assessment. For example, teachers of beginning-level foreign language courses may decide to focus on practicing sentence-level constructions in classroom activities and not to introduce activities that require the production of extended turns (e.g., storytelling) because the Guidelines emphasize "sentences" as characteristic of Intermediate speakers' talk. In any event, the level descriptions in the Guidelines should adequately reflect L2 speakers' IC in order to ensure their validity and positive influence on foreign language teaching and assessment.

The findings of this study indicate the importance of having an adequate theory of spoken interaction and empirical evidence for ACTFL OPI rating criteria. I recommend that future research should further investigate the issues discussed in this chapter. If findings are consistent, then recommendations for the revision of the Guidelines should be made so that the rating scale of the OPI better reflects actual candidate performance. It is hoped that the findings of this study contribute to the efforts to validate the proposed interpretations and uses of the OPI ratings, and contribute to the growing body of literature on L2 speakers' IC and the interviewer–candidate interaction in the OPI.

## Notes

1. As I discuss the OPI rating criteria in this chapter, I will focus on the written descriptions of the oral proficiency levels (ACTFL, 2012a, 2012b), rather than discussing how and to what extent these criteria are actually used by raters in rating OPIs.
2. While "connectors" in a broad sense includes a variety of linking words and phrases, I focus on the use of the *te*-form of the predicate, connective particles, and connectives in this study, as the present candidates most commonly used these resources as connectors.
3. The Japanese OPIs were conducted by the present author as she was the only ACTFL-certified tester on campus available for the research at the time of data collection. While it is ideal for validation research purposes to have several testers, it was not possible for this study. On the other hand, as the same interviewer conduct all the OPIs, interviewer variability was likely minimized.
4. The names of the candidates are pseudonyms.
5. In this and other excerpts, the notation of embodied actions is placed below the second tier (i.e., the interlinear word-by-word gloss tier). Due to space limitations, however, not all embodied actions are included. An asterisk (*) is used to indicate non-target-like forms.
6. In my Japanese OPI data, the interviewer most frequently used *aa soo desu ka* 'Oh I see/is that so' to acknowledge a candidate's response, which often elicited a minimal response from the candidate. In English OPIs, an interviewer may use 'okay' or 'I see' for acknowledgement, but may not elicit a verbal response from the candidate as regularly.
7. George utters *ichi*, which was probably meant as *hi* 'day' (in all, *tsugi no hi* 'next day'). He may also be trying to say *nichi*, another pronunciation of the kanji for 'day.'
8. It is not uncommon that *onsen* baths (and their associated changing rooms) alternate daily between male and female visitors. In line 61, George utters *t(hh) omodachi kara* 'from my friend,' which indicates that he is quoting his friend, though the quoting particle and verb are not produced in his utterance. The utterance is thus incomplete, but the interviewer claims understanding.
9. In the ACTFL OPI, the interviewer is encouraged to act monolingual, pretending as if they only speak and understand the target language. If the candidate codeswitches, the interviewer may ask for equivalent words or a circumlocution in the target language.
10. This phenomenon (the interviewer first uses the shorter version of the acknowledgement token *aa soo*, and then produces the longer version *aa soo desu ka* in a subsequent sequential slot) was also observed in other OPIs in my data. Therefore, with this interviewer, it seemed that *aa soo* showed the tentativeness of her analysis that the candidate's turn was completed.

# References

ACTFL. (2012a). *ACTFL oral proficiency interview familiarization manual.* Retrieved May 9, 2015, from http://www.languagetesting.com/wp-content/uploads/2012/07/OPI.FamiliarizationManual.pdf

ACTFL. (2012b). *ACTFL proficiency guidelines 2012.* Retrieved May 9, 2015, from http://www.actfl.org/sites/default/files/pdfs/public/ACTFLProficiencyGuidelines2012_FINAL.pdf

Bachman, L. F. (1988). Problems in examining the validity of the ACTFL oral proficiency interview. *Studies in Second Language Acquisition, 10*, 149–164.

Bachman, L. F., & Savignon, S. J. (1986). The evaluation of communicative language proficiency: A critique of the ACTFL oral interview. *The Modern Language Journal, 70*, 380–390.

Barnwell, D. (1993). Oral proficiency testing and the bilingual speaker. In A. Roca & J. M. Lipski (Eds.), *Spanish in the United States: Linguistic contact and diversity* (pp. 199–209). Berlin: Mouton de Gruyter.

Brown, A. (2003). Interviewer variation and the co-construction of speaking proficiency. *Language Testing, 20*, 1–25.

Brown, G., & Yule, G. (1983a). *Discourse analysis.* Cambridge, UK: Cambridge University Press.

Brown, G., & Yule, G. (1983b). *Teaching the spoken language: An approach based on the analysis of conversational English.* Cambridge, UK: Cambridge University Press.

Carroll, D. (2004). Restarts in novice turn beginnings: Disfluencies or interactional achievements? In R. Gardner & J. Wagner (Eds.), *Second language conversations* (pp. 201–220). London: Continuum.

Chambless, K. S. (2012). Teachers' oral proficiency in the target language: Research on its role in language teaching and learning. *Foreign Language Annals, 45*(S1), 141–162.

Firth, A. (2009). Doing not being a foreign language learner: English as a lingua franca in the workplace and (some) implications for SLA. *International Review of Applied Linguistics in Language Teaching, 47*, 127–156.

Ford, C. E., & Thompson, S. A. (1996). Interactional units in conversation: Syntactic, intonational, and pragmatic resources for the management of turns. In E. Ochs, E. A. Schegloff, & S. A. Thompson (Eds.), *Interaction and grammar* (pp. 134–184). Cambridge, UK: Cambridge University Press.

Goodwin, C. (1980). Restarts, pauses, and the achievement of mutual gaze at turn-beginning. *Sociological Inquiry, 50*, 272–302.

Goodwin, C. (1984). Notes on story structure and the organization of participation. In J. M. Atkinson & J. Heritage (Eds.), *Structures of social action* (pp. 225–246). Cambridge, UK: Cambridge University Press.

Gumperz, J. J., Kaltman, H., & O'Connor, M. C. (1984). Cohesion in spoken and written discourse: Ethnic style and the transition to literacy. In D. Tannen (Ed.), *Coherence in spoken and written discourse* (pp. 3–19). Norwood, NJ: Ablex.

Hall, J. K., Hellermann, J., & Pekarek Doehler, S. (Eds.). (2011). *L2 interactional competence and development*. Bristol, UK: Multilingual Matters.

Hall, J. K., & Pekarek Doehler, S. (2011). L2 interactional competence and development. In J. K. Hall, J. Hellermann, & S. Pekarek Doehler (Eds.), *L2 interactional competence and development* (pp. 1–15). Bristol, UK: Multilingual Matters.

Hauser, E. (2009). Turn-taking and primary speakership during a student discussion. In H. t. Nguyen & G. Kasper (Eds.), *Talk-in-interaction: Multilingual perspectives* (pp. 215–244). Honolulu, HI: University of Hawai'i, National Foreign Language Resource Center.

He, A. W., & Young, R. (1998). Language proficiency interview: A discourse approach. In R. Young & A. W. He (Eds.), *Talking and testing: Discourse approaches to the assessment of oral proficiency* (pp. 1–24). Amsterdam: John Benjamins.

Hellermann, J. (2008). *Social actions for classroom language learning*. Bristol, UK: Multilingual Matters.

Houston, T. (2005). Outcomes assessment for beginning and intermediate Spanish: One program's process and results. *Foreign Language Annals, 38*(3), 366–376.

Ishida, M. (2006). Interactional competence and the use of modal expressions in decision-making activities: CA for understanding microgenesis of pragmatic competence. In K. Bardovi-Harlig, J. C. Félix-Brasdefer, & A. Omar (Eds.), *Pragmatics and language learning* (Vol. 11, pp. 55–79). Honolulu, HI: University of Hawai'i, National Foreign Language Resource Center.

Ishida, M. (2009). Development of interactional competence: Changes in the use of *ne* in L2 Japanese during study abroad. In H. t. Nguyen & G. Kasper (Eds.), *Talk-in-interaction: Multilingual perspectives* (pp. 351–385). Honolulu, HI: University of Hawai'i, National Foreign Language Resource Center.

Ishida, M. (2011). Engaging in another person's telling as a recipient in L2 Japanese: Development of interactional competence during one-year study abroad. In G. Pallotti & J. Wagner (Eds.), *L2 learning as social practice: Conversation-analytic perspectives (pp. 45–85)*. Honolulu, HI: University of Hawai'i, National Foreign Language Resource Center.

Jefferson, G. (1978). Sequential aspects of storytelling in conversation. In J. Schenkein (Ed.), *Studies in the organization of conversational interaction* (pp. 219–248). New York, NY: Free Press.

Johnson, M. (2001). *The art of nonconversation: A reexamination of the validity of the oral proficiency interview*. New Haven, CT: Yale University Press.

Kagan, O., & Friedman, D. (2003). Using the OPI to place heritage speakers of Russian. *Foreign Language Annals, 36*, 536–545.

Kasper, G. (2006a). Beyond repair: Conversation analysis as an approach to SLA. *AILA Review, 19*, 83–99.

Kasper, G. (2006b). When once is not enough: Politeness of multiple requests in oral proficiency interviews. *Multilingua, 25*, 323–349.

Kasper, G. (2013). Managing task uptake in oral proficiency interviews. In S. J. Ross & G. Kasper (Eds.), *Assessing second language pragmatics* (pp. 258–287). Basingstoke, UK: Palgrave Macmillan.

Kasper, G., & Ross, S. J. (2003). Repetition as a source of miscommunication in oral proficiency interviews. In J. House, G. Kasper, & S. J. Ross (Eds.), *Misunderstanding in social life: Discourse approaches to problematic talk* (pp. 82–106). Harlow, UK: Longman/Pearson Education.

Kasper, G., & Ross, S. J. (2007). Multiple questions in oral proficiency interviews. *Journal of Pragmatics, 39*, 2045–2070.

Kasper, G., & Ross, S. J. (2013). Assessing second language pragmatics: An overview and introductions. In S. J. Ross & G. Kasper (Eds.), *Assessing second language pragmatics* (pp. 1–40). Basingstoke, UK: Palgrave Macmillan.

Kim, Y. (2009). Korean discourse markers -*nuntey* and -*kuntey* in native–nonnative conversation: An acquisitional perspective. In H. t. Nguyen & G. Kasper (Eds.), *Talk-in-interaction: Multilingual perspectives* (pp. 317–350). Honolulu, HI: University of Hawai'i, National Foreign Language Resource Center.

Kondo-Brown, K. (2012). *Nihongo kyooshi no tame no hyooka nyuumon* [Introduction to assessment for Japanese language teachers]. Tokyo: Kuroshio Shuppan.

Labov, W. (1972). *Language in the inner city.* Philadelphia, PA: University of Pennsylvania Press.

Lantolf, J. P., & Frawley, W. (1988). Proficiency: Understanding the construct. *Studies in Second Language Acquisition, 10*, 181–195.

Lazaraton, A. (2002). *A qualitative approach to the validation of oral language tests.* Cambridge, UK: Cambridge University Press.

Lee, S. H., Park, J. E., & Sohn, S. O. (2011). Expanded resources of English-speaking Korean heritage speakers during oral interviews. In G. Pallotti & J. Wagner (Eds.), *L2 learning as social practice: Conversation-analytic perspectives* (pp. 87–104). Honolulu, HI: University of Hawai'i, National Foreign Language Resource Center.

Lee, Y. (2006). Towards respecification of communicative competence: Condition of L2 instruction or its objective? *Applied Linguistics, 27*(3), 349–376.

Liddicoat, A. J. (2011). *An introduction to conversation analysis* (2nd ed.). London: Continuum.

Liskin-Gasparro, J. E. (1996a). Circumlocution, communication strategies, and the ACTFL proficiency guidelines: An analysis of student discourse. *Foreign Language Annals, 29*(3), 317–330.

Liskin-Gasparro, J. E. (1996b). Narrative strategies: A case study of developing storytelling skills by a learner of Spanish. *The Modern Language Journal, 80*, 271–286.

Makino, S., Kamada, O., Yamuchi, H., Saito, M., Ogiwara, C., Ito, T., ..., & Nakajima, K. (2001). *ACTFL-OPI nyuumon: Nihongo gakushuusha no "hanasu chikara" o kyakkantekini hakaru* [An introduction to the ACTFL OPI: Objective assessment of Japanese learners' speaking competence]. Tokyo: ALC.

Makino, S., & Tsutsui, M. (1986). *A dictionary of basic Japanese grammar.* Tokyo: The Japan Times.

McNamara, T. F. (2000). *Language testing.* Oxford, UK: Oxford University Press.

Ohta, A. S. (2001). A longitudinal study of the development of expression of alignment in Japanese as a foreign language. In K. R. Rose & G. Kasper (Eds.), *Pragmatics in language teaching* (pp. 102–120). Cambridge, UK: Cambridge University Press.

Okada, Y. (2010). Role-play in oral proficiency interviews: Interactive footing and interactional competencies. *Journal of Pragmatics, 42*(6), 1647–1668.

Okada, Y., & Greer, T. (2013). Pursuing a relevant response in oral proficiency interview role plays. In S. J. Ross & G. Kasper (Eds.), *Assessing second language pragmatics* (pp. 288–310). Basingstoke, UK: Palgrave Macmillan.

Pomerantz, A. (1984). Agreeing and disagreeing with assessments: Some features of preferred/dispreferred turn shapes. In J. M. Atkinson & J. Heritage (Eds.), *Structures of social action: Studies in conversation analysis* (pp. 57–101). Cambridge, UK: Cambridge University Press.

Raffaldini, T. (1988). The use of situation tests as measures of communicative ability. *Studies in Second Language Acquisition, 10,* 197–216.

Rifkin, B. (2003). Oral proficiency learning outcomes and curricular design. *Foreign Language Annals, 36*(4), 582–588.

Ross, S. J. (2007). A comparative task-in-interaction analysis of OPI backsliding. *Journal of Pragmatics, 39,* 2017–2044.

Ross, S. J., & Berwick, R. (1992). The discourse of accommodation in oral proficiency interviews. *Studies in Second Language Acquisition, 14,* 159–176.

Ross, S. J., & O'Connell, S. P. (2013). The situation with complication as a site for strategic competence. In S. J. Ross & G. Kasper (Eds.), *Assessing second language pragmatics* (pp. 311–326). Basingstoke, UK: Palgrave Macmillan.

Sacks, H., Schegloff, E. A., & Jefferson, G. (1974). A simplest systematics for the organization of turn-taking for conversation. *Language, 50,* 696–735.

Savignon, S. J. (1985). Evaluation of communicative competence: The ACTFL provisional proficiency guidelines. *The Modern Language Journal, 69,* 129–134.

Schegloff, E. A. (1982). Discourse as an interactional achievement: Some uses of "uh huh" and other things that come between sentences. In D. Tannen (Ed.), *Analyzing discourse: Text and talk* (pp. 71–93). Washington, DC: Georgetown University Press.

Schegloff, E. A. (1996). Turn organization: One intersection of grammar and interaction. In E. Ochs, E. A. Schegloff, & S. A. Thompson (Eds.), *Interaction and grammar* (pp. 52–133). Cambridge, UK: Cambridge University Press.

Schegloff, E. A. (2007). *Sequence organization in interaction.* Cambridge, UK: Cambridge University Press.

Schegloff, E. A., Jefferson, G., & Sacks, H. (1977). The preference for self-correction in the organization of repair in conversation. *Language, 53,* 361–382.

Schegloff, E. A., & Sacks, H. (1973). Opening up closings. *Semiotica, 8*, 289–327.
Schiffrin, D. (1987). *Discourse markers.* Cambridge, UK: Cambridge University Press.
Seedhouse, P. (2013). Oral proficiency interviews as varieties of interaction. In S. J. Ross & G. Kasper (Eds.), *Assessing second language pragmatics* (pp. 199–219). Basingstoke, UK: Palgrave Macmillan.
Stivers, T. (2008). Stance, alignment, and affiliation during storytelling: When nodding is a token of affiliation. *Research on Language and Social Interaction, 41*, 31–57.
Tominaga, W. (2013). The development of extended turns and storytelling in the Japanese oral proficiency interview. In S. J. Ross & G. Kasper (Eds.), *Assessing second language pragmatics* (pp. 220–257). Basingstoke, UK: Palgrave Macmillan.
Tominaga, W. (2014). *Validating the scoring inference of the Japanese OPI ratings: The use of extended turns, connective expressions, and discourse organization.* (Doctoral dissertation). Available from ProQuest Dissertations and Theses database. (UMI No. 3648599).
van Compernolle, R. A. (2011). Responding to questions and L2 learner interactional competence during language proficiency interviews: A microanalytic study with pedagogical implications. In J. K. Hall, J. Hellermann, & S. Pekarek Doehler (Eds.), *L2 interactional competence and development* (pp. 117–144). Bristol, UK: Multilingual Matters.
Watanabe, S. (2003). Cohesion and coherence strategies in paragraph-length and extended discourse in Japanese oral proficiency interviews. *Foreign Language Annals, 36*(4), 555–565.
Yoshimi, D. R. (2001). Explicit instruction and JFL learners' use of interactional discourse markers. In K. R. Rose & G. Kasper (Eds.), *Pragmatics in language teaching* (pp. 223-244). Cambridge, UK: Cambridge University Press.
Young, R., & He, A. W. (Eds.) (1998). *Talking and testing: Discourse approaches to the assessment of oral proficiency.* Amsterdam: John Benjamins.
Young, R., & Milanovic, M. (1992). Discourse variation in oral proficiency interviews. *Studies in Second Language Acquisition, 14*, 403–424.
Young, R., & Miller, E. R. (2004). Learning as changing participation: Discourse roles in ESL writing conferences. *The Modern Language Journal, 88*, 519–535.

# Developing Interactional Competence

# 9 Developing Recipient Competence During Study Abroad

Midori Ishida
*San José State University*

## Introduction

Previous studies of second language (L2) development in different learning contexts have shown a general advantage of study abroad over at-home study on overall oral proficiency, fluency, and sociolinguistic and pragmatic competences (e.g., Freed, 1995; Matsumura, 2001; Yang, 2016). However, the reality is more complicated, and greater development of L2 competences is not guaranteed (e.g., Collentine & Freed, 2004). Linguistic gains during study abroad are largely related to the amount of linguistic contact (e.g., Freed, Segalowitz, & Dewey, 2004) and the quality of social interaction in which L2 speakers engage (e.g., Kinginger, 2009), and social interaction is in turn diversely shaped, not merely by the attitudes of the learners themselves or those of the host community (e.g., Iino, 1999), but also through the dynamic relationships between them (e.g., Wilkinson, 2002). Using conversation analysis (CA), Wilkinson (2002), for example, documented how L2 speakers of French and their host families relied on classroom interactional patterns of questions, answers, and corrective feedback, and revealed that their interactions did not provide the L2 speakers with adequate opportunities to learn to converse beyond those opportunities L2 classroom learners have in the role of "students."

Following Wilkinson's CA study of social interaction during study abroad, this chapter uses CA to investigate how interaction with first language (L1) speakers of Japanese helps or prevents an L2 speaker's development of *interactional competence* (e.g., Hall & Pekarek Doehler, 2011; Young, 2011; henceforth, IC) in Japanese during a one-year study abroad sojourn. It specifically focuses on the L2 speaker's use of *receipts* (Jefferson, 1986, p. 162), by which I mean utterances that indicate receipt of the prior speaker's utterance. Since a recipient of a telling can indicate various stances toward the speaker's utterance through receipts (e.g., *soo desu ka* 'Really?'; *soo desu ne* 'That's true'; *soo soo* 'That's right') and thus steer the trajectory of the talk, this chapter regards providing receipts as an important aspect of an L2 speaker's IC. Partly as a response to Kinginger's (2009) call for studies that examine the interaction in which L2 speakers participate during study abroad and its relationship with long-term development, this chapter explores what features of social interaction might afford L2 speakers opportunities to "form new practices" (Pallotti & Wagner, 2011, p. 1), especially when using receipts.

## CA as an approach to investigating affordances of interaction for L2 learning

Research on the role of interaction for L2 learning began with Hatch's (1978) proposal that interaction with native speakers of the target language is more valuable for L2 learning than merely providing an opportunity for practicing previously obtained knowledge. Since then, a variety of approaches have been taken to investigate the issue of how engaging in interaction helps L2 learning, including the *cognitive-interactionist approach* (Ortega, 2009), sociocultural theory (Lantolf & Thorne, 2006), language socialization theory (Bronson & Watson-Gegeo, 2008), and situated learning theory (Lave & Wenger, 1991). Being the most long-lasting and prolific one within the field of second language acquisition (SLA) since the early 1980s, the cognitive-interactionist studies, motivated by Long's (1983, 1996) interaction hypotheses, have investigated the utility of modified input for comprehension and the effectiveness of corrective feedback on higher grammatical accuracy. However, there are fundamental problems with this approach due to its narrow view of "language" as an autonomous system, its conceptualization of language acquisition as cognitive processes, and its use of predetermined coding systems that dismantle language-mediated actions from their specific sequential contingencies (e.g., Firth & Wagner, 1997; Hauser, 2005). Moreover, because the approach focuses almost exclusively on lexical and morphosyntactic features and form-function mapping, other components of L2 speakers' competences, such as discourse, sociolinguistic, pragmatic, and interactional competences, are programmatically left outside the scope of its investigation. In addition, its data sets are typically taken in classrooms and (quasi-)experimental settings; thus, how L2 speakers develop their competences in naturally-occurring interactions is left to the hands of other approaches.

Meanwhile, based on the understanding of language as social action, *CA-SLA* (Kasper & Wagner, 2011) has offered valuable insights on how L2 speakers learn to use the L2 as a resource for engaging in interaction, based on meticulous analyses of naturally occurring interaction both inside and outside the L2 classroom. A number of CA-SLA studies have documented locally occasioned social practices of learning both inside and outside the L2 classroom (e.g., Koshik & Seo, 2012; Markee, 2000; Markee & Seo, 2009; Pallotti & Wagner, 2011; Seedhouse, 2004), where participants' "orientation to learning" (Gardner, 2008) is observable. There, participants engage in repair or "practices for dealing with problems or troubles in speaking, hearing, and understanding the talk in conversation" (Schegloff, 2000, p. 207), often focusing on linguistic matters, in which they "isolat[e] the correction, making it an interactional business" (Jefferson, 1987, p. 97). Meanwhile, there are other CA-SLA studies (e.g., Ishida, 2006; Kim, 2012), although still few in number, that address the issue of learning from a different perspective. They describe the details of interaction that appear to provide L2 learners with the opportunity to exhibit higher competence in the use of the L2 despite the absence of an orientation to L2 learning. The next two subsections will, in turn, review each of these two strands of previous CA-SLA studies on learning.

**Social practice of learning where learning becomes an interactional business**

A number of CA studies on L2 talk (e.g., Pallotti & Wagner, 2011; Sahlström, 2011; Theodórsdóttir, 2011a, 2011b) have documented ways in which "[t]he participants demonstrate for themselves and for each other that they 'do learning'" (Pallotti & Wagner, 2011, p. 4). Seo (2011), for example, delineates how an L2 speaker of English and her tutor engage in a long activity of recurrent repair in order to solve a lexical problem and arrive at an understanding as displayed by the tutee's *AH::::::::: I: understand*. In Seo's study and others, the practice of *repair* (Schegloff, Jefferson, & Sacks, 1977), or recovering a trouble that arises in interaction, is identified and regarded as "a learning mechanism" (Pekarek Doehler & Pochon-Berger, 2015, p. 249) for both comprehension (Markee, 2000) and production of grammar (e.g., Eskildsen & Wagner, 2015; Hellermann, 2009; Hauser, 2013b; van Compernolle, 2011) and vocabulary (e.g., Kim, 2012; Lee, 2010; Markee, 2008; Seo, 2011; Theodórsdóttir, 2011a), including word searches as forward-oriented repair (e.g., Brouwer, 2003; Hosoda, 2006; Koshik & Seo, 2012). When one of the participants flags a problem during interaction (e.g., a problem with understanding and putting it into words for others to understand), either the trouble-source speaker him/herself or another participant orients to the problem, and they attempt to fix it. This social practice of orienting to trouble and providing a solution to it is considered to provide an opportunity for learning.

However, repair is not a necessary condition or satisfactory condition for *learning as social practice* (Pallotti & Wagner, 2011). Theodórsdóttir (2011a) documented a case in which an L2 speaker of Icelandic, Anna, during her stay in Iceland, created a practice of learning by insisting on completing a turn construction units (TCU) even though intersubjectivity had already been achieved through her interlocutor's assistance. While Anna could have oriented to vocabulary learning when the L1-Icelandic clerk offered a word that was initially unavailable to her, she instead completed the previously cut-off TCU, and thus oriented to language learning, "to deliver a whole phrase in the second language" (Theodórsdóttir, 2011a, p. 204). This is a case in which the social practice of learning is achieved through diversion from a repair activity. Theodórsdóttir (2011b) also presents a case in which Anna counted her change aloud along with a baker, showing her orientation to learning how to count change in the target language. These findings illustrate that learning as a social practice is observable even without repair activities, when L2 speakers show orientation to learning the language.

L2 speakers' orientation to learning is, however, most frequently observed in repair. While self-initiated self-repair is preferred in naturally occurring mundane conversations, other-initiated repairs and other-repairs do occur with some features of reservation (e.g., Schegloff et al., 1977; Jefferson, 1987), and studies of interactions that involve L2 speakers (referred to as "L2 interactions" here) have detailed various circumstances and ways in which other-initiation of repair and other-repair are done. For example, Kurhila (2001) shows that while both the asymmetrical relationship between the L1 speaker and the L2 speaker and the kinds of trouble source (e.g., lexical, morphological) affect the occurrence of other-repair, L1 speakers tend to provide overt correction of morphological trouble that L2 speakers encounter, particularly when the trouble-source speaker displays uncertainty about morphology. In such cases, the L2 speaker indicates a change of state by saying *oh*, and sometimes displays his or her understanding. Such *exposed correction* is contrasted with situations in which the L2 speaker does not flag trouble: The L1 speaker discreetly makes a correction using *embedded correction* (Jefferson, 1987, p. 95) and the L2 speaker does not orient to it. Kurhila's finding of orientation toward exposed correction resonates with Hauser's (2001) finding that an L2 speaker of English orients to her L1-English interlocutor's provision of a grammatically correct version of her utterance as a correction when she has appealed for help.

These CA-SLA studies document learning as an *accountable* practice (Garfinkel, 1967). Learning is constructed as such in the actions of members themselves. Participants are considered to be engaging in the social activity of learning when they initiate repair on linguistic matters, engage in insertion sequences on the repairable, and resolve problems. Here, learning is not about cognition that resides in one's head, but rather about cognition that is *socially shared* through the documentation of participant understanding (Kasper, 2009). That is, learning is about *socially shared cognition* (Schegloff, 1991; Kasper & Wagner, 2014). While CA is agnostic "as an analytical *policy*" (Kasper, 2006, p. 84, emphasis in original) concerning cognition, CA can document the social practice of learning that is locally occasioned and therefore made public.

## Interactional contingencies that afford new practices without orientation to learning

### *Another view of* learning

Although learning as socially shared cognition can be observed in the social practice of learning, it may not be a prevalent practice within L2 interactions outside the educational context. While L2 speakers are more likely to orient to linguistic issues, L1 speakers are often found not to initiate repair on linguistic matters in L2 speakers' talk (e.g., Kim, 2012) and instead "let it pass" (Firth, 1996), especially when they are outside an educational context, out in the target-language community or at work (e.g., Brouwer & Wagner, 2004; Gardner & Wagner, 2004; Kurhila, 2001; Theodórsdóttir, 2011a, 2011b). Even when L1 speakers initiate repair, they usually focus on accomplishing intersubjectivity rather than on linguistic accuracy (e.g., Kim, 2012; Kurhila, 2001). A question arises here as to whether there can be any learning without repair or orientation to language form. Consider, for example, the following interaction taken from Kim's (2012) study of casual conversation between L1 and L2 speakers of English (In Excerpt 1, T is the L1 speaker and C the L2 speaker).

**Excerpt 1.** Attack (From Kim, 2012, p. 725)

```
964 C: I think (0.3) it will be very funny (.) if (0.6) he just
965    (0.3) comes out of the restroom, (0.8) and (0.9) standing
966    (0.8) in front of the stairs (0.8) and uh (.) cat jumps
967    [(0.7) into him
968 T: [mh heh heh ye(hh)ah atta(h)cks heh heh heh heh
       heh heh
969    (2.7)
970 C: I wanted to watch the movie meet the fockers,
971 T: yeah
. . .

988 C: I thinked (.) that (2.5) ((the sound of tap water
989    running)) maybe uh (0.6) m the cat (0.9) this cat can be
990    my side
. . .
```

```
998 T: how do you mean?
999 C: uh when he attacks him, (0.6)
1000 T: oh::
```

In line 968, while T affiliatively responds to C's telling of a funny situation with laughter, he uses the word *attack* as an alternative to the phrase *jump into*, which C used in his telling (lines 966–967). Although C does not show any immediate orientation to the word *attack*, in line 999 he adopts the word in his answer to T's question. Kim argues that, as evidenced in his use of the word in line 999, C must have registered the alternative word T used in line 968 even though he had not shown any immediate uptake. She regards this as an instance of learning, although she qualifies her argument by saying that "what he learned is to use that word in that particular context" (p. 725).

Here we can see a treatment of learning that is very different from that of learning as social practice: Learning is seen here not as socially shared cognition, but as forming "new practices" (Pallotti & Wagner, 2011, p. 1) through the "*adaptation of existing resources* to mutating interactional contexts" (König, 2013, p. 234). The formation of a new practice and adaptation of semiotic resources, including "linguistic resources that were not used on previous occasions to a particular context" (Hellermann, 2007 p. 86), constitute evidence of learning. In this chapter, I consider learning in this way. While *development* involves observable changes in competence demonstrated in samples of talk taken at different times, *learning*, as the formation of a new practice, occurs at a certain time and is reflected and manifested in developmental changes. Some CA-SLA researchers who track long-term development in L2 speakers' ICs (e.g., Brouwer & Wagner, 2004; Hellermann, 2007, 2008; König, 2013; Pekarek Doehler, 2010) define *learning* in a sense similar to what I call *development*, that is, changes over time. In contrast, I see learning as the formation of a new practice within interaction in one sitting, and in this chapter, I aim to delineate contingencies of interaction that provide an L2 speaker with the opportunity to form a new practice.

## *ICs as the objects of learning*

CA sees language as social action, and is primarily "concerned with the analysis of the competences which underlie ordinary social activities" (Heritage, 1984b, p. 241). Such competences, or ICs, can be investigated by focusing on *interactional practices* and how *linguistic* and other *semiotic resources* are used to accomplish these interactional practices (Hauser, 2013a; Kasper & Wagner, 2014). CA-SLA researchers have investigated the development of interactional practices (e.g., Hellermann, 2007, 2008, on task opening and closing; Ishida, 2011, on engaging at another's telling closing; Nguyen, 2011, on pharmaceutical advice giving), linguistic resources (e.g., Eskildsen, 2012, on negation; Hauser, 2013a, on direct reported speech) and other semiotic resources (e.g., Mori &

Hayashi, 2006, on embodied actions, gaze). However, the issue of learning in relation to these features of ICs has largely eluded investigation. The targets of learning that participants orient to during *doing learning* found in previous studies are mostly about gaining knowledge of linguistic resources (as reviewed above), with the exception of Waring's (2013) study, in which the teacher engages the students in learning how to respond to how-are-you questions. Kim's (2012) finding regarding the adaptation of a new word afforded within interaction without public orientation to learning (as presented above in Excerpt 1) also concerns linguistic resources rather than interactional practices. If this tendency is not the result of a skew in researchers' methodological or analytical choice, but reflects participants' non-engagement in isolated activities of learning about their ICs (especially with regard to interactional practices such as turn-taking and preference organization), CA-SLA researchers need to direct more attention to what is going on within interaction that drives participants' IC development or that helps L2 speakers form new interactional practices even without an orientation to learning.

In my previous study (Ishida, 2006) of a 10-minute interaction during a communicative task assigned to an L2 speaker of Japanese (Erica) and an L1-Japanese interlocutor (Mariko), I outlined interactional contingencies in which Erica changed her ways of engaging in decision-making activities when deciding on a list of hotels to recommend to tourists. The sequential structure of a decision-making activity that they established can be presented as follows:
1. The participants are discussing a hotel
2. One provides a *ne*-marked positive assessment (e.g., *ii ne* 'That sounds good, huh?')
3. The other provides a verbal agreement token (e.g., final-falling *nn* 'yeah')
4. One makes a decision-proposal ('Let's decide on it.')

At the first occurrence of this sequence, after #2 by Mariko, Erica said *nn* (#3), but did not align with Mariko's decision-proposal (#4) and instead suggested that they continue discussing the hotel in question. In the subsequent occurrence of this sequential structure, Erica provided no verbal affirmative token in the place of #3, and thus prevented Mariko from proceeding to #4. A comparison of these two instances shows the development in Erica's action at #3 in this particular sequence, with evidence of learning; that is, the formation of a new practice in what to do at this sequential position, i.e., say *nn* in order to allow closure of the discussion and do not say *nn* to continue discussing the item. This learning occurred not simply because of repeated participation or "situated" learning, but also due to Mariko's display of understanding in #4: Mariko's display reflexively indicated that Erica's *nn* was an agreement to move onto a decision grounded on agreement and a favorable assessment, and informed Erica of the *procedural consequentiality* (Schegloff, 1991) of a verbal agreement token (#3) in this particular context (after #1 and #2).

As Kasper and Wagner (2014) maintain, "[l]anguage, culture, and interaction are learnable because they are on constant public exhibition" (p. 194). Responding to a *ne*-marked assessment in that particular sequential context was learnable because the sequential consequentiality of a response was observable in Mariko's next turn action. Cicourel states that "[t]*he interpretive procedures and their reflexive features provide continuous instructions to participants such that members can be said to be programming each other's actions as the scene unfolds*" (1974/1999, p. 95, italics in original). Since people's public displays of their understanding inform others how others' actions are interpreted, interpretive procedures are the premise of "[t]he acquisition of language rules" (Cicourel, 1974/1999, p. 90). As seen in Cicourel's argument (see also Kasper, 2009), CA-based understanding of the public nature of discursive practices, represented by the reflexivity of language, provides us with a theoretical and methodological framework within which affordances of interaction for L2 learning and development can be investigated.

Although still few in number, some researchers have begun investigating how interaction affords L2 speakers' greater ICs (e.g., Ishida, 2006, 2011; Nguyen, 2011). Nguyen shows how a patient's response to a pharmacy intern's advice giving necessitated the intern to *recipient-design* his advice on one occasion, and how this newly formed practice paved a way for him to recipient-design his advice on later occasions as well. In my previous study (Ishida, 2011) on conversations between an L2 speaker of Japanese, Sarah, and her homestay host mother, I documented how the host mother's re-issuing of a turn completion point provided Sarah with the opportunity to present her opinion. Furthermore, Sarah's development in her use of assessment at the closure of the host mother's telling was observed after an occasion where the host mother's agreement to Sarah's assessment publicly indicated that the assessment was made at the right moment. Thus, CA analysis can delineate contingencies of interaction that help L2 speakers achieve greater ICs, and paves the way for future development.

## Receipting as the object of learning

This chapter investigates the way an L2 speaker learns how to use *receipts*. When a speaker provides a *telling* (turns in which the speaker imparts information or proffers opinions; e.g., Pomerantz, 1980), the audience members, as *recipients*, signal that they are following the teller and that the teller may continue talking, using next-turn repetition (Greer, Andrade, Butterfield, & Mischinger, 2009) and short lexical and non-lexical tokens without syntactic structures (e.g., *yeah, oh, right, mm hm*; see Gardner, 1998; Mori, 2006, on *hee* 'oh, wow' in Japanese).

Through prosody and vocal qualities, recipients can even indicate their *epistemic stance*, or their position with regard to their knowledge of the delivered information or proffered opinion. In German, for example, although *achso* 'oh, I see' and *ach* 'oh' are both acknowledging receipts, they differ as to whether the receipt indicates understanding or not (Golato, 2010). Similarly, in Japanese, *soo na n desu ka* 'I see' indicates acknowledgment with understanding, while *soo desu ka* 'Is that so/Really' highlights the newsworthiness of the information found in the telling rather than claiming understanding.

The combination of the anaphor *soo* 'so' and other linguistic forms is used also to indicate agreement. However, the selection of linguistic forms that follows *soo* helps the speaker accomplish different actions through indication of differentiated epistemic stances. For example, *soo desu ne* 'That's true'—which indicates the speaker's *epistemic subordination* (Heritage & Raymond, 2005), or the subordinate rights to claim the knowledge—is used as weak agreement before showing disagreement, as found by Mori (1999). On the other hand, as Kushida (2011) shows, when the first speaker confirms the second speaker's *candidate understanding* (Kurhila, 2006), the first speaker in the third turn uses *soo soo* 'That's right,' which indicates the speaker's *epistemic authority* (Heritage & Raymond, 2005), or the epistemic rights to claim his or her authority on a proposition. Because the choice of receipt forms is crucial for indicating a particular stance toward the previous telling, performing a specific social action, and determining the trajectory of subsequent interaction, receipting is an important aspect of IC that L2 speakers of Japanese need to develop.

## The Study

With the aim of delineating the contingencies of interaction that seem to either help or hinder the L2 speaker's learning of how to use receipts, the rest of this chapter reports on a CA-SLA study of conversations that feature an L2 speaker of Japanese during his one-year study abroad in Japan.

### Methodology

#### The data

The main data consist of 10 video-recorded casual conversations that an American university student, Steve, took part in once a month during his study-abroad year in Okinawa, Japan. Most of his interlocutors were Japanese people with whom he regularly interacted during his stay in Japan, including his longtime friend from high school (Tsuyoshi), his friend from the Japanese university (Ken), and his student mentor (Ikuko). Steve recorded the conversations in a variety of situations, including mealtimes and study sessions. The recordings are identified as SA1 through SA10.

An additional set of data consists of two 20-minute conversations Steve participated in at his home university in the U.S before and after studying abroad (April, 2005 and August, 2006), each with a Japanese person whom he was meeting for the first time. These first-encounter (FE) conversations, identified as FE1 and FE2, are deemed comparable in that in each conversation Steve was introduced to a Japanese university student and had to deal with first-encounter situations. Although the topics that the participants covered in their conversations and the ways in which they interacted differ, such contrasts make valuable objects for analysis.

### Analytical process

After transcribing all the data, I made a collection of segments in which Steve was primarily the recipient of his interlocutors' tellings. Although I had the broad intention of studying the use of modal expressions as part of one's IC before carrying out the original study (Ishida, 2010), I had not decided on any specified set of modal expressions or any sequential structures in which those modal expressions are used. After I began analyzing the data through *unmotivated looking* (Psathas, 1995, p. 45), I realized the wide range of interactional functions that responses to tellings serve, and modal expressions used in receipts, in particular, caught my attention. Once an object for analysis is identified in the data, it is the standard approach in CA to make a large collection (e.g., Heritage, 1984a, on *oh*) for aggregate analysis. Following this practice, I collected segments where Steve was the recipient of his interlocutor's tellings, and analyzed Steve's use and non-use of receipts. Observations of learning emerged only after this analysis of receipts with unmotivated looking.

## Findings

### Long-term development

Steve's recipient actions in the two FE conversations (FE1 and FE2) were remarkably different in several ways. In general, the FE1 conversation consisted mostly of information exchanges and Steve rarely oriented to his interlocutor's tellings as topicalizable. Although there were a few instances of assessments, they did not develop into assessment activities in which the participants agreed or disagreed with each other's assessments. On the other hand, in the FE2 conversation, both Steve and his interlocutor frequently indicated agreement with each other and also supplied supporting evidence. This tendency is clearly captured in his use of receipts, as summarized in Table 1.

## Table 1. Steve's use of receipts in the FE1 and FE2 conversations

| Acknowledging receipt form | FE1 | FE2 | Agreeing receipt form | FE1 | FE2 |
|---|---|---|---|---|---|
| ((Repetition))<br>'I know that you said ~' | 11 | 15 | | | |
| Soo desu ka<br>'Is that so?' | 3 | 7 | | | |
| Soo na (n desu ka)<br>'I see' | 2 | — | | | |
| Sokka<br>'I got it' | — | 4 | | | |
| Soo desu ne*<br>'I see' | 16 | — | Soo (desu) ne<br>'That's true' | — | 3 |
| Soo<br>'Is that so' | 1 | 2 | Soo<br>'Right' | — | 2 |
| Soo soo*<br>'Now I got it' | — | 4 | Soo soo¿<br>'That's true (afterthought)' | — | 1 |
| | | | Soo soo<br>'That's right' | — | 6 |
| | | | ((Repetition)) deshoo?<br>'Isn't that right?' | — | 1 |
| | | | ((Repetition)) desu yo<br>'That's how it is' | — | 1 |
| | | | Soo desu yo ne<br>'That's what I also knew/thought' | — | 1 |

*Note.* Numbers indicate frequency of use. Translations in single quotes are based on the way Steve used each receipt in context. An asterisk (*) indicates inapposite[1] use of an agreeing form of receipt as an acknowledging receipt. A reversed question mark (¿) indicates inappositeness in terms of indicated epistemic stance.

In the FE1 conversation, Steve used five receipt forms for indicating acknowledgment: bare repetition without the use of the proterm *soo*, *soo desu ka* 'Is that so?,' *soo na (n desu ka)* 'I see,' *soo desu ne* 'I see,' and the plain *soo* 'Is that so.' Although *soo desu ne* 'That's true' is a form of agreement, he used it inappositely as an acknowledging receipt in a way similar to *soo desu ka* 'Is that so?,' as illustrated in Excerpt 2.[2]

**Excerpt 2.** Working for Skyline Airlines (FE1 23'38", 4/28/2005)

In response to Steve (SV)'s question about her plans for after graduation, Hiroko (HK) has answered that she wants to work for an airline company, and named Skyline Airlines as one example.

```
1  HK  okaasan:    ga:.  (0.3)  sukairain de:.  (.)
       mother      S            Skyline    at
       ((looks at SV)) ((hand to chest)) ((finger on the table))
2      hataraiteim[as.
       work-CONT
       My mother works for Skyline Airlines.

3→ SV             [aa.  soo.  hai.  soo desu ne,=
                   CS   so    yes   so  CP   IP
                            ((a nod))((blinks, gaze away from HK))
                   Oh, is that right? Yes. I see [that's true].

4  HK  =nn.  nn.
        yeah yeah
        ((nodding))
        Yeah, yeah.

5      (0.6)
       ((HK looking down, smiling))

6  SV  aa.  (0.2)  nihon  kara
       um          Japan  from
                  ((looks at HK))
       Um, from Japan?
```

In response to Hiroko's informing, Steve first indicates a change of state by saying *aa* 'oh' (Heritage, 1984a) and acknowledges the information through *soo* 'Is that right?' and a nod. However, the form of the subsequent utterance *hai. soo desu ne* 'Yes, that's true' (line 3) seems incongruent with the epistemic stance previously marked with *aa*. A congruent alternative would be either *soo desu ka* 'Really?' or repetition-plus-*ne* 'I see, (you said) xx, right?' (e.g., *sukairain desu ne* 'I see, Skyline, right?'), which is a form of *registering receipt* (Schegloff, 1997; see also Morita, 2005 for Japanese examples). Although the form of Steve's receipt *soo desu ne* is inapposite here, it hearably functions as an acknowledging receipt. Steve's shifting gaze away from Hiroko when uttering *soo desu ne* (line 3) and his returning gaze back to Hiroko at the beginning of his question (line 6) suggest that the receipt acknowledges Hiroko's informing and thus closes the informing sequence temporarily before initiating a question-answer sequence related to the topic. Hiroko withdraws from her informing by responding to Steve's receipts with nods and tokens *nn. nn.* 'yeah, yeah' (line 4) and by shifting her gaze away from him.

While Steve did not use receipts to show agreement in his FE1 conversation, he used as many as seven forms of receipt for indicating agreement in the FE2 conversation, including the apposite use of *soo (desu) ne*, as illustrated in Excerpt 3.

**Excerpt 3.** Regions in Aichi Prefecture (FE2 6'43", 8/17/2006)

Steve (SV) and Miki (MK) have found out that they had lived in adjacent regions, Mikawa and Owari. Steve had lived in a part of the Mikawa region for three weeks and had been to Nagoya City in the Owari region on day trips. Miki had lived in Nagoya for four years.

```
1  SV   mikawa to:.  (.)  na[go:ya.   tottemo  chiga:u  °ne°
        Mikawa and        Nagoya      very     different IP
        ((hand to the right))   ((to the left))  ((wiggling hand))
        Mikawa and Nagoya are very different, aren't they?

2  MK                      [°nn.°
                            yeah
                            ((a nod, gaze at SV))
3         [nn    n:n.  chigau    n(e),
           yeah yeah different   IP
           ((looks down, nodding))
           Mm hh. Yeah, they are different.

4  SV   [( docchi to- )
           which    both
        Both of them...

5  SV   ahah hh

6  MK   nn nagoya sugoi tokai da °(kedo ne:,)°
        mm Nagoya very  urban CP  but   IP
        ((a nod))
        Um, Nagoya is very urban but...,

7                (0.3)

8  SV   [°soo s  ne,°]
         so  CP IP
        That's true.
```

```
 9  MK   [°nn;]   (0.2)   n:n.   nn°=
          mm              yeah mm
         ((a nod))        ((a nod)) ((a nod))
         Mm, yeah, mm.

10  SV   =°(         )°
```

((SV goes on to mention a dialect of Nagoya.))

In response to Steve's assessment of the Mikawa region and Nagoya City as quite different (line 1), Miki indicates agreement (line 3) and presents in line 6 the grounds on which she agrees: Nagoya is very urban while Mikawa is rural, the latter of which is implied by the use of the contrastive connective *kedo* 'but.' In line 8, Steve indicates agreement by saying *soo (de)s(u) ne*, and after line 10, further mentions a dialect of Nagoya as its distinctive character. This action subsequent to *soo desu ne* indicates reflexively that he does not have any contesting opinion about Nagoya being urban, and thus accepts Miki's characterization of the city. Steve's use of the receipt form *soo s ne*, which indicates epistemic subordination in having less experience and knowledge about the city, is thus considered apposite here.

The pattern of development from the initial inapposite use of *soo desu ne* for indicating understanding to its apposite use as an agreeing receipt has been unanimously found in previous studies on study abroad (e.g., Ishida, 2009; Masuda, 2011) and L2 classrooms (e.g., Ohta, 2001; Yoshimi, 1999).

While Steve's apposite use of *soo desu ne* in the FE2 conversation shows development, what is remarkable in the FE2 conversation is his frequent use of *soo soo* 'That's right.' An example of *soo soo* that Steve appositely used is shown in Excerpt 4.

**Excerpt 4.** Translation is difficult (FE2 21'35", 8/17/2006)

Steve (SV) has been telling Miki (MK) about his recent work on Japanese-English translation, and commented that it was difficult (*muzukashikatta*). He has given an example of translating a Japanese word that does not even exist in English, and said again that translating it was difficult (*muzukashikatta desu*).

```
1  SV   eego      made   honyaku     suru   (.)  shinikui.
        English   to     translate   do          do-difficult
                                                 ((looks at MK))
2       (°soo  s-°)=
         so    CP
        Translating into English. . . It's difficult. (It Is).
```

```
3  MK   =°aa°       sore  wa  ne:,=
         ah         that  TP  IP
         ((raises head))  ((gives a big nod))
         Ah, it is . . .

4→SV    =so(h)o hh so(h)[o(h).
         so          so
         Right. Right.

5  MK                    [muzukashii yo ne:,
                          difficult  IP IP
                         ((two nods))
                         Difficult, isn't it?
```

((SV says *soo desu yo* 'That's how it is,' and mentions the differences in terms of grammar and word order.))

In response to Steve's telling of his difficulty in translating Japanese documents into English (line 1), Miki says *aa sore wa ne:,* 'ah, it is. . .' with a big nod (line 3). Although the predicate of the sentence is missing, Steve displays his understanding, by saying *soo soo* 'Right. Right' (line 4), that Miki's utterance and her nod are indications of agreement. Here, Steve anticipates that Miki will agree with him and marks the achievement of mutual agreement through the use of *soo soo*. The choice of this receipt form is apposite here because he has the right to assume epistemic authority as the person who experienced the difficulty firsthand and has repeatedly stressed the difficulty in previous turns. Steve's understanding of the trajectory of Miki's turn is confirmed in line 5, where Miki provides an assessment using the word *muzukashii* 'difficult,' which Steve has used twice before and is a synonym of *shinikui*. This excerpt thus shows Steve's competence in the use of *soo soo* for indicating achievement of mutual agreement with an implication of epistemic authority.

Although Steve used *soo soo* frequently as a strong agreeing receipt, he also used it inappositely in contexts where other receipts would have been sequentially suitable. Excerpt 5 illustrates how he used *soo soo* as an indicator of *restored intersubjectivity* (Barnes, 2012), a just-solved problem of understanding (e.g., 'I got it').

**Excerpt 5.** ELS, not ISEC (FE2 13'42", 8/17/2006)

Steve (SV) has asked Miki (MK) if she had studied abroad before starting her graduate studies in the U.S., and Miki begins talking about her first study abroad after graduating from university.

```
1   MK    sotsugyoo    shite-kara:.  suguni:.  (.) ano
          graduation   do-and then   immediately   um
2         erusu  tte  shittemasu ka?[ano language school.
          ELS    QT   know        Q  um
          ((index finger upward))      ((index finger downward))
          Right after graduating, um, do you know ELS? Um, a language
          school.

3   SV                               [((opens mouth slightly))

4         (0.2)

5   SV    erusu.  (0.3) oo okkee.  aiseru  ja-nakute
          ELS           oh okay    ISEL    CP-NG-and
          ((looks down))           ((point finger extended))
6         erusu  (0.2) [to yuu
          ELS          QT  say
          ((hand at neck))
          ELS. Oh, okay. Not ISEL but (the one) called ELS?

7   MK                 [nn.   nn.   soo.  aiseru:
                        yeah  yeah  so    ISEL
                       ((chin up))  ((a nod)) ((a nod))
8         [mitai-na kanji [no °er-° (0.2)
           similar  feeling LK EL-
          Yeah, yeah. Right. Similar to ISEL, EL-

9→  SV    [°(erusu,)°         [soo    soo
            ELS                so      so
                              ((nodding))
10        so] [o
          so
          ELS. I got it [That's right].

11  MK         [erusu no hoo
                ELS   LK  side
               ((nodding, looking down))
               ELS, not the other one.
```

((MK says that she studied there for nine months.))

Just after Miki starts talking about the English school she previously attended, she initiates an *insertion sequence* (Schegloff, 1972) in order to help establish intersubjectivity with regard to the identification of the school, and therefore suspends her telling until line 11. In response to Miki's question of whether Steve knows the school by its name (line 2), Steve indicates his non-recognition through repetition of the name and lowered eye gaze (line 5), without any acknowledging nods, any immediate acknowledging response tokens (e.g., *aa* 'ah,' *hai* 'yes'), or any claims of knowledge (e.g., *shittemasu* 'I know that'). His comparison between ISEL and ELS (lines 5–6) and the formulation *erusu to yuu. . .* '(a school) called ELS' also suggest his unfamiliarity with ELS, in contrast to his familiarity with another language school called ISEL. In response to Steve's formulation of the identification of the school, Miki says *soo* 'right' and reformulates Steve's utterance in lines 7 and 8. Thus, she acknowledges Steve's formulation as helpful for accomplishing intersubjectivity (see Kushida, 2011). This is the moment when Steve claims, through successive nods and repetition of *soo*, that he has achieved understanding of what ELS is. Miki's subsequent actions (from line 11) also reflexively construct Steve's *soo soo* as an indication of restored intersubjectivity: Miki begins withdrawing from the insertion sequence through nods and lowered gaze, and then goes back to the telling that has been suspended since line 1. Although Steve's receipt marks restored intersubjectivity here, such use of repeated *soo* (i.e., *soo soo*) is a non-standard use of the form.[3] Restored intersubjectivity would have been better indicated with the combination of the change-of-state token *aa* 'oh' and an acknowledging receipt (e.g., *sokka* 'I got it').

Even if Steve already had the latent knowledge of *soo desu ne* and *soo soo* at the time of the FE1 conversation, he did not demonstrate his competence in appositely using them. Therefore, based on this comparison of the FE1 and FE2 conversations, I conclude that Steve showed development in using these two receipt forms, even though he was still developing competence in appositely using *soo soo* at the time of the FE2 conversation. In the next section, I will illustrate some features of interaction that potentially facilitate or hinder Steve's higher competence in using these receipt forms.

**Contingencies of interaction for learning how to use receipts**
In this section, I present three features of interaction that potentially foster or impede Steve's learning of how to use receipts: (a) the interlocutor's receipting actions in a particular sequential position, (b) the interlocutor's next-turn display of understanding, and (c) the interlocutor's non-orientation to inapposite receipt use. The selected examples are presented not for the purpose of claiming a general tendency, but for illustrating cases in which CA-based findings of interactional workings can address the issue of how interaction affords L2 speakers' greater ICs.

### The interlocutor's receipting actions in a particular sequential position

Analysis of the SA conversations uncovered that the functions of Steve's interlocutor's receipting actions were identifiable in a particular sequential position and in concert with her embodied actions (C. Goodwin, 2000; M. H. Goodwin, 2007), as illustrated in Excerpt 6.

**Excerpt 6.** Translation search (SA3 15'52", 12/19/2005)

In a library study room, Steve's (SV) tutor, Ikuko (IK), is helping him with his homework for his Okinawan language class. There is a dictionary in front of Ikuko, and there are worksheets in front of Steve. They have been trying to translate a Japanese phrase, *boonenkai o shite* 'hold an end-of-year party and,' into Okinawan.

```
1   SV   o shite?  (.)  shite    wa
         O do-and       do-and   TP
                           ((turning a page))
         How about "shite"? What's "shite"?

2        (1.1)
         ((IK looks at SV's worksheet))

3   SV   suru   wa   °shite,  shite,  shite,°
         to do  TP    do-and  do-and  do-and
         ((moving fingers around over the pages))
         "To do" becomes "shite," "shite," "shite."

4        (1.1)
         ((SV moves fingers away from the worksheet))

5→  SV   °nai  yo,°
          none IP
         It's not here.

6        (0.7)

7→  IK   haa:n.  nai  ne,
         ah      none IP
         ((narrowing eyebrows))
         Ah. There's none, yeah.

8        (2.8)
         ((SV turns the page))
         ((IK looks at her dictionary))
```

*Developing Recipient Competence During Study Abroad* 271

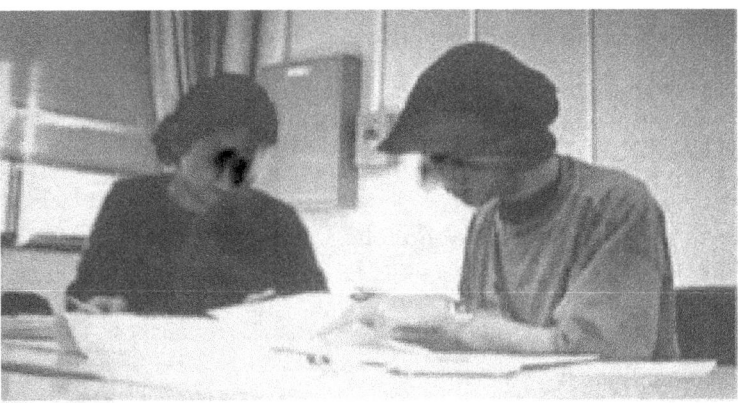

**Figure 1.** Steve runs his finger over the sheet at line 3.

Steve initiates a translation search in line 1 and finishes it in line 4. Although Ikuko joins in the search in line 2, she is a secondary participant in the activity, since Steve leads the search, as indicated via his embodied actions: Steve turns a page of the worksheet (line 1), runs his fingers over the sheet (line 3; see Figure 1), and marks the end of the activity by moving his hand away from the paper (line 4). By using the interactional particle *yo* 'I'm telling you' when reporting on the search result (*nai yo* 'There's no entry,' line 5), Steve indicates an assumption that he holds *epistemic primacy* (Raymond & Heritage, 2006), or in other words, the primary rights to claim knowledge on the content of the message (*nai* 'there's none') relative to the other person in the conversation (see also Hayano, 2011, on *yo*). Ikuko, who agrees with Steve's conclusion by repeating the word *nai*, aligns with this epistemic assumption. By adding *ne*, Ikuko accepts her epistemic subordination. Such indication of epistemic subordination is also evidenced through her subsequent actions: When Steve turns the page (line 8), Ikuko simply follows the completion of the search on that particular page and begins a new search in her dictionary. Through these embodied actions, she accepts Steve's proposition, *nai* 'there's none,' without contesting to his claim to epistemic primacy. Although Steve does not take any verbal action in response to the receipt, the action of turning the page demonstrates his understanding of her receipting.

Another example of Steve's interlocutor's use of a *ne*-marked receipt in response to Steve's *yo*-marked telling is shown below in Excerpt 7.

**Excerpt 7.** Similar languages and dialects (SA10 21'59", 7/2006)

Steve (SV) and Ken (KN) have been talking about the similarities between the Japanese and Ainu languages.[4] Steve (SV) has asserted that the Ainu language is a little different from the Japanese language. Then he begins comparing the Okinawan language to the Japanese language.

```
1→  SV   uchinaaguchi      de wa hotondo niteru    yo.
         Okinawa language  in TP mostly  resemble  IP
         ((looking sideways))                      ((looks at KN))
         I'm telling you, the Okinawan language is mostly similar to Japanese.

2        (0.5)
         ((SV and KN looking at each other))

3→  KN   niteru    ne,
         resemble  IP
         ((gaze away from SV, slightly nodding twice))
         Yeah, it's similar.

4        (0.5)

5   SV   sugu         iku wa ichun toka.
         right away   go  TP go    etc.
         ((gaze away from KN))
         ((KN looks down, fiddling with his fingers))
         "To go right away" in Japanese is "ichun" in Okinawan, for example.

6        (1.0)
         ((SV looks at KN))
         ((KN grins before saying "sore"))

7   KN   so↑re wa↓: (.) tada no (0.4) namari sa.
         that  TP       only LK       accent IP
         That's just an accent.
```

Steve, in line 1, proffers his opinion that the Okinawan language is similar to the Japanese language. Having taken a course on the Okinawan language at the university in Okinawa, he indicates his epistemic primacy concerning the close proximity between the two languages through his use of *yo*. In response, Ken indicates agreement through his repetition of the word *niteru* 'similar' followed by the interactional particle *ne* (line 3), while nodding. However, the fact that his gaze shifts away from Steve immediately after beginning the receipt and that this is followed by a subsequent 0.5-second pause suggest a lack of commitment to this agreeing action. Moreover, Ken's critical comment (line 7) about the example Steve gave in line 5 suggests that Ken does not have any evidence to support his agreement on the comparison. Such subsequent actions by Ken reflexively indicate that his utterance of *niteru ne* was not a wholehearted agreement, but a pro-forma one in response to the *yo*-marked proposition. With these indications of his epistemic subordination, Ken thus aligns with Steve's assumption of epistemic primacy. This example showed how the function of a *ne*-marked receipt is made identifiable by means of embodied actions and subsequent actions.

The analysis of Excerpts 6 and 7 revealed that the function of Ikuko's and Ken's *ne*-marked receipts are made identifiable within a particular sequential context and with accompanying embodied actions. This observation points to the possibility that monitoring the interlocutor's use of *ne*-marked receipts helps Steve learn, that is, form a new understanding of, how these receipts can be appositely used to indicate agreement while implying epistemic subordination.

### The interlocutor's next-turn display of understanding

Another feature of interaction that potentially fostered Steve's learning of how to use *soo soo* is found in the interlocutor's turn after Steve's receipt use, as illustrated in Excerpt 8.

**Excerpt 8.** Reading comic books (SA1 11'25", 10/30/2005)

Sitting side by side on the bed in his dorm room, Steve (SV) has told Tsuyoshi (TS) that it is still difficult and a little tiresome to read Japanese. In response to Tsuyoshi's question of whether it also applies to reading comic books, Steve agrees and continues after saying *tanoshii dakedo* 'it's fun, but.'

```
1   SV   chotto     manga        aru,
         a little   comic book   exist
         ((turns to the right))
         I have some comic books,

2        (0.9)
         ((SV and TS both turning gaze to the right))

3   SV   miseta:?
         show-PST
         ((turning to TS))
         Did I show them to you?

4        (0.4)

5   TS   et[to:  :   tabun:::      takahashi rumi[ko  (    )
         umm         probably-     Takahashi Rumiko
         ((looks at SV))           ((hand on the head))
         Mm, probably, Rumiko Takahashi
```

```
 6   SV      [tabun      sono  (>onna no<)        [takaha-
              probably   that  female LK           Takaha-
                                                   ((raises chin))
 7→          soo  soo  soo.
              so   so   so
              ((a nod))  ((a nod))
              Probably that woman. . . Takaha- That's right.

 8           (0.6)
             ((TS nodding))

 9→  TS      aa  a[a  aa.  >aa  yuu    yatsu  wa  yomeru    n  da.
              oh  oh   oh   that kind  stuff  TP  read-POT  N  CP
              ((nodding))       ((looks at SV))   ((opening and closing hands))
              Oh, oh, I see. You can read that stuff.

10   SV      [tomodachi  ga  (      )
              friend      S
                   ((hand at chest))
              My friend. . .

11   SV      soo.  (0.6)  aa:.  (.)  yonda     koto       ga  nai  kedo=
                                oh    read-PST  experience S   none but
              ((a nod)) ((looks away))          ((looks at TS))
              Right. Oh. I haven't read them, but...

12   TS      =aa[:.
              oh
              ((nodding))
              Oh.

13   SV      [tabun  (.)  yomitai,
              probably    read-want
                     ((gaze away from TS))
              I probably want to read them.
```

After Steve mentions that he has Japanese comic books in his dorm room (line 1), he and Tsuyoshi, in line 2, begin looking for those presumably stored on the bookshelf to their right. Although Steve asks whether he has shown them to Tsuyoshi before (line 3), Tsuyoshi does not directly answer the question, but instead offers a candidate name of the cartoonist (Rumiko Takahashi) whose book Steve might have. Overlapping with the reference to the cartoonist, Steve repeats the first part of the name, and says *soo* three times while nodding (line 7). This *soo soo soo* is hearably confirming the name, which he was trying to recall in the first half of line 6 (see Kushida, 2011, on *soo soo* for acknowledging another person's assistance with a formulation). Here, Tsuyoshi's utterance in his turn after Steve's *soo soo soo* reveals that Tsuyoshi regarded it as a confirmatory action and also demonstrates how he interpreted the relevance of the cartoonist within Steve's telling: That is, Tsuyoshi makes an inference (line 9) that Steve is capable of reading her comic books. Although Steve spontaneously confirms Tsuyoshi's inference by saying *soo* 'right' (line 11), he immediately indicates his realization of the trouble with *aa* 'oh' and enacts self-repair, saying that he has not read her books—disconfirming Tsuyoshi's inference. Continuing his turn onto line 13, Steve further clarifies that reading her books is something he hopes to do in the future, rather than a past experience. His post-*soo* actions in lines 11 and 13 exhibit Steve's higher competence in clarifying the action suggested with *soo*. Having realized a misunderstanding revealed in Tsuyoshi's understanding-display that stemmed from the ambiguous action indicated with the repetition of *soo* in line 7, Steve now competently offers a post-*soo* clarification, built in repair.

Another example of the interlocutor's next-turn display of understanding is shown in Excerpt 9.

**Excerpt 9.** The timing for job hunting (SA9 23'42", 06/26/06)

Tsuyoshi (TS), who is in his third year at a Japanese university, has been telling Steve (SV) about his plans to find a job: He will begin looking in his fourth year in order to start working immediately after graduation. Steve shows confusion about the year in which Tsuyoshi's job search will begin.

```
1   TS   nihon no daigaku (.)  wa soo >da (kara)<   sa, (.)
         Japan LK university   TP so   CP (because)  IP
         ((moving hand vertically))
2        sotsugyoo suru mae:  ni >shiken ukeru °wake°<
         graduation do  before in  test   take    that's why
                             ((moves hand to the left))
         Universities in Japan are like that. We take job-qualifying exams
         before we graduate. That's why.

3   SV   hontoo.=
         really
         Really?

4   TS   =amerika de wa (yappa)      sotsugyoo  shita
         America in TP as expected   graduation do-PST
                   ((hand toward SV))
5        ↑a↓to ja nai.
         after CP NG
         ((swiftly moves hand vertically))
         In the U.S., you guys do so after graduation, don't you?
```

```
 6→SV   aa:.         °soo soo°
        uh           so  so
        ((raises head))  ((a nod, looking in the midair))
        Uh. That's right.

 7      (0.2)
        ((SV looks at TS))

 8→TS   da  yo  ne,
        CP  IP  IP
        That's how it is, right?

 9  SV  (moo.) (.)  [°nn.  (soo.[       ]°
        already     yeah   so
        ((a nod))          ((a nod))
        (Already)... Yeah. Right. (    )

10→TS            [           [sotsugyoo  shita    ato   ni:.
                              graduation do-PST   after in
                 ((hand down)) ((hand up))        ((rightward))
11      shigoto  sagashiteru  [(°desho°)
        job      search-CONT    CP-probably
                 ((hand toward SV))  ((a nod))
        You guys usually look for jobs after graduation, (right?)

12→SV                        [soo soo.
                              so  so
                              ((two nods, looking at TS))
                              That's right.

13      (0.2)

14  TS  bokura wa:  (0.2)  sotsugyoo   suru
        we     TP          graduation  do
        ((hand at chest))
15      mae     ni  shigoto  sagasu   (wake)
        before  in  job      search   that's why
        ((hand leftward))    ((hand at chest))
        In Japan, we look for jobs before graduation.
```

When Tsuyoshi talks about the Japanese practices of job hunting, he makes public his epistemic authority through the use of *sa* 'that's that' (line 1),[5] and *wake* 'that's why' (lines 2 and 15). In contrast, when he talks about the American practice, he assigns epistemic authority to Steve by making a confirmation as the relevant next-turn response (*ja nai* 'isn't it?', line 5; *da yo ne* 'right?', line 8).[6] Steve's actions are in alignment with Tsuyoshi's epistemic indications. In response to Tsuyoshi's informing about the Japanese practices (lines 1–2),

Steve indicates that Tsuyoshi's informing provided new information by using the news-marker *hontoo* 'Really?' (line 3). Further, Steve says *soo soo* 'That's right' (lines 6 and 12) about the American practices, indicating that he has accepted epistemic authority. Although the employment of this receipt form (*soo soo*) is in exact alignment with Tsuyoshi's assignment of epistemic authority to Steve, the action that Steve takes by uttering *soo soo*—with his unfocused gaze and without a confirmatory *nn.* 'yeah' in line 6—is not clear enough for Tsuyoshi to return to the contrastive case in Japan, and thus Tsuyoshi initiates repair in line 8. Tsuyoshi projects an affirmative answer as the relevant next-turn response by saying *da yo ne* 'That's how it is, right?' (line 8), and elaborates on his earlier proposition *sotsugyoo shita ato* 'after graduation' (lines 4–5) by adding *shigoto sagashiteru* 'you look for jobs' (line 11). Such repair initiations from Tsuyoshi suggest that, even though he can tentatively regard Steve's utterance of *soo soo* as a confirming action, he still needs to ascertain its function before proceeding with his telling.[7] As Pomerantz (1984) notes, one of the options that participants can take for pursuing a response is to make sure the other party has comprehended the prior utterance. Through the reformulation of his prior proposition, Tsuyoshi makes himself better understood by Steve. In line 12, Steve firmly says *soo soo*, nodding twice while directly looking at Tsuyoshi. These coordinated actions clearly indicate that Steve is now making a confirmation. Tsuyoshi's next-turn continuation of his contrastive telling reflexively indicates that he now takes this *soo soo* as a satisfactory confirmatory receipt.

The analysis of Excerpts 8 and 9 illustrated how an "understanding-display device" (Sacks, Schegloff, & Jefferson, 1974) works in interaction: By making publicly visible his understanding of Steve's previous turn and what was going on at the moment, Tsuyoshi's post-*soo* action informed Steve how Steve's *soo soo* would work, not in the abstract, but at the very moment in that particular interaction. Thus, the action served as feedback both on the appositeness of the form choice and the ambiguity of its action. Moreover, Steve was provided with an interactional space in which he was able to perform a clearer action of confirmation.

### The interlocutor's non-orientation to inapposite receipt forms

While Steve's Japanese interlocutors occasionally initiated repair when the exact meaning of his receipt was ambiguous, this rarely occurred. They usually did not orient to such ambiguous receipts or inapposite forms of receipt from Steve. Excerpt 10 illustrates a case of this non-orientation.

**Excerpt 10.** Unfairness of the Winter Olympics (SA5 29'29", 2/27/2006)

While watching the Winter Olympics on TV, Tsuyoshi (TS) begins talking about his opinion of the Winter Olympics to Steve (SV).

```
1   TS   fuyu     no  orinpikku  wa:.   (1.7)  a:no::::  (0.5)
         winter   LK  Olympics   TP            well
         ((facing the TV))
2        okane   kakaru   jan.⁸
         money   cost     IP
         (((looks at SV))        ((a nod))
         The Winter Olympics are, well, costly, y'know.

3        (0.8)

4   SV   hontoo?
         really
         Really?

5        (0.7)
         ((TS turns back to TV))

6   TS   datte:   s:sukeeto  toka   (0.4)  sa:.
         because  skate      etc.          IP
         'Cuz, like skating,
```

((43 seconds of transcript omitted. TS gives examples of expensive sports goods and practice fees. SV says *dakedo* 'but' and refers to the availability of sponsors. TS says *dakedo* and states that sponsors are available only in rich countries. SV says that some countries are probably rich and adds *kedo* 'but.' Latching onto this connective, TS says *dakara* 'therefore' and states that only developed countries participate in the Winter Olympics.))

```
7   TS   afurika   toka   katenai      jan.
         Africa    etc.   win-POT-NG   IP
         ((looking at SV))
         Places like Africa can't win, right?

8        (0.3)

9→ SV    ee   soo  soo.
         mm   so   so
         Mm, yeah yeah [That's right].

10→      (1.1)
         ((TS turns to TV))
```

```
11→TS  >dakara<  (0.3)  ore  wa  hontoni
       so              I    TP  really
       So, I really feel,
```

((TS goes on to say that the Winter Olympics have failed to become a worldwide competition in the real sense.))

By using *jan* 'y'know' in line 2, Tsuyoshi indicates an assumption that Steve shares his knowledge about the cost for participating in the Winter Olympics. However, by saying *hontoo?* 'Really?,' Steve indicates that this is new information to him. From line 6, Tsuyoshi begins pursuing agreement on his view that participation in the Winter Olympics highly depends on the economic situation of a country. During the 53 seconds of talk from line 1 until Steve says *soo soo* in line 9, Tsuyoshi makes an agreement as a relevant next-turn action through repeated use of self-justification (e.g., *datte* '(be)cause,' Mori, 1999) and modal expressions *jan* 'y'know' (6 times) and *deshoo?* 'Isn't that right?' However, Steve disagrees each time. It is only after recurring exchanges that he indicates agreement in line 9. Although the agreeing action is in alignment with Tsuyoshi's *jan*-marked utterance 'y'know' (line 7), the form of the receipt (*soo soo*), which is associated with a claim to epistemic authority, is epistemically inapposite in this sequential environment: It is Tsuyoshi that is entitled to claim his epistemic authority over his arguments, not Steve. A form of receipt that implies the speaker's epistemic subordination (e.g., *soo da ne* 'That's true') would be more suitably used by a person who concedes to an opposing argument after iterated persuasion (Mori, 1999; Saft, 2001).[9] However, Tsuyoshi does not orient to such epistemic inappositeness: He treats Steve's action simply as a satisfactory indication of agreement, as reflexively indicated by his discontinuation of the persuasion sequence and the resumption of his telling in line 11.

This is clearly an example of the "let it pass" practice (Firth, 1996). This practice is frequently observed in the present data, as can be seen in Excerpts 2 and 5, as well as Excerpt 10. Without orientation to inappositeness of the agreeing forms of receipts, the interlocutors' subsequent turn suggests their acceptance of Steve's receipt as satisfactory, and thus might prevent Steve from overcoming his inapposite use of those forms.

## Discussion

The analyses above illustrated contingent features of social interaction that potentially have either facilitative or debilitative roles for learning how to use receipts. Although the present data set precludes a microgenetic analysis of how a new aspect of IC emerged, I will discuss in this section how these contingent features might have contributed to Steve's learning and long-term development in the use of *soo desu ne* and *soo soo*.

**Identifiability of the interactional function of the interlocutors' use of receipts**

The analysis of Excerpts 6 and 7 revealed that the function of the interlocutors' *ne*-marked receipts is made identifiable even in an untroubled interaction. *Ne* is a versatile particle that can be used for a variety of functions in diverse sequential contexts (Morita, 2015; e.g., in weak agreement as in *soo da ne* 'That's true'; as part of a filler, *soo ne:* 'let me see'; marking an intonation boundary as in *sore de ne* 'then'). Therefore, it is difficult for L2 speakers to learn the whole range of its usage (e.g., Masuda, 2011; Ohta, 2001; Yoshimi, 1999) by applying a single inclusive functional characteristic such as "display[ing] some interactional concern at that moment in terms of establishing or maintaining alignment to the ongoing activity" (Morita, 2005, p. 97). Nevertheless, when Steve's interlocutors (Ikuko and Ken) used *ne*-marked receipts, they make it public that they were agreeing to Steve's *yo*-marked assertion while indicating their epistemic status as subordinate to Steve's by (1) placing the *ne*-receipt in a particular sequential context (in this case, in response to Steve's *yo*-marked assertion), (2) initiating subsequent actions that do not indicate their strong commitment, and (3) using embodied actions that indicate retrieval from the current sequence. Steve was thus authorized to choose his subsequent action based on the understanding that his assertion received agreement.

By observing his interlocutors' use of receipts in such interactional contingencies and by responding to their actions, Steve plausibly developed an understanding of when and how he could use a *ne*-marked agreeing receipt, even without engaging in repair activities or social practice of learning. However, I am not intending to claim that Steve's long-term development of *ne*-marked receipts is the immediate result of these instances of interaction. Although Steve did show development in his use of *ne*-marked agreeing receipts between the FE1 and FE2 conversations, he had already stopped using *soo desu ne* inappositely as an acknowledging receipt and begun using the receipt form for indicating agreement in his first study-abroad conversation (SA1, 10/30/05). This suggests the need for future research to investigate the very early period of study abroad for microgenesis of receipt use. Nevertheless, the excerpts here illustrate that the sequential positioning of a receipt and associated embodied actions carry important clues to understanding the interactional function of a receipt.

In previous CA-SLA studies, L2 speakers were found to initiate repair on trouble sources concerning their understanding of the meaning of unfamiliar words that their interlocutors used (e.g., "cheese is *blowing*" in Firth & Wagner, 2007; *sneiða* 'cut' in Theodórdóttir, 2011a). Even when L2 speakers do not explicitly request assistance, L1 speakers may enact repair when L2 speakers show signs of uncertainty or trouble, by providing translation or circumlocution of the word at stake (e.g., Theodórdóttir, 2011a). CA-based analyses of these repair activities detail what cognitive-interactionist (e.g., Long, 1996) research would regard as *negotiation for meaning*,[10] in which *interactionally modified input* that L1 speakers provide solves L2 speakers' problems with understanding. In the present data, however, there is no instance in which Steve engaged in negotiation for the meaning of his interlocutors' receipts of his tellings.[11] Nonetheless, as shown in the analysis of Excerpts 6 and 7, important information that helps identify the meaning of the receipts is embedded in the sequential structure of the interaction and the interlocutors' embodied actions, and this is reflexively indicated via their subsequent actions.

## Candidate understanding and repair

In the findings of previous CA-SLA research, repair activities (including word-search activities as forward-oriented repair) are largely considered to be an important site for L2 learning. L2 speakers are often found to initiate repair on problems with the choice of words and their meanings, the correctness of grammar, and other linguistic matters, to orient to the linguistic expertise of L1 or more advanced speakers of the target language (e.g., Hosoda, 2006), and to get help from these speakers on correct alternatives. Repair activities on these problems include what cognitive-interactionist research has narrowly focused on as *confirmation checks* and *corrective feedback*. However, there are other kinds of repair: For example, by challenging the validity of the previous speaker's assertion, one can display a disaffiliative epistemic stance. Kasper and Prior (2015), for example, illustrate such cases, in which an interviewer displays a disaffiliative affective stance by saying *You said that?* in response to the interviewee's narrative reports of their own and others' speech. Furthermore, repair activities found in Excerpts 8 and 9 deal with the specific actions made with Steve's *soo soo*. I would like to argue here that these repair activities provided Steve opportunities for learning in ways different from the repair activities documented in previous CA-SLA research on learning.

In Excerpt 9, Tsuyoshi initiated other-repair on the ambiguity of the action made with Steve's *soo soo*. Since this repair was accomplished through re-doing the confirmation-seeking turn, Steve was offered the opportunity to re-do his confirming action. Furthermore, Tsuyoshi's display of his candidate understanding informed Steve that *soo soo* was, even tentatively, taken as an act of confirmation, and gave Steve a warrant to use the same linguistic resource (*soo soo*) as a form of confirmation. Steve thus used this receipt in the second instance with more clarity through prosody and direct gaze. Meanwhile, in Excerpt 8, the candidate understandings displayed in Tsuyoshi's post-*soo* turn informed Steve of a gap in understanding. After his realization of the misunderstanding, Steve initiated repair and specified what his previous *soo*

*soo* confirmed—that the name Tsuyoshi referred to is the name of the cartoonist whose books Steve wants to read, even though he has not read them yet.

Although we have seen the contingencies of interaction that afforded Steve's improved response to a confirmation-seeking turn, I am reluctant to claim that this provides an illustration of a microgenetic developmental process, since Steve had already started using *soo soo* for confirmation in his first study-abroad conversation (Excerpt 8, taken from SA1). Nevertheless, it does illustrate how the normal feature of talk-in-interaction that Sacks et al. (1974) call an "understanding-display device," in contrast to *learning as social practice*, helped Steve recognize the locally constructed meaning of his prior action, and further provided him with the opportunity for exhibiting his competence in formulating a clearer action.

**Orientation to progressivity**

As we observed in Excerpts 8 and 9, Steve and his interlocutor engaged in repair when intersubjectivity was threatened. However, as seen in Excerpt 10, along with Excerpts 2 and 5, Steve's interlocutors did not orient to the *incongruence* (Hayano, 2011) between the epistemic stance assumed in the particular sequential position and the epistemic stance indicated by the receipt form that Steve used. This practice of "letting-it-pass" (Firth, 1996) seems to be a consequence of the participants' orientation to the *progressivity* of talk (Lerner, 1996). Rather than repair matters irrelevant to the current trajectory of talk, they build on what has been achieved to move the talk forward. However, the indexical nature of receipting actions should also be taken into account when providing possible explanations for the rarity of repair on receipts. First, next-turn repair-initiation on receipts by the interlocutors is sometimes impractical because they cannot judge the aptness of a receipt at the time of its utterance. The meaning of a receipt can be made clear only in subsequent turns. By the time the interlocutor detects incongruence between the form of a receipt and its subsequent actions, the course of interaction has already proceeded and the interlocutor may find initiation of repair to be out of place. Furthermore, the choice of receipt forms indexes not only the speaker's epistemic stance, but also certain identities the speaker wants to project (e.g., Raymond & Heritage, 2006). *Soo soo* is an important linguistic resource with which an L2 speaker can claim equal or higher position on a matter at hand despite their conceivable linguistic disadvantage, and its use can enable an L2 speaker to engage in meaningful activities and claim certain identities (e.g., Ishida, 2010). Steve's interlocutors could have been being cautious not to threaten Steve's face by challenging his claim to higher epistemic status.

That being the case, how might such non-orientation to epistemically incongruent use of a receipt form have affected Steve's development of IC? In his FE2 conversation, there were still many cases of inapposite use of *soo*

*soo* even though his use of this receipt form became more natural over time. Steve's difficulty in overcoming its inapposite use could have been affected by his interlocutors' non-orientation to its unexpected sequential placement, which informed him that his use of this receipt was acceptable. However, his lingering overuse of *soo soo* could also be due to the demand for prompt receipting: It is possible that the presence of a wide variety of similar receipt forms involving different combinations of modal expressions overburdened him when choosing a particular receipt, and tempted him to rely on this particular receipt form as a convenient to-go form. If so, we can consider that the receipt form *soo soo* became an important linguistic resource for interaction, enabling him to participate in "expedient interaction" (Firth, 2009, p. 140). In addition, the interlocutors' non-orientation to epistemic incongruence allowed Steve's prompt receipting and "accomplishment of normality" (Firth, 1996), and contributed to Steve's "doing *not* being a language learner" (Firth, 2009). Thus, the present analysis has documented one aspect of interactional contingencies that worked for learning a language in and for social interaction, rather than for learning a language as acquisition of linguistic knowledge.

## Conclusion

For L2 speakers who study abroad, the ways in which they engage in conversations highly affect the kinds of L2 competences that they develop (e.g., Wilkinson, 2002). The present study has focused on one L2 speaker's use of two receipt forms and explored, through ethnomethodological CA, affordances of social interaction for developing his IC when in the role of a recipient. Cognitive-interactionist research has shown findings that interactionally modified input and corrective feedback provided during negotiation for meaning help L2 speakers pay selective attention to linguistic forms and thus facilitate acquisition. However, this scenario is considered for the learning of language as a self-contained system, and does not directly apply to the learning of how to use receipts. In the present CA-SLA study, interactionally modified input was not available with regard to Steve's interlocutor's receipts. The functions of their receipts, however, were made identifiable in a particular sequential position with accompanying embodied actions, and without interactional modification. Moreover, corrective feedback was not provided on Steve's use of receipts due to the indexical nature of receipting, although Steve's interlocutors did pursue clarification of his *soo*-marked actions. The interlocutors' understanding-display is "a vehicle of intersubjectivity" (Kurhila, 2006, p. 173), which helps Steve recognize threatened intersubjectivity and seems to provide an opportunity for him to be a competent participant in the social interaction.

Over the past decade, a growing number of CA-SLA studies have contributed to our understanding of the trajectories in which L2 ICs develop over time, both inside and outside the classroom. However, the explanations offered for the observed development of ICs—drawn on from exogenous theories of learning such as the theory of situated learning, sociocultural theory, and language socialization—tend to be general ones that relate to overall developmental paths rather than the specific instances analyzed. Only a handful of studies have examined contingencies of interaction that situate the formation of new practices. While such interactional contingencies have been extensively studied with regard to discrete linguistic features such as vocabulary, morphology, and syntax, this does not apply for ICs. The present study was aimed at filling this gap in research and unveiling affordances of social interaction for learning that help the development of ICs. Although this study revealed only some features of interaction that potentially help L2 speakers to learn how to use receipts and did not explore microgenesis of ICs, I hope this research has paved the way for future studies of ICs to explore this issue of learning in interaction.

## Notes

1. I use the term *appositeness* (e.g., Kasper & Kim, 2007) to describe when one's receipting action fits the sequential context. Since appositeness is about situational timeliness and properness, this adjective aligns well with CA's stance on sequential positioning.
2. All excerpts in the remainder of this chapter are taken from the data collected for my doctoral dissertation (Ishida, 2010). All names are pseudonyms.
3. My interpretation of inappositeness does not go against CA's analytical approach. In a CA study on the use of *that's right* by a person with aphasia, Barnes (2012) writes, "The identification of the restored intersubjectivity *that's right* also suggests that recipients can exploit the epistemic and actional characteristics of *that's right* to employ it in unexpected (and perhaps ad hoc) ways" (p. 258). His interpretation also suggests that a set of linguistic resources, instead of those that are sequentially expected, can be impromptly drawn on to deal with the immediate necessity to respond.
4. Ainu are the people native to northern Japan.
5. Morita (2005) argues that the turn-final particle *sa* indicates the *non-negotiability* of the utterance that precedes it.
6. Tsuyoshi's assignment of epistemic authority to Steve would also be indicated with *desho* 'isn't it?' in line 11. Although this part is inaudible because of the overlap, the video shows the movement of Tsuyoshi's mouth, which ends with an "o" sound.
7. Tsuyoshi's turn in line 5 ending with *ja nai* 'isn't it?' makes a confirmation a preferred response in the next turn. Therefore, Steve's *soo soo* is not a receipting action. My analysis, however, shows what epistemic stance is assumed in Steve's use of this linguistic form, which can be employed as a form of receipt.

8   Jan is one of the colloquial variants of the negative question form *de wa nai ka* 'isn't it,' along with *ja nai*, widely used throughout Japan. As such, it acts as a tag question.
9   Mori's (1999) excerpts contain many instances in which the recipient uses *soo da ne* 'That's true' after the teller pursues agreement with the use of "self-justification" (p. 168) and the modal expression *jan* 'isn't it.'
10  I use Long's (1996) term *negotiation for meaning* instead of the widely-used term *negotiation of meaning*. The former term is suitable for the cognitive-interactionist view of negotiation, which sees it as the process of communication for the purpose of identifying the meaning that one of the interlocutors intended to encode. The second term can be interpreted, if used in a discursive practice approach, as the process of discursively accomplishing shared meaning.
11  There are, however, many instances of other-initiations of repair when Steve's interlocutors answer his question, using the forms often drawn on as receipts (e.g., *soo soo* 'right,' *kamo shirenai* 'it could be true'). Steve requests they confirm their answers and they sometimes modify their initial answers. This finding suggests two points: (a) Steve's challenge against his interlocutor's response implies that he already understood the action that the interlocutor took; that is, the repair he initiated is not about a comprehension problem; and (b) Repair was called for because the validity of the interlocutors' response was relevant for the subsequent trajectory of the talk-in-interaction.

# References

Barnes, S. (2012). On *that's right* and its combination with other tokens. *Journal of Pragmatics, 44*, 243–260.
Bronson, M. C., & Watson-Gegeo, K. A. (2008). The critical moment: Language socialization and the (re)visioning of first and second language learning. In P. A. Duff & N. H. Hornberger (Eds.), *Encyclopedia of language and education* (2nd ed., Vol. 8: Language Socialization, pp. 43–55). Dordrecht, Netherlands: Springer.
Brouwer, C. E. (2003). Word searches in NNS-NS interaction: Opportunities for language learning? *Modern Language Journal, 87*(4), 534–545.
Brouwer, C. E., & Wagner, J. (2004). Developmental issues in second language conversation. *Journal of Applied Linguistics, 1*(1), 29–47.
Cicourel, A. V. (1999). Interpretive procedures. In A. Jaworski & N. Coupland (Eds.), *The discourse reader* (pp. 89–97). New York, NY: Routledge. (Reprinted from *Cognitive sociology: Language and meaning in social interaction*, pp. 51–58, by A. V. Cicourel, 1974, Harmondsworth, UK: Penguin Education)
Collentine, J., & Freed, B. F. (2004). Learning context and its effects on second language acquisition: Introduction. *Studies in Second Language Acquisition, 26*, 153–171.

Eskildsen, S. W. (2012). L2 negation constructions at work. *Language Learning, 62*(2), 335–372.

Eskildsen, S. W., & Wagner, J. (2015). Embodied L2 construction learning. *Language Learning, 65*(2), 268–297.

Firth, A. (1996). The discursive accomplishment of normality: On "lingua franca" English and conversation analysis. *Journal of Pragmatics, 26*, 237–259.

Firth, A. (2009). Doing *not* being a foreign language learner: English as a *lingua franca* in the workplace and (some) implications for SLA. *IRAL, 47*, 127–156.

Firth, A., & Wagner, J. (1997). On discourse, communication, and (some) fundamental concepts in SLA research. *Modern Language Journal, 81*(3), 285–300.

Firth, A., & Wagner, J. (2007). Second/foreign language learning as a social accomplishment: Elaborations on a reconceptualized SLA. *Modern Language Journal, 91*(5), 800–819.

Freed, B. F. (1995). *Second language acquisition in a study abroad context.* Amsterdam: John Benjamins.

Freed, B. F., Segalowitz, N., & Dewey, D. P. (2004). Context of learning and second language fluency in French. *Studies in Second Language Acquisition, 26*(2), 275–301.

Gardner, R. (1998). Between speaking and listening: The vocalisation of understandings. *Applied Linguistics, 19*(2), 204–224.

Gardner, R. (2008). Conversation analysis and orientation to learning. *Journal of Applied Linguistics, 5*(3), 229–244.

Gardner, R., & Wagner, J. (Eds.). (2004). *Second language conversations: Studies of communication in everyday settings.* London: Continuum.

Garfinkel, H. (1967). *Studies in ethnomethodology.* Englewood Cliffs, NJ: Prentice-Hall.

Golato, A. (2010). Marking understanding versus receipting information in talk: *Achso* and *ach* in German interaction. *Discourse Studies, 12*(2), 147–176.

Goodwin, C. (2000). Action and embodiment within situated human interaction. *Journal of Pragmatics, 32*, 1489–1522.

Goodwin, M. H. (2007). Participation and embodied action in preadolescent girls' assessment activity. *Research on Language and Social Interaction, 40*(4), 353–375.

Greer, T., Andrade, V. B. S., Butterfield, J., & Mischinger, A. (2009). Receipt through Repetition. *JALT Journal, 31*(1), 5–34.

Hall, J. K., & Pekarek Doehler, S. (2011). L2 interactional competence and development. In J. K. Hall, J. Hellermann, & S. Pekarek Doehler (Eds.), *L2 interactional competence and development* (pp. 1–15). Bristol, UK: Multilingual Matters.

Hatch, E. (1978). Discourse analysis and second language acquisition. In E. Hatch (Ed.), *Second language acquisition: A book of readings* (pp. 401–435). Rowley, MA: Newbury House.

Hauser, E. (2001). Corrective recasts in interaction: A case study. *Second Language Studies, 20*(1), 79–98.

Hauser, E. (2005). Coding "corrective recasts": The maintenance of meaning and more fundamental problems. *Applied Linguistics, 26*(3), 293–316.

Hauser, E. (2013a). Expanding resources for making direct reported speech. In T. Greer, D. Tatsuki, & C. Roever (Eds.), *Pragmatics and language learning* (Vol. 13, pp. 29–53). Honolulu, HI: University of Hawai'i, National Foreign Language Resource Center.

Hauser, E. (2013b). Stability and change in one adult's second language English negation. *Language Learning, 63*(3), 463–498.

Hayano, K. (2011). Claiming epistemic primacy: *Yo*-marked assessments in Japanese. In T. Stivers, L. Mondada & J. Steensig (Eds.), *The morality of knowledge in conversation* (pp. 58–81). Cambridge: Cambridge University Press.

Hellermann, J. (2007). The development of practices for action in classroom dyadic interaction: Focus on task openings. *Modern Language Journal, 91*(1), 83–96.

Hellermann, J. (2008). *Social actions for classroom language learning*. Clevedon, UK: Multilingual Matters.

Hellermann, J. (2009). Looking for evidence of language learning in practices for repair: A case study of self-initiated self-repair by an adult learner of English. *Scandinavian Journal of Educational Research, 53*(2), 113–132.

Heritage, J. (1984a). A change-of-state token and aspects of its sequential placement. In M. Atkinson & J. Heritage (Eds.), *Structures of social action: Studies in conversation analysis* (pp. 299–345). Cambridge: Cambridge University Press.

Heritage, J. (1984b). *Garfinkel and ethnomethodology*. Cambridge: Polity Press.

Heritage, J., & Raymond, G. (2005). The terms of agreement: Indexing epistemic authority and subordination in talk-in-interaction. *Social Psychology Quarterly, 68*(1), 15–38.

Hosoda, Y. (2006). Repair and relevance of differential language expertise in second language conversation. *Applied Linguistics, 27*(1), 25–50.

Iino, M. (1999). Language use and identity in contact situations: An ethnographic study of dinner table conversations between Japanese host families and American students. In L. F. Bouton (Ed.), *Pragmatics and language learning* (Vol. 9, pp. 129–162). Urbana-Champaign, IL: Division of English as an International Language, University of Illinois, Urbana-Champaign.

Ishida, M. (2006). Interactional competence and the use of modal expressions in decision-making activities: CA for understanding microgenesis of competence. In K. Bardovi-Harlig, C. Félix-Brasdefer, & A. S. Omar (Eds.), *Pragmatics and language learning* (Vol. 11, pp. 55–79). Honolulu, HI: University of Hawai'i, National Foreign Language Resource Center.

Ishida, M. (2009). Development of interactional competence: Changes in the use of *ne* in L2 Japanese during study abroad. In H. T. Nguyen & G. Kasper (Eds.), *Talk-in-interaction: Multilingual perspectives* (pp. 351–385). Honolulu, HI: University of Hawai'i, National Foreign Language Resource Center.

Ishida, M. (2010). *Development of interactional competence in L2 Japanese during study abroad: The use of modal expressions in recipient actions* (Doctoral dissertation). Available from ProQuest Dissertations and Theses database (AAT 3415909).

Ishida, M. (2011). Engaging in another person's telling as a recipient in L2 Japanese: Development of interactional competence during one-year study-abroad. In G. Pallotti & J. Wagner (Eds.), *L2 learning as social practice: Conversation-analytic perspectives* (pp. 45–85). Honolulu, HI: University of Hawai'i, National Foreign Language Resource Center.

Jefferson, G. (1986). Notes on 'latency' in overlap onset. *Human Studies, 9*, 153–183.

Jefferson, G. (1987). On exposed and embedded correction in conversation. In G. Button & J. R. E. Lee (Eds.), *Talk and social organization* (pp. 86–100). Clevedon, UK: Multilingual Matters.

Kasper, G. (2006). Beyond repair: Conversation analysis as an approach to SLA. *AILA Review, 19*, 83–99.

Kasper, G. (2009). Locating cognition in second language interaction and learning: Inside the skull or in public view? *IRAL, 47*(1), 11–36.

Kasper, G., & Kim, Y. (2007). Handling sequentially inapposite responses. In Z. Wei, P. Seedhouse, L. Wei & V. Cook (Eds.), *Language learning and teaching as social interaction* (pp. 22–41). Basingstoke, UK: Palgrave Macmillan.

Kasper, G., & Prior, M. T. (2015). "You said that": Other-initiations of repair addressed to represented talk. *Text & Talk, 35*(6), 815–844.

Kasper, G., & Wagner, J. (2011). A conversation-analytic approach to second language acquisition. In D. Atkinson (Ed.), *Alternative approaches to second language acquisition* (pp. 117–142). New York, NY: Routledge.

Kasper, G., & Wagner, J. (2014). Conversation analysis in applied linguistics. *Annual Review of Applied Linguistics, 34*, 171–212.

Kim, Y. (2012). Practices for initial recognitional reference and learning opportunities in conversation. *Journal of Pragmatics, 44*(6-7), 709–729.

Kinginger, C. (2009). *Language learning and study abroad: A critical reading of research*. Basingstoke, UK: Palgrave Macmillan.

König, C. (2013). Topic management in French L2: A longitudinal conversation analytic study. *EUROSLA Yearbook, 13*, 226–250.

Koshik, I., & Seo, M.-S. (2012). Word (and other) search sequences initiated by language learners. *Text & Talk, 32*(2), 167–189.

Kurhila, S. (2001). Correction in talk between native and non-native speaker. *Journal of Pragmatics, 33*(7), 1083–1110.

Kurhila, S. (2006). *Second language interaction*. Amsterdam: John Benjamins.

Kushida, S. (2011). Confirming understanding and acknowledging assistance: Managing trouble responsibility in response to understanding check in Japanese talk-in-interaction. *Journal of Pragmatics, 43*(11), 2716–2739.

Lantolf, J. P., & Thorne, S. L. (2006). *Sociocultural theory and the genesis of second language development*. Oxford: Oxford University Press.

Lave, J., & Wenger, E. (1991). *Situated learning: Legitimate peripheral participation.* Cambridge: Cambridge University Press.

Lee, Y-A. (2010). Learning in the contingency of talk-in-interaction. *Text & Talk, 30*(4), 403–422.

Lerner, G. H. (1996). On the "semi-permeable" character of grammatical units in conversation: Conditional entry into the turn space of another participant. In E. Ochs, E. A. Schegloff, & S. A. Thompson (Eds.), *Interaction and grammar* (pp. 238–245). Cambridge: Cambridge University Press.

Long, M. H. (1983). Linguistic and conversational adjustments to non-native speakers. *Studies in Second Language Acquisition, 5*(2), 177–193.

Long, M. H. (1996). The role of the linguistic environment in second language acquisition. In W. C. Ritchie & T. K. Bhatia (Eds.), *Handbook of second language acquisition* (pp. 413–468). San Diego, CA: Academic Press.

Markee, N. (2000). *Conversation analysis.* Mahwah, NJ: Lawrence Erlbaum.

Markee, N. (2008). Toward a learning behavior tracking methodology for CA-for-SLA. *Applied Linguistics, 29*(3), 404–427.

Markee, N., & Seo, M.-S. (2009). Learning talk analysis. *IRAL, 47,* 37–63.

Masuda, K. (2011). Acquiring interactional competence in a study abroad context: Japanese language learners' use of the interactional particle *ne. Modern Language Journal, 95*(4), 519–540.

Matsumura, S. (2001). Learning the rules for offering advice: A quantitative approach to second language socialization. *Language Learning, 51*(4), 635–679.

Mori, J. (1999). *Negotiating agreement and disagreement in Japanese: Connective expressions and turn construction.* Amsterdam: John Benjamins.

Mori, J. (2006). The workings of the Japanese token *hee* in informing sequences: An analysis of sequential context, turn shape, and prosody. *Journal of Pragmatics, 38,* 1175–1205.

Mori, J., & Hayashi, M. (2006). The achievement of intersubjectivity through embodied completions: A study of interactions between first and second language speakers. *Applied Linguistics, 27*(2), 195–219.

Morita, E. (2005). *Negotiation of contingent talk: The Japanese interactional particles* ne *and* sa. Amsterdam: John Benjamins.

Morita, E. (2015). Japanese interactional particles as a resource for stance building. *Journal of Pragmatics, 83,* 91–103.

Nguyen, H. T. (2011). Achieving recipient design longitudinally: Evidence from a pharmacy intern in patient consultations. In J. K. Hall, J. Hellermann, & S. Pekarek-Doehler (Eds.), *Interactional competence and development* (pp. 173–205). Bristol, UK: Multilingual Matters.

Ohta, A. S. (2001). *Second language acquisition process in the classroom: Learning Japanese.* Mahwah, NJ: Lawrence Erlbaum.

Ortega, L. (2009). *Understanding second language acquisition.* New York, NY: Hodder Education.

Pallotti, G., & Wagner, J. (Eds.). (2011). *L2 learning as social practice: Conversation-analytic perspectives*. Honolulu, HI: University of Hawai'i, National Foreign Language Resource Center.

Pekarek Doehler, S. (2010). Conceptual changes and methodological challenges: On language and learning from a conversation analytic perspective on SLA. In P. Seedhouse, S. Walsh, & C. J. Jenks (Eds.), *Conceptualizing 'learning' in applied linguistics* (pp. 105–126). New York, NY: Palgrave MacMillan.

Pekarek Doehler, S., & Pochon-Berger, E. (2015). The development of L2 interactional competence: Evidence from turn-taking organization, sequence organization, repair organization and preference organization. In T. Cadierno & S. W. Eskildsen (Eds.), *Usage-based perspectives on second language learning* (pp. 233–267). Berlin: Mouton de Gruyter.

Pomerantz, A. (1980). Telling my side: "Limited access" as a "fishing" device. *Sociological Inquiry, 50*(3-4), 186–198.

Pomerantz, A. (1984). Pursuing a response. In M. Atkinson & J. Heritage (Eds.), *Structures of social action: Studies in conversation analysis* (pp. 152–163). Cambridge: Cambridge University Press.

Psathas, G. (1995). *Conversation analysis: The study of talk-in-interaction*. Thousand Oaks, CA: Sage.

Raymond, G., & Heritage, J. (2006). The epistemics of social relations: Owning grandchildren. *Language in Society, 35*, 677–705.

Sacks, H., & Schegloff, E. A. (1979). Two preferences in the organization of reference to persons in conversation and their interaction. In G. Psathas (Ed.), *Everyday language: Studies in ethnomethodology* (pp. 15–21). New York, NY: Halsted (Irvington).

Sacks, H., Schegloff, E. A., & Jefferson, G. (1974). A simplest systematics for the organization of turn-taking for conversation. *Language, 50*, 696–735.

Saft, S. (2001). Displays of concession in university faculty meetings: Culture and interaction in Japanese. *Pragmatics, 11*(3), 223–262.

Sahlström, F. (2011). Learning as social action. In J. K. Hall, J. Hellermann, & S. Pekarek-Doehler (Eds.), *Interactional competence and development* (pp. 45–65). Bristol, UK: Multilingual Matters.

Schegloff, E. A. (1972). Notes on a conversational practice: Formulating place. In D. Sudnow (Ed.), *Studies in social interaction* (pp. 75–119). New York, NY: Free Press.

Schegloff, E. A. (1991). Conversation analysis and socially shared cognition. In L. B. Resnick, J. M. Levine, & S. D. Teasley (Eds.), *Perspectives on socially shared cognition* (pp. 150–171). Washington, DC: American Psychological Association.

Schegloff, E. A. (1997). Practices and actions: Boundary cases of other-initiated repair. *Discourse Processes, 23*, 499–545.

Schegloff, E. A. (2000). When "others" initiate repair. *Applied Linguistics, 21*(2), 205–243.

Schegloff, E. A., Jefferson, G., & Sacks, H. (1977). The preference for self-correction in the organization of repair in conversation. *Language, 53*(2), 361–382.

Seedhouse, P. (2004). The interactional architecture of the language classroom: A conversation analysis perspective. *Language Learning, 54*(S1), 1–300.

Seo, M-S. (2011). Talk, body, and material objects as coordinated interactional resources in repair activities in one-on-one ESL tutoring. In G. Pallotti & J. Wagner (Eds.), *L2 learning as social practice: Conversation-analytic perspectives* (pp. 107–134). Honolulu, HI: University of Hawai'i, National Foreign Language Resource Center.

Theodórsdóttir, G. (2011a). Language learning activities in real-life situations: Insisting on TCU completion in second language talk. In G. Pallotti & J. Wagner (Eds.), *L2 learning as social practice: Conversation-analytic perspectives* (pp. 185–208). Honolulu, HI: University of Hawai'i, National Foreign Language Resource Center.

Theodórsdóttir, G. (2011b). Second language interaction for business and learning. In J. K. Hall, J. Hellermann, & S. Pekarek-Doehler (Eds.), *Interactional competence and development* (pp. 93–118). Bristol, UK: Multilingual Matters.

van Compernolle, R. A. (2010). Incidental microgenetic development in second-language teacher-learner talk-in-interaction. *Classroom Discourse, 1*(1), 66–81.

Waring, H. Z. (2013). "How was your weekend?": Developing the interactional competence in managing routine inquiries. *Language Awareness, 22*(1), 1–16.

Wilkinson, S. (2002). The omnipresent classroom during summer study abroad: American students in conversation with their French hosts. *Modern Language Journal, 86*(2), 157–173.

Sacks, H., Schegloff, E. A., & Jefferson, G. (1974). A simplest systematics for the organization of turn-taking for conversation. *Language, 50*, 696–735.

Yang, J.-S. (2016). The effectiveness of study-abroad on second language learning: A meta-analysis. *The Canadian Modern Language Review. La Revue Canadienne Des Langues Vivantes, 72*(1), 66-94.

Yoshimi, D. R. (1999). L2 language socialization as a variable in the use of *ne* by L2 learners of Japanese. *Journal of Pragmatics, 31*, 1513–1525.

Young, R. F. (2011). Interactional competence in language learning, teaching, and testing. In E. Hinkel (Ed.), *Handbook of research in second language teaching and learning* (Vol. 2, pp. 426–443). New York, NY: Routledge.

# 10

# Becoming a Conversationalist at the Dinner Table: Topic Management Practices by a JFL Student Living in Foreign Language Housing

Junko Mori
*University of Wisconsin-Madison*

Yumiko Matsunaga
*University of Colorado Boulder*

## Introduction

Since Firth and Wagner's (1997) call for the reconceptualization of second language (L2) learning and the expansion of L2 data for investigation, the last two decades have seen a growing number of studies that investigate L2 speakers' conduct as observed in various types of social interaction. By using conversation analysis (CA) as a central tool for analysis, these studies have explicated how L2 speakers utilize linguistic and other semiotic resources to accomplish social actions, and how they demonstrate, through their conduct, orientation towards the institutional or non-institutional nature of activities in progress (e.g., Cadierno & Eskildsen, 2015; Gardner & Wagner, 2004; Hall, Hellermann, & Pekarek Doehler, 2011; Markee, 2004; Mori & Markee, 2009; Nguyen & Kasper, 2009; Pallotti & Wagner, 2011, to name several edited volumes and special issues featuring a collection of such studies). A cross-section of these studies also elucidates how interactional contingencies experienced by L2 speakers, and consequently affordances for L2 learning, differ from one occasion to another. As discussed by Eskildsen and Theodórsdóttir (2017), the interactional work conducted by participants to set up and ensure L2 learning and teaching activities differs for classroom and non-classroom contexts as well. The current study situates itself within this body of research and examines one specific type of out-of-classroom interaction, dinner table conversation held in a Foreign Language Housing (FLH) setting (a kind of residential learning program that has long been instituted at colleges and universities in the United States).[1] Through the close examination of two episodes of dinner table conversation, the study considers how mundane conversation at this FLH is organized and what kind of L2 learning it occasions. More specifically, by focusing on the performance of one focal participant, Michael (a pseudonym), one of the most active students in the program, this chapter considers how this particular student managed to take advantage of opportunities presented by this program.

Notwithstanding some variations in their organization and stated objectives, FLH programs generally share the goal of increasing student residents' exposure to the target language and culture beyond the language classroom (Bown, Dewey, Martinsen, & Baker, 2011; Martinsen, Baker, Bown & Johnson, 2011; Martinsen, Baker, Dewey, Bown, & Johnson, 2010; Matsunaga, 2012). To attain this goal, these programs typically offer official activities such as dinner table conversations, cultural events and classes, and office hours with L1-speaking facilitators and resident faculty, although precise arrangements for these activities vary from one program to another. In addition, student residents may also hold unofficial activities, such as movie nights and cooking parties. In other words, the participants in each FLH program—both L2-speaking student residents and L1-speaking facilitators—are the ones who determine and co-construct particular kinds of spaces for L2 learning through these various activities. Thus, FLH activities, which are situated outside of the classroom but still within educational institutions, can be seen as occupying a unique place in between the language classroom, where L2 learning is foregrounded and L2 learner status takes prominence, and out-of-classroom contexts, where L2 learning is not at the forefront and other aspects of the participants' identities may become more salient.

Despite the extensive history of FLH programs and their reported effectiveness in providing more opportunities for L2 use than classrooms and traditional study abroad programs (Martinsen et al., 2011; Martinsen et al., 2010), the realities of FLH activities and the nature of the L2 learning that takes place in these contexts have not been thoroughly investigated. In particular, while the importance of dinner table conversation for the residents' L2 use and development has been frequently pointed out by both researchers and the participants themselves, to our knowledge, few studies have investigated actual audio- or video-recorded conversations that occur at the FLH dinner table. One notable exception is Bown et al. (2011), who studied several FLH programs at an American university by using participant observation, interviews with residents, and analysis of video-recorded conversation at the dinner table. The findings generated from these multiple data sources indicate that the residents' level of L2 proficiency, the closeness of the residents, and the maturity of each program as a community were among the factors that affected the quality of the dinner table conversation. For instance, they reported that dinner table conversation in the Japanese FLH program, which had relatively lower-level L2 speakers compared to the other programs, was mostly dominated by two L1-speaking resident facilitators. The student residents' L2 production was generally limited to simple observations about their surroundings, simple questions, commonly used greetings and other set phrases. Bown et al. linked their observation of this outcome to an interview comment by one of the participants, who pointed out that the low proficiency level of the student residents and the lack of scaffolding provided by the resident facilitator and advanced-level speakers impeded efforts to speak Japanese. With no transcript of the video-recorded interaction made available, however, it is not clear exactly how the interaction unfolded and what kinds of scaffolding might have been possible.

In contrast to what is reported by Bown et al. (2011), our focal participant, Michael, demonstrated active contributions to the ongoing development of interaction, despite the fact that he was only a first-year Japanese student at the time. As alluded to by the example from Bown et al., becoming active conversationalists at the dinner table can present a major hurdle for L2 speakers who have only experienced L2 use in the beginning-level language classroom. Nevertheless, unless they make the shift from responding to the agenda set by instructors to initiating and pursuing talk on a range of topics, student residents cannot take advantage of the unique opportunities presented at the dinner table that differ from traditional classroom interaction. Through the close examination of two episodes of FLH dinner table conversation, the current study explores how the participants engage in this out-of-classroom, unstructured, multi-party conversation, and create opportunities for L2 learning. In particular, we pay close attention to the nature of interactional competence (IC) exhibited by Michael, as it pertains to topic management, and how it enabled him to create spaces for L2 learning not frequently available in the beginning-level language classroom. By juxtaposing the two episodes, which occurred four months apart, we also consider how Michael expanded the L2 resources he used for discussing similar topics and how he improved his efficacy in calibrating L2 resources.

## Interactional competence, topic management, and L2 learning

In the field of applied linguistics, the notion of IC was first introduced by Schmidt (1983), whose study of a Japanese speaker of English, Wes, is widely recognized as the earliest longitudinal study of L2 pragmatic development. Since then, the conceptualization of IC has been further advanced thanks to the work of Kramsch (1986), Hall (1993, 1995), McNamara (1997), He and Young (1998), and Young (2003, 2009), among others. In contrast to the previously dominant conceptualization of L2 competence that puts emphasis on an individual's static, cognitive properties, IC sheds light on dynamic, context-specific practices that are carried out in coordination with other parties involved in interaction. To investigate the nature of L2 speakers' IC, a growing number of applied linguists have turned to CA, which aims at "describing and explicating the competences which ordinary speakers use and rely on when they engage in intelligible, conversational interaction" (Heritage, 1984, p. 241). The competences uncovered by the first generation of CA researchers concern fundamental procedural infrastructures such as turn-taking organization, sequence organization, preference organization, repair organization, and topic organization. The understanding of these organizational mechanisms has been brought to bear in explicating the ways in which L2 speakers participate in a range of activities in interaction.

For L2 speakers, IC serves "double duty as both a fundamental condition for and object of learning" (Kasper & Wagner, 2011, p. 119). IC serves as a basic condition for learning as it enables the participants to construct learning as a social activity, whether it is situated in the classroom, everyday interaction, or the workplace. In this paradigm, learning is conceptualized as "an accountable, public, and locally occasioned process" (Koschmann, 2013, p. 1039), following the ethnomethodological tradition. Lee (2006), for instance, claims that "L2 instruction is organized *in and as* the members' competent language use" (p. 369, emphasis in original). That is, the participants, teachers and students alike, rely on their existing IC in regard to issuing and responding to questions, undertaking repairs, and so on, to understand each other's conduct and develop the activity of teaching and learning. Theodórsdóttir (2011), on the other hand, reports how an L2 speaker of Icelandic engaging in service encounters creates opportunities for learning specific L2 linguistic items in the course of interaction with an L1-speaking store clerk. In this case, too, what allows the L2 speaker to participate in the interaction is her available IC, and the specific L2 linguistic items emerge as objects of learning within the process of taking care of some other business.

The IC that L2 speakers bring with them is an enabling device for learning; as Pekarek Doehler and Pochon-Berger (2015, p. 235) note, however, IC "is not simply transferred from the L1 to the L2, but is recalibrated, adapted in the course of L2 development." An increasing number of studies have demonstrated how L2 speakers' conduct in specific interactional procedures changes over time, showing increased efficacy and complexity. Procedures that have been investigated by recent applied linguistic studies of IC include openings of telephone conversations (Brouwer & Wagner, 2004), taking turns at talk (Cekaite, 2007), managing conversational openings (Hellermann, 2007), telling stories (Hellermann, 2008), and introducing new topics or achieving topic shifts (König, 2013; Lee & Hellermann, 2014). The last of these, topic shift, is also the focus of the current study.

CA approaches the issue of topic management by examining what a particular stretch of talk is doing rather than what it is about. It explicates procedures through which participants nominate a new topic, sustain topical coherence, or shift topical focus (e.g., Button & Casey, 1984, 1985; Holt & Drew, 2005; Jefferson, 1984, 1993; Maynard, 1980; Maynard & Zimmermann, 1984; Sacks, 1992; Schegloff & Sacks, 1973). These studies illustrate that conversational participants regularly exhibit their understanding of prior talk by designing their current turn-at-talk in such a way that it fits the interaction up until that point. That is, topics generally shift in a stepwise manner, while disjunctive topic shifts tend to be marked with specific prefaces such as *by the way* or *actually* (Crow, 1983). Rather abrupt topic changes, however, can occur in specific environments. According to Maynard (1980), one such environment is when the occurrence of a series of silences indicates that the prior topic no longer generates any further talk from any party involved. Under such a circumstance, a participant may initiate a complete topic change as a solution to failed speaker transition.

Building on these CA studies of topic management, several recent studies have examined L2 speakers' practices in initiating topic shift, especially in relation to longitudinal development. Lee and Hellermann (2014), for instance, documented how an L2 speaker of English managed topic shifts. The focal participant, a middle school English teacher in South Korea, initially made an abrupt topic shift without any explicit marking, even though she demonstrated awareness of her procedural inadequacy through her subsequent conduct. After 10 months of participation in weekly conversation practice sessions, this same person exhibited the ability to employ various devices to mark a disjunctive topic shift that she initiated. Likewise, a study by König (2013) of an L2 French-speaking au pair conversing with her host-family illustrated how this advanced speaker changed the ways in which she initiated new topics. From the beginning of the data collection, König's participant was able to initiate a new topic, having recognized closing implicative features of the previous sequence that suggested the appropriateness of a topic change for regenerating speaker transitions (Maynard, 1980). On the other hand, she developed the ability to exploit various linguistic and prosodic resources to achieve smooth topic introduction over the course of a few months.

While these relatively advanced L2 speakers studied by Lee and Hellermann (2014) and König (2013) demonstrated the ability to initiate topic shifts, other studies have indicated that less proficient L2 speakers tend to assume the role of responder rather than initiator of new topics, even when they were provided with opportunities to act as an initiator. For instance, Nguyen (2011), who examined openings of five weekly office hour interactions between an L1 English-speaking teacher and an intermediate-level L2 English student from Vietnam, showed how the student's responses to the teacher's topic proffers became more elaborate and prompt over the course of the five sessions. The same student, however, initiated a topic only once during these five sessions. Wilkinson (2002), who studied American students' interaction with their French hosts during a summer study abroad program, also noted how the intermediate-level students, as well as their hosts, tended to adopt patterns reminiscent of classroom exchanges to organize their interaction. One of the features of this "omnipresent classroom" is topic management. That is, in the absence of a teacher who typically determines topics or assigns the topic initiator role to a particular party, some students participating in interactions with their hosts often deferred to them to initiate the next topic, or to identify who should initiate the next topic.

As Wilkinson's characterization suggests, participants in classroom interaction typically, though not always, orient to their institutional roles such as teachers and students (e.g., Markee, 2000; Seedhouse, 2004). Topics tend to be pre-determined and initiated by teachers, exhibiting participants' orientation towards their asymmetrical rights as conferred by their respective institutional roles. Pair- or group-work sessions in the classroom demonstrate different types of speech exchange systems from teacher-led plenary sessions, but what needs to be accomplished during non-plenary sessions is still often determined in advance by the teacher. As students engage in pair- or group-work, they may initiate topics. According to Stokoe (2000) and Markee (2005), however, participants regularly monitor the legitimacy of nominated topics and their relevance to the externally imposed agenda. Overall, in classroom interactions, students have limited opportunities to initiate topics of their choice.

Outside of the classroom, L2 speakers encounter various occasions where they can more actively contribute to topic management. However, as reported by Wilkinson (2002) and Nguyen (2011), this is not always an easy task for L2 speakers to accomplish. The context of the current data, dinner table conversations at the Japanese FLH program, shares some characteristics with the L2 speakers' interactions with host family members studied by Wilkinson (2002), König (2013), and others. That is, unlike the language classroom, there is no set lesson plan pre-determined for each meeting. The FLH residents simply get together to eat dinner and converse in Japanese as much as possible. Similar to *Gesprächsrunde,* a dyadic conversation-for-learning examined by Kasper (2004), "what exactly should be learned is not specified, but the general pedagogical idea is that, at the very least, through TL [target language] practice, the participating learners will improve their L2 fluency, and at best, they will make unpredictable but specific gains in their L2 lexis, morpho-syntax, pragmatics, or discourse ability" (p. 554). Thus, during dinner table conversation, the ability to initiate, pursue, and sustain topics can serve as a critical procedural infrastructure for FLH student residents to create spaces for learning L2 lexis and morpho-syntax. At the same time, this ability can be seen as an object of learning in its own right, considering the results of the previous studies that suggest novice L2 speakers' apparent difficulty in this area.

## The Study

### The Japanese FLH program

The Japanese FLH program examined in the current study was located inside a residential hall at a large Midwestern American university, along with several other FLH programs, as well as a non-language specific, international-focus program. The program's three stated main objectives were to develop language skills, to enhance student exposure to and knowledge of the Japanese culture, and to prepare students for future travel and study abroad, and its core activities included dinner table conversation, cultural events, cultural classes, and office hours held by an L1-speaking graduate coordinator. The program required students to sign a contract in order to ensure their participation in these activities and to encourage them to use the L2, but the degree of enforcement of L2 use varied from year to year, depending on group dynamics.

Exit interviews that the second author conducted with the Japanese FLH student residents revealed that their initial expectations for the FLH generally fell into the following three categories: (a) to develop Japanese competency, (b) to learn about the Japanese culture, and (c) to enjoy living with people who share the same interests (Matsunaga, 2012). As discussed by Bown et al. (2011), this third expectation, consistently listed as crucial for FLH residents, often comes into conflict with the first expectation, due to residents' limited and varying levels of L2 proficiency. This was the case at the current FLH as well. As a result, the student residents sometimes resorted to English, even during official activities. Nevertheless, at the dinner table, most student residents appeared to have tried speaking Japanese more than during other official activities, and all student residents uniformly stated in the exit interviews that their aim during dinner table conversation had been to develop speaking skills.

Although the fieldwork was conducted by the second author for three consecutive academic years (see Matsunaga, 2012 for further details of this ethnographic study), the current study focuses on the third year of fieldwork, when the residents' overall L2 proficiency was considerably lower than that of previous years' groups. Only one of the 17 student residents was an advanced L2 speaker enrolled in fourth-year Japanese courses, while the other student residents were novice to intermediate L2 speakers (four at the first-year level and twelve at the second-year level). The L1-speaking graduate coordinator, Shiori, lived in the same section of the residential hall with the student residents, and coordinated the official activities mentioned above. She was a first-year graduate student who had just moved to the U.S. She had previously taught Japanese in Japan, as well as in other countries, but this type of program was a new experience for her. The program was only in its third year, and there were no set guidelines for the coordinator as to how to run FLH activities. Shiori received some information from her predecessors about their experiences, but was told by her supervisors that she could approach FLH activities based on her own ideas. In addition to Shiori, the second author participated in FLH activities, including dinner table conversation, throughout the year. Further, Japanese-speaking guests, including a graduate student of Japanese, teaching assistants from the Japanese program, and some exchange students from Japanese universities, were often invited to participate in the activities. The arrangements may be considered somewhat similar to the *Gesprächsrunde* studied by Kasper (2004) or the conversation table studied by Mori (2003). However, unlike *Gesprächsrunde,* which is a dyadic interaction, FLH dinner table conversation involved a large number of participants and often experienced "schisming and merging" (see Egbert, 1997). Unlike the conversation table examined by Mori (2003), the majority of L1-speaking participants in the current data were language instructors who had experience in teaching beginning-level Japanese language courses.

Dinner table conversations were held two to three times per week in one of the university's cafeterias where different languages were spoken depending on the table. Over the course of the academic year, conversations at the Japanese table were video-recorded fifteen times; the total length of the resulting videos was approximately 10.5 hours. To ensure the quality of audio, selected participants (Shiori, the coordinator, and three student residents) were asked to wear pin-microphones, and an IC audio recorder was also placed on the table to collect backup audio data. One student was recruited from each level of the Japanese courses: the first-year student was Michael, the second-year student was Victoria, and the fourth-year student was Lucas. Among the multiple students in the first- and second-year Japanese courses, Michael and Victoria regularly attended the dinner table, enrolled in the Japanese courses for the entire academic year, and were willing to be video-recorded.

**The focal participant, Michael**
Field notes and interviews with the student residents, and the graduate coordinator, indicated that Japanese use and linguistic gains varied widely from student to student. One of the most notable differences was their level of engagement in dinner table conversations, which also appeared to correspond to the levels of the participants' perceived L2 use and linguistic gains. As mentioned

earlier, our focal participant, Michael, was someone who established himself as an active participant in dinner table conversation. Michael was a freshman at the time of data collection and was taking first-year Japanese courses. Despite his apparent lack of certain basic vocabulary and grammar, manifest in his frequent requests for assistance addressed to his peers taking higher-level courses, Michael was often more engaged in dinner table conversation than those students from whom he received linguistic assistance.

A systematic examination of the entire set of video-recordings with regard to the initiators of new topics and the types of topics initiated further revealed the difference in patterns of participation between Michael and the rest of the students. The procedures and the results of this examination are provided in the Appendix. Overall, the graduate coordinator and the Japanese-speaking guests initiated topics roughly twice as often as the student residents. Among the student residents, Michael was the one who most frequently initiated topics, whereas other students tended to wait until they were nominated as next speaker by the coordinator or the guests. In addition to the frequency of his topic initiation, the variety of topics introduced by Michael differed from those introduced by the other students. To illustrate, the student residents commonly talked about the weather, their health or mood, weekend plans, school issues, FLH activities, or FLH members. These topics can be characterized as the kinds of themes that are often covered in beginning-level language classrooms, or those that can be discussed by adopting vocabulary and grammatical expressions already introduced and practiced in the classroom—as gauged by the textbooks adopted by the first-year Japanese language courses at the university at the time, *Genki I and II* (Banno, Ohno, Sakane, & Shinagawa, 1999; Banno, Ohno, Sakane, Shinagawa, & Tokashiki, 1999), and the authors' familiarity with the curriculum of these courses. On the other hand, Michael tackled a wider variety of topics, including his observation of various linguistic and cultural traits. He also attempted to deliver extended tellings of personal stories more frequently than the other students.

## Data Analysis

This section will provide an analysis of two episodes that exemplify how Michael presented himself as an active participant, maximizing the linguistic and non-linguistic resources available to him. In both episodes, recorded four months apart, he introduced similar topics, focused on the understanding of linguistic variations that he gained through his friendship with an international student from England. On both occasions, Michael introduced these topics by recognizing a possible closing of the prior sequence and initiating a new sequence that built on the immediate, local context of interaction. While sharing these similarities, the two episodes differed in some other respects, including who the co-participants were and under what circumstances these topics were brought up. As discussed by Hall and Pekarek Doehler (2011), Kasper and Wagner (2014), and Koschmann (2013), among others, whether or not sets of interactional data taken from two different points in time can be used as evidence of longitudinal development demands careful consideration. In fact, we found it challenging to find truly comparable sets of segments from the current data of naturally occurring FLH dinner table conversation. The primary focus of our analysis, thus, is to illustrate how Michael uses his available IC to participate in dinner table conversation and thereby generates opportunities to practice, explore, and solidify L2 linguistic resources useful to discuss matters of his interest. We will discuss, however, possible implications that can be drawn from these two episodes in regard to Michael's longitudinal development.

**Episode 1: "Line"**
The first episode was recorded at the end of October, approximately two months into the academic year. Prior to this segment, the graduate coordinator, Shiori, had been asking multiple students about their experience at a local Halloween event. The episode can be divided into four different phases: (a) Michael's attempt to pursue topical talk on the Halloween event; (b) Shiori's abrupt introduction of a new topic; (c) Michael's attempt to generate a new sequence based on the topic proffered by Shiori; and, (d) Michael and Shiori's exchange of opinions about their common experiences. As shown in Figure 1, Michael was sitting next to Shiori and five other students were present at the table.[2] In addition to Michael, three other students (Will, Heather, and Rachel) had all responded to Shiori's question regarding what kinds of costumes they enjoyed seeing at the event. However, the students struggled to describe the costumes in Japanese. Further, Shiori's lack of knowledge regarding some popular culture references made it more difficult for the students to explain some of the costumes that they liked. During the stretch of interaction, Marcus, Heather, Will, and Rachel left the table one by one to return their trays, and eventually Michael became Shiori's lone interlocutor, while Young, who was sitting far from Shiori and Michael, remained silent.

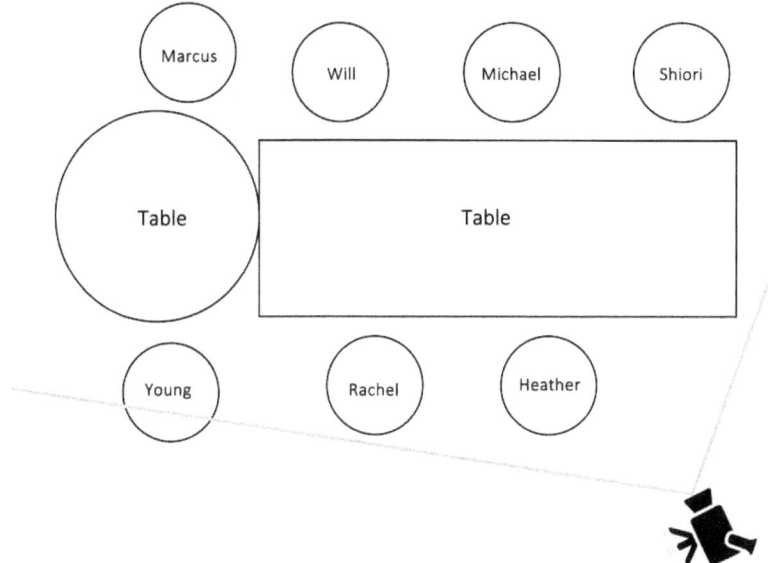

**Figure 1.** Seating arrangement for Episode 1.

Excerpt 1 begins at the end of the costume exchange, where Shiori provides a possible pre-closing assessment of the Halloween event (line 1). This excerpt exemplifies how Michael (M) tries to pursue topical talk with his limited set of L2 resources and how Shiori (S) validates Michael's contribution

**Excerpt 1.**[3]

```
01 S:  hu::n demo omoshiro[katta.
       hmm   but  interesting-PST
       Hmm, but it was interesting.

02 M:                 [°(un    un    soo ne)°
                       mmhm  mmhm  so  IP
                       Mmhm mmhm yeah.

03 S:  hu::n
       hmm

04     (0.5)
```

```
                                          |((S and M establish mutual gaze))
05 S:   tch demo,  atashitachi::(0.4)|hayaku itta kara|::,
            but    we                  early   went because
        Tch, but we went there early and so,
                                                                |((M
                                                                |nods))

06      saisho wa amari   omoshirokunakute::|:,
        first  TP little  interesting-NG-and
        at first it was not very interesting and uhm,
                                     |((M nods))

07      hito    ga sukunakatta kara::|:,(0.7)
        people  S  few-PST     because
        because there weren't many people,
                                     |((M nods))

08      demo atode motto hito    ga fuete::|:,
        but  later more  people  S  increase-and
        But more people came later, and
                                         |((M nods))

09      tanoshiku natta  ke|do::,
        fun              became but
        it got more fun, but
                         |((M nods and moves his gaze away from S))

10      (3.0)/((S nods several times))
              /((M brings his right hand up to his left shoulder and takes
                 an inaudible inbreath))

                 |((M covers his mouth with his right arm))
11 M:   hh. h|h.

12      (0.2)

13 S:   [un
         mmhm
                                                       |((M crosses
                      |((M moves his left hand under the table))  | his arms))
14 M:   [tomodachi::|o,  (0.4) minna no tomo- tomoda|chi wa::
         friends     O          all   LK   friends        TP
        (My) friends, everyone's frie- friends...
```

```
                                   |((M directs his gaze to S))
15     .hhh (0.6) ta- totemo samu|katta [°(desu.)°
                         really  cold-PST        CP
       .hhh were re- really cold.

16 S:                                   [samu|katta|nn:::
                                         cold-PST    yeah
                                        Cold. Yeah.
                                              |((M looks down))
                                                  |((M nods))

17     soo omou:.
       so  think
       I think so.

18     (0.5)

       |((S nods))
19 S:  |°hh hh°

20     (1.0)/((M shakes his head horizontally))

       |((M raises his shoulders))
21 M:  |.hhhhh

22 S:  °mmhm°

       |((M looks down))|((M brings his right hand up to his forehead))
23 M:  |boku wa dai|joobu.
        I    TP   okay
       I (was) okay.

24     (1.0)

25 S:  |demo samukatta |yo: kinoo.
        but  cold-PST   IP  yesterday
       But it was cold yesterday.
       |((M looks away from S))
                        |((M looks down))

       |((S begins to bring up her arm)) |((S's arm and finger fully extended))
26     |.hhh sugoi      retsu |ne,=
             remarkable line   IP
       That's quite a line.
```

With no one else taking a turn after her closing-relevant token in line 3, Shiori continues to describe her experience at the event (lines 5–9), selecting Michael as her addressed recipient through her gaze direction. During Shiori's talk, Michael demonstrates his recipiency by gazing at her and slightly nodding during each of the elongated clause chaining markers produced during her turn. Shiori's description does not necessarily contain many newsworthy elements, and returns to another assessment (*tanoshikunatta* 'got more fun') similar to her earlier possible pre-closing assessment (*omoshirokatta* 'it was interesting') that summarizes the experience. The elongated connective particle *kedo* produced in a trailing-off manner (line 9), together with the head nods that she produces during the subsequent silence (line 10), suggest that Shiori is yielding speakership to Michael (see Aoki, 2011). As the silence goes on without Shiori's continuation of talk, Michael is faced with the decision either to remain silent or to initiate a next turn.

After an outbreath that sounds and looks like a forced cough (lines 10–11), Michael finally manages to produce a full-fledged turn, stating that all of his friends were feeling cold, although his formulation of this is somewhat unnatural (i.e., *tomodachi wa minna* would be a more natural word order in Japanese) (lines 14–15). Although no obvious "tying structures" (Sacks, 1992, Vol. 1, p. 540) that link the turn to the prior talk were used in this case, Shiori treats Michael's turn as a description of his friends' experience at the same Halloween event by enacting agreement through next-turn repetition of Michael's assessment (lines 16–17).

After a series of silences and nonverbal vocalizations, Michael pursues the topic further by stating that he was okay (line 23). However, unlike in his previous turn, he keeps his gaze down during the entire turn and does not direct his gaze to Shiori at all. This, along with his gaze movements (away from Shiori and then down) during Shiori's next turn in line 25, appears to indicate either his difficulty in continuing the talk on this topic or his readiness to close this sequence. It is under this circumstance that Shiori suddenly takes an audible inbreath and introduces a completely new topic, by gazing and pointing to a corner of the cafeteria (line 26).

Excerpt 1 thus illustrates how Michael, who has been selected as the lone addressee of Shiori's talk, manages to display his recipiency and contribute to the pursuit of topical talk. Excerpt 2, on the other hand, shows that when Shiori's talk does not indicate any specific addressed recipient it fails to elicit a significant response from the students. By the time Shiori produces the setting talk (Maynard & Zimmermann, 1984) concerning the line of people, Will (W) and Rachel (R) have returned to the table and have settled down in their chairs. Neither Shiori's talk nor her nonverbal conduct in line 26, however, selects anyone as the primary addressed recipient

## Excerpt 2.

```
25 S:  |demo samukatta |yo: kinoo.
        but  cold-PST    IP  yesterday
       But it was cold yesterday.
       |((M looks away from S))
                            |((M looks down))


       |((S begins to bring up her arm))|((S's arm and finger fully extended))
26     |.hhh sugoi       retsu |ne,=
             remarkable  line   IP
       That's quite a line.

27    =|nagai  |ne.
        long    IP
       It's so long.
       |((M directs his gaze to the pointed area))
            |((Figure 2 -- W and R also direct their gaze to the same area))

28     (1.8)/((S brings her arm back to the home position))

                    |((S leans back to examine further the area she pointed to))
29 S:  |minna ai|sukuriimu?
        all     ice cream
       Are they all lined up for ice cream?
       |((W looks down at the table))
       |((M brings his left hand to his mouth, maintaining his gaze direction))

30     (0.6)

       |((M maintains his gaze towards the pointed area))
31 M:  |hn

32     (0.2)

       |((S smiles))
33 S:  |hh hh

34     (2.8)/((M looks up in the air and makes a thinking face))

       |((S slightly nods a few times))
35 S:  |sokka
        so Q
       I see.
```

**Figure 2.** Line 27.

Shiori's setting talk refers to a feature of the surroundings accessible to all parties involved. Immediately after Shiori's turn in line 26, Michael directs his gaze to the area at which she is pointing. Shortly after, Will and Rachel also shift their gaze to the same area, as shown in Figure 2. While all three student residents are eligible to take the next turn to comment on her public display of noticing, or to initiate a repair, none of them offers any immediate verbal response (line 28). Given Shiori's use of the final particle *ne*, which works to solicit the co-participants' agreement, acknowledgement, or confirmation (e.g. Morita, 2005; Tanaka, 2000), the absence of responses is particularly notable.

Facing a lack of uptake, Shiori further pursues a response from the student residents by formulating her next utterance in line 29 as a question through the use of rising intonation. At the same time, Will brings his gaze down to the table and thereby displays that he is not willing to be selected to respond to Shiori (see Mortensen, 2008). In the meantime, Michael and Rachel keep their gaze towards the area Shiori pointed to, rather than turning to Shiori herself. Michael's minimal token produced in line 31 appears ambiguous as to whether it indicates his affirmative response to Shiori's earlier question or his independent noticing. In either case, he does not produce any additional talk to clarify his intent. After these unsuccessful attempts to elicit the student residents' talk, Shiori produces a third-turn receipt in line 35, effectively closing the sequence.

The development thus far exemplifies how challenging it is for these FLH residents to build on and develop a topic through the successive transfer of speakership. Oftentimes, Shiori, the graduate coordinator, as well as other language expert guests, assume responsibility for initiating new topics, or shifting topical focus, to elicit responses from the student residents. Identifying topics to which the students can contribute with their level of Japanese appears to be a challenging task. As shown in Excerpt 2, the attempts by the coordinator and Japanese-speaking guests are often unsuccessful, especially when they do not specifically select the next speaker.

As shown in Excerpt 3, however, Michael eventually makes a move to resolve the failed speaker transition. While he begins this move in Japanese, in order to convey his intended meaning, he also draws on other resources, including his L1 and hand gestures.

**Excerpt 3.**

```
            |((S smiles))
33 S:       |hh hh

34          (2.8)/((M looks up in the air and makes a thinking face))

            |((S slightly nods a few times))
35 S:       |sokka
             so  Q
             I see.

36          (1.2)

                                    |((M gazes at S and points in the
                                    | direction of the line))
37 M:   nn:: ee::- eigo    |de nn  (0.6)  sore wa nani.
        mmhm     English   in             that TP  what
        Um, er in English um, what's that?

38          (1.0)
```

```
            |                |
39 M:       |you call it a   |line?
```

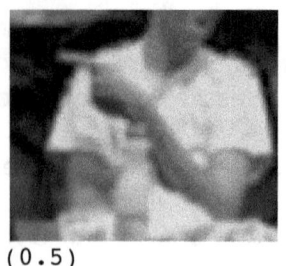

```
40        |(0.5)

          |((S nods a few times))
41  S:    u|::n
          uhhuh
```

```
42        |(1.2)

43  M:    aa:: aa::  (1.0) um::  (0.5)
          uhm  uhm         um
          Yeah, yeah, yeah.

                      |((M puts his
            |((M gazes| right hand on |((M creates some beat gestures
            | at S))   | his head))    | with his left hand in the air))
44        Eng|lish?   |(0.5)          |jin     no tomodachi?
                                       person  LK  friend
          English? My English friend?

45        (0.5)

          |((M looks away
          | and makes a    |((M gazes at S and begins to create some
          | thinking face)) | beat gestures by using both hands))
46  M:    |aa::: chigau|::=
          uhm    different
          Um different,
```

```
47 S:  =queue=
                     |((M points to S with
                     | the thumb of              |((M crosses
                     | his left hand))|((M nods))| his arms))
48 M:  =queue |queue         |un      shitte(h)|iru?
                              uhhuh    know
       Queue, queue, uhuh. Do you know it?

             |((S begins to lean
             | forward towards M))|((S points to her chest with his left hand))
49 S:        |watashi  oosuto |raria [ni ita    ka[ra::,
              I        Australia     in be-PST  because
       Because I lived in Australia.

                                                 |((M nods))
50 M:                                  [aha    [ |ha::i
                                                 Yes

             |((S leans back to her earlier position))
51 S:  [itsumo:|queue
        always
       Always queue.

                 |((M looks down))
52 M:  [e- queu|e? uh:m
        what
       What- queue? Uhm.

                         |((M brings his right hand to his mouth))
53 M:  hh hh omoshi|roi.=
              interesting
       Hh hh interesting.
```

After Shiori's sequence-closing third (line 35), another silence emerges. Thereafter, however, Michael asks Shiori what the thing she pointed to is called in English (line 37). The link between this turn and her prior talk is indicated by the use of the demonstrative *sore* 'that' and the pointing gesture that duplicates Shiori's earlier pointing gesture. This move by Michael appears to have been in preparation for some time: During the silence in line 34, he suddenly looks up in the air and makes a thinking face, which he maintains until he begins his turn in line 37.

It may appear rather atypical that an L1 English speaker asks an L1 Japanese speaker about English vocabulary in this Japanese-speaking event. Indeed, the silence in line 38 seems to indicate Shiori's bewilderment in regard to the intent of Michael's question. With no response from Shiori, Michael reformulates his question in line 39 by switching to English and offering a candidate English word, "line." As shown in the first image embedded in the transcript, Michael points with his left hand in the same direction to which Shiori pointed earlier to clarify the referent, and at the same time, he also points to Shiori with his right hand to indicate that she is indeed the addressed recipient. Shiori responds with a delayed affirmative answer, offered through the lengthened response token *u::n* and head nods (line 41). The timing and the design of her response appear to indicate her continuing uncertainty concerning the intent of Michael's question.

Faced with Shiori's delayed, minimal response, Michael begins a solitary search of some sort, as indicated by his gaze direction, posture, and facial expression (line 42). It appears that he is preparing for his next turn in order to respond to Shiori's apparent confusion. Subsequently, he begins his turn with *English?,* produced as an English word with rising intonation. He then produces the Japanese suffix *-jin* '-people/person', a morpheme which is added to the name of a country to describe nationality, and then goes on to construct the rest of the utterance in Japanese. After the noun phrase, produced with rising intonation, another short silence emerges (line 45). However, he eventually adds the predicate *chigau* 'different', minimally conveying that he had an English friend and that something was different (lines 43–46). As he produces the word *chigau* 'different', he also begins to create beat gestures with both hands in the air, which seems to indicate that he is searching for the next item due. Despite the disfluent and fragmented nature of this turn, the addressed recipient, Shiori, figures out Michael's intent as soon as she hears the word *chigau* 'different', and offers *queue,* an alternative English word for *retsu* 'line' (line 47). By doing so, Shiori indicates that she has heard Michael's turn in lines 43 to 46 as an account for his earlier question (lines 37–39), rather than as a turn unrelated to the prior talk. Michael immediately repeats the word offered by Shiori and explicitly confirms her knowledge of it (line 48). Shiori responds to this question by referring to the fact that she used to live in Australia, and therefore knows the word *queue*, which is also used in Australia.

Excerpt 3 reveals how Michael, despite his limited L2 resources, attempts to take up an opportunity presented by Shiori's setting talk to introduce a new, but related topic of interest to him. To this end, Michael calibrates available resources, including his L1 and L2, gaze, and hand gestures. Although the intended meanings of the gestures produced in lines 39 and 40 may not have been immediately clear at the moment of their production, after Michael's talk progresses to line 46 where his interest in different varieties of English becomes clear, the possible intent of his thumbs-up gesture in line 39 becomes available in retrospect. Namely, it appears that Michael used the thumbs-up gesture to indicate that "line" is one possible, but not the only English equivalent for the Japanese word *retsu*, and at the same time the gesture allowed him to use his index finger for the purpose of pointing. Such an impromptu manipulation of linguistic and non-linguistic resources to produce a timely contribution for the ongoing development of topic characterizes the type of IC Michael frequently exhibits during dinner table conversations.

The number of gaps between turns becomes notably fewer after line 47 when Shiori indicates her understanding of Michael's attempt to regenerate topical talk building on the topic Shiori had proffered earlier. In this fashion, Michael effectively accomplishes a stepwise transition from the setting talk offered by Shiori to the discussion of different varieties of English, which yields a lively exchange. Following the segment shown in Excerpt 3, Shiori and Michael's interaction on the different varieties of English continues for a while, each sharing their respective experiences regarding confusion with British English words in the case of Michael, and with American English words in the case of Shiori, who had just moved to the U.S. two months prior to this recording.

As noted earlier, after Shiori's setting talk, any of the student residents at the table could have taken the opportunity to respond and develop subsequent interaction in a variety of directions. While the others did not take up this opportunity, Michael, through his effective use of a variety of resources, managed to extend the interaction by introducing a topic of interest to him and properly situated it in the ongoing development of talk. In this episode, neither Michael nor Shiori displays a visible orientation towards the learning of any specific linguistic items. Yet, by sustaining the interaction with Shiori through this effective topic shift and by attending to the ongoing interactional contingencies of the talk, Michael gains opportunities to perform a range of actions in his L2, including confirming the recipient's understanding, demonstrating recipiency, offering an assessment, and reporting his past experience.

**Episode 2: "English man"**

The second episode to be examined in this section was video-recorded at the end of February, approximately six months into the academic year and four months after the episode introduced above. The context of this episode differed from the previous one in several respects. Although Shiori was the only L1-speaking participant in the previous episode, in this episode, three Japanese-speaking graduate students attended the dinner table conversation, in addition to Shiori. Further, in the middle of the conversation, a non-Japanese-speaking friend of Michael's, Tim, stopped by the table, and began to converse with Michael in English. (The seating arrangement for this occasion is shown in Figure 3.) Despite these differences, this episode was selected for close examination because Michael introduced the topic of linguistic variations again and thereby created a space for L2 learning. In this second episode, the interaction eventually leads to an L2 learning activity, in which Michael checks his understanding of a Japanese suffix and learns a new vocabulary item.

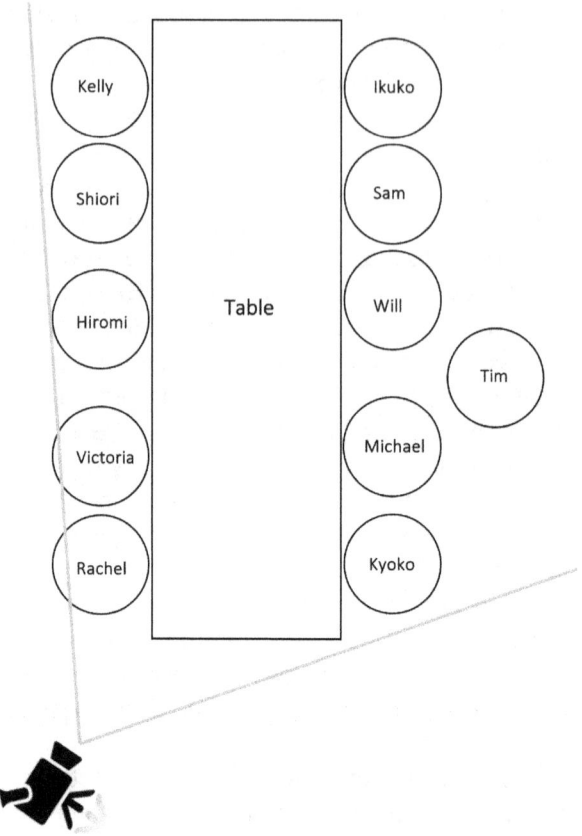

**Figure 3.** Seating arrangement for Episode 2.

Prior to Excerpt 4, Tim, who was not a member of the Japanese FLH program or a student officially learning Japanese, had been carrying out a conversation with Michael entirely in English. During that time, Victoria and Rachel were talking with each other and Kyoko (K) was quietly eating her dinner, as shown in Figure 4. Excerpt 4 begins when Michael (M) and Tim (T) initiate a closing, leave-taking sequence. The excerpt demonstrates how Michael successfully achieves a transition from his interaction with Tim in English back to his interaction with Kyoko in Japanese.

**Figure 4.** Line 6 "Sir."

**Excerpt 4.**

```
01 M: excellent.

02 T: yeah.

03     (2.0)

                              |((M reaches his right hand out to T))
04 M: cool. well (0.3)|good luck again.

05     (0.2)/((M and T shake hands))

       |((Figure 4 – M salutes to T))
06     |sir.=

                |((T salutes back to M))
07 T: =|ariga|to:
       thank you
       Thank you.
       |((K directs her gaze to M and T))

08 M: do it for (   ).|study your balls off for (   )
                      |((T starts to stand up))

09 T: (   my balls off)
```

```
10  M:  hh hh ca(h)tch you la(h)te(h)r du(h)de

11      hh [.hh .hh hhh hhh hhh

12  T:     [enjoy your (enjoy your dinner)

           |((M moves his chair closer to the table))
13  M:     |un=
           |((T's gaze meets with K's gaze))

14  K:  =|sayonara  ((addressing T))
          good bye
          Good bye.
          |((T brings his right hand up, gazing at K))
          |((M gazes at K))

15  T:   |sayonara=  ((addressing K))
          good bye
          Good bye.
          |((M looks back to the direction of T))

16  M:  =|haha[hahaha
          |((M and K gaze at each other))
          |((T leaves the table))

17  K:         [huhuhaha

                             |((M points to the direction of
         |((Figure 5))       | T with his left hand thumb))
18  M:   |ano: igiri|sujin? de[su?
          well  Englishman    CP
          Well, he is British?
```

**Figure 5.** Line 18 *"anoo igirisu jin desu?"*

Immediately after Kyoko hears Michael's *Sir* in line 6, she moves her gaze from the dinner table to the direction of Michael and Tim. Tim responds to Michael by using a commonly known Japanese phrase, *arigato:* 'thank you' (line 7), demonstrating his understanding that Michael is participating in the Japanese-speaking event. Tim's sudden use of Japanese in some sense reciprocates Michael's marked choice of the address term produced with the saluting gesture (Figure 4), and together they create a playful leave-taking exchange. After additional joking exchanges between Michael and Tim in English, Tim's gaze meets with Kyoko's as he is about to leave the table (line 13). At this point, Tim raises his right hand to create a good-bye gesture, gazing at Kyoko. In the meantime, Kyoko produces another commonly known Japanese phrase, *sayonara* 'good bye', addressing Tim (line 14). With a smile on his face, Tim greets Kyoko back by using the same Japanese phrase. This unexpected yet playful use of Japanese by a non-member of the Japanese-speaking group is treated as laughable by Michael and Kyoko, who also establish mutual gaze. During this joint laughter, Tim finally leaves the table, and immediately after his departure, Michael engages in some setting talk in Japanese, describing Tim as a British person (line 18).[4] Michael formulates this turn while gazing at Kyoko, as shown in Figure 5, with their relative posture directions indicating that they have established mutual orientation. Michael's introduction of the setting talk is timely and fitted to the immediate, local context, in which Michael has (a) just completed his leave-taking sequence with Tim in English, (b) observed that Kyoko has also exchanged parting greetings in Japanese with Tim, and (c) jointly treated Tim's use of Japanese as laughable. In this manner, Michael accomplishes a fluent transition from his interaction with Tim in English back to his interaction with Kyoko in Japanese.

Excerpt 5 demonstrates how Michael builds on the topic he introduced in Excerpt 4 and creates opportunities to try out different expressions to describe his friend, Tim.

**Excerpt 5.**

```
                          |((M points to the direction of
             |((Figure 5))  | T with his left hand thumb))
18  M:       |ano: igiri|sujin? de[su?
             well  Englishman    CP
             Well, he is British?

19  K:                               [a,  soo na n desu ka?
                                      oh  so  CP N CP   Q
                                      Oh, really?

20  M:  u:n
        uhhuh

21  K:  huun
        hmm

                     |((M smiles))
22  M:  chotto::    |hen.
        a little     strange
        A bit strange.

23  K:  [e? (soo desu ka)
         what so  CP    Q
         Huh? (Really?)

24  M:  [hen      hen      hen'ni hh
         strange  strange  strangely
         Strange, strange, strangely hh

                          |((M performs a gesture of something coming
                          | out of the mouth by using both of his hands))
25       chotto    hen|ni::   hanashimasu.
         a little  strangely  speak
         He speaks a bit strangely.
```

```
26  K:  a igirisu   no  aku|sen[to
        oh England  LK   accent
        Oh, British accent.
                                  |((M looks up))
                                                    |((M waves his
                                                    | right hand out))
27  M:                           [hen- hen|janai.
                                      strange-NG
                                  Stra- not strange.

                | ((M rotates hands | ((M performs a gesture of something
                |  a few times))    |  coming out of the mouth))
28      demo:[ |:(0.5)           [ |chigau hh
        but                          different
        But  different. Hh.

29  K:          [igirisu  no    [akusento?=
                 England  LK     accent
                 British accent?

            |((M nods and smiles))
30  M:  =|soo.
         so
         Right.

31      (1.0)/((K nods))
```

Michael's initial description of Tim, *chotto:: hen* 'a little strange' (line 22), which can be interpreted as referring to Tim's personality, is met with Kyoko's open-class repair initiator, *e?* 'What?' (line 23). Michael then repairs his underspecified description. After a few repetitions of *hen* 'strange', the adjective, he adds the morpheme *-ni* to make the expression into the adverb *hen'ni* 'strangely' (line 24). He then reformulates his description by re-introducing the adverb *chotto* 'a little' and adding the verb *hanashimasu* 'speak' (line 25). Simultaneously, he produces a hand gesture to indicate something coming out of the mouth, emphasizing that Tim's way of speaking is the target of description.

Kyoko responds to Michael's second try with the change of state token *a* 'oh' and her candidate understanding of Michael's intended meaning (line 26). As soon as Michael hears Kyoko's turn, he negates the descriptor he introduced earlier, *hen* 'strange' (line 27). Furthermore, with the prefaced contrastive marker *demo* 'but', he begins to create a hand gesture indicative of his search for another expression, and eventually produces an alternative, *chigau* 'different' (line 28), which is less pejorative than his earlier word choice, *hen* 'strange'. In overlap with Michael's latest version of the repaired description, Kyoko repeats her same candidate expression (line 29). This time, Michael acknowledges Kyoko's assistance in solving the trouble that he has encountered (line 30) by producing the token *soo* 'right' (see Kushida, 2011).[5]

Excerpt 5 demonstrates how the new topic, which can be considered a type of setting talk that comments on a person seen at the site of interaction, is expanded. Through the process, Michael performs a series of self-repairs in refining the description of his friend. He also gains his co-participant's assistance in his search for a suitable expression. Although the sequence about Tim's accent appears to reach a possible closing in lines 30 and 31, Excerpt 6 shows Michael further pursuing an alternative expression to the one provided by Kyoko that includes the use of the English loanword *akusento* 'accent'. This last excerpt illustrates how Michael, in pursuing topical talk, transforms the interaction in such a way that L2 learning becomes a central activity.

**Excerpt 6.**

```
29  K:         [igirisu no    [akusento?=
                England LK     accent
                British accent?

               | ((M nods and smiles))
30  M:    =| soo.
             so
             Right.

31       (1.0)/((K nods))

             | ((M makes a serious face))
32  M:    | igirisu ben? (iie/ne)?
            England         no/right
            England-ben? (No/Right)?

33  K:    °iya° [hh hh hh
           no
          No. Hh hh hh.

34  M:         [is that [wrong? dialect? no?

35       (0.8)/((K shakes her head))

36  M:  hh chiga(h)i(h)ma[(h)su?
              different
        Hh. That's wrong?
```

```
37  K:                    [igi(h)ri(h)su(h)[ben(h)
                           England
                           England-ben.

                                              |((M raises both hands
                                              | with the palms up))
38  M:                                        [|hhh  hahaha

        |((M leans forward towards the researcher (R) behind the camera.
        | Gazing at the researcher, M puts his right hand behind his right
        | ear. He holds his hand here until line 45))
39  M:  |e?


40      igirisu nani?
        England what
        England what?

41  R:  namari
        accent
        Accent.

42  M:  nama?

43  R:  namari
        accent
        Accent.

        |((M shifts his gaze to K))
44  M:  |namai?

45  K:  namari
        accent
        Accent.

46  M:  namari:

47  K:  namari
        accent
        Accent.

        |((M raises his left hand half way up with the palm up))
48  M:  |ben wa: na(h)ni?
             TP   what
        What is ben?
```

```
                        |((M moves his right hand back and forth))
49      do(h)oshi(h)te  |chiga(h)i(h)ma(h)su?
        why              different
        Why are they different?
```

Michael's attempt to combine the name of a country and the suffix *-ben* (line 32) is met by Kyoko with the negative response token *iya* 'no' and laughter (line 33). The Japanese suffix *-ben* can be attached to the name of a specific region in Japan to refer to a regional dialect of Japanese, but *-ben* is not generally used for non-Japanese dialects. Michael apparently knows this suffix and tries it to refer to his friend's British accent, but Kyoko treats this as something laughable. As soon as Michael hears Kyoko's negative response, he momentarily switches to English to ask Kyoko if his use of the term *-ben* to mean "dialect" is wrong (line 34). Although it is not captured in the audio data, it appears that the researcher, who is video-recording the conversation, says something at this point, having observed Michael's confusion. Michael's repair initiator and gaze shift in lines 39–40 suggests this possibility. The researcher (R) then introduces an alternative expression, *namari* 'accent' (line 41), and with the assistance of Kyoko (line 45), Michael eventually confirms the pronunciation of the newly introduced vocabulary item. The interaction between these three participants on the difference between *-ben* and *namari* continues for another half a minute or so. Then, having confirmed his understanding of the difference between *-ben* and *namari,* Michael incorporates the newly learned word, *namari,* to state that there are different accents in America, and that he finds the Midwestern accent to be interesting. This last excerpt shows how Michael pursues topical talk, shifting its focus from the description of his British friend's way of speaking to an exploration of vocabulary items that capture different varieties of a given language. Through the process, he creates opportunities to clarify his understanding of the suffix that he already knows and to acquire a new vocabulary item.

**Summary**
The two episodes examined in this section exhibit the following aspects of Michael's IC concerning topic management practices:
   a. The ability to attend to the development of the prior speaker's talk and to recognize the possible closing of a prior sequence, where, among various actions that can be taken, the initiation of a new sequence through a topic shift is possible;
   b. The ability to identify a topic that concerns an element of the prior talk and the setting of the interaction, and to make a sequence-initiating move, indicating how it fits to the ongoing development of the interaction; and,
   c. The ability to mobilize L1, L2, and non-linguistic resources to accomplish sequence-initiating moves and pursuit of topical talk.

In both episodes, Michael's sequence-initiating turns are not particularly complex in their formulation: *eigo de sore wa nani* 'in English what's that?' (Episode 1), and *anoo igirisujin desu* 'well, he is British' (Episode 2). What matters is not the complexity of the L2 utterances, but rather the timely delivery of these turns which generates further interaction when the prior sequence appears to have reached a possible closing. Indeed, this is what sets Michael's performance apart from the performances of the rest of the students, as illustrated in Excerpts 2 and 3.

These episodes also demonstrate how sequence-initiating moves open up further possibilities for L2 use and learning *in and as* interaction. That is, Michael, together with his co-participants, expand the sequences that he initiated by further clarifying the intention behind the sequence-initiating question (Episode 1) or elaborating on the initial description of his friend (Episode 2). His utterances in these subsequent turns are not always delivered smoothly, requiring the calibration of L1, L2, and non-linguistic resources (Episode 1), or a series of self-repairs to refine the formulation of L2 talk (Episode 2). However, Michael manages to express himself, in collaboration with the attentive co-participants who treat him as a competent interactant: Shiori responds to Michael's question despite the uncertainty of its intent and interprets his subsequent talk as his attempt to clarify his intended meaning (Episode 1); Kyoko offers a repair initiation to Michael's description of his friend and a candidate understanding of his intended meaning, as Michael engages in self-repair and a word search (Episode 2). Moreover, upon establishing the understanding of intended meanings, Michael and his co-participants further extend their talk on the topic of Michael's choice, by sharing respective experiences with different varieties of English (Episode 1) or exploring alternative expressions to describe the British accent in Japanese (Episode 2). In this fashion, Michael utilizes his IC concerning topic management practices as an enabling device for generating opportunities to use his L2 to discuss topics of his interest and to create spaces for L2 learning specific to his own purpose.

The two cases also show some differences in the quality of his L2 use, which are suggestive of his L2 development:

a. A more prompt delivery of the sequence-initiating turn in Episode 2;
b. Fewer pauses and delaying devices in Episode 2 of the kind observed in Michael's utterances in Episode 1;
c. The expression of his friend's nationality using the full-fledged L2 word (*igirisujin*) in Episode 2 as opposed to the mixture of L1 and L2 (*English? jin?*) in Episode 1.

Some may consider the apparent improvements described in (a) and (b) to be Michael's development of IC in terms of its efficacy, but these differences may also be due to the relative ease of indicating the connection between the newly introduced topic and the immediate, local context in the latter episode (i.e., issuing the setting talk about his friend who has just left the table seems to be an easier task than introducing an English vocabulary matter by expanding the setting talk offered by the prior speaker). Given the lack of assurance of comparability between these two episodes, we are hesitant to call the contrast between them evidence of development of Michael's IC. However, we would like to note that these differences in Michael's performance seen in the two episodes correspond to the overall impression of his growth in the amount of talk, fluency, and timely production of responses to co-participants, generated from the second author's fieldwork and review of the entire set of video-recoded interactions. We argue that the kind of IC Michael exhibited in these episodes allowed him to gain opportunities for putting his L2 into use at the FLH dinner table conversations, and this manner of participation in turn contributed to his L2 development.

## Conclusion

Previous studies have shown that FLH programs, as well as FLH student residents, unvaryingly consider dinner table conversation to be the most important site for the development of L2 oral proficiency, but researchers have not fully documented how this activity is utilized by student residents. To fill this gap, the current study provided a closer look at one aspect of dinner table conversation, topic management. In line with the findings of Bown et al. (2011) on FLH dinner table conversation, and Wilkinson's (2002) study on American students' interactions with their French host family members, the overall tendency at the current FLH dinner table, especially during the early months, was that the L1-speaking graduate coordinator and other language expert guests more frequently initiated topics that were familiar to the student residents in an attempt to facilitate their L2 use. The creation of learning opportunities distinct from the classroom, an intended outcome of the program, however, cannot happen only through the graduate coordinator's efforts. Student residents' voluntary initiation of new topics and topic shifts is necessary to change the quality of their participation and to provide them with opportunities to use their L2 in action and to create a space for L2 learning related to their specific interests. Michael's episodes attest to the fact that L2 speakers with relatively limited vocabulary and grammar can indeed achieve this form of participation and become active conversationalists at the dinner table. These episodes also reaffirm the understanding that IC is a fundamental condition for learning, whether the learning entails trying out available L2 resources to accomplish a broader set of actions that they have not yet tried in their L2, or focusing on the exploration of particular L2 forms that will be added to their interactional tool kit. At the same time, the type of IC exhibited by Michael may be viewed as a learning target for the other students in the Japanese FLH program, who rarely initiated a topic shift on their own.

We must acknowledge, however, that it is not certain whether the less active participants did not have this type of IC, or whether they instead simply treated these conversations differently from the way Michael did. The aspects of Michael's IC summarized in the previous section are so fundamental that they can be exercised in any other types of interactions where L2 speakers are not institutionally expected to take a particular role. As discussed above, the FLH program is unlike the traditional language classroom, but it is still an institutional program organized by the university, run by the graduate coordinator, and assisted by the guests, many of whom specialized in Japanese language education. These unique characteristics of the FLH dinner table conversation— outside of the classroom, but still within an educational institution—might have impacted on how the student participants treated the dinner table conversations, causing them to act accordingly. In other words, in different types of settings, with different co-participants, the other students might have exhibited the type of IC demonstrated by Michael. Kasper and Wagner (2014) indeed point out that challenges in conducting CA research on IC development stem from (a) "the nature of interactional competence as a competence that cannot be reduced to an individual participants' competence" (p. 198) and (b) the fact that "interactional competence development cannot be separated from the development of the participants' social relations" (p. 199). Thus, rather than suggesting his inherent superiority over the others, we consider Michael's IC as described in this study to be tightly related to how he treated these particular conversations and how he established his relationship with the other FLH members and guests.

In the spirit of applied CA (see Antaki, 2011), we would like to end this chapter by offering several points for consideration with regard to FLH management, as well as language pedagogy more generally. First, while FLH programs usually consider applicants' linguistic competence to be a crucial factor for selection, L2 competence determined by traditional methods such as standardized tests may not be a good predictor of L2 learners' success in FLH. As demonstrated by Michael's performance, even a novice- or intermediate-level learner with the ability to draw on existing IC can take advantage of the unique opportunities offered by FLH. Second, given that not all lower-level learners actively participated in the dinner table conversations, their purpose may need to be clarified among the participants, including the students, coordinator, and guests. Students may also be encouraged to reflect on, observe, and practice how to initiate and/or pursue topical talk (see Wong & Waring, 2010). Finally, considering what has been reported by recent CA studies on L2 talk and reconfirmed by the current study, it is essential to encourage students to envision themselves not as "L2 learners" with a communicative deficiency, but as "L2 users" with potential. In this light, the nature of classroom instruction should also be reconsidered to aspire for a balance between the development of accuracy and fluency, on the one hand, and confidence in participating in real-life interactions, on the other.

**Notes**

1. According to Jordan (1937), as cited by Bown et al. (2011), FLH has been in existence since as early as 1917.
2. The dinner conversation began with 11 student residents and Shiori, but by the time the current episode started, several students had already left the table.
3. Transcripts in this chapter are prepared by generally following the volume guidelines. The vertical bar ( | ) is used to indicate the onset of participants' embodied actions. The notations for the current speaker's concurrent embodied actions are placed above the first tier, whereas those for non-speaking co-participants' conduct are placed below the third tier. The diagonal line ( / ) after a silence is used to introduce participants' embodied actions that occurred during the silence. We provide third tier translation for each line, which corresponds to a prosodic unit, rather than placing it at the end of a multi-unit turn. With this arrangement, we hope to make it easier for the reader who is not familiar with Japanese to follow the development of ongoing talk and the onset of co-participants' linguistic or non-linguistic responses. Some of the original Japanese utterances are translated in unnatural or incomplete English sentences in order to convey the manner in which the original Japanese utterances are produced.
4. In fact, Tim was the British friend whom Michael mentioned in the previous episode on "line" versus "queue".
5. According to Kushida (2011), "[b]y responding with a *soo*-type token in response to an offer of a candidate understanding, the trouble-source speaker can display his/her stance to the fact that the recipient has assisted in solving a trouble in speaking and that s/he (the speaker) is responsible for the trouble" (p. 2716). It appears that Michael's use of *soo* in this context corresponds to Kushida's description.

# References

Antaki, C. (Ed.). (2011). *Applied conversation analysis: Intervention and change in institutional talk.* Basingstoke, UK: Palgrave Macmillan.

Aoki, H. (2011). Some functions of speaker head nods. In J. Streeck, C. Goodwin & C. LeBaron (Eds.), *Embodied interaction: Language and body in the material world* (pp. 93–105). New York, NY: Cambridge University Press.

Banno, E., Ohno, Y., Sakane, Y., & Shinagawa, C. (1999). *Genki I: An integrated course in elementary Japanese.* Tokyo: The Japan Times.

Banno, E., Ohno, Y., Sakane, Y., Shinagawa, C., & Tokashiki, K. (1999). *Genki II: An integrated course in elementary Japanese.* Tokyo: The Japan Times.

Bown, J., Dewey, D. P., Martinsen, R. A., & Baker, W. (2011). Foreign language houses: Identities in transition. *Critical Inquiry in Language Studies, 8*(3), 203–235.

Brouwer, C., & Wagner, J. (2004). Developmental issues in second language conversation. *Journal of Applied Linguistics, 1*, 29–47.

Button, G., & Casey, N. (1984). Generating topic: The use of topic initial elicitors. In J. Atkinson & J. Heritage (Eds.), *Structures of social action: Studies in conversation analysis* (pp. 167–190). New York, NY: Cambridge University Press.

Button, G., & Casey, N. (1985). Topic nomination and topic pursuit. *Human Studies, 8*, 3–55.

Cadierno, T., & Eskildsen, S. W. (Eds.). (2015). *Usage-based perspectives on second language learning*. Berlin: Mouton de Gruyter.

Cekaite, A. (2007). A child's development of interactional competence in a Swedish L2 classroom. *The Modern Language Journal, 91*(1), 45–62.

Crow, B. K. (1983). Topic shifts in couples' conversation. In R. T. Craig & K. Tracy (Eds.), *Conversational coherence* (pp. 137–156). Beverly Hills, CA: Sage.

Egbert, M. (1997). Schisming: The collaborative transformation from a single conversation to multiple conversations. *Research on Language and Social Interaction, 30*(1), 1–51.

Eskildsen, S. W., & Theodórsdóttir, G. (2017). Constructing L2 learning spaces: Ways to achieve learning inside and outside the classroom. *Applied Linguistics, 38*(2), 143–164.

Firth, A., & Wagner, J. (1997). On discourse, communication, and (some) fundamental concepts in SLA research. *The Modern Language Journal, 81*, 285–300.

Gardner, R., & Wagner, J. (Eds.). (2004). *Second language conversations*. London: Continuum.

Hall, J. K. (1993). The role of oral practices in the accomplishment of our everyday lives: The sociocultural dimension of interaction with implications for the learning of another language. *Applied Linguistics, 14*(2), 145–166.

Hall, J. K. (1995). (Re)creating our worlds with words: A sociohistorical perspective of face-to-face interaction. *Applied Linguistics, 16*(2), 206–232.

Hall, J. K., Hellermann, J., & Pekarek Doehler, S. (Eds.). (2011). *L2 interactional competence and development*. Bristol, UK: Multilingual Matters.

He, A. W., & Young, R. F. (1998). Language proficiency interviews: A discourse approach. In R. F. Young & A. W. He (Eds.), *Talking and testing: Discourse approaches to the assessment of oral proficiency* (pp. 1–24). Amsterdam: John Benjamins.

Hellermann, J. (2007). The development of practices for action in classroom dyadic interaction: Focus on task openings. *The Modern Language Journal, 91*(1), 83–96.

Hellermann, J. (2008). *Social actions for classroom language learning*. Clevedon, UK: Multilingual Matters.

Heritage, J. (1984). *Garfinkel and ethnomethodology*. Cambridge, UK: Polity Press.

Holt, E., & Drew, P. (2005). Figurative pivots: The use of figurative expressions in pivotal transitions. *Research on Language and Social Interaction, 38*(1), 35–62.

Jefferson, G. (1984). On stepwise transition from talk about a trouble to inappropriately next-positioned matters. In J. Atkinson, & J. Heritage (Eds.), *Structures of social action: Studies in conversation analysis* (pp. 191–222). New York, NY: Cambridge University Press.

Jefferson, G. (1993). Caveat speaker: Preliminary notes on recipient topic-shift implicature. *Research on Language and Social Interaction, 26*(1), 1–30.

Jordan, E. L. (1937). German language houses. *The Modern Language Journal, 21*(5), 354.

Kasper, G. (2004). Participant orientations in German conversation-for-learning. *The Modern Language Journal, 88*(4), 551–567.

Kasper, G., & Wagner, J. (2011). A conversation analytic approach to second language acquisition. In D. Atkinson (Ed.), *Alternative approaches to second language acquisition* (pp. 117–142). New York, NY: Taylor and Francis.

Kasper, G., & Wagner, J. (2014). Conversation analysis in applied linguistics. *Annual Review of Applied Linguistics, 34*, 171–212.

König, C. (2013). Topic management in French L2: A longitudinal conversation analytic study. *EUROSLA Yearbook, 13*, 226–250.

Koschmann, T. (2013). Conversation analysis and learning in interaction. In K. Mortensen & J. Wagner (Eds.), *Conversation analysis*. In C. A. Chapelle (Ed.), *The encyclopedia of applied linguistics* (pp. 1038–1043). Malden, MA: Wiley-Blackwell.

Kramsch, K. (1986). From language proficiency to interactional competence. *The Modern Language Journal, 70*, 366–372.

Kushida, S. (2011). Confirming understanding and acknowledging assistance: Managing trouble responsibility in response to understanding check in Japanese talk-in-interaction. *Journal of Pragmatics, 43*(11), 2716–2739.

Lee, Y. (2006). Towards respecification of communicative competence: Condition of L2 instruction or its objective? *Applied Linguistics, 27*(3), 349–376.

Lee, Y., & Hellermann, J. (2014). Tracing developmental change through conversation analysis: Cross-sectional and longitudinal analysis. *TESOL Quarterly, 48*(4), 736–788.

Markee, N. (2000). *Conversation analysis*. Mahwah, NJ: Lawrence Erlbaum.

Markee, N. (Ed.). (2004). Special issue: Classroom talks. *The Modern Language Journal, 88*(4), 491–616.

Markee, N. (2005). A conversation analytic perspective on off-task classroom talk: Implications for second language acquisition studies. In K. Richards & P. Seedhouse (Eds.), *Applying conversation analysis* (pp. 187–213). Basingstoke, UK: Palgrave MacMillan.

Martinsen, R. A., Baker, W., Bown, J., & Johnson, C. (2011). The benefits of living in foreign language housing: The effect of language use and second-language type on oral proficiency gains. *The Modern Language Journal, 95*(2), 274–290.

Martinsen, R. A., Baker, W., Dewey, D. P., Bown, J., & Johnson, C. (2010). Exploring diverse settings for language acquisition and use: Comparing study abroad, service learning abroad, and foreign language housing. *Applied Language Learning, 20*(1/2), 45–69.

Matsunaga, Y. (2012). *Learner investment, identity, and imagined communities: A study of Japanese language house community* (Doctoral dissertation). Available from ProQuest Dissertations and Theses database. (UMI No. 3512833)

Maynard, D. W. (1980). Placement of topic changes in conversation. *Semiotica, 30*(3/4), 263–290.

Maynard, D. W., & Zimmerman, D. H. (1984). Topical talk, ritual and the social organization of relationships. *Social Psychology Quarterly, 47*(4), 301–316.

McNamara, T. F. (1997). 'Interaction' in second language performance assessment: Whose performance? *Applied Linguistics, 18,* 446–466.

Mori, J. (2003). The construction of interculturality: A study of initial encounters between Japanese and American students. *Research on Language and Social Interaction, 36*(2), 143–184.

Mori, J., & Markee, N. (Eds.). (2009). Special issue: Language learning, cognition, and interactional practices. *International Review of Applied Linguistics in Language Teaching, 47*(1), 1–156.

Morita, E. (2005). *Negotiation of contingent talk: The Japanese interactional particles* ne *and* sa. Amsterdam: John Benjamins.

Mortensen, K. (2008). Selecting next speaker in the second language classroom: How to find a willing next speaker in planned activities. *Journal of Applied Linguistics, 5*(1), 55–79.

Nguyen, H. t. (2011). A longitudinal microanalysis of a second language learner's participation. In G. Pallotti & J. Wagner (Eds.), *L2 learning as social action: Conversation analytic perspectives* (pp. 17–44). Honolulu, HI: University of Hawai'i, National Foreign Language Resource Center.

Nguyen, H. t., & Kasper, G. (Eds.). (2009). *Talk-in-interaction: Multilingual perspectives.* Honolulu, HI: University of Hawai'i, National Foreign Language Resource Center.

Pallotti, G., & Wagner, J. (Eds.) (2011). *L2 learning as social practice: Conversation-analytic perspectives.* Honolulu, HI: University of Hawai'i, National Foreign Language Resource Center.

Pekarek Doehler, S., & Pochon-Berger, E. (2015). The development of L2 interactional competence: Evidence from turn-taking organization, sequence organization, repair organization and preference organization. In T. Cadierno & S. Eskildsen (Eds.), *Usage-based perspectives on second language learning* (pp. 233–268). Berlin: Mouton De Gruyter.

Sacks, H. (1992). *Lectures on conversation.* Oxford, UK: Blackwell.

Schegloff, E., & Sacks, H. (1973). Opening up closings. *Semiotica, 7,* 289–327.

Schmidt, R. W. (1983). Interaction, acculturation, and the acquisition of communicative competence: A case study of an adult. In N. Wolfson & E. Judd (Eds.), *Sociolinguistics and language acquisition* (pp. 137–174). Rowley, MA: Newbury House.

Seedhouse, P. (2004). *The interactional architecture of the language classroom: A conversation analysis perspective.* Malden, MA: Blackwell.

Stokoe, E. H. (2000). Constructing topicality in university students' small-group discussion: A conversation analytic approach. *Language and Education, 14*(3), 184–203.

Tanaka, H. (2000). The particle *ne* as a turn-managing device in Japanese conversation. *Journal of Pragmatics, 35*(8), 1135–1176.

Theodórsdóttir, G. (2011). Second language interaction for business and learning. In J. K. Hall, J. Hellermann & S. Pekarek-Doehler (Eds.), *Interactional competence and development* (pp. 93–118). Bristol, UK: Multilingual Matters.

Wilkinson, S. (2002). The omnipresent classroom during summer study abroad: American students in conversation with their French hosts. *The Modern Language Journal, 86*(2), 157–173.

Wong, J., & Waring, H. Z. (2010). *Conversation analysis and second language pedagogy: A guide for ESL/EFL teachers.* New York, NY: Routledge.

Young, R. F. (2003). Learning to talk the talk and walk the walk: Interactional competence in academic spoken English. *North Eastern Illinois University Working Papers in Linguistics, 2,* 26–44.

Young, R. F. (2009). Discursive practice in language learning and teaching. *Language Learning, 58*(Supplement 2), 1–267.

## Appendix: Topic initiators and topics

| Topics | Initiators | | Total |
|---|---|---|---|
| | Graduate Coordinator, TAs, Guests | Student residents (Michael) | |
| Health, weather, weekend | 61 | 15 (4) | 76 |
| Food, clothes, attendants at the dinner table | 46 | 31 (9) | 77 |
| Classes, homework, exams | 45 | 19 (2) | 64 |
| Activities & members of the Japanese House | 37 | 4 (2) | 41 |
| Personal stories | 18 | 12 (11) | 30 |
| Languages | 13 | 15 (10) | 28 |
| Japanese culture | 14 | 7 (2) | 21 |
| Non-Japanese-specific culture | 7 | 9 (5) | 16 |
| Other | 5 | 8 (4) | 13 |

The entire database of video-recorded conversations (approximately 10.5 hours) was reviewed by paying attention to who initiated new topics and what kind of topics were introduced. Cases of topic changes and topic shifts with clear sequential boundaries were identified following Maynard (1980). Considering the difficulty of capturing dinner table conversations in their entirety, we do not claim that the numbers given in this table are conclusive. However, we also consider these numbers to be informative, as they illustrate an overall tendency in topic management.

# 11 "Daijoobu desu ka?": Use of Formulaic Expressions by One Novice L2 Japanese Teacher

Yumiko Tateyama
*University of Hawai'i at Mānoa*

## Introduction

Conversation Analysis (CA) studies on interactional practices in the second language (L2) classroom have examined repair practices (Hellermann, 2011; Seedhouse, 2004), sequence organization such as IRF (Initiation-Response-Feedback) (Lee, 2007; Waring, 2008), and word searches during pair work activities (Mori & Hasegawa, 2009), among others. These studies have raised our awareness of the emerging and context-sensitive nature of interactions that take place in the L2 classroom, be they between student and teacher, or between student peers. In particular, analysis focusing on the sequence of turns at talk reveals the interactional resources that participants deploy, as well as orientations they display during the talk.

Recently, CA research has also looked at novice L2 teachers' interactional practices in the classroom (Hosoda & Aline, 2010; Leyland, Greer, & Rettig-Miki, 2016; Rine & Hall, 2011). Unlike the surveys or interviews that are frequently employed in examining teacher development, microanalysis of classroom interactions from a CA perspective reveals the teacher's situated, local display of competence. This chapter pursues this line of research by investigating the interactional competence (IC) of one novice L2 Japanese teacher with respect to his classroom practices. While there are a number of CA studies that examine the L2

IC of learners of Japanese (e.g., Ishida, 2009, 2011; Tominaga, 2013), few to date have investigated novice L2 Japanese teachers' interactional practices in the classroom. This chapter seeks to address this research gap by examining the interactional practices of one novice Japanese teacher (an L1 speaker of Chinese) in a beginning Japanese as a foreign language (JFL) class offered at a university in the United States. In particular, this study examines the sequential environment in which the focal teacher deploys the formulaic expression *daijoobu desu ka* 'Are you all right?', the actions he accomplishes by using this expression, and how these actions change over the course of the semester. The analysis also examines multimodal resources such as gesture, gaze, body positioning, and objects that are deployed in conjunction with the verbal resources in the instructor's interactions with students. While teachers frequently deploy questions such as 'Are you okay?' to check student understanding, few studies have examined the nature of such questions via the details of actual episodes during classroom interaction (Waring, 2012). It is hoped that insights obtained from the analysis in the current study will be useful, even in a small way, when implementing teacher training for novice teachers in order to improve student-teacher interactions in the L2 classroom.

## Background

### Student-teacher interactions in the L2 classroom

The significance of interaction in the L2 classroom has been widely discussed. For instance, van Lier (1996) considers interaction as the most important element in the curriculum. In particular, contingent interaction and joint construction by all participants are noted as features of an organic and holistic curriculum. More recently, Walsh (2011, 2013) argues that when teachers make effective use of interaction, learners are more engaged and involved in classes. Walsh (2011) introduces the notion of classroom interactional competence (CIC), which he defines as "teachers' and learners' ability to use interaction as a tool for mediating and assisting learning" (p. 165). As Walsh notes, when interaction is put at the center of teaching and learning, CIC results in improved learning and opportunities for learning.

Studies that investigate classroom interaction from a CA perspective reveal that student-teacher interactions are dynamic and that the teacher makes contingent and ad hoc decisions while monitoring and acting on what becomes available within the sequence of interaction (Lee, 2007). This contingent decision-making is consistent with the way Young (2011) conceptualizes IC and highlights the significance of the sequential structure of talk in sense-making. Participants in any given instance of talk show their understanding of previous turns and actions in the way their next action is designed (Kasper & Wagner, 2014; Schegloff, 1992).

While a growing body of research has examined the development of L2 speakers' IC when they engage in situated, discursive practices (e.g., Brouwer & Wagner, 2004; Cekaite, 2007; Hellermann, 2008, 2011; Ishida, 2009, 2011; Markee 2008; Young & Miller 2004), recent CA studies have also examined the development of novice teachers' interactional practices in the classroom. Rine and Hall (2011) conducted a longitudinal case study of one international teaching assistant (ITA) who participated in a semester-long ITA training course. Their study showed how the ITA learned to use the interactional resources, both verbal and nonverbal (e.g., gesture, gaze, and body positioning) at his disposal, indicating an increased orientation to his role as teacher. Hosoda and Aline (2010) examined the development of the classroom interactional practices of two Japanese English as a Foreign Language (EFL) teacher trainees who were undertaking a pre-service practicum at an elementary school in Japan. Initially, both trainees oriented to their role as a teaching assistant; however, as they were socialized into the classroom culture, they displayed characteristics conventionally associated with teachers. Through interaction, they learned how to deploy assessments and directives in socially and culturally meaningful ways, thereby showing their increased orientation to their role as the teacher.

Leyland, Greer, and Rettig-Miki (2016) documented the interactional practices of one novice tester in a series of group discussion tests among EFL students in Japan. A teaching assistant (TA), who served as the tester, initially utilized a rhetorical discourse structure whereby she played the devil's advocate in order to elicit follow-up turns from her students. Through a detailed sequential analysis, Leyland et al. found that such strategies did not generate significant follow-up turns. Over the course of successive engagement in the group discussion tests, the TA was found to increasingly align her turn design with that of the EFL students, which contributed to generating follow-up turns from the students. That is to say, instead of simply transferring her available IC or linguistic resources, the TA adapted to the local contingencies and deployed more interactionally acceptable conduct (see Nguyen, 2012).

The studies reviewed above show how a novice can gain competences as a teacher or a tester through the iterative process of interacting with students. Kasper and Ross (2013) note that "participation in interaction is both constrained and enabled by the co-participant's actions" and that "the co-participant's prior turn opens up an opportunity space for the current speaker's actions" (p. 11). This statement can be applied to classroom interaction as well. By closely monitoring the student's prior turn and aligning with it, the teacher can show sensitivity to the local context. Such sensitivity allows the teacher to interact with students more fully.

**Teacher questions in the L2 classroom**
Teacher questions are ubiquitous in the L2 classroom. Earlier studies on teacher questions (Long & Sato, 1983; Pica & Long, 1986) found that teachers ask more display questions than referential questions. Display questions attempt to elicit known information, whereas referential questions request unknown information. Referential questions were generally considered to be more effective than display questions, as shown by Brock (1986), who found referential questions elicited student responses that were longer and more grammatically complex. However, some researchers (e.g., van Lier, 1988) have questioned the relevancy of this distinction between the two types of questions. Studies that examine teacher questions from a CA perspective (e.g., Koshik, 2010; Lee, 2006; 2008; Markee, 1995) demonstrate that a teacher's display questions generate different interpretations and actions depending on where in the sequence such questions are uttered. Lee (2006) argued that display questions serve as central resources for teachers and students to organize their lessons through the production of interactional exchanges. For instance, through the questioning process the teacher can assess what students know at any given moment to determine the next course of action (Lee, 2008). Koshik (2010) found that during L2 one-on-one writing conferences a teacher's "reversed polarity question," a yes-no question produced after targeting a portion of a student's written text as problematic, conveys a negative assertion and thereby helps students to carry out self-correction.

These CA studies shed new light on what teacher questions do depending on the interactional context and the sequential location in which such questions are uttered. This chapter focuses on questions that the teacher asks in order to check student understanding: a topic which has received less attention in the existing literature than perhaps it deserves. Following Waring (2012), I call these questions understanding checks. In English, questions such as "Are you okay?" and "Do you understand?" are used to check student understanding. Japanese equivalents of these expressions are *ii desu ka* and *wakarimasu ka.* They are the first pair part of an adjacency pair. As Waring (2012) notes, these questions elicit claims, rather than demonstrations, of understanding.

While a growing body of CA studies have examined teacher questions in the L2 classroom (e.g., Hosoda, 2014; Hosoda & Aline, 2013), the one which is most relevant to the current study is Waring (2012), which examines teacher questions to check student understanding. Waring found that understanding checks are not always produced to invite questions, and are not always treated as such. At activity boundaries, they serve the dual role of checking student understanding and launching a possible activity closing sequence. Waring also notes that students orient to understanding check questions as preferring "no problem" as a response and that the teacher also treats no problem responses as preferred. While understanding checks in Waring (2012) include a variety of questions that the teacher produces to check student understanding, the current study primarily focuses on the Japanese expression *daijoobu desu ka* 'Are you all right?' and its alternative expressions, such as *ii desu ka* 'Are you okay?'.

The importance of teacher questions in classroom interaction has been discussed in L2 pedagogy texts (e.g., Brown, 2007; Richards & Lockhart, 1996). However, there is little empirical research on the interactional work that teacher questions do in ongoing classroom talk, especially when the target language is Japanese. The current study contributes to this literature. Teacher trainees may also benefit from insights obtained from empirical studies that examine the minute details of unfolding student-teacher interaction in the classroom. In order to uncover the inner workings of interaction that unfold moment-by-moment and the orientations displayed by the teacher and students during class interaction when the teacher produces understanding checks, I turn to CA. CA's radically emic perspective allows us to see orientations displayed by the participants in the interaction and the actions these orientations accomplish.

CA studies on classroom interaction have shown how embodied action, objects, and spatial practices interface with verbal productions (e.g., Markee, 2011; Mori & Hasegawa, 2009; Sert, 2013). Focusing on the formulaic expression *daijoobu desu ka* 'Are you all right?', the present study also uses multimodal CA to explicate how interactions between one novice JFL teacher and his students unfold moment-by-moment during teacher-fronted class sessions, and how the teacher's use of the expression changes over the course of the semester.

## The Study

### Data

The data for the current study consist of six class sessions (50 minutes each) video-taped at approximately two to three week intervals in a beginning-level first-semester JFL class (JPN101) that was offered at a university in the U.S. during the spring semester of 2012. The teacher, a male graduate student at the university, was an L1 speaker of Chinese who was highly proficient in spoken and written Japanese. He will be referred to as Tao (a pseudonym) throughout this study. After Tao successfully completed a mandatory teaching practicum, he was assigned to teach JPN101 in the subsequent semester. A camcorder was placed in the back of the classroom to video-record class interactions. Since the camera was focused on the teacher, most student utterances were only available in audio format.[1] On most days that were recorded, 10 to 12 students were present. The researcher was also present in class during the recordings and also took field notes. A total of six lessons in the textbook were covered during the semester. Topics included self-introductions, conversations in a post office and a restaurant, asking the whereabouts of things and people, and asking about unfamiliar words. Approximately eight days were allocated for each lesson, and recordings were conducted towards the end of each lesson as indicated by the course schedule. The class followed a common course syllabus prepared by the department. Instructional items consisted of a set of grammatical structures and communicative situations where those structures were utilized. Tao's teaching style was communicative: He usually created a meaningful context in which students could practice newly introduced grammatical patterns. He also introduced Japanese orthography, including *kanji* (Japanese characters of Chinese origin), and relevant cultural information as appropriate.

**Selection of focal sections**
An exploratory review of the data via "unmotivated looking" (Psathas, 1995) revealed that one of the noticeable features of Tao's talk was his frequent use of *daijoobu desu ka* 'Are you all right?'. According to Japanese dictionaries,[2] *daijoobu* 'okay; all right' describes a state in which worries or uncertainties are resolved. Thus, its question form, *daijoobu desu ka*, is commonly directed towards someone who appears to be concerned about something. For instance, to someone who looks pale, one could say *daijoobu desu ka* 'Are you all right?'. Or, to someone who is concerned about time, one could say *jikan daijoobu desu ka* 'Are you okay for time?'. While L1 Japanese speaking teachers may also ask students *daijoobu desu ka* during class to check student understanding, a more typical question is *ii desu ka*,[3] which similarly means 'Are you okay?' or 'Is everything all right?', but does not convey the nuance of a worry-free state. By producing *ii desu ka*, a teacher can check student understanding, and also confirm whether students are following his or her talk. In some contexts, the expression may also be used to elicit agreement from the interlocutor.

A total of 171 cases of *daijoobu desu ka* were found in the current data set. I examined each occurrence of *daijoobu desu ka* and then compared Tao's use of this expression across class sessions. I also examined his use of the alternative expressions, *ii desu ka* 'Are you okay?' and *wakarimasu ka* 'Do you understand?', to check student understanding. The current analysis seeks to explicate the following:

1. In what sequential environments does Tao use *daijoobu desu ka* and what actions are achieved by using this expression?
2. Are there any changes in Tao's use of *daijoobu desu ka* over the course of the semester?
3. How does Tao use alternative expressions and how does his use of these expressions develop?

# Analysis

In this section I will first examine the functions of Tao's use of *daijoobu desu ka* while paying close attention to the sequential environment in which Tao produces this question. Next, I will briefly discuss some of the changes over the course of the semester in Tao's use of *daijoobu desu ka*. Finally, I will present an analysis of his use of alternative questions when he checks for student understanding.

## Actions Tao performed through the use of *daijoobu desu ka*

Tao's use of *daijoobu desu ka* was observed in the following sequential environments: (a) at activity closings during teacher-fronted activities; (b) at transitions from teacher-fronted to student-centered activities; and (c) at transitions from student-centered to teacher-fronted activities. My analysis of sample excerpts from these sequential environments is presented below.

### At activity closing during teacher-fronted activities

Tao often used *daijoobu desu ka* at activity or topic boundaries during teacher-fronted activities. One of the most frequently observed placements of *daijoobu desu ka* was after IRF sequences (Excerpts 1 and 2). He also produced *daijoobu desu ka* after extended teacher talk (Excerpts 3 and 4). In both cases, there were instances where Tao used *daijoobu desu ka* to check student understanding and then subsequently went on to close the activity (Excerpts 1 and 3). He also used *daijoobu desu ka* to close an activity without displaying an orientation to checking student understanding (Excerpt 2). There were also instances where Tao produced *daijoobu desu ka* multiple times after an extended episode of teacher-led talk in order to first check student understanding and then subsequently close the activity (Excerpt 4). Detailed analyses of these excerpts follow.

### After IRF sequences

One of the commonly observed placements of *daijoobu desu ka* was after IRF sequences in which Tao asked a question, students provided a response, and then Tao provided feedback. Prior to Excerpt 1 below, Tao had been reviewing a model conversation about sending a package at a post office.

**Excerpt 1.** (2/8) Air mail (T: Tao; S: Student)
A dialogue set in a post office is shown on the screen via a PowerPoint slide.

```
1    T:   |((leans towards screen and left hand
              touches a sentence with left hand, LH))
2         |so if you finally decide to send the package

3         (0.4)/((T returns to base position))

4         by sea- uh by air mail °okay°

5         kookuubin de onegaishimasu.
          air mail   by please
          By airmail please.

6         (1.5)/((T leans towards screen, points
          to de on screen*, shifts gaze from screen
          to students))
```

 *Figure 1

```
7    T:   what does this de mean here?

8         (1.2)/((T returns to base position))

9    T:   kookuubin de onegaishimasu.
          air mail   by please
          By airmail please.

10        (0.8)

11   S:   °by°
            by
            by

12   T:   |((shifts gaze between screen and Ss))
13        |by (.) yeah. (.) by (.) by airmail.

14        kookuubin de onegaishimasu.
          air mail   by please
          By airmail please.
```

```
15→     ((looking at Ss)) daijoobu  desu ka¿**
                         all right CP   Q
                         All right?
```

```
                                                  ** Figure 2

16      (1.5)

17      so by the means of (.) by.

18      kookuubin  de onegaishimasu. hai.
        air mail   by please         okay.
        By airmail please. Okay.

19      (1.5)/((T looks at the handout))

20      okay, so please look at the steps.
```

In this excerpt, Tao asks the class to explain the function of the particle *de* in the sentence *kookuubin de onegaishimasu* 'by air mail please' (line 7). Prior to asking this question, Tao first touches the sentence projected on the screen (line 1), explains when the expression is used (i.e., when sending a package by air) (lines 2–4), and then reads aloud the focal sentence (line 5). Following this, Tao points to the particle *de* in the sentence projected on the screen (Figure 1) and shifts his gaze away from the screen to the students before he asks the question. This indicates that he is making sure that the students are co-orienting to the character to which he is pointing (Goodwin, 2007). Tao's question is followed by a 1.2 second gap of silence, during which no response from the students is forthcoming. In the meantime, Tao returns to the position right behind the desk in the front of the classroom where a computer monitor and a keyboard are stored (line 8). I will refer to this classroom location as the base position because Tao's instruction centers around this area, starting and ending activities at this physical location. In line 9, instead of reformulating the question he posed earlier in order to elicit a response from the students, his repair is done by repeating the focal sentence, *kookuubin de onegaishimasu* 'by airmail please'. Following a 0.8 second silence, a student whispers the answer (line 11). In the next turn, Tao provides a receipt to confirm the student's answer by repeating it, and then offers an acknowledgment token, "yeah" (see Schegloff, 1996) (line 13). After repeating the focal sentence one more time (line 14), Tao says *daijoobu desu ka¿* 'all right?'[14] with a slight rising intonation (line 15, Figure 2). Although Tao's earlier question about the meaning of *de* (line 7) was issued to the entire class, only one student responded to this question and did so in a soft voice (line 11), suggesting that the student was not very confident about his answer. Thus, by formulating *daijoobu desu ka* after receipting the student's response, Tao can check if both the focal student and the rest of the class have understood the meaning of the particle *de* that he introduced. This is followed by a 1.5 second gap of silence, during which no verbal response from the students is heard. Tao's repetition of the meaning of the particle *de* (line 17) appears to be oriented to the absence of a response, that is, the missing second pair part from the students to his question *daijoobu desu ka* (the first pair part).[5] After this, Tao repeats the focal sentence one last time (line 18). The acknowledgement token *hai* 'okay' that follows projects an upcoming transition to a new activity (Ikeda & Ko, 2011). In sum, this sequence shows that Tao uses *daijoobu desu ka* to check student understanding, and subsequently, to close the activity, during which time his gaze was directed towards the students when he used this expression, as shown in Figure 2.

There were also instances in which Tao produced *daijoobu desu ka* to close an activity while not showing an orientation to checking student understanding after the IRF sequence. One is shown in Excerpt 2, which took place approximately five minutes before Excerpt 1 above.

**Excerpt 2.** (2/8) Sea mail (T: Tao; Ss: Students)
A dialogue is written on a handout and is also shown on the screen.

```
1      T:  |((reading from the handout he is holding))
2          |funabin   de   ikura      desu ka¿
            sea mail  by   how much   CP   Q
           How much is it by sea mail?

3          so he asked for how much th- (1.2) sea mail

4          cost, okay.

5      T:  |((touches screen with LH; shifts gaze to Ss))
6          |funabin de ikura      desu ka¿*
            boat    by how much CP     Q
           How much is it by boat?
```

*Use of Formulaic Expressions by One Novice L2 Japanese Teacher* 343

*Figure 3

```
7            (3.0)

8    Ss:     °sen     en°
             thousand yen
             One thousand yen.

9    T:      ((shifts gaze back to paper he is holding))
10           hai sen         en    desu ne, sen       en    desu ne.
             yes thousand    yen   CP   IP  thousand  yen   CP   IP
             Yes, one thousand yen. One thousand yen.

11           so he asked th- (.) how much it cost

12           respectively to decide °okay° (.) which one

13           (1.5)/((T leans towards keyboard, looks down))

14           |((extends right hand, RH, towards keyboard))
15           |funabin   de   ikura        desu ka¿
             sea mail   by   how much     CP   Q
             How much is it by boat?

16           |((stands straight, while gazing at handout))
17→          |daijoobu desu ka.**
             okay     CP   Q
             All right.
```

**Figure 4

```
18           (3.5)/((T continues to look at handout))**
```

```
19   T:   |((shifts gaze to screen, points to sentences
              with LH))
20        |hai   jaa   minna   isshoni   yomimashoo.
           okay  well  all     together  read-VOL
           Okay, so, let's read it together.
```

In this excerpt, Tao is going over an expression from a conversation that takes place at a Japanese post office. The teacher and students have a written copy of the conversation, and the dialogue also appears on a PowerPoint slide projected on the screen at the front of the classroom (see Figure 3). In line 2, Tao reads aloud the new expression, *funabin de ikura desu ka* 'How much is it by boat?', from his handout. After providing an English explanation of the expression (lines 3–4), he repeats the same sentence in line 6 (Figure 3). Tao's left hand is touching the screen where the second pair part is written as he shifts his gaze towards the students, an embodied action indicating that he is asking a question this time around. After a 3.0 second gap of silence, a few students respond with *sen en* 'one thousand yen,' although their voices are soft (line 8). The teacher approves the answer with a turn initial *hai* 'yes', followed by repetition (line 10), and provides an additional explanation in English (lines 11–12). During this time (lines 9–12), Tao is looking at the handout of the conversation that he is holding in his left hand. During the 1.5 second gap of silence that follows, he leans forward and looks further down (line 13), extends his right hand towards the keyboard (line 14), and repeats *funabin de ikura desu ka* 'How much is it by boat?' (line 15). This is followed by *daijoobu desu ka* 'all right' produced with falling intonation (line 17), as Tao changes his posture to a straight up position with his eyes still looking at his handout (Figure 4). Tao continues to look at his handout during the 3.5 second gap of silence that follows. Tao's absence of gaze towards the students and his production of *daijoobu desu ka* with a falling intonation during this sequence (lines 9–17) suggest that he is not checking student understanding. Rather, he is using *daijoobu desu ka* as an activity-closing device. Subsequently, the acknowledgement token *hai* 'okay' and the transition device *jaa* 'well' together with his gaze shift to the screen (lines 19–20) project a transition to a new activity.

In Excerpt 1, Tao's gaze was directed towards his students when he produced *daijoobu desu ka* to check their understanding. He then waited a few seconds before he repeated the key point of that particular sequence. In Excerpt 2, as we have just observed, there was no indication that Tao was checking student understanding after he said *daijoobu desu ka*, in spite of the 3.5 second gap of silence that followed, since he was still looking at his handout. Tao's embodied actions in conjunction with his use of verbal resources provide important clues for understanding what he is doing via his interaction with students (see Markee, 2011; Sert, 2013)

*After extended talk*

There were also some instances in which Tao used *daijoobu desu ka* after an extended turn in English or in Japanese. In Excerpt 3 below, Tao produces *daijoobu desu ka* after a lengthy English explanation in order to check student understanding and at the same time to indicate an activity closing. Prior to the excerpt, the students had practiced a dialogue on asking how to say something in English, as a choral reading activity. The script of the dialogue that the students had just practiced and a picture of a Ferris wheel is shown on the screen. The focal word, "Ferris wheel", is written in English in the Japanese dialogue.

**Excerpt 3.** (4/3) Ferris wheel

```
1    T:   |((extends LH to the focal word))
2         |okay here

3         |((shifts gaze to Ss, smiling))
4         |you just say english okay?*
```

*Figure 5

```
5         |((withdraws hand, still smiling))
6         |don't say (.) don't say that in katakana °okay°.

7         |((extends LH again, still smiling))
8         |this is english. you can see english °okay°.
9          say it in english.

10         ((shifts gaze downward and then towards Ss))
11→        daijoobu desu ka¿**
           all right   CP  Q
           All right?
```

**Figure 6

```
12        (.)

13       |((moves both hands.))
14       |hai.  ja switch roles.
          okay well
         Okay. Now switch roles.
```

Here, Tao tells his students that they should pronounce the word "Ferris wheel" in English, not in Japanese as would be the case for a word written in *katakana*.[6] Tao's verbal and nonverbal actions mutually elaborate what he is doing in his interaction with the students. For instance, in line 1, Tao makes his reference point clear by extending his left hand to the picture of the Ferris wheel that appears on the screen. Shifting his gaze to the students, he tells them to pronounce the word in English (lines 3–4, Figure 5). After withdrawing his left hand (line 5), he extends it one more time to the focal word (line 7) while again directing the students to pronounce it in English (lines 8–9). After this, he momentarily shifts his gaze downward, but immediately looks towards the students and checks their understanding using *daijoobu desu ka* (lines 10–11, Figure 6), delivering the turn with a slightly rising intonation. Student nonverbal response to the question is not clear due to non-availability of student video data. However, Tao's next utterance *hai* 'okay', which projects an upcoming transition to a new activity, suggests that he assessed the students' understanding to be sufficient. The next utterance, "*ja* ('now') switch roles," clearly indicates that the class will be embarking on a new activity. Similar sequences were observed when Tao introduced cultural information about Japan or when he provided additional comments on newly introduced Japanese structures in English. He would produce *daijoobu desu ka* following his English explanation, first to check student understanding and then subsequently to close a sequence once he judged their comprehension was adequate.

In Excerpt 3 above, Tao gave an extended explanation in English. There were also instances in which Tao produced prolonged spates of talk in Japanese, such as reading a dialogue aloud from the textbook or a handout. On such occasions, Tao checked the students' understanding before he came to the close of his talk. Prior to Excerpt 4 below, Tao went over the expression *are nihongo de nante yuu n desu ka* 'What do you call that in Japanese?'. In the excerpt, Tao is reading aloud a dialogue that is projected on the screen. A picture of a telephone box is also shown on the screen.

**Excerpt 4.** (4/3) Telephone box

```
1    T:   |((reading from dialogue on screen))
2         |are nihongo    de nan  te  yuu n desu ka?*
           that Japanese  in what QT  say N CP   Q
          What do you call that in Japanese?
```

*Figure 7

```
3         (3.7)/((T shifts gaze down to computer monitor))

4    T:   |((looks at screen; extends and withdraws LH))
5         |ah  denwa bokkusu desu yo.
           ah  phone box     CP   IP
          Ah, that's a telephone box.

6         aa  denwa bokkusu desu ka¿
          oh  phone box     CP   IP
          Oh, telephone box.

7         hai soo desu. ((looks at handout))
          yes so  CP
          Yes, that's right.

8         doomo.
          thank you
          Thank you.

9         iie.
          no.
          No problem.

10        (1.3)/((T looks at students))

11   T:   |((looking at students))
12 →      |daijoobu   desu ka?**
           all right  CP   Q
          All right?
```

**Figure 8

```
13        (1.2)/((T continues to look at Ss))

14   T:  |((looking at students))
15   →   |°imi     wa daijoobu  desu ka¿°
          meaning TP all right  CP    Q
          Are you all right with the meaning?

16        (1.4)/((T shifts gaze from Ss to screen))

17   T:  |((looking at and reading from screen))
18       |are  nihongo  de nan te yuu n desu ka?
          that Japanese in what QT say N CP   Q
          What do you call that in Japanese?

19       |((shifts gaze to students))
20   →   |un (.) daijoobu desu ka.*** hai, ja.
          yeah   all right  CP    Q    okay then.
          Yeah, all right. Okay, next.
```

***Figure 9

Tao reads aloud line by line a dialogue in which one person asks the other what "that thing over there" is called in Japanese and the other person provides the response "telephone box" (lines 1–9). Following a 1.3 second gap of silence in line 10 after he finishes reading the dialogue, Tao asks *daijoobu desu ka* while looking at the students (line 12, Figure 8). The 1.2 second gap of silence that follows suggests that Tao is monitoring the students' response to his question. Perhaps not being able to receive a clear indication of understanding from the students' nonverbal action, Tao once again produces *daijoobu desu ka* in line 15, asking whether the students are all right with the meaning this time around. This *daijoobu desu ka* was produced in a soft voice with a slightly rising intonation. During the 1.4 second silence that follows, he continues to look at the students, perhaps monitoring their embodied response, and then shifts his gaze to the screen (line 16). After reading aloud the key expression from the dialogue one more time (line 18), he produces *un* 'yeah', suggesting that he has assessed that there is sufficient understanding of the expression. His formulation of *daijoobu desu ka* and *hai jaa* 'okay, next' that follows (line 20) indicates that he is closing the current activity and embarking on a new one. As this excerpt shows, production of *daijoobu desu ka* as an understanding check before moving into activity closing was accompanied with Tao's gaze towards students.

In sum, when Tao used *daijoobu desu ka* at the activity boundary, it had the dual function of accomplishing both an understanding check and an activity closing. When Tao wanted to specifically check student understanding, he produced *daijoobu desu ka* multiple times before he closed the activity, as shown in Excerpt 4. When Tao produced *daijoobu desu ka* to check student understanding, his gaze was directed towards them. When his gaze was not directed towards them, as shown in Excerpt 2, Tao did not seem to be checking student understanding, but rather was simply closing the activity at hand.

### At transition from teacher-fronted to student-centered activities

In addition to producing *daijoobu desu ka* while standing at the front of the classroom in the base position during teacher-fronted activities, Tao also used the same phrase during transition times from teacher-fronted to student-centered activities. Prior to Excerpt 5 below, Tao demonstrated how to write *kanji* such as *sensee* 'teacher,' *ni* 'two,' and *san* 'three.' In Excerpt 5, he erases the characters he has written on the whiteboard and then demonstrates how to write *yonensee* '4th year student,' which is also projected on the board.

**Excerpt 5.** (1/23) Writing *kanji*
T is standing at the front of the room with a marker pen in his hand.

```
1    T:  hai  ja  isshoni    kakimashoo.
         okay now together   write-VOL
         Okay, now let's write it together.

2        (4.2)/((T erases characters written on board))

3    T:  yonensee desu ne.
         4th year  CP   IP
         It's senior.
```

```
4          |((points to the kanji for yonensee on screen))
5          |please write this.

6          |((writes the kanji for yonensee on the board))
7          |yonensee.  hai.   °yo° (2.2)  °nen°  (3.5)  °see°*
            4th year   okay  four         year          student
           Senior. Okay. Fourth-year student.
```

*Figure 10

```
8          (1.8)/((T shifts body position towards Ss))

9     T:|((points to the kanji he just wrote))
10       |yonensee**
          4th year
         Senior.
```

**Figure 11

```
11         (2.8)/((T shifts gaze to board and then to Ss))

12    T:|((walks towards students))
13→     |daijoobu desu ka¿***
         all right   CP   Q
         All right?
```

***Figure 12

```
14         (2.5)/((T looks at a student's writing))
15     T: hai.
           okay.
           okay
```

After announcing a new activity (line 1) and erasing the characters that he wrote earlier (line 2), Tao carefully prepares for his demonstration of how to write *yonensee* 'senior' in *kanji*: He verbalizes the word (line 3) and then points to the characters for *yonensee* projected on the screen (line 4). This pointing gesture indicates what "this" in his verbal directive "please write this" (line 5) refers to. Tao verbalizes the word *yonensee* again while he is writing it (line 7, Figure 10) and one last time when he finishes writing it as he points to the word (lines 9–10, Figure 11). Tao's verbal and nonverbal actions provide students with important clues to make sense of what the teacher is doing during this particular sequence. After issuing the directive "please write this" (line 5), Tao checks if the students are following his directions for writing the newly introduced characters. He walks towards the students as he asks *daijoobu desu ka* with slightly rising intonation (lines 12–13, Figure 12), which suggests that Tao is making sure that the students do not have any questions about the *kanji* or the task of writing them. At the same time, he indicates that he is transitioning from the teacher-fronted activity to the student-centered activity (i.e., writing *kanji*) by saying *daijoobu desu ka* and leaving the base position, directing attention to individual students. He then checks each student's writing and offers an acknowledgement token *hai* 'okay' (lines 14–15). Tao's use of *daijoobu desu ka* at the time of transitioning from the teacher-fronted activity to the student-centered activity was observed throughout the semester.

### At transition from student-centered to teacher-fronted activities

Tao also produced the phrase *daijoobu desu ka* when transitioning from student-centered activities, such as pair-based conversation practice or individual reading or writing practice, to teacher-fronted activities. Prior to Excerpt 6 below, Tao had been reviewing the Japanese names of things that can be found inside a building, such as stairs, classrooms, and vending machines. Tao then placed the students into pairs. As the excerpt begins they are practicing conversations with their partners, asking the whereabouts of things and people based on the picture shown on the screen.

**Excerpt 6.** (3/14) Pair practice

Tao has just returned to the base position after moving around the classroom.

```
1  Ss:   ((practicing conversation in loud voices))

2  T:   |((looks towards Ss))
3  →    |°hai° daijoobu  desu ka?*
         okay all right  CP   Q
         Okay, all right?
```

*Figure 13

```
4       (7.8)/ |((Ss continue talking fairly loudly))
5              |((T continues looking at Ss*; then
6                  shifts gaze to handout he is holding**))
```

** Figure 14

```
7  T:   |((shifts gaze from handout to Ss))
8  →   |hai  daijoobu  desu ka?***
        okay all right  CP   Q
        Okay, all right?
```

***Figure 15

```
9       |((moving LH to picture on screen))
10      |konpyuutaa wa nankai    ni arimasu ka.
         computer   TP what floor on exist    Q
         What floor is the computer on?
```

11  S:  °yonkai.° ((some pairs still practicing))
        fourth floor
        The fourth floor.

12  T:  hai konpyuutaa wa yonkai     ni arimasu.
        yes computer     TP 4th floor on exist
        Yes, the computer is on the 4$^{th}$ floor.

In this excerpt, by utilizing *daijoobu desu ka* after *hai* 'okay,' where *hai* projects a change of activity, Tao attempts to get student attention while at the same time checking to see if they are ready for the next activity. At the beginning, while students continue practicing their conversations with their partners in fairly loud voices, Tao looks towards them and produces *hai* 'okay' in a soft voice. This is followed by the question *daijoobu desu ka* (line 3, Figure 13). However, the students do not attend to his question, and instead continue with their partner conversations (line 4). During this time, Tao continues looking at the students, perhaps checking to see if they are ready for the next activity.[7] Then, he shifts his gaze to the handout he is holding (line 6, Figure 14), suggesting that he has determined that the students need some more time. After shifting his gaze back to the students, he repeats *hai daijoobu desu ka* (line 8, Figure 15); this time *hai* is pronounced louder than on the first occasion. Instead of checking the students' reaction, however, as he did in line 5, Tao immediately moves his left hand towards the picture on the screen and asks where the computer is located (line 10). This time he gets a response from one student (line 11).

The fact that the students continue talking in line 4 suggests that they are not providing the second pair part response to the question *daijoobu desu* ka. Therefore, either verbally or nonverbally, they are not orienting to Tao's initiating action. This may be partly attributable to the fact that Tao utters *hai* in a soft voice (line 3). When he produced the *daijoobu desu ka* expression the second time around, the *hai* that came before it was louder, and he did manage to get a response to his question on the location of the computer, although the response was uttered in a soft voice. At this time, some students were still practicing their conversations, apparently not orienting to the teacher's question. This may be due to the fact that Tao did not give sufficient time to check whether students were ready for the next activity when he produced *daijoobu desu ka* the second time.

To sum up, Tao's use of *daijoobu desu ka* was observed at activity closings, such as after IRF sequences and after extended episodes of talk by Tao. On these occasions, *daijoobu desu ka* often had the dual function of checking student understanding and initiating the end of the activity. When Tao specifically checked student understanding, he produced more than one *daijoobu desu ka* before the activity came to a close, and his gaze was directed towards the students. When his gaze was not directed towards the students, Tao was simply closing the activity. Tao also used *daijoobu desu ka* during the transition from teacher-fronted to student-centered activities. For this, he often produced the expression while he was walking towards the students. Tao's use of *daijoobu desu ka* was also observed during the transition from student-centered to teacher-fronted activities: Tao produced *daijoobu desu ka* to draw student attention and get them ready for the next activity that he had prepared.

### Changes in Tao's use of daijoobu desu ka and emergence of alternative expressions

While Tao used *daijoobu desu ka* throughout the semester, fewer instances were observed as the semester progressed. There was, however, an increased use of the alternative expression, *ii desu ka* 'Are you all right?', which appears in a similar sequential environment to *daijoobu desu ka*. *Ii desu ka* is frequently deployed by L1 Japanese-speaking teachers in order to check student understanding, close an activity, or transition from student-centered to teacher-fronted (or from teacher-fronted to student-centered) activities. A notable change in Tao's instructional practices is his use of *ii desu ka* during the time of transition from teacher-fronted to student-centered activities (observed on 4/3 and 4/23), and from student-centered to teacher-fronted activities (observed on 3/14, 4/3, and 4/23). There was no use of the expression for these functions during the first half of the semester.

In Excerpt 6 above, we observed that Tao used *daijoobu desu ka* when transitioning from student-centered to teacher-fronted activities. His attempt to draw student attention was not initially successful as evidenced by the students' continuous talk when he first produced the expression. Excerpt 7 below shows an instance in which Tao uses *ii desu ka* at the time of transitioning from student-centered to teacher-fronted activities. The students have been practicing conversations in pairs, asking about the names of food items shown on the screen, and at this point their voices are fairly loud.

**Excerpt 7.** (4/3) Food

```
1   Ss:  ((practicing conversation in loud voices))

2    T:  |((standing in base position, looking at Ss))
3→       |hai (.) ii   desu ka?*
          okay    good CP   Q
         Okay. All right?
```

*Figure 16

```
4        (0.5)/((Ss stop talking))

5    T: |((shifts gaze to screen; extends LH
6           to a picture on screen))
7→      |ii   desu ka?**
         good CP   Q
         All right?
```

**Figure 17

```
8        hai  jaa (.) ee   kore=**
         okay well       uhm this

9        ((withdraws hand, shifts gaze to Ss))
10       =nihongo  de  nan  te  yuu  n desu ka.***
          Japanese in  what QT  say  N CP   Q
          Okay, well, um how do you say this in Japanese?
```

***Figure 18

```
11   S:  okonomiyaki desu.
         Okonomiyaki CP
         It's okonomiyaki.

12   T:  ((smiles, extends RH towards S who responded))
13       u:n.  okonomiyaki desu ne.
         R     okonomiyaki CP   IP
         Yeah, it's okonomiyaki.
```

While the students are still practicing their conversations in pairs (line 1), Tao looks toward them and produces *hai ii desu ka?* 'Okay. All right?,' attempting to get them ready for the upcoming activity that he has planned (line 3, Figure 16). His voice is clearly heard by the students, because during the 0.5 second gap of silence that follows, the students stop talking, displaying their orientation towards a possible transition to the next activity. As Tao shifts his gaze towards the screen and extends his left hand to the picture, he says *ii desu ka* one more time (line 7, Figure 17), drawing the students' attention to the activity that he is about to begin. This is followed by *hai* 'okay' and *jaa* 'well' (line 8), which further project topic transition. These verbal and nonverbal actions provide the students with sufficient time to get ready for Tao's next action. When Tao asks about the Japanese name of the picture to which he was just pointing (line 10, Figure 18), one of the students provides the answer (*okonomiyaki*) right away (line 11), and Tao receipts and confirms this response (line 13).

This excerpt demonstrates how Tao successfully had the students transition from the paired activity to the teacher-fronted activity. Comparing this to his approach in Excerpt 6 where he was not so successful, there are a couple of significant points to note. First, in Excerpt 7 Tao produced *hai, ii desu ka* in a louder voice so that all students could hear it well. He waited for half a second to make sure that the students had stopped the paired activity. He then produced *ii desu ka* one more time along with *hai* and *jaa* to further project the onset of a different action, which gave the students verbal warning to attend to the remainder of his turn-in-progress. Tao's embodied actions of pointing to the object projected on the screen and directing his gaze at the students when he asked the question also contributed to his successful elicitation of the answer. Second, in Excerpt 6, there were still some students practicing in pairs even after Tao received an answer from one student. In Excerpt 7, no pair voices were heard, suggesting that all the students were attending to Tao's question as well as the subsequent answer provided by a student.

Excerpt 8 below shows an instance in which Tao used *ii desu ka* to close an activity. Prior to the excerpt, Tao had explained the sentence structure, A *janakute* B *desu* 'It's not A, but B.' Students were expected to use this structure when answering his question about their hometown. Tao had already asked one student about his hometown. In Excerpt 8, he asks another student about her hometown. A map is projected on the screen.

*Use of Formulaic Expressions by One Novice L2 Japanese Teacher* 357

**Excerpt 8.** (4/23) Hometown

```
1 T:      |((raises RH towards S))
2      hai |eeto S san* (.) S san no goshusshin    wa
       okay uhm  S AT       S AT  LN hometown-HON TP
```

*Figure 19

```
3 T:      |((touches LH upper middle part of map))
4      etto | um hareiwa desu ka.**
       uhm    um Haleiwa  CP   Q
       Okay uhm, Ms. S, are you from um, um, Haleiwa?
```

**Figure 20

```
5      (1.5)

6 S:  harei- ie ha[rei]wa janakute
      Halei- no Haleiwa   CP-NG-and
      No, I'm not from Haleiwa, but...

7 T:                  [hai].
                      uh huh
                      Uh huh
8 T:  hai
      uh huh
      Uh huh

9      (1.2)

10 S: °hono-°
```

```
11     (5.2)/((T looking towards S))

12  S: honoruru (.) desu.
       Honolulu      CP
       I'm from Honolulu.

13  T:      |((smiles; raises RH quickly towards S))
14     hai |ii   desu ne. honoruru desu.***
       okay good CP   IP  Honolulu CP
       Okay, good. You're from Honolulu.
```

***Figure 21

```
15     |((shifts posture towards Ss; still smiling))
16→    | hai.  ii   desu ka, minasan.
         okay good  CP   Q  everyone
         Okay. All right, everyone.

17     (1.0)****
```

****Figure 22

Tao nominates a student as he raises his right hand towards her (lines 1–2, Figure 19). His left hand then touches the upper middle part of the map as he asks if the student is from Haleiwa (lines 3–4, Figure 20). These embodied actions make it clear who or what he is referring to. Following a 1.5 second gap of silence, the nominated student formulates an answer (lines 6–12). Once the answer is completed, Tao acknowledges it and offers an assessment as he smiles and quickly raises his right hand towards the student who provided the answer (lines 13–14, Figure 21). As he shifts his torso towards the entire class, he says *hai* 'okay,' which projects the next activity. With the utterance of *ii desu ka, minasan* 'All right, everyone' that follows, Tao broadens the participation framework to include the overhearing students in the class, checks the entire group's understanding of the activity so far, and then closes the sequence. In a similar context in earlier class sessions, Tao produced *daijoobu desu ka*. Here, however, he deploys *ii desu ka* instead. The combined use of the assessment token *ii desu ne* 'good' and the understanding check *ii desu ka* is frequently observed among L1 Japanese speaking teachers and seems to suggest that Tao's classroom instructional practices have become more like those of other Japanese teachers. Another thing that should be noted here is his embodied actions, such as raising his right hand as he nominated a student and shifting his posture towards the entire class when he was addressing them all. These embodied actions, when combined with talk, provide important clues to the students so that they can make sense of what the teacher is doing at a particular moment during class activities. Further, Tao's smile, which was hardly ever observed during earlier lessons, seems to suggest that his affective stance towards his students has changed.[8]

## Discussion

Focusing on the Japanese formulaic expression *daijoobu desu ka* 'Are you all right?', this study examined one novice Japanese teacher's interactional practices in a JFL classroom and how they changed over the course of a semester. While the teacher, Tao, an advanced L2 speaker of Japanese, used *daijoobu desu ka* throughout the semester, fewer instances of this usage were observed as the semester progressed. Instead, an alternative expression, *ii desu ka* 'Are you all right?', was deployed more frequently during the second half of the semester. In this section, I will discuss the focal questions posed earlier based on the analysis I have conducted.

The first question is concerned with the sequential environments where Tao used *daijoobu desu ka* and the actions he achieved by using this expression. Tao deployed *daijoobu desu ka* most frequently during teacher-fronted instruction at the boundaries of activities, such as after an IRF sequence or after an extended teacher explanation. By doing so, Tao achieved the dual function of initiating both an understanding check and an activity closing (Excerpts 1 and 3). This is consistent with Waring (2012), who noted that understanding checks are not always produced and treated as inviting questions. This finding suggests that depending on its sequential location, its prosody, and the design of the turn in which it is housed, a question that is generally considered to check student understanding can accomplish a range of actions (see Koshik, 2010; Lee, 2006, 2008). Further, the fact that there was no instance in which the students responded to the *daijoobu desu ka* question with a negative answer is also consistent with Waring (2012). That is, a positive response is a preferred second pair part to understanding check questions. Affirming understanding aligns with the teacher's project and thus advances the activity; claiming understanding problems would delay the progress of the activity because those problems would have to be dealt with. Hence, there is a preference for a positive response for both the teacher and the students.

The analysis showed that when Tao produced *daijoobu desu ka* while directing his gaze towards his students, he was checking student understanding. As shown in Excerpt 4, there were instances in which Tao produced *daijoobu desu ka* multiple times before the activity came to a close, first checking student understanding and then closing the activity. On such occasions, he usually waited for a second or two after he said *daijoobu desu ka*. Then, in order to ensure student understanding, he repeated the key word or expression he had already presented. Tao's repetition of words or sentences within the sequence was frequently observed, and this accommodation was recipient-designed (Sacks, Schegloff, & Jefferson, 1974): Tao produced repetitions specifically for his students, taking into account their knowledge of Japanese. As recipients of his talk, the students can "presume that the action addressed to them is designed to be interpretable specifically for them" (Kasper & Burch, 2016, p. 202).

Tao also closed an activity using *daijoobu desu ka* while not showing an orientation to checking student understanding. Evidence for this distinction is his lack of gaze direction towards his students (Excerpt 2), and of embodied action associated with checking understanding. This is significant when considering gaze and the mutual monitoring of gaze as basic elements for participating in social interaction (e.g., Goodwin, 1980). Instead of looking at his students, Tao directed his gaze towards objects, such as the handout he was holding, the screen, or the keyboard or computer monitor stored beneath the desk. When Tao produced *daijoobu desu ka* in conjunction with this embodied action (i.e., not directing his gaze towards his students), it served as a boundary resource to foreshadow his next activity. Goodwin (2000) argues that human action is built through the simultaneous deployment of different kinds of semiotic resources. In his classroom practices, Tao's gaze and other embodied actions became an important indicator of what actions he was projecting and achieving.

Tao also used *daijoobu desu ka* during the transition from teacher-fronted to student-centered activities. To do so, he often produced the expression while he was walking towards the students, as shown in Excerpt 5 when he transitioned from a demonstration of *kanji* writing to having the students write the *kanji* themselves. Tao's use of *daijoobu desu ka* was also observed during the transition from student-centered to teacher-fronted activities: He produced *daijoobu desu ka* to draw the students' attention and prepare them for the next planned activity. In Excerpt 6, we observed that Tao produced *daijoobu desu ka* when transitioning from a pair-based conversation activity to a teacher-fronted activity. In that excerpt, some students continued talking in pairs even after the teacher shifted to the whole class activity. Although he produced *daijoobu desu ka* while directing his gaze towards the students, he did not allocate time to monitor the students' next turn for their readiness for his next action. Instead, he immediately asked a question following his production of *daijoobu desu* ka, meaning that some students were still engaged in their pair work. This indicates the importance of the teacher's orientation to a second pair part after producing a first pair part. In one-on-one interaction such as in a tutoring session (e.g., Young & Miller, 2004), the tutor needs to focus only on the tutee's next turn. In a classroom setting where the teacher has to deal with multiple students, being able to align with the class as a whole to move onto the next activity becomes an important part of the teacher's IC.

The second and third focal questions are concerned with changes in Tao's use of *daijoobu desu ka* over the course of the semester, and his use of alternative questions. There was a high occurrence of *daijoobu desu ka* during the early part of the semester. Its frequency decreased as the semester progressed, although Tao still continued to produce the expression. Table 1 gives a rough summary of how many times Tao used *daijoobu desu ka* and *ii desu ka*. A higher occurrence of *daijoobu desu ka* was observed during the first two sessions (35 instances on January 23, and 40 instances on February 8). As the semester progressed, its frequency decreased; the lowest occurrence was observed on April 23, with 20 instances. Throughout the semester, activity closing was most frequently achieved through the expression *daijoobu desu ka* (approximately 20 instances each on 1/23 and 2/8, with fewer instances on the rest of the days). Although not as frequent as activity closing, Tao also used *daijoobu desu ka* to transition from teacher-fronted to student-centered activities, as well as from student-centered to teacher-fronted activities.

**Table 1. Tao's use of *daijoobu desu ka* and *ii desu ka* '(Are you) all right?'**

| | Dates | | | | | |
|---|---|---|---|---|---|---|
| | 1/23 | 2/8 | 2/22 | 3/14 | 4/3 | 4/23 |
| daijoobu desu ka | 35 | 40 | 27 | 23 | 26 | 20 |
| ii desu ka | 4 | 0 | 0 | 2 | 10 | 5 |

The more frequent use of the alternative expression *ii desu ka* '(Are you) all right?' was observed during the second half of the semester with the highest occurrence on April 3 (10 instances). In particular, production of this expression for transitioning from teacher-fronted to student-centered activities as well as from student-centered to teacher-fronted activities was observed only during the second half of the semester. As we observed in Excerpt 7, Tao was successful in getting students to transition from paired conversation practice to teacher-fronted activity when he produced *ii desu ka* along with *hai* in a louder voice and also when he monitored the students' response before he began his next action. This shows that Tao became more skillful at employing context-sensitive conduct; he developed the ability to project upcoming actions and foreshadow trajectories of action by means of prefatory work (Pekarek Doehler & Pochon-Berger, 2015). With regard to the other alternative expression, *wakarimasu ka* 'Do you understand?', only two instances were observed. Tao employed the expression to check student familiarity with a topic he mentioned rather than checking understanding.[9]

In their discussion of one ITA's development of IC as a teacher, Rine and Hall (2011) note the ITA's increasing use of teacher-specific actions and spatial and nonverbal orientation to the role of teacher, as exemplified by the changes in body positioning and gaze in addition to verbal cues. Instances such as Tao's increasing ability to project upcoming action, as well as his combined use of the assessment phrase *ii desu ne* 'good' addressed to individual students and the subsequent understanding check *ii desu ka* addressed to the entire class (Excerpt 8), indicate the development of Tao's professional IC as a teacher. Changes in his affective stance towards his students (e.g., smiling) may also be considered as part of his growing classroom interactional competence.

One final point that should be noted is that although Tao was already a highly proficient L2 speaker of Japanese when he started teaching the class and was familiar with different types of understanding check expressions, he used *daijoobu desu ka* almost exclusively during the first half of the semester. He started to use the alternative expression *ii desu ka* as the semester progressed. This indicates that Tao expanded the interactional purposes he could accomplish with the expression *ii desu ka* (Pekarek Doehler & Pochon-Berger, 2015) and that its use became more stabilized. Along with his use of *ii desu ka,* Tao developed his competence to closely monitor the student turn, which, as we saw in Excerpt 7, led to a smoother transition from student-centered to teacher-fronted activity. This evidence suggests that Tao developed his CIC through his use of understanding check questions that were more locally adapted as well as with his nonverbal conduct, such as a close monitoring of a student's turn. Whether he developed such competence through his classroom interaction with his students alone or in conjunction with the development of his own L2 IC in Japanese is not clear. Regardless, the analysis suggests that Tao became more adept at contingent and ad hoc decision making while monitoring and acting on what became available within the sequence of interaction in his classroom practices (Walsh, 2013; Young, 2011).

## Concluding remarks

This study examined the development of one novice JFL teacher's interactional practices in a beginning Japanese class by focusing on the formulaic expression *daijoobu desu ka* '(Are you) all right?'. The teacher, Tao, who was an advanced L2 speaker of Japanese, used the expression throughout the semester to perform actions such as checking understanding, closing activities, and transitioning from student-centered to teacher-fronted activities or from teacher-fronted to student-centered activities. As the semester progressed, however, fewer instances of its use were observed and he started to utilize the alternative expression *ii desu ka* for the same functions. This transition was particularly apparent during the second half of the semester. In addition to the changes in his word choice, Tao became adept at closely monitoring the student-focused second pair part to make contingent decisions for his third turn. The analysis also showed that Tao's gaze and other embodied actions became important indicators of what actions he was projecting and achieving.

With its microanalytic orientation, CA allowed us to scrutinize the focal teacher's instructional practices, including his verbal and nonverbal conduct, deployment of semiotic resources, turn allocation, and sequence organization. Details obtained from the analysis also helped us understand how his actions resulted from the unique coordination of available resources. Additionally, we were able to observe changes in Tao's instructional practices through the examination of his class sessions over the course of a semester.

Hauser (2013) argues that instead of drawing on exogenous theory, learner development can be examined through the increased use of resources that are available to the learner. In the current study, Tao's increased use of the expression *ii desu ka* 'Are you all right?' for actions that he initially performed almost exclusively with *daijoobu desu ka*, suggests that he became adept at utilizing resources more skillfully in his interaction with his students, and this demonstrates a clear development of his IC in the classroom. His expanding interactional repertoire included monitoring students' next turns and using an increasing variety of semiotic resources.

Limitations of the current study include the lack of student video data. Future studies should include such data so that students' embodied conduct can also be closely examined. In terms of teacher training, novice teachers can be reminded of various expressions that are available for checking student understanding and closing activities. Experienced JFL teachers also use *wakarimashita ka* 'Did you understand?' to check student understanding, a phrase which was absent in Tao's instructional practices.[10] It can also be helpful for novice teachers to video record their own teaching, transcribe selected segments, and examine how interactions with students unfold. Conscious attention to their interaction through transcription and guided reflection on their performance (Yagi, 2007; Young,

2011) can contribute to developing their competence to carefully monitor student turns and act upon what becomes available within the sequence of interaction.

**Notes**

1　The non-availability of video data for students is a limitation in the current study.
2　Japanese dictionaries consulted include *Daijirin* published by Sanseido. An online version is available via Weblio at the following link: http://www.weblio.jp/content/%E5%A4%A7%E4%B8%88%E5%A4%AB.
3　This observation is based on classroom interaction data involving L1 Japanese-speaking teachers that the researcher has collected for another research project.
4　I use "All right" as a more idiomatic translation of *daijoobu desu ka* in the excerpts.
5　While it is possible that some students showed their understanding through the use of nonverbal resources such as nodding during the 1.5 second gap of silence in line 16, non-availability of the student video data limits analysis of exactly what they were doing during the silence.
6　*Katakana* is a Japanese syllabary commonly used to write loanwords and foreign names.
7　Tao might also be orienting to time at this junction: Checking if students are ready can also function to hurry them along so that he can have enough time to fit the next activity into the class.
8　Tao's smile was observed in Excerpts 3 and 7 as well; both excerpts came from the April 3rd class session.
9　When Tao used *wakarimasu ka*, he was checking whether or not students were familiar with a certain item rather than checking their understanding. For instance, when he showed a picture of *kendo* (a Japanese martial art), he asked the class, *kore wakarimasu ka?* 'do you know this?.'
10　This is based on the researcher's analysis of the data collected from L1 Japanese speaking teachers. These teachers also use specific expressions such as *chotto yamete kudasai* 'stop (it) for now' when they want to transition from student-centered to teacher-fronted activities.

# References

Brock, C. A. (1986). The effect of referential questions on ESL classroom discourse. *TESOL Quarterly, 20*(1), 47–59.
Brouwer, C. E., & Wagner, J. (2004). Developmental issues in second language conversation. *Journal of Applied Linguistics, 1*(1), 29–47.
Brown, D. H. (2007). *Teaching by principles: An interactive approach to language pedagogy* (3rd ed.). New York, NY: Pearson Longman.
Cekaite, A. (2007). A child's development of interactional competence in a Swedish L2 classroom. *The Modern Language Journal, 91*(1), 45–62.

Goodwin, C. (1980). Restarts, pauses, and the achievement of mutual gaze at turn-beginning. *Sociological Inquiry, 50* (3/4), 272–302.

Goodwin, C. (2000). Action and embodiment within situated human interaction. *Journal of Pragmatics, 32,* 1489–1522.

Goodwin, C. (2007). Participation, stance, and affect in the organization of activities. *Discourse and Society, 18*(1), 53–73.

Hauser, E. (2013). Expanding resources for marking direct reported speech. In T. Greer, D. Tatsuki & C. Roever (Eds.), *Pragmatics and language learning* (Vol. 13, pp. 29–53). Honolulu, HI: University of Hawai'i, National Foreign Language Resource Center.

Hellermann, J. (2008). *Social actions for classroom language learning.* Clevedon, UK: Multilingual Matters.

Hellermann, J. (2011). Members' method, members' competences: Looking for evidence of language learning in longitudinal investigations of other-initiated repair. In J. K. Hall, J. Hellermann & S. Pekarek Doehler (Eds.), *L2 interactional competence and development* (pp.147–172). Bristol, UK: Multilingual Matters.

Hosoda, Y., & Aline, D. (2010). Learning to be a teacher: Development of EFL teacher trainee interactional practices. *JALT Journal, 32*(2), 119–147.

Hosoda, Y. (2014). Missing response after teacher question in primary school English as a foreign language classes. *Linguistics and Education, 28,* 1–16.

Hosoda, Y., & Aline, D. (2013). Two preferences in question-answer sequences in language classroom context. *Classroom Discourse, 4*(1), 63–88.

Ikeda, K., & Ko, S. (2011). Choral practice patterns in the language classrooms. In G. Pallotti & J. Wagner (Eds.), *L2 learning as social action: Conversation analytic perspectives* (pp. 163–184). Honolulu, HI: University of Hawai'i, National Foreign Language Resource Center.

Ishida, M. (2009). Development of interactional competence: Changes in the use of *ne* in L2 Japanese during study abroad. In H. T. Nguyen & G. Kasper (Eds.), *Talk-in-interaction: Multilingual perspectives* (pp. 351–385). Honolulu, HI: University of Hawai'i, National Foreign Language Resource Center.

Ishida, M. (2011). Engaging in another person's telling as a recipient in L2 Japanese: Development of interactional competence during one-year study abroad. In G. Pallotti & J. Wagner (Eds.), *L2 learning as social action: Conversation analytic perspectives* (pp. 45–85). Honolulu, HI: University of Hawai'i, National Foreign Language Resource Center.

Kasper, G., & Burch, A. R. (2016). Focus on form in the wild. In R. A. van Compernolle & J. McGregor (Eds.), *Authenticity, language, and interaction in second language contexts* (pp. 198–232). Bristol, UK: Multilingual Matters.

Kasper, G., & Ross, S. J. (2013). Assessing second language pragmatics: An overview and introductions. In G. Kasper & S. J. Ross (Eds.), *Assessing second language pragmatics* (pp. 1–40). Basingstoke, UK: Palgrave Macmillan.

Kasper, G., & Wagner, J. (2014). Conversation analysis in applied linguistics. *Annual Review of Applied Linguistics, 34,* 171–212.

Koshik, I. (2010). Questions that convey information in teacher-student conferences. In A. F. Freed & S. Ehrlich (Eds.), *"Why do you ask?" The function of questions in institutional discourse* (pp. 159–186). Oxford, UK: Oxford University Press.

Lee, Y. A. (2006). Respecifying display questions: Interactional resources for language teaching. *TESOL Quarterly, 40*(4), 691–713.

Lee, Y. A. (2007). Third turn position in teacher talk: Contingency and the work of teaching. *Journal of Pragmatics, 39,* 1204–1230.

Lee, Y. A. (2008). Yes-no questions in the third-turn position: Pedagogical discourse processes. *Discourse Processes, 45*(3), 237–262.

Leyland, C., Greer, T., & Rettig-Miki, E. (2016). Dropping the devil's advocate: One novice language tester's shifting interactional practices across a series of speaking tests. *Classroom Discourse, 7*(1), 85–107.

Long, M. H., & Sato, C. J. (1983). Classroom foreigner talk discourse: Forms and functions of teachers' questions. In H. W. Seliger & M. H. Long (Eds.), *Classroom oriented research in second language acquisition* (pp. 268–285). Cambridge, MA: Newbury House.

Markee, N. (1995). Teachers' answers to students' questions: Problematizing the issue of making meaning. *Issues in Applied Linguistics, 6*(2), 63–92.

Markee, N. (2008). Toward a learning tracking methodology for CA-for-SLA. *Applied Linguistics, 29*(3), 404–427.

Markee, N. (2011). Doing, and justifying doing, avoidance. *Journal of Pragmatics, 43,* 602–615.

Mori, J., & Hasegawa, A. (2009). Doing being a foreign language learner in a classroom: Embodiment of cognitive states as social events. *IRAL, 47,* 65–94.

Nguyen, H. T. (2012). *Developing interactional competence. A conversation-analytic study of patient consultations in pharmacy.* Basingstoke, UK: Palgrave Macmillan.

Pekarek Doehler, S., & Pochon-Berger, E. (2015). The development of L2 interactional competence: Evidence from turn-taking organization, sequence organization, repair organization, and preference organization. In T. Cadierno & S. Eskildsen (Eds.), *Usage-based perspectives on second language learning* (pp. 233–268). Berlin: Mouton De Gruyter.

Pica, T., & Long, M. (1986). The linguistic and conversational performance of experienced and inexperienced teachers. In R. R. Day (Ed.), *Talking to learn* (pp. 85–98). Rowley, MA: Newbury House.

Psathas, G. (1995). *Conversation analysis: The study of talk-in-interaction.* Thousand Oaks, CA: Sage.

Richards, J. C., & Lockhart, C. (1996). *Reflective teaching in second language classrooms.* Cambridge: Cambridge University Press.

Rine, E. F., & Hall, J. K. (2011). Becoming the teacher: Changing participant frameworks in international teaching assistant discourse. In J. K. Hall, J. Hellermann & S. Pekarek Doehler (Eds.), *L2 interactional competence and development* (pp.244 274). Bristol: Multilingual Matters.

Sacks, H., Schegloff, E.A., & Jefferson, G. (1974). A simplest systematics for the organization of turn-taking for conversation. *Language, 50*(4), 696–735.

Schegloff, E. A. (1992). Repair after next turn: The last structurally provided defense of intersubjectivity in conversation. *American Journal of Sociology, 97*(5), 1295–1345.

Schegloff, E. A. (1996). Issues of relevance for discourse analysis: Contingency in action, interaction, and co-participant context. In E. Hovy & D. Scott (Eds.), *Computational and conversational discourse: Burning issues—an interdisciplinary account* (pp. 3–38). Heidelberg, Germany: Springer.

Seedhouse, P. (2004) *The interactional architecture of the language classroom: A conversation analysis perspective*, Malden, MA: Blackwell.

Sert, O. (2013). 'Epistemic status check' as an interactional phenomenon in instructed learning settings. *Journal of Pragmatics, 45,* 13–28.

Tominaga, W. (2013). The development of extended turns and storytelling in the Japanese oral proficiency interview. In G. Kasper & S. J. Ross (Eds.), *Assessing second language pragmatics* (pp. 220–257). Basingstoke, UK: Palgrave Macmillan.

van Lier, L. (1988). *The classroom and the language learner.* London: Longman.

van Lier, L. (1996). *Interaction in the language curriculum: Awareness, autonomy and authenticity.* New York, NY: Longman.

Walsh, S. (2011). *Exploring classroom discourse: Language in action.* New York, NY: Routledge.

Walsh, S. (2013). *Classroom discourse and teacher development.* Edinburgh: Edinburgh University Press.

Waring, H. Z. (2008). Using explicit positive assessment in the language classroom: IRF, feedback, and learning opportunities. *The Modern Language Journal, 92*(4), 577–594.

Waring, H. Z. (2012). "Any questions?": Investigating the nature of understanding-checks in the language classroom. *TESOL Quarterly, 46*(4), 722–752.

Yagi, K. (2007). The development of interactional competence in a situated practice by Japanese learners of English as a second language. *Hawaii Pacific University TESL Working Paper Series, 5*(1). Retrieved February 18, 2016 from http://www.hpu.edu/CHSS/English/TESOL/ProfessionalDevelopment/200720TWPspring07/yagi_5-1.pdf

Young, R. F. (2011). Interactional competence in language learning, teaching, and testing. In E. Hinkel (Ed.), *Handbook of research in language learning and teaching* (pp. 426–443). New York, NY: Routledge.

Young, R. F., & Miller, E. R. (2004). Learning as changing participation: Discourse roles in ESL writing conferences. *The Modern Language Journal, 88*(4), 519–535.

# 12

# L1 Speaker Turn Design and Emergent Familiarity in Opening Sequences of Second Language Japanese Interaction

Tim Greer
*Kobe University*

## Introduction

Whenever we meet someone for the first time we adjust the way we talk based on our emergent understandings of our interlocutor, and therefore in subsequent meetings we may greet them in a different way based on what we have learned about them. The way we formulate each turn makes public our growing familiarity with the person with whom we are talking. This may be displayed through such features of the talk as the politeness expressions we choose, the content of what we say, or even the speed at which we talk.

It is not uncommon for first language (L1) speakers in an initial encounter with a second language (L2) speaker to alter the way they might otherwise formulate a turn in order to facilitate communication. In first encounters, expert speakers may hyper-compensate for perceived language difficulties through what has been called *foreigner talk* (Ferguson, 1971, 1975), a way of speaking that may include simplifications, modifications, and deletions at the syntactic, lexical, and morphological levels. This phenomenon has also been studied within applied linguistics through research into accommodation (e.g., Zuengler, 1991), and is related to similar speech adjustments that foreign language teachers use in the classroom, or what has been called *teacher talk* (Early, 1987).

Conversation Analysis (CA) can offer additional insight via its emic micro-interactional concern for the details of turn design, particularly with respect to turn constructional changes across sequential episodes involving a central participant initiating the same action to different recipients. Some examples from the literature include when one person phones multiple participants in succession and formulates a request in slightly different ways according to the person she is talking to (Drew, 2013), when one person answers the door to different people within a matter of minutes, greeting one as a friend and another as a stranger (Pillet-Shore, 2012), or when a caller makes a second or third call to a helpline and adapts her formulation of the opening sequence to present herself accordingly (Shaw & Kitzinger, 2007). CA frames its understanding of turn design in terms of formulation (Deppermann, 2011; Schegloff, 1972), recipient design (Schegloff, 1986), and turn construction (Sacks, Schegloff, & Jefferson, 1974). Central to each of these are the interactional practices of description when choosing a particular set of words for a particular recipient and a particular instance of talk. Depperman (2011) notes that formulations are selective, contingent, relevant, and inference-rich, and the way a speaker chooses to formulate a turn reveals their understanding of the situation. Recipient design, the way a turn is formulated based on the speaker's knowledge of the recipient, makes public various aspects of the interactants' relationship.

Turn design, therefore, is often sensitive to temporality, in that a turn is formulated in relation to earlier episodes of talk. Longitudinal CA research by Nguyen (2011, 2012) documents changes in recipient design over time by examining how novice pharmacists begin to adjust the way they formulate advice for different customers. From an L2 learning perspective, Brouwer and Wagner (2004) track a novice L2 speaker as he learns and applies language items across a series of business telephone calls that took place over a matter of hours or days rather than years. Although the CA approach did not originally aim to account for such interactional changes over time, a small but growing number of researchers are adopting this sort of longitudinal approach to the micro-details of talk, particularly in language learning settings (e.g., Hall, Hellermann, & Pekarek Doehler, 2011; Lee & Hellermann, 2014; Leyland, Greer, & Rettig-Miki, 2016).

This chapter will adopt such a longitudinal CA perspective to explore recipient design and turn construction among L1 and L2 speakers of Japanese during a series of four successive haircuts. The four clients were a Japanese female, an American male, a Chinese male, and a Bolivian male, and the initial haircut (T1) was the first time the clients had met the hairdresser and his assistant (both L1 speakers of Japanese). One segment of each opening sequence that is highly accommodation-laden is the initial greet-and-seat sequence. By focusing on such openings the analysis will investigate how the two hairdressers formulate their turns during these initial moments of contact with new clients and how they adjust their turns based on the clients' responses in that time and place (Mortensen & Hazel, 2014).

In addition, the study will compare these first-time openings to the hairdressers' formulations in similar opening sequences in the second and subsequent haircuts in order to investigate how their greetings change as they begin to discover more about their interlocutors. Elsewhere, analysis in this project has revealed that over time the hairdresser and a client who speaks very little Japanese work together to adopt a dual-receptive pattern of language alternation in which each participant speaks his preferred language (Greer, 2013). The current study extends this research by observing how the focal participants (the L1 Japanese-speaking hairdressers) interact with other L1 and L2 Japanese speakers, particularly with respect to the way their talk reflects and reifies their growing familiarity as they move from complete strangers to an established hairdresser-client relationship. As such, the focus here is primarily on the L1 speakers and how they adapt their turn design as they accommodate to the linguistic proficiencies of their clients and become increasingly familiar with one another.

The investigation is therefore situated in L2 talk, by which I mean interaction that involves one or more second language users. In other words, even though the focus is largely on the L1 users, the aim in doing so is to examine how they adapt their language to novice speakers across time. The data also allow for a convenient base analysis in that one of the sets of recordings involves the hairdressers speaking with a Japanese client, and a comparison of this talk to that with the novice Japanese speakers will underpin the argument for adaptive formulations across interlocutors. In short, the current study is concerned with L2 talk, defined as interaction that involves an L2 speaker, rather than focusing on the L2 speakers alone.

## Background to the data

The data were recorded over a period of four months, approximately once a month beginning in May, 2011. The data collection site was a small neighborhood hairdressing salon in western Japan, and the staff consisted of Yoh[1] (the owner and head stylist) and Yumi, his assistant. Both were L1 speakers of Japanese in their late twenties. The four clients were all students at a large national university; a summary of their backgrounds is provided in Table 1. They were recruited for the project by the researcher, but were not given any particular instructions, except that they were to behave as they would normally do when getting their hair cut. None of the clients had previously been to this salon and prior to the clients' arrival the hairdressers were not aware of which (or even how many) of the clients were Japanese.

**Table 1. Participant backgrounds**

| Pseudonym | Nationality | Gender | Age | Languages (Self-reported proficiency) | Number of haircuts recorded |
|---|---|---|---|---|---|
| Aki | Japanese | F | 20 | Japanese (Native), English (Intermediate) | 4 |
| Tye | American | M | 22 | English (Native), Japanese (Intermediate) | 4 |
| Jay | Chinese | M | 23 | Chinese (Native), Japanese (Beginner) | 3 |
| Emil | Bolivian | M | 27 | Spanish (Native), English (Advanced), Japanese (Beginner) | 4 |

The researcher set up two or three cameras and an audio device around the salon on each occasion, but was not present during the recording. This process facilitated an efficient data collection process, enabling the researcher to record four haircuts in one day, two in the morning and two in the afternoon. One drawback, however, was that the researcher set up the appointment times directly with the hairdresser, and this may have impacted the naturalness of the data; in retrospect, it would have been better to have had the clients call and make an appointment themselves. This remains one of the study's limitations.

## Emergent familiarity in greeting sequences

Despite the vast array of institutional and mundane interaction that takes place in hairdressing salons, very few CA studies have explored the constraints and affordances of communication in this setting. Toerien and Kitzinger (2007) investigate emotional labor and multiple involvements in beauty salons, in which the beauty specialist must simultaneously engage in mundane talk with the client as well as carry out the haircut procedure and initiate interaction related to it. Oshima (2007) conducts a multimodal CA study of the service-assessment sequence in a variety of Japanese and American hairdressing salons, finding that the client displays her satisfaction with the service through both spoken and embodied assessments, making the haircut an "interactional product" (Oshima, 2007, p. 10). The current study aims to contribute to this discussion by investigating the opposite end of the hairdressing service encounter, the opening sequence.

Openings have been widely studied by CA researchers, most famously in telephone calls (e.g., Schegloff, 1979), but also in face-to-face greetings (e.g., Pillet-Shore, 2012). As a crucial part of opening sequences, greetings are one of the fundamental sites in which familiarity work gets accomplished. Greetings are a means by which people acknowledge each others' existence and establish their readiness for a more extended conversation (Goffman, 1971). According to Pillet-Shore (2012), "[g]reetings are microcosmic encapsulations of social relationships critical to parties' (re)creation and maintenance of social solidarity" (p. 396). The myriad of ways in which greetings get done can also be seen as an interactional means of recognizing the other person, and therefore (re)affirming and reifying their identities and their social relationships. Pillet-Shore (2012) showed that speakers use a variety of multi-modal resources including proximity, gesture, gaze, and prosody to display stance in greeting sequences, providing recipients with clues to their current mood and making public claims about the nature of their relationship.

One basic consideration for any greeting sequence, then, is whether or not it is a first time encounter or if the participants have some sort of "history" together (Schegloff, 1986); this becomes visible through the way the greeting is recipient designed for that person in that time and place as the interactants "display an orientation and sensitivity to the particular other(s) who are the coparticipants" (Sacks et al., 1974, p. 42).

Given the enormity of social relationship-building work that is achieved in these brief moments, greetings and opening sequences more generally are an important interactional locus for the current investigation, especially considering that in the initial recordings they represent the very first time the participants meet each other and later go on to re-establish the developing client-hairdresser relationship in subsequent meetings. At the same time, other aspects of the participants' relative identities such as gender or linguistic heritage can also be brought to the fore, and my analysis will consider these where the participants make them relevant to the talk. One opportune aspect of the current data set is that the head stylist (Yoh) and his assistant (Yumi) are present in each of the encounters, so in addition to changes over time, we are also able to compare and contrast ways their greetings are fitted to different recipients, particularly with respect to the clients' perceived and demonstrated Japanese proficiency. As such, the current study represents a response to Brouwer and Wagner's (2004) call for more research that examines data collected from talk between the same speakers across episodes. This section will begin by looking at how the hairdressers formulate their greetings in the opening sequences with Aki, another L1 speaker of Japanese, and then go on to compare these with the greeting sequences in their service encounters with Tye, Jay and Emil, who are all novice speakers of Japanese.

## Aki

I will begin by comparing several fragments of talk taken from the longer excerpts that will appear later in the chapter. These first few seconds involve the greetings as the Japanese client, Aki, enters the door and before she has even sat down. Comparing these moments across episodes will reveal the participants' growing familiarity with each other.

**Fragment 1.** taken from Excerpt 1 Aki T1 Greetings

```
01              ((bells on door ring; door opens))

02  Yumi        $i[r↑asshaimase:]$
                come-HON
                Welcome.

03  Yoh         $[irasshaimase ]$
                come-HON
                Welcome.

04  Yumi        $konnichiwa::$
                hello
                Hello.

05              (2.1)/((Aki enters))

06  Yumi        onimotsu $oazu[karishimasu$
                HON-bag       take-HON
                Let me take your bag for you.
```

Yumi and Yoh initiate the sequence the first time (T1, Fragment 1) with a vigorously delivered *irasshaimase*, a routine honorific greeting that is common in most Japanese service encounters and roughly translates as "welcome." Yumi then follows this immediately with *konnichiwa* 'hello,' a more standard greeting. *Konnichiwa* is routinely used as a first pair part (FPP, a sequence-initiating action), and therefore a second pair part (SPP) response becomes relevant from the recipient in next turn. *Irasshaimase*, on the other hand, does not normally receive any response action and arguably this contributes to maintaining the social distance between the server and the customer. By adding *konnichiwa* as a kind of follow-up greeting, Yumi is moving to ameliorate this distance by initiating a non-service opening sequence in which the recipient is sequentially obliged to participate.

However, no SPP is forthcoming from Aki in line 5, the slot at which a response would normally be done. This may indicate that Aki still views the interaction primarily as a service encounter, and is therefore working to preserve the server-client relationship.[2] This said, Aki is out of shot at this point, and it is possible that she used some sort of embodied action such as a head nod to respond to Yumi in a minimal fashion. Compare this opening with that in Fragment 2, taken from the start of Aki's third appointment. Having talked for over two hours across two separate occasions, Aki is now well acquainted with Yoh and Yumi, and in fact it is she who initiates the opening with *ohayo gozaimas* 'good morning', another standard (i.e., non-service encounter) greeting.

**Fragment 2.** taken from Excerpt 3 Aki T3 Greetings

```
07  Aki      $O↑Hayohgozai[ma:::s]$
                  good morning

08  Yoh                  [oHAYOh]gozai[ma s : : : ]
                                       good morning

09  Yumi                              $[oh↑ayogozai]ma::s$=
                                              good morning

10  Yoh      =irassha↓:i.
             come-HON
             Welcome!
```

The recipients reply quickly, overlapping their SPP greetings in a way that is hearably affiliative. Yoh follows this with *irasshai*, a truncated version of the institutional greeting that is more familiar than the full version he used in T1, but one that still denotes the sequence as service encounter talk. Even from these very brief initial moments, we can see that there have been some changes in the way the opening greetings are performed, and that the participants seem to be displaying a different level of familiarity, albeit one that still employs polite formulations. Pillet-Shore (2012) calls these "large" greetings, in that they sound "big, substantial, [and] effusive" (p. 383), and therefore treat the addressed recipient as familiar or the encounter as special. She identifies a cluster of prosodic features that are typical of large greetings, including lengthening, audible smiling, higher onset pitch, increased volume, and wider pitch span, many of which are observable in Aki's later greeting sequences. In addition, the participants work to produce their greetings simultaneously, by lengthening the vowels to enable affiliative overlap and by latching additional TCU's to deliver multiple greeting terms. By contrast, at the first appointment, Aki gave no audible response at all to the hairdressers' greetings, even though Yoh and Yumi's turn design contained many of these prosodic features, providing evidence to suggest that Aki was not treating them with familiarity at that point.

Similar tendencies can be observed in the opening sequences of the third appointment between the hairdressers and their non-Japanese clients (Fragments 3 and 4), with non-institutionally formulated greetings reciprocated in overlap and institutional greetings shortened to give a slightly less formal impression (Fragment 3, line 4).

**Fragment 3.** taken from Excerpt 9 Jay T3 Greetings

```
01  Yumi      ((walking toward door))
02            $↑KONnichi[wa$
                hello
              Hello.

03  Jay                  [kon ni chiwa[:]

04  Yoh                  [↑KONNIchiwa [i]ra[sshai
                           hello          come-HON
                         Hello, welcome.

05  Yumi                                     [heh heh
06            (0.8)/((sound of bell on door))
```

**Fragment 4.** taken from Excerpt 7 Emil T3 Greetings

```
01  Emil     $[Kon[nichiwa:]$
               hello
             Hello.

02  Yui      $[Kon[nichiwa:]$

03  Yoh           $[nchwa:  :]$

04  Emil     ↑hello

05           (.)

06  Yui      $hello$ heh ha ha

07  Emil     $Nice to see you.$

08           (.)

09  Yui      heh
```

In Emil's case (Fragment 4), the hairdressers have, by this point, acquired knowledge of his preference for English over Japanese, and so repeat the initial greetings in English. Reciprocation in greeting sequences is a feature of mundane talk (Schegloff, 2007, p. 199) and while it is not always required in service encounters, the fact that Emil and Jay come to do this in their later appointments demonstrates they are becoming more familiar and friendly with Yoh and Yumi.

I will now return to Aki's first appointment and explore what happened immediately after the initial greetings. As a basic rule, when a client enters the salon, Yoh and Yumi carry out the following sequence of procedural activities:
1. Greet the client;
2. Take the client's hat and/or bag; and,
3. Guide the client to the styling chair.

Of course, there is any number of other eventualities that could derail this routine, and frequently a comment from the customer will result in a brief opportunity for talk that can serve to reduce the distance between the participants. In Excerpt 1, for example, Yumi's attempt to deal with Aki's bag is briefly delayed while Aki removes her mobile phone (lines 10 and 11).

**Excerpt 1.** Aki T1 Greetings

```
01              ((bells on door ring; door opens))

02 Yumi         $i[r↑asshaimase:]$
                come-HON
                Welcome.

03 Yoh          $[irasshaimase ]$
                come-HON
                Welcome.

04 Yumi         $konnichiwa::$
                hello

05              (2.1)/((Aki enters))

06 Yumi         onimotsu $oazu[kari shimasu$
                HON-bag    take-HON
                Let me take your bag for you.

07 Aki                         [aa.) hai °onegai shimas°=
                                CS   yes  please-HON
                                Oh, yes, thanks.

08 Yumi         =ha:i
                yes

09              (0.4)

10 Aki          (chotto) keitai[(    )
                just     mobile
                I'll just get my mobile.
```

| | | |
|---|---|---|
| 11 | Yumi | [ah (.) hai dohzo<br>    CS     yes go-ahead<br>Oh, yes, please do. |
| 12 | | (4.1)/((Aki takes mobile out of bag)) |
| 13 | | (3.8)/((Yumi takes Aki's bag to back room)) |
| 14 | Yoh | irasshaimase<br>come-HON<br>Welcome. |
| 15 | | (.) |
| 16 | Yoh | hai<br>yes<br>Alright. |
| 17 | | (1.1) |
| 18 | Yoh | (gotsui) des ne (.) okaban=<br> big    CP  IP     HON-bag<br>Your bag is huge, huh? |
| 19 | Aki | =hah[ah |
| 20 | Yoh |     [haha |
| 21 | Aki | (jugyo tak'san at[te)<br> class many  have-and<br>I have a lot of classes. |
| 22 | Yoh |                  [a::h (se   ya ne)<br>                  CS     so    CP IP<br>                Oh, I see. |
| 23 | | (0.6) |
| 24 | Yoh | hai (.) dewa kochira  ni [(onegai itashimas)<br>okay   well here-POL to  please-HON<br>Okay, so over here if you would. |
| 25 | Yumi |                                [dohzo::<br>                                go ahead<br>                              This way please. |
| 26 | | (0.6)/((Aki sits)) |

The hairdressers often use the opening sequence to make a connection with the client, such as commenting on their appearance, clothing, or possessions. Yoh's noticing in line 18 is an apparent assessment related to the size and form of Aki's backpack. Aki treats this as an account initiation and responds first with laughter and then an explanation (line 21), to which Yoh provides immediate uptake in line 22. These seemingly minor remarks are by no means inconsequential. Despite the fact that they have known each other for less than ten seconds, Yoh has found a topic that is within both his and Aki's spheres of experience. Although it is not completely audible, it seems that Yoh's turn formulation at line 22 is delivered in plain form, perhaps indicating it is primarily directed at himself. Yet, it is also a receipt of Aki's turn and even though Aki can be normatively understood to have heard it, there is nothing in the subsequent talk to indicate she treats it as rude or over-familiar. Rather, Yoh's mention of the bag is bracketed off from the official work of the service greeting, and therefore constitutes Yoh's first bid for rapport with his new client. Immediately following this, when directing Aki to the chair Yoh returns to honorific Japanese turn constructions (such as *dewa* rather than *jaa*, *kochira* rather than *kocchi* or *koko*, and *itashimasu* rather than *shimasu*, in lines 24 to 26), an activity that is hearable as part of the routine that would be applicable to any customer.

Naturally, what follows this is the haircut itself, along with approximately one hour of talk in which Aki, Yoh, and Yumi get to know each other. It is impossible to document here each of the many moves that contributes to their growing familiarity over that hour, but instead what I will do is compare Excerpt 1 with the opening sequence of Aki's second appointment, approximately one month later (Excerpt 2). Here the initial greeting sequence pattern is largely missing due to a visibly available cue that Yumi and Yoh treat as so noticeable as to waylay the delivery of a formal greeting: Aki has cut her hair short, even though during the first appointment it was long and she had told Yoh she wanted to leave it that way.

**Excerpt 2.** Aki T2 Greetings

```
01 Yumi      (    )

02 Yoh       ↑eh? ah homma  y(h)a,  $zenzen     ch'au       yan.$
             huh  CS  really CP      totally     different   CP
             Huh? You're right. It looks totally different.

03           ((Aki enters))

04 Yoh       a[hah    hah]
```

```
05  Yumi    $[ohayo goz]aimas$
                good morning-POL

06  Aki     $sarani kitchaimash'ta$
             more    cut-(regret)-POL-PST
             I ended up cutting some more off.

07  Yumi    [(                    )]=

08  Yoh     [kitchaimash'ta       ne]
             cut-(regret)-POL-PST IP
             You sure did.

09  Aki?    =heh

10  Yumi    heh heh ha

11  Aki     hai
             yes

12          (.)

13  Aki     heh h[eh

14  Yoh          [kitchaimash'ta kedo
                  cut-POL-PST    but

15          nobash'tetta    n  janakatta des ka.
             grow-PROG-PST  N  CP-NG-PST CP  Q
             You cut it, but weren't you letting it grow?

16  Aki     >iya< nanka %moh     kirita::(i)%
             well  H    IP       cut-want
17          to omottara    kirimash'ta.
             QT think-CND  cut-PST
             Y'know, um, I just thought I want to cut it, so I did.

18  Yoh     aa, aa, aa
19          ((Yoh takes bag))

20  Yoh     kyoh   kiru toko  ga  nai    des ne
             today  cut  place S   is-NG  CP  IP
             There's nothing to cut today then, is there?

21  Aki     eh? demo kono hen  (.) ki ni iranakute
             huh but  this area      like-NG-and
             Huh? But I don't like this bit.
```

Delivered just prior to Aki's entrance, lines 1 and 2, the noticing of Aki's short hair, appear to be primarily designed as between Yumi and Yoh; although Yumi's utterance is inaudible, Yoh treats it as a telling, marking it as an unexpected departure with "eh?" (Hayashi, 2009) and producing a laughed-through agreement in plain form Kansai dialect. Aki is just outside the door and can be seen by them, and can also see (and probably overhear) this segment of talk. Yoh is laughing when Aki enters (line 4), and although Yumi delivers a polite greeting in line 5, this is not reciprocated by Aki, who instead makes explicit the laughable (line 6). As it turns out, the participants treat the newsworthiness of this event as taking precedence over the need for institutional opening sequences, and Yoh does not formally greet Aki on this occasion. Instead, the noticing and its account take priority (Bilmes, 2011), and the interactional work that goes on between Yoh and Aki to accomplish this noticing serves the function of displaying familiarity both through laughter and a claimed history of co-experiences. As such, their relative institutional identity categories as hairdresser and client are being made relevant to the talk at this point; however, they are doing so in a way that is friendly and affiliative, and this may help to avoid any possible loss of face that could arise from the fact that Aki has had her hair cut elsewhere, after Yoh had cut it previously.

The opening sequences of Aki's third appointment (Excerpt 3) are more subdued, but nonetheless provide interactional evidence for the growing bond between the hairdressers and their client. As outlined above, the initial moments are carried out with "large" greetings initiated by Aki rather than the hairdressers (lines 7–10), and this displays both a positive stance and a claim of solidarity. In addition, Aki carries out a noticing sequence from line 12 that acts as a further display of affiliation.

**Excerpt 3.** Aki T3 Greetings

```
01                ((Yoh looks to door))

02  Yoh           |((walking to door))
03                |ah   tsuita      ne
                   CS   arrive-PST  IP
                   Oh, she's here.

04                (0.4)

05  Yoh           |hehheh (0.4)
06                |((bells on door ring; Aki entering))

07  Aki           $O↑Hayohgozai[ma:::s]$
                   good morning-POL
                   Good morning.
```

```
08  Yoh                    [oHAYOh]gozai[ma s : : : ]
                           Good morning.

09  Yumi                                       $[oh↑ayogozai]ma:s$=
                                               Good morning.

10  Yoh     =irassha↓:i.
            come-HON
            Welcome.

11          (0.4)

12  Aki     wa! nanka metcha hiroi.
            CS  H         very  spacious
            Wow! Like, it looks bigger.

13          (.)

14  Aki     °des ne.°
            CP   IP
            Doesn't it?

15  Yoh     oh-

16  Yumi    hah-

17  Yoh     kizuita?
            notice-PLN-PST
            You noticed?

18  Yumi    hhah [heh heh HA Ha

19  Aki          [HAH HAh HAh hah

20  Yumi    komaka[(kai) koto ni  kizuite]
            fine         thing to notice-and
            You have a fine eye for details.

21  Yoh           [(                     )]

22  Aki     eh? itsumo demo (.) shittemash'ta
            IP  always  but      know-CONT-PST
            Huh, but I always knew.

23  Yumi    ma- eh [hah hah ]

24  Aki            [(       ]       )
```

```
25  Yoh        |((moves seat to Aki))
26             |((to Yumi))(°    °)

27             (0.8)

28  Yumi       |((taking Aki's bag))
29             |ah- ha::i (.) $oaz'karishima:s$
               CS   okay           take-HON
               Oh, okay, let me take your bag.

30             (1.4)/((Aki walks to chair))

31  Yoh        °dohzo°
               go ahead
               This way.
```

As she walks into the salon, Aki initiates the noticing sequence in line 12, first with a response cry (Goffman, 1981), *Wa!* 'Wow!,' and then an explication that specifies the target of her surprise, *metcha hiroi* 'heaps of room,' which appears to be an assessment of the recent rearrangement of the salon's entrance space. Since the entrance way is in fact not particularly spacious, such an assessment is hearable as comparative, in that Aki is implying that there appears to be more space than there used to be. Implicit to this assessment is the knowledge of the previous furniture arrangement, which is therefore evidence of Aki's ongoing history of visiting this salon, and her expression of this realization therefore indexes the growing familiarity between her and the hairdressers. Yoh and Yumi initially receipt Aki's noticing in quick succession with brief change-of-state tokens (lines 15 and 16), followed by Yoh's mock-clarification initiator delivered with a casual, plain form verb (line 17), which is met with laughter from both Yumi and Aki. In line 20, Yumi then compliments Aki on her observant eye, which again accomplishes closeness; arguably such a sequence would be unlikely to occur on the client's initial visit since Yumi's compliment claims some knowledge of Aki's personality and is predicated on her prior visit.

By tracking the initial opening sequences of a series of hair appointments, this subsection has therefore mapped out the progressive display of increasing familiarity between the hairdressers and one of their Japanese customers, moving from complete strangers to friendly acquaintances. One aspect of this interaction that has thus far gone largely unstated (in the analysis as well as in the talk itself) is that the participants are interacting with each other as fully proficient speakers of Japanese. The participants do not orient to this feature of the talk because it does not cause any particular problem for them. Documenting the way Yoh and Yumi interact with Aki provides a kind of baseline that will be useful in comparing and contrasting the way that they interact with the non-Japanese clients as shown in the following subsections.

**Jay**

I will begin by examining the opening sequences of Jay's appointments. When Jay arrives on the first day, Yoh is at the back of the salon dealing with another customer, but Yumi comes to the door to greet him (Excerpt 4).

**Excerpt 4.** Jay T1 Greetings

```
01  Yumi      $konnichiwa:$
              hello
              Hello.

02  Yoh       (yoroshiku onega-)
              well       pleas-

03            (.)

04  Yoh       >konnichiwa<

05  Yumi      $konnichiwa$

06            (1.3)

07  Yumi      tim  sensei:?
              name professor
              Are you Tim's?

08  Jay       hai t[im ]sensei    no (.) uh (.)
              yes  name professor LK

09  Yumi           [hah]
                    CS

10  Jay       gakusei des.
              student CP-POL
              Yes, I'm Tim's student.

11  Yumi      hai yoroshiku onegaishimasu.
              yes well-POL  HON-please
              Okay, nice to meet you.

12            onimotsu    o (.) >okaban< oazukari sh'te
              HON-baggage O     HON-bag  take-HON-and
              I'll just take your baggage, your bag.
```

```
13                  (.)

14  Yumi            $hai.$  >eheh heh h[eh]<
                    yes
                    Please.
15  Jay                                 [ah] dohzo.
                                         CS  please
                                        Oh, here you are.

16                  (0.3)

17  Jay             [arigatoh arigatoh]
                     thank you thank you

18  Yumi            [hai        hai      ]
                     okay       okay
                    Okay, got it.
```

In this case, Yumi and Yoh give multiple versions of standard (non-service) greetings (lines 1–5), but Jay does not reciprocate in the slot where a SPP is due (line 6), perhaps because he is orienting to this as a service encounter nonetheless. In line 7, Yumi instead initiates a clarification sequence, giving the name of the researcher, who had set up the initial appointment for Jay. In one sense, this referral from another customer is a form of familiarity, in that a connection between the two people is assumed before they meet, and Yoh and Yumi orient to this in the talk by raising it as a recognitional even at this early stage in the conversation. Even though Yumi formulates the name as just a single referent, Jay demonstrates that he hears the turn-final rising intonation as marking a question and responds to it as such, first with an affirmative token and then by completing the elided segment of Yumi's just-prior turn (lines 8 and 10). After this, Yumi uses the formal phrase *yoroshiku onegaishimasu* 'nice to meet you,' which marks this as first-time talk between strangers who are entering into some sort of relationship, in this case that of service-provider and customer. In line 12, Yumi also offers to take Jay's bag for him, as she did with Aki in Excerpt 1, line 6, but notice that her formulation of this turn involves a self-initiated repair in which she redoes *onimotsu* 'your baggage' as *okaban* 'your bag', a term that is narrower and more specific, and therefore likely to be more easily understood. When Yumi formulated the same offer for Aki, she used only the more general term, and Aki accepted the offer so quickly that it was delivered in overlap (Fragment 5).

**Fragment 5.** taken from Excerpt 1: Aki T1 Greetings

```
06  Yumi      onimotsu $oazu[karishimasu$
              HON-bag    take-HON
              Let me take your bag for you.

07  Aki                  [ah (.) hai °onegaishimas°=
                          CS     yes  please-HON
                          Oh, yes, thanks.
```

For Jay, on the other hand, the uptake was slightly delayed, first after the initial formulation of *your baggage* (line 12) and then after the remainder of the offer was completed (line 13). Such gaps of silence, coming as they do post-FPPs (line 6 and line 13), are Yumi's first potential indication of Jay's limited Japanese proficiency, or perhaps his limited familiarity with Japanese hair salons.

Yumi then has Jay fill out his name and phone number on a customer profile card while Yoh deals with another client. A few minutes later, Yumi returns to collect the card and guide him to the styling chair (Excerpt 5).

**Excerpt 5.** Jay T1 Greetings

```
01  Yumi      Lee- (0.3) Lee san?
                              AT
              Lee- Mr. Lee?

02  Jay       Lee [Jay.

03  Yumi          [eh?

04  Yumi      Lee Jay, (.) san.
                            AT
              Mr. Jay Lee.

05  Jay       ha[i
              yes

06  Yumi        [ha:i. yoroshiku onegai[shimasu  ]
                 yes   well            please-HON
              Okay, nice to meet you.

07  Yoh                                 >[|hai dohzo]<
                                          yes go ahead
                                          Here, have a seat.
                                         |((moves chair))

08            (3.6)
```

```
09  Yumi        kochira [no seki.          ]
                this-POL LK seat
                This seat please.

10  Yoh                 [kochira ni   doh]zo
                         this-POL PT  go ahead
                         This way please.

11              (2.8)/((Jay walks to chair))

12  Jay         |thank you
                |((sitting))

13  Yoh         ha:↑i↓
                yes
                There you are.
```

Reading from the profile card Jay has just written, Yumi attempts to pronounce Jay's name. In line 1, the cut-off intonation demonstrates that she can pronounce his family name, but not his given name. Jay says it aloud for her and she repeats it in line 4, leading to a second version of the first-time-talk marking expression *yoroshiku onegaishimasu* in line 6. Again, there is a missing SPP as Jay does not respond to this during the gap of silence in line 8, a slot where he could have reciprocated. In many service situations in Japan, such as in a convenience store or at a train station, this lack of response from the customer is quite normal; however, a hairdresser may be something of an exception, since it is understood that the hairdresser and client will be engaging in conversation over an extended period of time. That is, the hairstylists occupy a position somewhere between friend and service provider.

As they guide Jay to the chair on this first encounter, Yoh and Yumi both use high politeness registers (lines 7–10), which again is completely normative for an initial encounter between a service provider and a customer in Japanese. Compare this, however, with the opening moments of Jay's third appointment two months later in Excerpt 6.

**Excerpt 6.** Jay T3 Greetings (July 21)

```
01  Yumi        |((walking toward door))
02              |$↑KONnichi[wa$
                            hello

03  Jay                    [kon ni chiwa[:]
                            hello
```

```
04  Yoh                [↑KONNIchiwa  [i]ra[sshai
                        hello         come-HON
                       Hello, welcome.

05  Yumi                                        [heh heh

06             (0.8)/((sound of bell on door))

07  Yumi       (    )

08  Jay        (thank you)

09  Yumi       $ha↑:i.$
               yes
               Not at all.

10             (0.3)

11  Yumi       $dohzo$
               go ahead
               This way.

12             (0.9)/((Yoh walks to chair, turns it around))

13  Yoh        dohzo
               go ahead
               Have a seat.

14             (0.2)/((Jay walks quickly to chair-->))

15  Yoh        hai   maido      arigato
               okay  every time thanks
               Okay, good to see you again.

16             (1.0)/((Jay sits down))
```

Jay responds to Yumi's greeting in a timely fashion, overlapping his SPP with the end of her FPP (lines 2 and 3) in a far more sociable way. There is a lot more implied familiarity with the situation, with Jay demonstrating that he is aware where he will be sitting and walking directly to the chair. Yumi and Yoh have also elided their invitations from *kochira no seki* 'this chair' and *kochira ni dohzo* 'this way please' (Excerpt 5, lines 9–10) to simply *dohzo* 'please' (Excerpt 6, lines 11 and 13), rightly displaying that they believe this recipient will understand the meaning of the invitation through his familiarity with the context. This suggests that one of the turn constructional manifestations of familiarity is seen in elision and the decreasing need for fully explicit formulations.

In addition, Yoh's use of expressions like *maido* 'every time' (line 15) clearly orient to Jay as a repeat customer. This word is regularly used in customer-server opening sequences, but only when the customer is clearly recognized by the server. In this way, the hairdressers' category-specific expressions cast Jay as "a regular" at this point, and therefore function to display an intimacy that did not exist in the initial appointment.

**Emil**

In the case of Emil, by the third appointment, in Excerpt 7, this elision has progressed to the extent that there is no invitation in Japanese from the hairdressers at all, and the client walks straight to the chair while producing a formulaic greeting (line 26).

**Excerpt 7.** Emil T3 Greetings (July 21)

```
01 Emil       $[kon[nichiwa:]$
                  hello

02 Yumi       $[kon[nichiwa:]$
                  hello

03 Yoh              $[nchwa:  :]$
                      'llo

04 Emil       ↑hello

05            (.)

06 Yumi       $hello$ heh ha ha

07 Emil       $nice to see you.$

08            (.)

09 Yumi       heh

10 Emil       ↑hello

11            (.)

12 Yumi       hello heh ha ha

13 Emil       nice to see you.

14            (.)
```

```
15  Yumi    heh

16  Yoh     come in.

17  Emil    thank you.

18          (1.0)

19  Emil    how are you today.=

20  Yoh     =hai.  ja-    genki des yo.
             yes   okay-  fine  CP  IP
            Okay- Yes, I'm fine.

21          (.)

22  Emil    ((laugh))

23  Yoh     bery guddo
            very good

24  Yumi    (    )

25  Yoh     ((laughs))

26  Emil    ojamashima::s
            interrupt-HON
            Pardon me.

27  Yoh     hai.
            yes

28          ((Emil sits, exhales deeply))

29  Emil    it's very hot.

30  Yoh     ah-hah ha, soh  des ne.
                       that CP  IP
                       It is, isn't it?

31          (.)

32  Emil    so (    ) ((Shakes head))

33  Yoh     mo::h         (0.3)   kore kara:,
            stance marker         this from
```

```
34              motto atsuku narimas yo:
                more  hot    become   IP
                Shoot, and it's going to get hotter from now on.

35  Emil        |°oh god°   heh heh ha
                |((smiles, looks upwards))

36  Yoh         demo (.) natsu  wa:,
                but      summer TP
37              (0.3)/((establishes eye contact in mirror))

38              kaeru  n des ka? bolivia.
                return N CP  Q
                But, are you going home to Bolivia in the summer?

39  Emil        ((shakes head)) no::

40  Yoh         ah  kaeranai   n ya.
                CS  return-NEG N CP
                Oh, you're not.

41  Emil        (    )
```

Yoh gives an invitation in English (line 16), something he does not do for any of the other clients. As I have documented in detail elsewhere (Greer, 2013), Emil's Japanese is the least proficient of the four customers, and therefore he and Yoh eventually adopt a pattern of dual-receptive language alternation, in which each party uses his preferred language. While Yoh generally speaks in Japanese and Emil responds in English, that pattern is relaxed somewhat in the greeting sequence, perhaps because the level of language proficiency required by both is not high. The choice of language itself constitutes part of Yoh's knowledge concerning Emil, and this language pattern is therefore an integral part of the way he recipient designs his turns for this client.

Since "how-are-you sequences" are a common part of English greetings (Schegloff, 2007, p. 199), these reciprocated greetings go on for longer than they do with the other three clients, where Japanese is the medium of communication. Despite his lack of Japanese proficiency, Emil seems to have established a good rapport with Yoh, initiating action sequences through FPPs throughout the opening moments (lines 1, 4, 7, 13, 19 and 29) and aligning to Yoh's turns in a timely fashion (e.g., line 39), which displays that he understands much of the Japanese even if he cannot produce it. Emergent familiarity, therefore, is not simply a function of growing understanding of the language; it also involves an increasing understanding of the situation, the participants, and the routines. By taking part in several iterations of the same procedure, the clients are engaged in a process of becoming familiar with the institutional practices of this particular hair salon and the people who run it. This process is carried out on a turn-by-turn basis and involves not just the clients, but the hairdressers as well, as they adapt their practices to meet the needs of their clients, adjusting the formulation of their turns for the recipient who currently occupies the chair. In addition, by orienting to information obtained in earlier episodes, such as when Yoh asks about Bolivia in line 38, the participants make relevant the personal details they know about each other, and therefore use their developing familiarity as a resource to carry out interactional tasks, such as proffering a topic.

## Tye

Tye's initial appointment was somewhat atypical with respect to the opening sequence in that he arrives while the hairdressers are busy and is obliged to wait roughly 25 minutes while Yumi washes Aki's hair and Yoh deals with another customer. As it turns out, Tye apparently knows Aki from university,[3] and so she recognizes him from the chair when he enters (Excerpt 8.1). Understandably, Aki greets Tye as a friend, not as a client, and this provides a convenient opportunity for comparing the familiarity of her greeting with that of Yumi, who is meeting Tye for the first time.

**Excerpt 8.1.** Tye T1 Greetings

```
01              ((Yumi is blowdrying Aki's hair and does not
02                react when the bells on the door ring))
03              ((Yumi stops the dryer and looks to the door))

04 Tye          o[negaishima:s
                    please-HON
                Hello?

05 Yumi         |[$konnichiwa$
                    hello
                |((head bow))

06              (0.6)

07 Yoh          ((looks to Tye))  konnichi[wa
                                     hello

08 Aki →        ((looking to Tye))         [ah- tye da
                                            CS       CP
                                           Oh, it's Tye!

09 Tye →        ↑o:::h
                awe-receipt
                Oh hey!
```

```
10  Yumi      >heh hah<

11  Aki       ((gives two short waves, smiling))

12  Yumi      |irasshaimase
               come-HON
               Welcome!
              |((walking toward door))

13            (0.5)

14  Tye       yoyaku       arimasen  des   kedo:
              reservation  CP-NEG    CP    but
              I don't have a booking but...

15  Yumi      ah    hai
              CS    yes
              Oh yes.

16            (0.3)

17  Tye       a:(g)h (0.8) er! sanpatsu (ga shitai)
                                haircut   S  do-want
              ...umm, er, I'd like a haircut.

18  Yumi      |kami:   (.) no  ke    des  ne.  ha:i.
               hair        LK  hair  CP   IP   yes
               Your hair, yes.
19            |((makes a scissor-cut gesture near her head))

20  Tye       (    )

21  Yumi      hai.  $wakarimash'ta.$
              yes   understand-PST
              Okay, certainly.

22            (1.3)/((Tye sits))

23  Yumi      omachi       kudasa::i.
              HON-wait     please
              One moment please.
```

Yumi's greetings are not significantly different to those she uses with the other clients in their initial appointments, including both service encounter greetings (line 12) and standard greetings (line 5). They are delivered with a smile voice and her embodied actions align to Tye's arrival as a customer as she moves quickly to the door to greet him and take his bag. Aki on the other hand does not get out of the chair, reaffirming her situated identity as a client. However, upon seeing Tye in line 8 she does produce a brief change-of-state token and utters his name, with the copula verb in plain form, directing it primarily at herself or a close acquaintance. Tye responds in kind in next turn, with an extended awe-marked response token (Greer, 2016), demonstrating not only that he recognizes Aki, but that he is somehow surprised or amazed to see her here. With these few words, Tye and Aki have made it public that they know each other, and the two brief pulses of laughter from Yumi in line 10 provide evidence to suggest that she is now also aware of this. While Tye and Aki do not openly greet each other with a formulaic greeting like *konnichiwa*, this noticing seems to substitute for the greeting, again perhaps demonstrating their pre-existing familiarity, yet still orienting to their situated identities as customers.

Although she seems to recognize the connection between Aki and Tye, Yumi continues to adhere to the institutional greeting script, treating Tye as a client (line 12). In lines 14 and 17 it seems that Tye has prepared an initial service request that includes the word *sanpatsu* 'haircut', a vocabulary item of Chinese origin that is now generally less commonly heard than the English loanword *katto* 'cut',[4] a word which should have been easier for Tye to remember and produce. That said, Tye's use of *sanpatsu* is situationally intelligible and Yumi does not initiate repair on it in any direct way. Instead, in line 18 she confirms her understanding of what Tye is trying to convey, reformulating *sanpatsu* 'haircut' to *kami no ke* 'hair' and coupling it with a scissor-like cutting gesture, thus subtly demonstrating an assumption of Tye's relatively low Japanese language proficiency (Bolden, 2014), and therefore possibly ascribing him an identity as a novice speaker.

After this brief incident there is an extended period of time in which Tye sits in the waiting room filling out a customer profile card and waiting for the hairdressers to finish with the other customers. After 25 minutes, Aki's haircut is done and she is at the entrance (Excerpt 8.2). Yoh has just returned her bag to her and while she is paying for the haircut she again has a brief chat with Tye. This provides an additional chance to observe how the participants design their turns based on their relative familiarity: Aki treats Tye as a friend, and Yoh treats him as a first-time client.

**Excerpt 8.2.** Tye T1

```
01 Yoh      |((slight bow to Tye))
02          |chotto omachi    kudasai
             just    HON-wait please
            Just a moment please.

03          (3.2)/((takes calculator out of drawer))
```

```
04  Yoh     eh::[to:]
            HM
            Umm...

05  Aki         [Tye] mijikaku su'n    no?
                      shorten  do-PLN  IP
                Are you gonna cut it short, Tye?

06              (.)

07  Tye     hm?

08  Aki →   |mijikaku suru?
             shorten  do-PLN
             Cut it short?
09          |((makes scissor gesture on own hair))

10  Tye     un.
            yeah

11  Aki     ↑e::::h (.) tanoshimi     ni sh'tokoh.
               wow      anticipating  PT do-FTR-PLN-VOL

12  Yoh     heh h'n

13  Aki     $raishuu.$
             next week
            Wow! I'm looking forward to seeing that next week.

14          (0.8)

15  Yoh     (°        °)

16  Aki     hai
            yes

17  Yoh     sanzen gohyaku gojuu en  des:.
            3000   500     50    yen CP
            That'll be 3550 yen.

18          ((Aki takes money out of purse))

19  Tye     hakkagetsu    mae (°    °)
            eight months  before
            (   ) eight months ago.

20          ((Aki pays Yoh))
```

```
21  Yoh        |ikkagetsu mae     des ka
               one month before   CP  Q
               One month ago was it?
22             |((holding one finger up))

23  Tye        hakkagetsu    des
               eight months  CP
               Eight months.

24  Yoh        ah  hachikagetsu mae    des [ka]
               CS  eight months before CP  Q
               Oh, eight months ago, was it?

25  Aki                                      ↑[ha]chikagetsu?!
                                              eight months

26  Yoh        ↑ha(h)chika(h)ge(h)tsu
                eight months

27  Aki        °sugo:i°
               incredible
               Wow!

28             (1.3)

29  Aki        ja amerika de?
               so America  PT
               So, in the US?

30  Tye        u:n.
               yeah

31  Yoh →     $sorya    sungoi      ss ne$
              that-TP  incredible   CP IP
              That is incredible, yeah?

32             (0.3)

33  Yoh        heh [heh heh h]eh

34  Aki            [su:goi!    ]
                    incredible
                    It is.
```

The difference between familiar clients and relative strangers is evident in the way that Aki and Yoh address Tye. Yoh uses polite language like the formal request form (line 2) and *desu/masu* form (line 21), whereas Aki uses phonetically elided plain verb forms (lines 5, 8, 11). Both make use of gestures to add meaning to questions they direct at Tye: Aki in a self-repair in line 8, and Yoh in an initiation of repair in line 22. One major difference is that some of Aki's turns allude to an ongoing relationship away from the salon, such as when she says she looks forward to seeing Tye's haircut next week (lines 11–13). It is through such turns that Yoh can begin to see that Tye and Aki know each other, and although Yoh does not question them about it at this time, later while cutting Tye's hair he does in fact ask him about it.

Contrast this with Yoh's greetings during Tye's second appointment, as outlined in Excerpt 9.

**Excerpt 9.** Tye T2 Greetings

```
01              ((Tye enters))

02              (1.9)/((Yumi walks toward door))

03 Yumi         konnichiwa:::↑
                hello

04 Yoh          ((walking toward door)) konnichiwa::=
                                        hello

05 Yumi         =irrashaimase
                come-HON
                Welcome!

06              (2.0)

07 Yumi         (kaban) o oaz'karishimashoo ka?
                bag     O take-HON-VOL      Q
                Shall I take your bag for you?

08 Tye          (hai)
                yes

09 Yumi         ha:i.
                yes
                Here.

10 Yoh          heh heh ha

11 Yoh →        ohisashiburi       des
                HON-a long while   CP
                Long time no see.

12              (.)
```

```
13 Yoh      eheh heh heh

14 Tye      (         )

15          (3.4)/((Yoh takes bag to side room))

16 Yoh      dohzo
            go ahead
            Come in.

17          |(4.4)
            |((Yoh walks to chair. Tye walks in and sits))

18 Yoh →    sakki   mata, (.) aki    san kitemashita    kedo,
            before  again    (name)  AT  come-CONT-PST  but

19 Tye      un
            RT
            mm

20          (0.3)

21 Yoh      aimashita, asoko de?
            meet-PST   there PT
            Aki was here again just before. Did you see her out there?

22 Tye      un
            yeah

23 Yumi     °heh heh hn.°

24 Tye      |atchi  de
             there  PT
             Up there.
            |((points up))

25 Tye      (or) sono-          tabun,
                 demonstrative  probably

26          (.)

27 Tye      daigaku     ni  ir- ah iru         chu.⁵
            university  to      H  exist-PLN   during*
            Um- she's probably on the way to university.

28          (0.9)/((Yoh stops, looks at Tye in mirror))
```

```
29  Tye        iku     chu.⁵
               go-PLN  during*
               Going there now.

30  Yoh  →    ↑↑oh::↓ iku       toki ne.
               CS      go-PLN    when IP
               Oh, when she was going, yeah.

31             (1.7)
```

Although both the institutional and standard greetings are present in lines 3 to 5, Yoh follows this with *ohisashiburi des* 'long time no see' in line 11, indicating that this is not a first-time meeting. By employing this formulation at this point, Yoh is able to link this second conversation with the talk that went on in the first session a month earlier, and therefore *talk into being* an ongoing human connection as well. Shaw and Kitzinger (2007) note that parties commonly orient to such mutual remembering in the opening sequences of second or subsequent service interactions, and the complete absence of such re-establishment of prior encounters is perhaps only a feature in initial encounters; to not refer to information learned in the prior haircuts would be tantamount to treating the client as a first-time customer.

Yoh initiates a first topic in lines 18 to 21 by referencing Aki, who is known to both Yoh and Tye and therefore represents a joint epistemic domain. Since Aki has just left the salon after finishing her second appointment, Yoh asks Tye if he saw her on the street when he came in. By initiating this turn in line 18 with *sakki mata* 'again, just before,' Yoh employs a time formulation that links this event with the one that happened in the first appointment, in which Aki also finished her haircut just as Tye began hers. In knowing this fact and publically displaying this knowledge to Tye at this point, Yoh makes a bid for co-membership via a non-present mutual acquaintance. In line 18, he begins with a my side telling (Pomerantz, 1980) and follows this with a question that assigns epistemic primacy (Heritage & Raymond, 2005) to Tye (line 21) by asking about what happened after Aki left the salon, a point that can be normatively understood to be beyond Yoh's domain of experience, since he has been in the salon since then.

Tye's response is aligned with Yoh's FPP in that it treats it as a yes/no question (line 22); however, when he goes on to extend the talk by providing an account (of where Aki was going), Tye evidently experiences difficulty in accessing the grammar he is trying to use (lines 25–29). It is likely that he was trying to say *iku tochuu* 'she was on the way', but while he self-repairs his misused verb (from *iru* to *iku*) he does not repair the temporal noun, leaving it as *chuu* 'in, during' instead of *tochuu* 'on the way.' Yoh is monitoring Tye's turn-in-progress and stops preening in line 28 to instead look at Tye through the mirror, paying attention to Tye's attempts at self-repair. In next turn, Yoh uses other-correction to replace *chuu* with *toki* 'the time when', but he embeds it within receipt, making a claim that he has understood, even though Tye's turn was not a completely standard formulation (Jefferson, 1987). Just as Yumi did in Excerpt 8.1, line 18, Yoh has enacted repair in an affiliative manner that does not delay the progressivity of the talk (Antaki, 2012).

Finally, it is worth examining the role of second and multiple assessments in establishing affiliation and therefore fostering rapport. Parties use assessments to evaluate or express an opinion about something, and when another speaker proffers a type-conforming second assessment it constitutes agreement (Pomerantz, 1984). Clark, Drew, and Pinch (2003) note that salespeople build rapport by using second assessments to affiliate with their customers' assessments, and it seems that a form of this practice is evident in the opening sequence of Tye's fourth appointment (Excerpt 10), which took place on a hot summer's day. Tye is sweating as he comes in and is carrying a paper fan.

**Excerpt 10.** Tye T4 Greetings

```
01              ((bell on door rings))

02              (1.2)

03 Yoh          konnichiwa:
                hello

04 Yumi         konnichiwa aheh heh heh
                hello

05 Tye          heh-heh

06              (1.0)

07 Yoh →        atsui    ne
                hot-PLN  IP
                Hot, huh?

08              (.)

09 Tye          sugoku    atsui.
                terribly  hot-PLN
                Really hot.

10 Yoh          heh heh h[eh

11 Yumi                  [h-heh heh HA
```

```
12  Tye          hontoni  natsu   nigate
                 really   summer  difficult
                 I really can't handle summer.

13  Yoh          heh heh h[eh

14  Yumi                  [h-heh heh HA

15               (.)

16  Yumi →       atsu sugite
                 hot  too-and
                 Because it's too hot.

17  Tye          un=
                 yeah

18  Yoh          =$hai   dohzo$
                   okay  go ahead
                 Okay, have a seat.

19               (2.1)/((Tye walks to chair and sits))

20  Tye          |arghh
                 |((hand to nose))

21               (2.2)

22  Yoh          dokka       itteta          n des ka
                 somewhere   go-CONT-PST     N CP  Q
                 Did you go somewhere today?

23               (1.2)

24  Tye          kyo?
                 today
                 Today?

25  Yoh          un
                 yeah

26  Tye          wa (tto kyoh  wa) boku no saigo no ryoh  ni
                 TP  H   today TP  I    LK last  LK dorm  in
27               sunderu     hi  kara[:, ]=
                 live-CONT   day because
                 Um today's my last day living in the dorm, so...
```

```
28  Yumi                      [oh!]

29  Yoh                       [un:]
                              RT
                              mm

30  Tye          =to   kyoh  wa  sohji      sh'ta   dake.
                  and  today TP  cleaning   do-PST  just
                 ...and today I was just cleaning.

31  Yoh          nohn  sohji.
                 RT    cleaning
                 Oh, cleaning!

32  Tye          [un]
                 yeah

33  Yoh →        [ u]wogh:  sore  wa  yokeini    (0.3)
                 RT         that  TP  extra
                 Woah! That's even more so.

34  Tye          ehah

35  Yumi         u[goite      atsu]katta  [(desho)ne.]
                 move-and     hot-PST      CP       IP
                 Moving makes you even hotter, right?

36  Yoh          [heh   ha   hah]

37  Yoh                                 [    yokee]ni  ugoite
                                             extra     move
                                        Extra movement

38  Yoh          (3.4)/((Yoh cools Tye's neck with hairdryer))
```

Although it can normatively be understood as part of a greeting sequence at this time of year, Yoh's initial assessment in line 7, *atsui ne* 'hot, huh?,' is also partly made relevant by the visibly available cues from the just-arrived client, including his sweaty head and the paper fan he is holding. Tye upgrades this assessment in next turn, which is hearable as a strong agreement, and therefore one that affiliates with Yoh's opinion. Note that both are delivered in plain form (i.e., without a polite copula), giving them an affect-laden, visceral feel. In addition, Yoh formulates his initial assessment with a post-positioned *ne* particle, which makes acknowledgement relevant in next turn (Tanaka, 2000) and sets the groundwork for Tye's preferred agreement through second assessment. In line 12 then, Tye produces another initial negative assessment, which broadens the topic from "today's heat" to summer in general. Yumi then follows this with a second assessment in line 16 that echoes the pair just produced by Tye and Yoh, allowing her to affiliate and therefore help to build rapport. By formulating it as a post-positioned account (an adjective in -*te* form), she implies an understanding of Tye's stance, and therefore claims affiliation with it. *Atsusugite* 'too hot' with the -*te* form suggests a reason for the subsequently following clause, and that the implied content in the missing clause is likely to be the same as what Tye said in line 12. In other words, this collaborative turn sequence (Lerner, 2004) uses an affiliating utterance to extend the TCU by providing an elided account. When Tye reveals that he is moving out of his dormitory that day and has been cleaning just prior to the appointment (lines 26–30), Yoh receipts this as news and he and Yumi collaboratively upgrade their prior assessments by reworking this information into an additional account for why Tye is looking hot, and thereby accomplish a deeper display of affiliation.

The initial moments in the opening sequence of each appointment constitute a highly pertinent locus for rapport work. In addition to allowing the speakers to gauge each other's current moods, they are also opportunities to display their emerging familiarity with each other. From a business standpoint, this is a vital means of promoting a customer relationship, ensuring that the client feels comfortable and will want to return for future haircuts. Naturally, in the very first appointments, the hairdresser and client were virtually strangers and this was reflected through the polite-yet-distant choice of verb endings and formulaic expressions. However, as they became more familiar with their clients, their formulations reflected and reified their growing relationship. Although they increasingly used plain form verb endings or non-service greeting formulae, these were not the only ways they had of displaying their rapport. The hairdressers also designed their turns as claims to familiarity by (a) referring to past encounters and topicalizing shared knowledge, (b) proffering affiliative second assessments, and (c) embedding other-repair within claims of comprehension.

## Second language use, emergent familiarity and longitudinal CA

As an initial investigation, this study's focus on greetings on first and subsequent occasions has only begun to scratch the surface. There are undoubtedly many other interactional practices left to explore in the wider data set and future research within this project will look at such issues as repair, requests and participation frameworks. Yet even in these brief opening moments of the hairdressing corpus, we have been able to witness the gradual development of social relationships from complete strangers to a relaxed and friendly server-client bond. By tracking the interaction between two hairdressers and four of their customers we were able to collect both vertical data, showing changes across episodes between the same speakers, and horizontal data, enabling us to compare the way two expert speakers of Japanese communicate with interlocutors with varying interactional competence in that language. Even though the openings all featured the same general practices, the way that Yoh and Yumi locally managed them as formulated for a particular recipient at a particular time demonstrated their growing knowledge about that client's Japanese ability. Emergent familiarity was also seen in the way institutional and service-like greetings were gradually replaced with more standard greetings that involved the customer in responding and therefore helped establish rapport. All of this became visible to us as analysts as it did to the participants themselves in real-time via the organization of sequence, turn construction, and formulation.

Like any interaction, the excerpts here naturally involved both parties in co-constructing the talk. The main focus of this study, however, has not been so much on the novice speakers' acquisition of target language competencies, as on the way that the expert speakers adapt and adjust their talk to reflect their growing knowledge of the novice. In so doing, it is possible to consider this kind of accommodation itself as a developing interactional competence from the perspective of the L1 speaker, not in the sense of acquiring new language, but with respect to how the L1 speaker learns to design a turn for a given interlocutor with limited Japanese proficiency. As Nguyen (2011, p. 201) notes, the increasing ability to produce recipient-designed turns is both locally and temporally accomplished, and so we can see changes within and across conversations. Developing interactional competence, therefore, is not just an issue for learners and novice language users.

Moreover, all of this rapport work is accomplished within the greater context of establishing a business relationship. A competently-achieved greeting helps set the mood for the remainder of the conversation. Part of that competence relies on the speaker designing the greeting for a specific recipient, and thus displaying his or her knowledge of the recipient. Not all of the recipient design work that the hairdressers do orients to the L2 users as novice Japanese speakers; indeed, to do so overtly would be counter-productive to their goals of establishing and maintaining rapport. Accommodation then is accomplished through the practices of formulation, wherein the hairdressers adapt their talk based on the clients' immediately prior turn as well as the knowledge they have acquired about that person in earlier appointments. In so doing, the hairdressers do not often overtly talk to them as "foreigners", treating them instead first and foremost as clients. In fact, the notion of "foreigner talk" should perhaps be better viewed as just one form of much broader interactional practices, such as formulation, recipient-design, and categorization, and should therefore be seen as a subset of the notion that speakers formulate any particular turn to accommodate what they know (or believe to be true) about their audience.

## Notes

1. Pseudonyms are used throughout the study.
2. Recently, convenience stores and other similar businesses seem to use the same approach of following *irasshaimase* with *konnichiwa*, although customers do not generally respond to either greeting.
3. This was not an intentional part of the research design, but it was a fortuitous one.
4. A reviewer pointed out, for instance, a blog where the Japanese writer related an account in which a hairdresser other-initiated repair on the client's use of *sanpatsu* to *katto*, the connotation being that the former is a little old fashioned, and therefore lacks prestige in current Japanese. http://blog.livedoor.jp/shuji55slisla/archives/50430632.html
5. Tye's use of *verb+chu* in lines 27 and 29 is not grammatical. He seems to be using it to indicate the action is happening in the present, something like the *noun+chu* formulation (e.g., *benkyo chu*).

## References

Antaki, C. (2012). Affiliative and disaffiliative candidate understandings. *Discourse Studies* 14(5), 531–547.

Bilmes, J. (2011). Occasioned semantics: A systematics approach to meaning in talk. *Human Studies*, 34(2), 155–181.

Bolden, G. (2014). Negotiating understanding in "intercultural moments" in immigrant family interactions. *Communication Monographs*, 81(2), 208–238.

Brouwer, C. E., & Wagner, J. (2004). Developmental issues in second language conversation. *Journal of Applied Linguistics, 1*(1), 29–47.

Clark, C., Drew, P., & Pinch, T. (2003) Managing prospect affiliation and rapport in real-life sales encounters, *Discourse Studies, 5*(1), 5–31.

Deppermann, A. (2011). The study of formulations as a key to interactional semantics. *Human Studies*, 34(2), 115–128.

Drew, P. (2013). Turn design. In J. Sidnell & T. Stivers (Eds.), *The handbook of conversation analysis* (pp. 131–149). Malden, MA: Wiley-Blackwell.

Early, M. (1987). Linguistic input and interaction in the content classroom, *TESL Canada Journal, 4*(2), 41–58.

Ferguson, C. (1971). Absence of copula and the notion of simplicity: A study of normal speech, baby talk, foreigner talk and pidgins. In D. Hymes (Ed.), *Pidginization and creolization of languages* (pp.141–50). New York, NY: Cambridge University Press.

Ferguson, C. (1975). Towards a characterization of English foreigner talk. *Anthropological Linguistics, 17*, 1–14.

Goffman, E. (1971). *Relations in public: Microstudies of the public order.* New York, NY: Harper & Row.

Goffman, E. (1981). Response cries. In E. Goffman (Ed.), *Forms of talk* (pp. 78–122). Oxford, UK: Blackwell.

Greer, T. (2013). Establishing a pattern of dual-receptive language alternation: Insights from a series of successive haircuts. *Australian Journal of Communication 40*(2), 47–61.

Greer, T. (2016). On doing Japanese awe in English talk. In G. Kasper & M. Prior (Eds.), *Talking emotion in multilingual settings*. Amsterdam: John Benjamins.

Hall, J. K., Hellermann, J., & Pekarek Doehler, S. (Eds.). (2011). *L2 interactional competence and development*. Bristol, UK: Multilingual Matters.

Hayashi, M. (2009). Marking a 'noticing of departure' in talk: *Eh*-prefaced turns in Japanese conversation. *Journal of Pragmatics, 41*(10), 2100–2129.

Heritage, J., & Raymond, G. (2005). The terms of agreement: Indexing epistemic authority and subordination in talk-in-interaction. *Social Psychology Quarterly, 68*(1), 15–38.

Jefferson, G. (1987). On exposed and embedded correction in conversation. In G. Button & J. R. E. Lee (Eds.), *Talk and social organization* (pp. 86–100). Clevedon, UK: Multilingual Matters.

Lee, Y-A., & Hellermann, J. (2014). Tracing developmental changes through conversation analysis: Cross-sectional and longitudinal analysis. *TESOL Quarterly, 48*(4), 763–788.

Lerner, G. (2004). Collaborative turn sequences. In G. Lerner (Ed.), *Conversation analysis: Studies from the first generation* (pp. 225–256). Amsterdam: John Benjamins.

Leyland, C., Greer, T., & Rettig-Miki, E. (2016). Dropping the devil's advocate: One novice language tester's shifting interactional practices across a series of speaking tests. *Classroom Discourse 7*(1), 1–21.

Mortensen, K., & Hazel, S. (2014). Moving into interaction: Social practices for initiating encounters at a help desk. *Journal of Pragmatics, 62*, 46–67.

Nguyen, H. T. (2011). Achieving recipient-design longitudinally: Evidence from a pharmacy intern in patient consultations. In J. K. Hall, J. Hellermann & S. Pekarek Doehler (Eds.), *L2 interactional competence and development* (pp. 173–205). Clevedon, UK: Multilingual Matters.

Nguyen, H. T. (2012). *Developing interactional competence: A conversation-analytic study of patient consultations in pharmacy*. Basingstoke, UK: Palgrave-Macmillan.

Oshima, S. (2007). A multimodal analysis of the service-assessment sequence in haircutting interactions. *Texas Linguistics Forum, 51*. Retrieved from http://studentorgs.utexas.edu/salsa/proceedings/2007/Oshima.pdf

Pillet-Shore, D. (2012). Greeting: Displaying stance through prosodic recipient design. *Research on Language & Social Interaction, 45*(4), 375–398.

Pomerantz, A. (1980). Telling my side: "Limited access" as a "fishing device". *Sociological Inquiry, 50*(3–4), 186–198.

Pomerantz, A. (1984). Agreeing and disagreeing with assessments: Some features of preferred/dispreferred turn shapes. In J. M. Atkinson & J. Heritage (Eds.), *Structures* of social action: Studies in conversation analysis (pp. 57–101). Cambridge, UK: Cambridge University Press.

Sacks, H., Schegloff, E., & Jefferson, G. (1974). A simplest systematics for the organization of turn-taking for conversation. *Language, 50*(4), 696–735.

Schegloff, E. (1972). Notes on a conversational practice: Formulating place. In D. Sudnow (Ed.), *Studies in social interaction* (pp. 75–119). New York, NY: Free Press.

Schegloff, E. (1979). Identification and recognition in telephone conversation openings. In G. Psathas (Ed.), *Everyday language: Studies in ethnomethodology* (pp. 23–78). New York, NY: Irvington.

Schegloff, E. (1986). The routine as achievement. *Human Studies, 9*, 111–151.

Schegloff, E. (2007). *Sequence organization in interaction*. Cambridge, UK: Cambridge.

Shaw, R., & Kitzinger, C. (2007). Memory in interaction: An analysis of repeat calls to a home birth helpline. *Research on Language and Social Interaction, 40*(1), 117–144.

Tanaka, H. (2000). The particle *ne* as a turn-management device in Japanese conversation. *Journal of Pragmatics, 32*, 1135–1176.

Toerien, M., & Kitzinger, C. (2007). Emotional labour in action: Navigating multiple involvements in the beauty salon. *Sociology, 41*(4), 645–662.

Zuengler, J. (1991). Accommodation in native-nonnative interactions: Going beyond the "what" to the "why" in second-language research. In H. Giles, J. Coupland & N. Coupland (Eds.), *Contexts of accommodation* (pp. 223–244). Cambridge, UK: Cambridge University Press.

# Index

## A
accommodation   360, 369-371, 404
accountability   168, 171, 256, 296, 360
accounts   29, 42, 99, 129, 203, 312, 379, 403
acknowledgment   55, 68, 122, 163, 167, 261, 274, 280
ACTFL Guidelines   211-213, 216, 241-243
affiliation   81, 103, 107, 192-193, 381, 400
affordances   146, 157, 163, 254-260
agreement   22, 23, 29-36, 41, 193, 259-263, 265-267, 271-273, 279-280
alignment   125, 259, 280, 284, 335, 399
assessment in education   211, 243
assessments, interactional   98, 105, 162, 215, 220, 259, 260, 262, 303, 306, 335, 358, 359, 362, 372, 383, 400, 402-403
    self-assessment   20, 21-23, 28-30, 33, 35, 36, 40-42

## B
*boke* and *tsukkomi*   82, 85-95, 100, 103, 105-111

## C
candidate   105, 192-194, 196-199, 204-206, 312, 320
   completion   28
   solution   54, 61
   understanding   131, 134, 261, 281-282, 319, 321, 326
categorization   404
   categories   7, 212, 381, 389
   *See also* membership categorization analysis
change-of-state token   29, 60, 68, 119, 126-129, 130, 135, 167, 256, 264
classroom interaction   181, 255, 298, 333-335, 337, 362
codeswitching   143, 144, 203, 220, 242, 243

comedic performance  81, 107
compliments  23, 35, 36, 40, 383
connective expressions  122, 230, 236, 241, 242, 266
continuers  118, 153, 214, 218, 221, 225, 229, 235, 240
conversation-for-learning  298
correction  64, 67, 75, 255, 256, 336, 400

## D
development
    of IC  43, 52, 180, 205, 258-260, 262, 266, 269, 280, 282, 284, 295-297, 323-326, 335, 362, 363, 401
    of talk  99, 104, 107, 111, 115, 117-118, 313, 322
dinner table talk  293-295, 298-302, 324-325
disagreement  23, 29, 30, 35, 41, 261, 262, 279
dispreference  22, 23, 39, 41, 42

## E
embodiment  24, 49, 117
    embodied action  86, 91, 108, 115, 128, 162, 225, 240, 259, 270-273, 280, 281, 344, 356, 358-360, 361, 374, 393
    embodied completion  43
    embodied interaction  20, 39, 142, 182-189
epistemics  203, 279, 283, 399
    epistemic authority  261, 267, 276, 277, 279
    epistemic primacy  271, 272, 273
    epistemic stance  81, 98, 101, 102, 261, 263, 264, 281, 282
    epistemic status  168, 280, 282
    epistemic subordination  261, 266, 271, 273, 279
ethnomethodology  144-146, 283, 296

## F
familiarity  51, 75, 87, 204, 269, 324, 362, 364, 338, 369-404
F-formation  160, 163
formulaic expressions  97, 333-363, 403
formulation  20, 22, 27-42, 119, 125, 182, 220, 269, 306, 349, 370-404
    extreme case formulation  27, 28, 42
    reformulation  60, 128, 192, 276, 311, 319

## G
gesture  41, 43, 149, 153, 168, 309, 319, 335, 373, 394
greetings  10, 97, 98, 295, 317, 370-404

## H
hesitation markers   22, 23, 124, 151, 176, 179, 184, 218, 220, 221, 225, 235, 240, 242, 243
humor   90, 99, 111

## I
identity   21-23, 39, 40-42, 68, 381, 393, 394
initial encounters   369, 370-399
internship   55, 260
intersubjectivity   20, 52, 144, 147, 169, 257, 267, 269, 282-284
interview   115-137, 181, 299, 300
IRF sequence   333, 339, 342, 353, 359

## J
Japanese as a foreign language (JFL)   6, 7, 9, 180, 204, 293, 334, 337, 359

## L
language alternation   5, 371, 391
laughter   8, 9, 32, 36, 39, 68, 70, 81-85, 87-90, 92-95, 97, 99-111, 115, 192-193, 203-204, 206, 218, 229, 242, 258, 317, 322, 379, 381, 383, 394
learning   2, 28, 51-56, 58-61, 63, 65, 71-73, 75-76, 279
    as a social practice   5, 52, 255-257, 280, 282
    as socially shared cognition   257
    interactional competence   52, 71-72, 213-214, 258-260, 296, 324, 334
    L2 learning   5, 28, 42, 52-53, 142-143, 170, 254-261, 280-283, 293-296, 320, 323, 324
    opportunities   10, 52-75, 256, 281, 296, 324, 334
    orientations to learning   5, 53-54, 58, 65, 255-256, 313
    vocabulary learning   8, 10, 52, 54, 299
longitudinal
    longitudinal CA   4, 6, 9-10, 24, 335, 370, 403
    longitudinal development   43, 296, 297, 302, 403

## M
membership categorization analysis   20
multilingual workplace   54-55, 62, 72
multimodal   86, 92, 142, 144, 146, 149, 198, 204, 334, 337, 372
multiparty interaction   141, 144, 148, 153, 163, 168

## N
nods   39, 76, 115, 122, 125, 225, 235-236, 240, 243, 264-265, 267, 269, 272, 274, 277, 306, 312, 364, 374

## O

objects
    of learning   204, 258-261, 296, 299
    of searches   176, 178
objects, material   75, 143, 146-147, 334, 337, 356, 360
openings   296-298, 370-404
OPI.   *See* Oral Proficiency Interview (OPI)
Oral Proficiency Interview (OPI)   20-21, 28, 144, 146, 211-216, 230-231, 240-244

## P

participation   116, 133-136, 143-144, 212-213, 259, 324, 335
    audience participation   81-82, 105, 108, 117, 212
    participation framework   71, 147, 358, 403
    patterns of participation   182, 301
precision timing   83, 108, 123, 128, 136, 160, 184-185, 188, 198
preference organization   7-8, 20-23, 40-42, 359-360
progressivity   3, 5, 54, 55, 56, 65, 95, 126, 135-136, 148, 282-283, 360, 400
projection   83, 95, 98, 122, 125, 149, 156, 157, 159, 168, 177, 193, 196, 277, 342, 344, 346, 353, 356, 358, 360, 362, 363
prosody   261, 281, 359, 373

## R

rapport   379, 391, 400, 403, 404
receipt   29, 32, 39, 74, 98, 153, 221, 254, 260-285, 341, 342, 356, 379, 383, 400, 403
    receipt token   71, 115, 118, 119, 122, 128, 132, 159, 162
recipient design   6, 175, 177, 193, 197-198, 199, 204, 260, 360, 370, 373, 391, 404
repair   3-4, 29, 39, 154, 176, 255, 256, 280-282, 296, 341, 400
    forward-oriented   54, 176
    other-initiated   64, 123, 256, 285, 405
    other-repair   32, 62, 70, 256, 281, 285, 403, 405
    repair initiation   4, 36, 123, 126, 240-241, 243, 256, 257, 277, 280, 281-282, 308, 319, 322, 323, 394, 397
    self-initiated   123, 133, 256, 385
    self-repair   27, 57, 62, 71, 134, 188, 191, 206, 256, 275, 319-320, 323, 397, 399
repetition   55, 68, 116-117, 191, 198, 263-264, 269
    other-repetition   119-126, 260, 272, 344
    self-repetition   97, 274, 341-342, 344, 360
rephrasing   129-136, 178, 203
resource   23, 28, 29, 39, 40-41, 42, 54, 82, 103, 116, 160, 177-180, 182, 189-198, 204-205, 213-215, 220, 242, 244, 336
    interactional   20, 21, 42, 136, 144, 205, 215, 225, 235, 243, 333, 335

    linguistic   23, 125, 143, 154, 175, 177-179, 205, 215, 220, 236, 242, 255, 258, 259,
        281-283, 284, 295, 301-303, 312, 324, 334, 335, 344
    non-linguistic   23, 76, 83 106, 117, 119, 146, 163, 176, 198, 204, 297, 309, 313, 322-
        323, 334, 360, 364, 373
    semiotic   56, 58, 60, 72, 75, 115, 142-144, 146, 167, 169, 178, 213, 258, 293, 360,
        363
response
    embodied (non-linguistic)   39, 326, 349
    minimal   225, 244, 312
    recipient   8, 116-118, 119, 125, 126, 129, 133-135, 137

## S
self-deprecation   7, 8, 19-23, 29, 30, 35, 40-42
semiotic field   146, 163, 168
sequence   4, 19, 20, 33, 41, 43, 54-56, 58, 71, 83, 133, 135, 154, 157, 159, 160, 168,
    169, 178, 179, 181-183, 185, 187, 197, 201-205, 221, 240, 264, 279, 334, 336, 372,
    403
    closing   229, 230, 258, 301, 306, 308, 314, 317, 322, 323, 336, 346
    insertion   4, 257, 269
    opening   10, 220, 242, 258, 370-375, 379, 381, 383, 384, 389, 392, 399, 400, 403
    proffering new   35, 302, 322
    question-answer   201-202, 205, 215, 225, 264
    repair.   See repair
    search   5, 176-178, 189, 204, 206
    sequence-closing third   201, 221, 311
    sequence-initiating turn   4, 205, 322, 323, 374
    sequence organization   3, 4, 109, 296, 333, 363
    word search.   See word search
storytelling   5, 8, 9, 82, 84, 89, 107, 211-243
study abroad   9, 10, 253-283, 294, 298, 299

## T
TCU.   See turn construction unit (TCU)
teacher questions   259, 336-337
technical terms   6, 51-77
topic   32, 43, 58, 63, 129, 130, 133, 134, 152, 154, 175, 179, 181, 197, 201, 203, 205,
    226, 230, 231, 240, 264, 339, 356, 362
    setting talk   306, 308, 312, 313, 317, 320, 324
    topic initiation   262, 297, 298, 301, 306, 308, 324, 325, 379, 392, 399
    topic management   76, 295, 297, 298, 323, 324, 331, 402
    topical talk   6, 10, 24, 181, 193, 221, 226, 230, 302, 303, 306, 313, 320, 322, 325
transition relevance place (TRP)   214, 221, 240

TRP. *See* transition relevance place (TRP)
turn construction unit (TCU)   97, 99, 105, 106, 128, 156, 176, 214, 221, 227, 229, 230, 235, 256, 375, 403
turn design   297, 312, 335, 369-404
turn-taking   67, 154, 198, 259, 296, 297

## U
understanding checks   336, 337, 349, 359, 362

## W
workplace interaction   7, 51-77, 296
word search   5, 8, 28, 32, 43, 54-77, 176-178, 189-190, 203-204, 221, 229, 235, 236, 255, 323, 333

# Pragmatics & Interaction
*Gabriele Kasper, Series Editor*

Pragmatics & Interaction ("P&I"), a refereed series sponsored by the University of Hawai'i National Foreign Language Resource Center, publishes research on topics in pragmatics and discourse as social interaction from a wide variety of theoretical and methodological perspectives. P&I welcomes particularly studies on languages spoken in the Asia-Pacific region.

### Interactional Competence in Japanese as an Additional Language
*Tim Greer, Midori Ishida, & Yumiko Tateyama (Editors), 2017*

In the research literature on interactional competence in talk among second language speakers and their coparticipants, this volume of Pragmatics & Interaction is the first to focus on interaction in Japanese. The chapters examine the use and development of interactional practices in a wide range of social settings, from everyday talk among friends to service encounters, workplace interaction, and a rakugo performance to various activities in Japanese language classrooms and oral language assessment. Conducted from the shared perspective of conversation analysis, the studies show in detail how the activities are accomplished through the generic methods of interactional organization, multimodal practices, and the specific linguistic resources of Japanese.

450 pp.  ISBN 978-1-64007-188-9          $30.

### Pragmatics of Vietnamese as Native and Target Language
*Carsten Roever & Hanh thi Nguyen (Editors), 2013*

The volume offers a wealth of new information about the forms of several speech acts and their social distribution in Vietnamese as L1 and L2, complemented by a chapter on address forms and listener responses. As the first of its kind, the book makes a valuable contribution to the research literature on pragmatics, sociolinguistics, and language and social interaction in an under-researched and less commonly taught Asian language.

282 pp.  ISBN 978-0-9835816-2-8          $30.

**L2 Learning as Social Practice: Conversation-Analytic Perspectives**
*Gabriele Pallotti & Johannes Wagner (Editors), 2011*

This volume collects empirical studies applying Conversation Analysis to situations where second, third, and other additional languages are used. A number of different aspects are considered, including how linguistic systems develop over time through social interaction, how participants 'do' language learning and teaching in classroom and everyday settings, how they select languages and manage identities in multilingual contexts, and how the linguistic-interactional divide can be bridged with studies combining Conversation Analysis and Functional Linguistics. This variety of issues and approaches clearly shows the fruitfulness of a socio-interactional perspective on second language learning.

380 pp.   ISBN 978-0-9800459-7-0             $30.

**Talk-In-Interaction: Multilingual Perspectives**
*Hanh thi Nguyen & Gabriele Kasper (Editors), 2009*

This volume offers original studies of interaction in a range of languages and language varieties, including Chinese, English, Japanese, Korean, Spanish, Swahili, Thai, and Vietnamese; monolingual and bilingual interactions; and activities designed for second or foreign language learning. Conducted from the perspectives of conversation analysis and membership categorization analysis, the chapters examine ordinary conversation and institutional activities in face-to-face, telephone, and computer-mediated environments.

420 pp.   ISBN 978-09800459-1-8             $30.

# Pragmatics & Language Learning
*Marta González-Lloret, Series Editor*

Pragmatics & Language Learning ("PLL"), a refereed series sponsored by the National Foreign Language Resource Center, publishes selected papers from the International Conference on Pragmatics & Language Learning under the editorship of the conference hosts and the series editor. Check the NFLRC website for upcoming PLL volumes.

**Pragmatics & Language Learning, Volume 14**
*Kathleen Bardovi-Harlig & César Félix-Brasdefer (Editors), 2016*

This volume contains a selection of papers presented at the 2014 International Conference of Pragmatics and Language Learning at Indiana University. It includes fourteen papers on a variety of topics, with a diversity of first and second languages, and a wide range of methods used to collect pragmatic data in L2 and FL settings. The articles advance our understanding of second language pragmatics with regard to learning and the use of pragmalinguistic resources necessary to produce and comprehend speech acts, conventional expressions, discourse markers, relational talk to develop L2 symbolic competence, and polite expressions in language textbooks.

402 pp.   ISBN 978-0-9835816-8-0          $30.

### Pragmatics & Language Learning, Volume 13
*Tim Greer, Donna Tatsuki, & Carsten Roever (Editors), 2013*

Pragmatics & Language Learning, Volume 13 examines the organization of second language and multilingual speakers' talk and pragmatic knowledge across a range of naturalistic and experimental activities. Based on data collected among ESL and EFL learners from a variety of backgrounds, the contributions explore the nexus of pragmatic knowledge, interaction, and L2 learning outside and inside of educational settings.

292 pp.   ISBN 978-0-9835816-4-2          $30.

### Pragmatics & Language Learning, Volume 12
*Gabriele Kasper, Hanh thi Nguyen, Dina R. Yoshimi, & Jim K. Yoshioka (Editors), 2010*

This volume examines the organization of second language and multilingual speakers' talk and pragmatic knowledge across a range of naturalistic and experimental activities. Based on data collected on Danish, English, Hawai'i Creole, Indonesian, and Japanese as target languages, the contributions explore the nexus of pragmatic knowledge, interaction, and L2 learning outside and inside of educational settings.

364 pp.   ISBN 978-09800459-6-3          $30.

### Pragmatics & Language Learning, Volume 11
*Kathleen Bardovi-Harlig, César Félix-Brasdefer, & Alwiya S. Omar (Editors), 2006*

This volume features cutting-edge theoretical and empirical research on pragmatics and language learning among a wide variety of learners in diverse learning contexts from a variety of language backgrounds and target languages (English, German, Japanese, Kiswahili, Persian, and Spanish). This collection of papers from researchers around the world includes critical appraisals on the role of formulas in interlanguage pragmatics, and speech-act research from a conversation analytic perspective. Empirical studies examine learner data using innovative methods of analysis and investigate issues in pragmatic development and the instruction of pragmatics.

430 pp.   ISBN 978-0-8248-3137-0          $30.

# NFLRC Monographs
*Julio C Rodriguez, Series Editor*

Monographs of the National Foreign Language Resource Center present the findings of recent work in applied linguistics that is of relevance to language teaching and learning (with a focus on the less commonly taught languages of Asia and the Pacific) and are of particular interest to foreign language educators, applied linguists, and researchers. Prior to 2006, these monographs were published as "SLTCC Technical Reports."

### Student Learning Outcomes Assessment in College Foreign Language Programs
*John M. Norris & John McE. Davis (Editors), 2015*

Changes in accreditation policies and institutional practices have led to the emergence of student learning outcomes assessment as an important, increasingly common expectation in U.S. college foreign language programs. This volume investigates contemporary outcomes assessment activity, with a primary focus on useful assessment, that is, assessment that is put to use proactively by foreign language educators. Authors approach the topic from distinct perspectives, ranging from a study of national trends in outcomes assessment practices, to reflections on assessment experiences by program leaders, to case studies highlighting language educators' implementation and uses of outcomes assessment for diverse curricular and pedagogical purposes.

274 pp.   ISBN  978-1-943281-37-4 (paperback)   $25.
          ISBN  978-1-943847-15-0 (eBook)        $10.

### *Cultura*-Inspired Intercultural Exchanges: Focus on Asian and Pacific Languages
*Dorothy M. Chun (Editor), 2014*

Although many online intercultural exchanges have been conducted based on the *Cultura* model, most to date have been between and among European languages. This volume presents several chapters with a focus on exchanges involving Asian and Pacific languages. Many of the benefits and challenges of these exchanges are similar to those reported for European languages; however, some of the difficulties reported in the Chinese and Japanese exchanges might be due to the significant linguistic differences between English and East Asian languages. This volume adds to the body of emerging studies of telecollaboration among learners of Asian and Pacific languages.

183 pp.   ISBN  978-0-9835816-7-3 (paperback)   $25.
          ISBN  978-1-63443-578-9 (eBook)        $10.

## Noticing and Second Language Acquisition: Studies in Honor of Richard Schmidt
*Joara Martin Bergsleithner, Sylvia Nagem Frota, & Jim Kei Yoshioka (Editors), 2013*

This volume celebrates the life and groundbreaking work of Richard Schmidt, the developer of the influential Noticing Hypothesis in the field of second language acquisition. The 19 chapters encompass a compelling collection of cutting-edge research studies exploring such constructs as noticing, attention, and awareness from multiple perspectives, which expand, fine tune, sometimes support, and sometimes challenge Schmidt's seminal ideas and take research on noticing in exciting new directions.

374 pp.   ISBN 978-0-9835816-6-6           $25.

## New Perspectives on Japanese Language Learning, Linguistics, and Culture
*Kimi Kondo-Brown, Yoshiko Saito-Abbott, Shingo Satsutani, Michio Tsutsui, & Ann Wehmeyer (Editors), 2013*

This volume is a collection of selected refereed papers presented at the Association of Teachers of Japanese Annual Spring Conference held at the University of Hawai'i at Mānoa in March of 2011. It not only covers several important topics on teaching and learning spoken and written Japanese and culture in and beyond classroom settings but also includes research investigating certain linguistics items from new perspectives.

208 pp.   ISBN 978-0-9835816-3-5           $25.

## Developing, Using, and Analyzing Rubrics in Language Assessment with Case Studies in Asian and Pacific Languages
*James Dean Brown (Editor), 2012*

Rubrics are essential tools for all language teachers in this age of communicative and task-based teaching and assessment—tools that allow us to efficiently communicate to our students what we are looking for in the productive language abilities of speaking and writing and then effectively assess those abilities when the time comes for grading students, giving them feedback, placing them into new courses, and so forth. This book provides a wide array of ideas, suggestions, and examples (mostly from Māori, Hawaiian, and Japanese language assessment projects) to help language educators effectively develop, use, revise, analyze, and report on rubric-based assessments.

212 pp.   ISBN 978-0-9835816-1-1           $20.

## Research Among Learners of Chinese as a Foreign Language
*Michael E. Everson & Helen H. Shen (Editors), 2010*

Cutting-edge in its approach and international in its authorship, this fourth monograph in a series sponsored by the Chinese Language Teachers Association features eight research studies that explore a variety of themes, topics, and perspectives important to a variety of stakeholders in the Chinese language learning community. Employing a wide range of research methodologies, the volume provides data from actual Chinese language learners and will be of value to both theoreticians and practitioners alike. *[in English & Chinese]*

180 pp.   ISBN 978-0-9800459-4-9           $20.

## Manchu: A Textbook for Reading Documents (Second Edition)
*Gertraude Roth Li, 2010*

This book offers students a tool to gain a basic grounding in the Manchu language. The reading selections provided in this volume represent various types of documents, ranging from examples of the very earliest Manchu writing (17th century) to samples of contemporary Sibe (Xibo), a language that may be considered a modern version of Manchu. Since Manchu courses are only rarely taught at universities anywhere, this second edition includes audio recordings to assist students with the pronunciation of the texts.

418 pp.    ISBN 978-0-9800459-5-6                $36.

## Toward Useful Program Evaluation in College Foreign Language Education
*John M. Norris, John McE. Davis, Castle Sinicrope, & Yukiko Watanabe (Editors), 2009*

This volume reports on innovative, useful evaluation work conducted within U.S. college foreign language programs. An introductory chapter scopes out the territory, reporting key findings from research into the concerns, impetuses, and uses for evaluation that FL educators identify. Seven chapters then highlight examples of evaluations conducted in diverse language programs and institutional contexts. Each case is reported by program-internal educators, who walk readers through critical steps, from identifying evaluation uses, users, and questions, to designing methods, interpreting findings, and taking actions. A concluding chapter reflects on the emerging roles for FL program evaluation and articulates an agenda for integrating evaluation into language education practice.

240 pp.    ISBN 978-0-9800459-3-2                $30.

## Second Language Teaching and Learning in the Net Generation
*Raquel Oxford & Jeffrey Oxford (Editors), 2009*

Today's young people—the Net Generation—have grown up with technology all around them. However, teachers cannot assume that students' familiarity with technology in general transfers successfully to pedagogical settings. This volume examines various technologies and offers concrete advice on how each can be successfully implemented in the second language curriculum.

240 pp.    ISBN 978-0-9800459-2-5                $30.

## Case Studies in Foreign Language Placement: Practices and Possibilities
*Thom Hudson & Martyn Clark (Editors), 2008*

Although most language programs make placement decisions on the basis of placement tests, there is surprisingly little published about different contexts and systems of placement testing. The present volume contains case studies of placement programs in foreign language programs at the tertiary level across the United States. The different programs span the spectrum from large programs servicing hundreds of students annually to small language programs with very few students. The contributions to this volume address such issues as how the size of the program, presence or absence of heritage learners, and population changes affect language placement decisions.

201 pp.    ISBN 0-9800459-0-8                    $20.

## Chinese as a Heritage Language: Fostering Rooted World Citizenry
*Agnes Weiyun He & Yun Xiao (Editors), 2008*

Thirty-two scholars examine the sociocultural, cognitive-linguistic, and educational-institutional trajectories along which Chinese as a Heritage Language may be acquired, maintained, and developed. They draw upon developmental psychology, functional linguistics, linguistic and cultural anthropology, discourse analysis, orthography analysis, reading research, second language acquisition, and bilingualism. This volume aims to lay a foundation for theories, models, and master scripts to be discussed, debated, and developed, and to stimulate research and enhance teaching both within and beyond Chinese language education.

280 pp.   ISBN 978-0-8248-3286-5     $20.

## Perspectives on Teaching Connected Speech to Second Language Speakers
*James Dean Brown & Kimi Kondo-Brown (Editors), 2006*

This book is a collection of fourteen articles on connected speech of interest to teachers, researchers, and materials developers in both ESL/EFL (ten chapters focus on connected speech in English) and Japanese (four chapters focus on Japanese connected speech). The fourteen chapters are divided up into five sections:

- What do we know so far about teaching connected speech?
- Does connected speech instruction work?
- How should connected speech be taught in English?
- How should connected speech be taught in Japanese?
- How should connected speech be tested?

290 pp.   ISBN 978 0 8248 3136 3     $20.

## Corpus Linguistics for Korean Language Learning and Teaching
*Robert Bley-Vroman & Hyunsook Ko (Editors), 2006*

Dramatic advances in personal-computer technology have given language teachers access to vast quantities of machine-readable text, which can be analyzed with a view toward improving the basis of language instruction. Corpus linguistics provides analytic techniques and practical tools for studying language in use. This volume provides both an introductory framework for the use of corpus linguistics for language teaching and examples of its application for Korean teaching and learning. The collected papers cover topics in Korean syntax, lexicon, and discourse, and second language acquisition research, always with a focus on application in the classroom. An overview of Korean corpus linguistics tools and available Korean corpora are also included.

265 pp.   ISBN 0-8248-3062-8     $25.

## New Technologies and Language Learning:
## Cases in the Less Commonly Taught Languages
*Carol Anne Spreen (Editor), 2002*

In recent years, the National Security Education Program (NSEP) has supported an increasing number of programs for teaching languages using different technological media. This compilation of case study initiatives funded through the NSEP Institutional Grants Program presents a range of technology-based options for language programming that will help universities make more informed decisions about teaching less commonly taught languages. The eight chapters describe how different types of technologies are used to support language programs (i.e., web, ITV, and audio- or video-based materials), discuss identifiable trends in e-language learning, and explore how technology addresses issues of equity, diversity, and opportunity. This book offers many lessons learned and decisions made as technology changes and learning needs become more complex.

188 pp.   ISBN 0-8248-2634-5                    $25.

## An Investigation of Second Language Task-Based Performance Assessments
*James Dean Brown, Thom Hudson, John M. Norris, & William Bonk, 2002*

This volume describes the creation of performance assessment instruments and their validation (based on work started in a previous monograph). It begins by explaining the test and rating scale development processes and the administration of the resulting three seven-task tests to 90 university-level EFL and ESL students. The results are examined in terms of (a) the effects of test revision; (b) comparisons among the task-dependent, task-independent, and self-rating scales; and (c) reliability and validity issues.

240 pp.   ISBN 0-8248-2633-7                    $25.

## Motivation and Second Language Acquisition
*Zoltán Dörnyei & Richard Schmidt (Editors), 2001*

This volume—the second in this series concerned with motivation and foreign language learning—includes papers presented in a state-of-the-art colloquium on L2 motivation at the American Association for Applied Linguistics (Vancouver, 2000) and a number of specially commissioned studies. The 20 chapters, written by some of the best known researchers in the field, cover a wide range of theoretical and research methodological issues, and also offer empirical results (both qualitative and quantitative) concerning the learning of many different languages (Arabic, Chinese, English, Filipino, French, German, Hindi, Italian, Japanese, Russian, and Spanish) in a broad range of learning contexts (Bahrain, Brazil, Canada, Egypt, Finland, Hungary, Ireland, Israel, Japan, Spain, and the US.).

520 pp.   ISBN 0-8248-2458-X                    $30.

## A Focus on Language Test Development:
## Expanding the Language Proficiency Construct Across a Variety of Tests
*Thom Hudson & James Dean Brown (Editors), 2001*

This volume presents eight research studies that introduce a variety of novel, non-traditional forms of second and foreign language assessment. To the extent possible, the studies also show the entire test development process, warts and all. These language testing projects not only demonstrate many of the types of problems that test developers run into in the real world but also afford the reader unique insights into the language test development process.

230 pp.   ISBN 0-8248-2351-6                    $20.

## Studies on Korean in Community Schools
*Dong-Jae Lee, Sookeun Cho, Miseon Lee, Minsun Song, & William O'Grady (Editors), 2000*

The papers in this volume focus on language teaching and learning in Korean community schools. Drawing on innovative experimental work and research in linguistics, education, and psychology, the contributors address issues of importance to teachers, administrators, and parents. Topics covered include childhood bilingualism, Korean grammar, language acquisition, children's literature, and language teaching methodology. *[in Korean]*

256 pp.   ISBN 0-8248-2352-4               $20.

## A Communicative Framework for Introductory Japanese Language Curricula
*Washington State Japanese Language Curriculum Guidelines Committee, 2000*

In recent years, the number of schools offering Japanese nationwide has increased dramatically. Because of the tremendous popularity of the Japanese language and the shortage of teachers, quite a few untrained, nonnative and native teachers are in the classrooms and are expected to teach several levels of Japanese. These guidelines are intended to assist individual teachers and professional associations throughout the United States in designing Japanese language curricula. They are meant to serve as a framework from which language teaching can be expanded and are intended to allow teachers to enhance and strengthen the quality of Japanese language instruction.

168 pp.   ISBN 0-8248-2350-8               $20.

## Foreign Language Teaching and Minority Language Education
*Kathryn A. Davis (Editor), 1999*

This volume seeks to examine the potential for building relationships among foreign language, bilingual, and ESL programs towards fostering bilingualism. Part I of the volume examines the sociopolitical contexts for language partnerships, including:

- obstacles to developing bilingualism;
- implications of acculturation, identity, and language issues for linguistic minorities; and
- the potential for developing partnerships across primary, secondary, and tertiary institutions.

Part II of the volume provides research findings on the Foreign Language Partnership Project, designed to capitalize on the resources of immigrant students to enhance foreign language learning.

152 pp.   ISBN 0-8248-2239-0               $20.

## Designing Second Language Performance Assessments
*John M. Norris, James Dean Brown, Thom Hudson, & Jim Yoshioka, 1998, 2000*

This technical report focuses on the decision-making potential provided by second language performance assessments. The authors first situate performance assessment within a broader discussion of alternatives in language assessment and in educational assessment in general. They then discuss issues in performance assessment design, implementation, reliability, and validity. Finally, they present a prototype framework for second language performance assessment based on the integration of theoretical underpinnings and research findings from the task-based language teaching literature, the language testing literature, and the educational measurement literature. The authors outline test and item specifications, and they present numerous examples of prototypical language tasks. They also propose a research agenda focusing on the operationalization of second language performance assessments.

248 pp.   ISBN 0-8248-2109-2                              $20.

## Second Language Development in Writing:
## Measures of Fluency, Accuracy, and Complexity
*Kate Wolfe-Quintero, Shunji Inagaki, & Hae-Young Kim, 1998, 2002*

In this book, the authors analyze and compare the ways that fluency, accuracy, grammatical complexity, and lexical complexity have been measured in studies of language development in second language writing. More than 100 developmental measures are examined, with detailed comparisons of the results across the studies that have used each measure. The authors discuss the theoretical foundations for each type of developmental measure, and they consider the relationship between developmental measures and various types of proficiency measures. They also examine criteria for determining which developmental measures are the most successful and suggest which measures are the most promising for continuing work on language development.

208 pp.   ISBN 0-8248-2069-X                              $20.

## The Development of a Lexical Tone Phonology
## in American Adult Learners of Standard Mandarin Chinese
*Sylvia Henel Sun, 1998*

The study reported is based on an assessment of three decades of research on the SLA of Mandarin tone. It investigates whether differences in learners' tone perception and production are related to differences in the effects of certain linguistic, task, and learner factors. The learners of focus are American students of Mandarin in Beijing, China. Their performances on two perception and three production tasks are analyzed through a host of variables and methods of quantification.

328 pp.   ISBN 0-8248-2068-1                              $20.

## New Trends and Issues in Teaching Japanese Language and Culture
*Haruko M. Cook, Kyoko Hijirida, & Mildred Tahara (Editors), 1997*

In recent years, Japanese has become the fourth most commonly taught foreign language at the college level in the United States. As the number of students who study Japanese has increased, the teaching of Japanese as a foreign language has been established as an important academic field of study. This technical report includes nine contributions to the advancement of this field, encompassing the following five important issues:

- Literature and literature teaching
- Technology in the language classroom
- Orthography
- Testing
- Grammatical versus pragmatic approaches to language teaching

164 pp.   ISBN 0-8248-2067-3                 $20.

## Six Measures of JSL Pragmatics
*Sayoko Okada Yamashita, 1996*

This book investigates differences among tests that can be used to measure the cross-cultural pragmatic ability of English-speaking learners of Japanese. Building on the work of Hudson, Detmer, and Brown (Technical Reports #2 and #7 in this series), the author modified six test types that she used to gather data from North American learners of Japanese. She found numerous problems with the multiple-choice discourse completion test but reported that the other five tests all proved highly reliable and reasonably valid. Practical issues involved in creating and using such language tests are discussed from a variety of perspectives.

213 pp.   ISBN 0-8248-1914-4                 $15.

## Language Learning Strategies Around the World: Cross-Cultural Perspectives
*Rebecca L. Oxford (Editor), 1996, 1997, 2002*

Language learning strategies are the specific steps students take to improve their progress in learning a second or foreign language. Optimizing learning strategies improves language performance. This groundbreaking book presents new information about cultural influences on the use of language learning strategies. It also shows innovative ways to assess students' strategy use and remarkable techniques for helping students improve their choice of strategies, with the goal of peak language learning.

166 pp.   ISBN 0-8248-1910-1                 $20.

## Telecollaboration in Foreign Language Learning: Proceedings of the Hawai'i Symposium
*Mark Warschauer (Editor), 1996*

The Symposium on Local & Global Electronic Networking in Foreign Language Learning & Research, part of the National Foreign Language Resource Center's 1995 Summer Institute on Technology & the Human Factor in Foreign Language Education, included presentations of papers and hands-on workshops conducted by Symposium participants to facilitate the sharing of resources, ideas, and information about all aspects of electronic networking for foreign language teaching and research, including electronic discussion and conferencing, international cultural exchanges, real-time communication and simulations, research and resource retrieval via the Internet, and research using networks. This collection presents a sampling of those presentations.

252 pp.   ISBN 0-8248-1867-9                 $20.

### Language Learning Motivation: Pathways to the New Century
*Rebecca L. Oxford (Editor), 1996*

This volume chronicles a revolution in our thinking about what makes students want to learn languages and what causes them to persist in that difficult and rewarding adventure. Topics in this book include the internal structures of and external connections with foreign language motivation; exploring adult language learning motivation, self-efficacy, and anxiety; comparing the motivations and learning strategies of students of Japanese and Spanish; and enhancing the theory of language learning motivation from many psychological and social perspectives.

218 pp.    ISBN 0-8248-1849-0                                $20.

### Linguistics & Language Teaching:
### Proceedings of the Sixth Joint LSH-HATESL Conference
*Cynthia Reves, Caroline Steele, & Cathy S. P. Wong (Editors), 1996*

Technical Report #10 contains 18 articles revolving around the following three topics:
- Linguistic issues—These six papers discuss various linguistic issues: ideophones, syllabic nasals, linguistic areas, computation, tonal melody classification, and wh-words.
- Sociolinguistics—Sociolinguistic phenomena in Swahili, signing, Hawaiian, and Japanese are discussed in four of the papers.
- Language teaching and learning—These eight papers cover prosodic modification, note taking, planning in oral production, oral testing, language policy, L2 essay organization, access to dative alternation rules, and child noun phrase structure development.

364 pp.    ISBN 0-8248-1851-2                                $20.

### Attention & Awareness in Foreign Language Learning
*Richard Schmidt (Editor), 1995*

Issues related to the role of attention and awareness in learning lie at the heart of many theoretical and practical controversies in the foreign language field. This collection of papers presents research into the learning of Spanish, Japanese, Finnish, Hawaiian, and English as a second language (with additional comments and examples from French, German, and miniature artificial languages) that bear on these crucial questions for foreign language pedagogy.

394 pp.    ISBN 0-8248-1794-X                                $20.

### Virtual Connections:
### Online Activities and Projects for Networking Language Learners
*Mark Warschauer (Editor), 1995, 1996*

Computer networking has created dramatic new possibilities for connecting language learners in a single classroom or across the globe. This collection of activities and projects makes use of email, the Internet, computer conferencing, and other forms of computer-mediated communication for the foreign and second language classroom at any level of instruction. Teachers from around the world submitted the activities compiled in this volume—activities that they have used successfully in their own classrooms.

417 pp.   ISBN 0-8248-1793-1              $30.

## Developing Prototypic Measures of Cross-Cultural Pragmatics
*Thom Hudson, Emily Detmer, & J. D. Brown, 1995*

Although the study of cross-cultural pragmatics has gained importance in applied linguistics, there are no standard forms of assessment that might make research comparable across studies and languages. The present volume describes the process through which six forms of cross-cultural assessment were developed for second language learners of English. The models may be used for second language learners of other languages. The six forms of assessment involve two forms each of indirect discourse completion tests, oral language production, and self-assessment. The procedures involve the assessment of requests, apologies, and refusals.

198 pp.   ISBN 0-8248-1763-X              $15.

## The Role of Phonological Coding in Reading Kanji
*Sachiko Matsunaga, 1995*

In this technical report, the author reports the results of a study that she conducted on phonological coding in reading kanji using an eye-movement monitor, and draws some pedagogical implications. In addition, she reviews current literature on the different schools of thought regarding instruction in reading kanji and its role in the teaching of nonalphabetic written languages like Japanese.

64 pp.   ISBN 0-8248-1734-6              $10.

## Pragmatics of Chinese as Native and Target Language
*Gabriele Kasper (Editor), 1995*

This technical report includes six contributions to the study of the pragmatics of Mandarin Chinese:

- A report of an interview study conducted with nonnative speakers of Chinese; and
- five data-based studies on the performance of different speech acts by native speakers of Mandarin—requesting, refusing, complaining, giving bad news, disagreeing, and complimenting.

312 pp.   ISBN 0-8248-1733-8              $20.

## A Bibliography of Pedagogy and Research in Interpretation and Translation
*Etilvia Arjona, 1993*

This technical report includes four types of bibliographic information on translation and interpretation studies:

- Research efforts across disciplinary boundaries—cognitive psychology, neurolinguistics, psycholinguistics, sociolinguistics, computational linguistics, measurement, aptitude testing, language policy, decision-making, theses, and dissertations;

- training information covering program design, curriculum studies, instruction, and school administration;
- instructional information detailing course syllabi, methodology, models, available textbooks; and
- testing information about aptitude, selection, and diagnostic tests.

115 pp.    ISBN 0-8248-1572-6                    $10.

## Pragmatics of Japanese as Native and Target Language
*Gabriele Kasper (Editor), 1992, 1996*

This technical report includes three contributions to the study of the pragmatics of Japanese:
- A bibliography on speech-act performance, discourse management, and other pragmatic and sociolinguistic features of Japanese;
- a study on introspective methods in examining Japanese learners' performance of refusals; and
- a longitudinal investigation of the acquisition of the particle *ne* by nonnative speakers of Japanese.

125 pp.    ISBN 0-8248-1462-2                    $10.

## A Framework for Testing Cross-Cultural Pragmatics
*Thom Hudson, Emily Detmer, & J. D. Brown, 1992*

This technical report presents a framework for developing methods that assess cross-cultural pragmatic ability. Although the framework has been designed for Japanese and American cross-cultural contrasts, it can serve as a generic approach that can be applied to other language contrasts. The focus is on the variables of social distance, relative power, and the degree of imposition within the speech acts of requests, refusals, and apologies. Evaluation of performance is based on recognition of the speech act, amount of speech, forms or formulae used, directness, formality, and politeness.

51 pp.    ISBN 0-8248-1463-0                    $10.

## Research Methods in Interlanguage Pragmatics
*Gabriele Kasper & Merete Dahl, 1991*

This technical report reviews the methods of data collection employed in 39 studies of interlanguage pragmatics, defined narrowly as the investigation of nonnative speakers' comprehension and production of speech acts, and the acquisition of L2-related speech-act knowledge. Data collection instruments are distinguished according to the degree to which they constrain informants' responses, and whether they tap speech-act perception/comprehension or production. A main focus of discussion is the validity of different types of data, in particular their adequacy to approximate authentic performance of linguistic action.

51 pp.    ISBN 0-8248-1419-3                    $10.

www.ingramcontent.com/pod-product-compliance
Lightning Source LLC
Chambersburg PA
CBHW050325230426
43663CB00010B/1740